Hitler's Ostkrieg
and the Indian Wars

CAMPAIGNS AND COMMANDERS

GENERAL EDITOR
Gregory J. W. Urwin, *Temple University, Philadelphia, Pennsylvania*

ADVISORY BOARD
Lawrence E. Babits, *Greenville, North Carolina*
James C. Bradford, *Texas A&M University, College Station*
Robert M. Epstein, *U.S. Army School of Advanced Military Studies, Fort Leavenworth, Kansas (retired)*
David M. Glantz, *Carlisle, Pennsylvania*
Jerome A. Greene, *Denver, Colorado*
Victor Davis Hanson, *Hoover Institution of Stanford University, Stanford*
Herman Hattaway, *Leawood, Kansas*
J. A. Houlding, *Rückersdorf, Germany*
Eugenia C. Kiesling, *U.S. Military Academy, West Point, New York*
Timothy K. Nenninger, *National Archives, Washington, D.C.*
Bruce Vandervort, *Virginia Military Institute, Lexington*

Hitler's Ostkrieg and the Indian Wars
Comparing Genocide and Conquest

Edward B. Westermann

University of Oklahoma Press | Norman

This book is published with the generous assistance of The Kerr Foundation, Inc.

Library of Congress Cataloging-in-Publication Data

Name: Westermann, Edward B., author.
Title: Hitler's Ostkrieg and the Indian wars : comparing genocide and conquest / Edward B. Westermann.
Description: Norman : University of Oklahoma Press, 2016. | Series: Campaigns and commanders | Includes bibliographical references and index.
Identifiers: LCCN 2016005057 | ISBN 978-0-8061-5433-6 (cloth) ISBN 978-0-8061-6467-0 (paper)
Subjects: LCSH: Manifest Destiny. | United States—Territorial expansion—History—19th century. | Indians of North America—Wars—West U.S.) | Indians, Treatment of—West (U.S.)—History—19th century. | Massacres—West (U.S.)—History—19th century. | World War, 1939-1945—Campaigns—Soviet Union. | World War, 1939-1945—Atrocities—Soviet Union. | World War, 1939-1945—Atrocities—Europe, Eastern. | Genocide—Europe, Eastern—History—20th century. | Germany—Territorial expansion—History—20th century.
Classification: LCC E179.5 .W49 2016 | DDC 973.1/4—dc23
LC record available at https://lccn.loc.gov/2016005057

Hitler's Ostkrieg and the Indian Wars: Comparing Genocide and Conquest is Volume 56 in the Campaigns and Commanders series.

The paper in this book meets the guidelines for permanence and durability of the Committee on Production Guidelines for Book Longevity of the Council on Library Resources, Inc. ∞

Copyright © 2016 by the University of Oklahoma Press, Norman, Publishing Division of the University. Paperback published 2019. Manufactured in the U.S.A.

All rights reserved. No part of this publication may be reproduced, stored in a retrieval system, or transmitted, in any form or by any means, electronic, mechanical, photocopying, recording, or otherwise—except as permitted under Section 107 or 108 of the United States Copyright Act—without the prior written permission of the University of Oklahoma Press. To request permission to reproduce selections from this book, write to Permissions, University of Oklahoma Press, 2800 Venture Drive, Norman, OK 73069, or email rights.oupress@ou.edu.

*To Suzann Westermann and Karl Meyer,
in loving memory of those who will always be with us*

Contents

List of Illustrations ix
Acknowledgments xi

Introduction 3
1. Visions of Conquest: Manifest Destiny and Lebensraum 17
2. National Policies of Race and Space 53
3. Strategy and Warfare 114
4. Massacre and Atrocity 159
5. War in the Shadows: Guerrilla Warfare in the
   West and the East 200
   Conclusion 249

Notes 261
Bibliography 289
Index 311

Illustrations

Figures

Columns of cavalry, artillery, and supply wagons, Black Hills Expedition	101
Slaughtered buffalo	102
Indians drawing rations at Camp Supply, Indian Territory	103
Looking Glass of the Nez Perce on an Indian pony	104
Apache scouts at Fort Wingate, New Mexico	105
Chiricahua Apaches under guard en route to Fort Pickens, Florida	106
A group of girls praying at the Phoenix Indian School, Arizona	107
German soldiers marching through a burning Soviet village	108
Prisoners at forced labor, Mauthausen concentration camp, Austria	109
Jewish children on the streets of the Warsaw ghetto	110
German forces executing Soviet civilians at a mass grave	111
Hungarian Jews on the selection ramp at Auschwitz-Birkenau, Poland	112
German police and auxiliaries with a group of Jewish women	113

Maps

The Great Plains	126–27
German Military Operations on the Eastern Front, June 22–September 30, 1941	147
The Desert Southwest	204–205
Partisan Operations and Bases on the Eastern Front, Winter 1941–1942	234

Acknowledgments

There is a saying related to comparative history that it "involves twice the work for half the credit." Although not exactly true, there are some unique challenges faced by the historian when undertaking a comparative historical analysis. Indeed, the clear differences in chronology, timespan, scale, and scope involved in the prosecution of these two national projects should offer considerable cause for consideration in attempting such an ambitious study. Such a project confronts the historian with a literal avalanche of source materials that encompass several major fields of study, including but not limited to Holocaust history, Native American studies, borderlands history, military history, and the history of the American West. Not only is the diversity of the historiography and the number of sources seemingly overwhelming, but also the attempt seems extraordinarily ambitious in an age when, in the words of Elisabeth Lasch-Quinn, "overspecialization has become so common that it is now valid for historians to devote their whole careers to the study of only one brief time period, a particular confined locale, or a single aspect of the past."

Despite the challenges associated with a comparative study, I would contend that there are several advantages to such an approach in general and, specifically, with respect to the processes of conquest associated with the Nazi East and the American West. From an intellectual perspective as a trained European historian, the examination of the process of westward expansion between 1850 and 1890 not only exposed me to a large and rich historiography outside my primary field but also provided me with new insights and perspectives for thinking about events in eastern Europe between 1939 and 1945. In truth, it also allowed me to confront and shed some of my biases concerning the *longue durée* of European history versus the comparatively "short" history of the United States. In the end, it is my hope that this comparison will provide valuable insights for historians across both disciplines.

Because of the amount of historiography that needed to be covered to write this book, I am indebted to a number of friends and colleagues for their support, suggestions, and insights. First, I would like to extend my appreciation to my colleague and friend Amy Porter, a historian of the southwest borderlands, who from the start of this project provided encouragement and shared her expertise as I ventured ever deeper into this fascinating field. Likewise, I am indebted to Francis Galan, another borderlands historian, who shared his insights and provided expert advice on locating key sources during my research. Amy and Francis also served as eager and enthusiastic discussion partners as I conceptualized this comparison. In my search for sources, the entire library staff at Texas A&M University–San Antonio deserves special mention for their enthusiastic and unflagging support of my many interlibrary-loan requests. I am especially grateful to Jacob Sherman, Emily Bliss-Zaks, and Sarah Timm for their efforts in support of my research.

During the research for this project, I benefited from a President's Circle Research Grant as well as the support of numerous individuals at the university. I owe special thanks to Maria Hernandez Ferrier, our inaugural university president, and my department head, Bill Bush, for his support in garnering research funds for this project. The staffs at the National Archives and Records Administration and the Library of Congress provided friendly and expert assistance during research in Washington, D.C. Likewise, the special-collections staff at the U.S. Military Academy at West Point provided rapid and professional assistance.

A number of individuals deserve special mention for their willingness to review the manuscript during various stages of its development. Gerhard Weinberg, my dissertation coadviser, scholarly role model, and mentor, read the entire manuscript and, with his usual perspicacity, provided critical inputs that sharpened the argument. Likewise, Jürgen Matthäus and Thomas Kühne both took time from very busy schedules to share their thoughts and insights on the manuscript. The following individuals also took time to listen to my argument or to point me in the direction of additional sources: Alex Alvarez, Volker Benkert, Rebecca Brown, Erika Bsumek, Steve Chiabotti, Rob Citino, Graham Cox, Ovidiu Creanga, Hilary Earl, Mark Erickson, Don Fixico, Geoffrey Giles, Maureen Hiebert, Chris Jocks, Jerry Jones, Pete Kakel, Thomas Pegelow Kaplan, Steven Katz, Eugenia Kiesling, Björn Krondorfer, Mike Leggiere, Brian Linn, Wendy Lower, Geoff Megargee, Al Mierzejewski, Katherine Osburne, Chris Rein, Carol Rittner, Joaquín Rivaya-Martínez, Lauren Faulkner

Rossi, Andrea McComb Sanchez, Rebecca Schloss, Adam Seipp, Dennis Showalter, Gerald Steinacher, Ursula Mindler-Steiner, Alan Steinweis, and Frank Usbeck.

I also would like to thank Greg Urwin and Chuck Rankin for their support. Greg proved to be an early and ardent supporter of this project. I remain indebted to him not only for championing my work but also for his expert insights and suggestions as I went through the revision process. Likewise, Chuck Rankin remains the consummate professional and a superb editor whose advice and support proved essential to bringing this book to press. I want to thank Brittney Berling for her enthusiastic and expert editorial assistance as well as Bill Nelson for his assistance in the creation of the maps of the American West. Likewise, Kevin Brock did a superb job in the copyediting of the manuscript. I especially would like to express my appreciation to the anonymous readers who provided valuable comments and suggestions that materially improved the final manuscript. Whatever success I have achieved in this journey I owe to the many colleagues and friends who have supported this effort, while any of the flaws or weaknesses are mine alone.

Finally, I would like to thank my wife, Brigitte, and my two daughters, Sarah and Marlies, for their unflagging encouragement and support.

Hitler's Ostkrieg
and the Indian Wars

INTRODUCTION

As he prepared for and waged his war of annihilation on the eastern front, Adolf Hitler repeatedly drew parallels between the Nazi quest for lebensraum, or living space, in the East and the concept of manifest destiny and the treatment of Native Americans during the United States' expansion into the West. Drawing this comparison in a conversation in October 1941, Hitler offered his vision of a "German East" populated by former soldiers settled on millions of homesteads, remarking, "Our Mississippi must be the Volga, not the Niger."[1] In other conversations he used the term "redskins" to describe the peoples of eastern Europe and asserted that the American West had been won after the settlers had "shot down the millions of redskins to a few hundred thousand." In Hitler's imagination the conquest of the American West provided an existing precedent for the murderous activities of Reich Leader of the SS and Chief of the German Police Heinrich Himmler and his SS and police legions as they swept forward behind the Wehrmacht deep into the Soviet Union, killing millions literally one bullet at a time.[2] The philosophical and ideological underpinnings of the westward march of the American empire and the displacement of Native Americans provide parallels with the Nazi conquest of the East and the conduct of a racial war of extermination against the Slavic and Jewish populations of eastern Europe and western Russia. This work examines these two historical events in order to determine whether the "wild East" between 1939 and 1945 had a historical precursor in the events of the American conquest of the West in the nineteenth century beyond the grandiose imaginings of Hitler and his dreams of a millennial world empire.

In her classic work *The Legacy of Conquest*, Patricia Nelson Limerick asserted, "Conquest forms the historical bedrock of the whole nation [the United States], and the American West is a preeminent case study in conquest and its consequences." She continued, "Conquest [in the case of the United States] was a literal, territorial form of economic growth." Limerick also remarked on the value of using the American West to study "comparative conquests" in an attempt to "knit the fragmented history of the planet back together." In a similar vein the German historian Jürgen Kocka, while warning of the risks associated with asymmetric historical comparisons, still stressed the value of such comparisons in "motivating empirical research to uncover initially one-sided or distorted assumptions."[3] His emphasis on "empirical research" is a critical point because it is only with a sufficient level of detail that the similarities and dissimilarities between historical cases can be truly explored and evaluated.

Limerick's use of the term "comparative conquest" in 1986 coincided with an emerging field of study focused on genocide as a distinct historical phenomenon. Initially, "genocide studies" was closely tied to the events involving the destruction of the European Jews, a natural linkage based on the immediacy and residual effects of the Final Solution; in fact, it was the Holocaust and its aftermath that provided the impetus for United Nations (UN) Resolution 260 and the passage of the Convention on the Prevention and Punishment of the Crime of Genocide in 1948. In keeping with its commitment to prevention, genocide studies has adopted a "predominant social science–positivistic orientation" focused on "discerning commonalities and general principles about the phenomenon of genocide." In this sense the field has embraced a comparative methodology under the assumption that "to rely on the insights afforded by just one genocide is to parochialize genocide scholarship and condemn it to a corpus of disconnected monographic studies." One scholar even goes so far as to argue that without a methodology of comparative genocide studies, "there can be *no* meaningful theoretical work and in-depth analysis."[4] This trend includes works that focus on commonalities between the Holocaust and the experiences of indigenous peoples, including Native American tribes.

The comparison between the Holocaust and the decimation of Native American tribes in the United States has been made most notably in the writings and speeches of the controversial Ward Churchill. Churchill drew this explicit parallel in 1993 with the contention that Hitler based his concept of lebensraum "directly upon U.S. practice against American Indians." In a later work, *A Little Matter of Genocide*, he equated the annihilation of Native Americans by European settlers with the Nazi campaign against the Poles and Jews. In other examples, the historian David Stannard and the sociologist Russell Thornton examined the whole course of European and Native American interaction in separate works. Stannard's *The American Holocaust* explicitly equated Nazi measures against the European Jews with the U.S. treatment of the Indian tribes. Similarly, in an earlier work devoted to examining and explaining the demographic collapse of Native American populations, *American Indian Holocaust and Survival*, Thornton invoked the specter of the Shoah and contended that "the holocaust of the North American tribes was, in a way, even more destructive than that of the Jews, since many American Indian peoples became extinct.[5]

In a more recent example, S. C. Gwynne's bestselling *Empire of the Summer Moon* drew a veiled allusion to the Holocaust by characterizing the response of the U.S. Army to the "Comanche empire" as "the beginning of the final solution." Similarly, Gary Anderson provocatively titled one chapter in *The Conquest of Texas* "Reservations or Concentration Camps?" but ultimately concluded that Anglo Texans supported a "policy of ethnic cleansing" with regard to the state's nonwhite populations.[6] In a more explicit comparison, Carroll P. Kakel provided an extended scholarly analysis of the similarities between Nazi plans for conquest and domination and that of the American West: "Violence and American expansion progressed hand in hand across the North American continent. . . . [M]uch [of the] Nazi genocidal violence and many of the events we have come to call the Holocaust were a radicalized blend of several forms of mass political violence whose patterns, logics, and pathologies can be found in the Early American project." Unfortunately, Kakel's focus on theoretical constructs, including the "logics" and "optics" of genocide, came at the cost of providing sufficient empirical detail to support his argument. In fact, one reviewer described this work as suffering from "perilous overextended comparisons, which confuse analogies with equivalences, inflate similarities, marginalize differences, view the past through the lens of later events, and sever events from their proper contexts."[7]

In contrast to these works, most scholars have refrained from direct comparisons between Nazi Germany's murder of the European Jews and the treatment of the Native Americans, but many have adopted the term "genocide" in discussing the latter. For example, Jeffrey Ostler described the "ideological underpinnings" of the U.S. Army's campaigns against the Indian tribes as carrying "genocidal impulses" and "genocidal tendencies." Building upon his study of Texas, Gary Anderson looked beyond that state at the broader scope of Anglo–Indian interaction and concluded that the United States pursued a policy of "ethnic cleansing," not "genocide," against the tribes. In another work, *Native America and the Question of Genocide*, Alex Alvarez offered a thoughtful and balanced account on the whole course of Euro-American interactions with American Indians, concluding, "the question of genocide in the Americas is a much more complicated issue than has often been suggested." Some of the factors "complicating" this discussion include the diversity and status of the actors, whether European or American, state or nonstate, as well as the various tribes, the role of disease in this process, the time frame considered, and the question of intent. Perhaps the key factor confusing this discussion relates to the definition of genocide itself. As the genocide scholar Dan Stone aptly pointed out in a 2010 publication, "genocide ... is not a stable concept; indeed it epitomizes what is meant by the phrase 'essentially contested concept.'"[8] In the proceeding five years the term "genocide," if anything, has become a more contested concept despite the existence of the legal definition under UN Resolution 260. Contemporary scholarly discussions have broadened the concept to include not only acts of premeditated physical extermination but also cases of "biological genocide" and even "cultural genocide." Other historians have employed a neo-Marxian perspective by embracing postcolonial theory and the concept of "colonial genocide" or "settler colonialism" as explanatory models linking historical cases of European settlement in the Americas, Australia, and Africa to the purported genocide of indigenous peoples.[9] For example, in a work devoted to examining the practice of "settler colonialism" in U.S. history, Walter Hixson described the settlement of the American West and concurrent reform efforts in the nineteenth century as "fundamentally ethnocentric and genocidal" and designed "to destroy the Indian way of life."[10]

This study focuses on the aptness and appropriateness of the comparison of Nazi genocide in the European East with the actions of the U.S. government, the U.S. Army, settlers, and the Native tribes in the conquest of the American West. It compares the overarching philosophies of subjugation, including lebensraum and manifest destiny; the role of government policy; the military strategies involved in conquest; the function of massacre and atrocity; and the nature of German antipartisan warfare in eastern Europe with the U.S. Army's campaign against the Apaches in the Desert Southwest.

In this analysis it is critical to move beyond theoretical constructs and to provide a discussion of specific historical events and the historical context that shaped the political philosophies, racial beliefs, economic factors, and military strategies framing the dynamic of American westward expansion between 1850 and 1890 and the Nazi war of conquest in eastern Europe between 1939 and 1945. This comparative and empirical approach provides a means for examining experience across time and space in order to determine if there are specific elements that link both national projects—the U.S. conquest of the West and Hitler's *Ostkrieg* (war in the East)—from the perspective of genocidal intent and execution.

Although scholars and researchers formulated concepts related to genocide as early as the 1920s, it was the destruction of the European Jews during World War II that brought the issue into the arena of a global discourse. Still under the shadow of the Holocaust, UN Resolution 260 not only defined genocide as a crime but also created a positive obligation on the part of member nations to prevent its occurrence and to punish those involved. The United Nations defined the crime of genocide as including: "(a) Killing members of the group; (b) Causing serious bodily or mental harm to members of the group; (c) Deliberately inflicting on the group conditions of life calculated to bring about its physical destruction in whole or in part; (d) Imposing measures intended to prevent births within the group; or (e) Forcibly transferring children of the group to another group." Importantly, this definition also includes the requirement concerning the "intent to destroy, in whole or in part, a national, ethnical, racial or religious group."[11]

The question of defining intent, or even including it as a prerequisite, has remained a central point of debate within the field of genocide studies almost since the advent of the field itself. Interestingly, the man credited with coining the term "genocide," Raphael Lemkin, not only was instrumental in the creation and passage of UN Resolution 260 but also was a scholar in his own right, having published a work in 1944 that argued, "Genocide has two phases: one the destruction of the national pattern of the oppressed group: the other, the imposition of the national pattern of the oppressor." In Lemkin's view, results with respect to targeted populations proved more important than the question of deliberate intent.[12] Contemporary definitional debates have resulted in the emergence, by one scholar's count, of at least "21 different definitions of genocide."[13]

In the last decade genocide scholars have increasingly pushed for a much broader definition, including one proposal that describes genocide as "the more or less coordinated attempt to destroy a dehumanized and excluded group of people [in whole or in part] because of who they are." In the words of genocide scholar Alexander Hinton, such an approach "open[s] the door to cultural genocide, genocide committed by non-state agents, genocide by neglect, and genocide of political, economic, social, and other groups as constituted in specific historical and cultural contexts." Some scholars even advocate redefining or eliminating the concept of intent as a prerequisite.[14] Obviously, disregarding intent and broadening the definition to this degree would have profound implications for any historical comparison.

When examined closely, these definitions reveal the broad range of possibility associated with the concept of genocide in general. For example, the UN definition considers intent as equally important to the successful consummation of the act itself. Furthermore, it broadens the concept of genocide to include physical violence and acts of social and eugenic restructuring. Lemkin's definition expands this model by allowing for the imposition of cultural hegemony versus the objective of physical annihilation or extermination as the standard. In contrast, the Holocaust historian Steven Katz restricted his definition of genocide to apply "only when there is an actualized intent, however, successfully carried out, to physically destroy an entire group."[15] Obviously, this definition sets a much higher standard that requires the intent to "physically destroy" the entire target population, thus attempts to annihilate parts of a group would not qualify.

Defining genocide is not an empty academic exercise but provides the fundamental basis upon which any comparison exists. In this sense, definitions that disregard intent threaten to widen the aperture of genocide to a point where the term loses its effective meaning. Any such change in definition also has profound implications for the way in which scholars define such acts of mass murder. The Holocaust historian Omer Bartov observed, "It may make us feel morally superior, or provide us with some political capital, to insist that every case of unjustifiable violence and mayhem is genocide but in fact such rhetorical exercises diminish our ability not only to understand but also to prevent genocide."[16] In the final analysis, it is critical to examine both the actions and the intent of the state actors involved in both national projects in order to reach a judgment on the question of genocide.

If both actions and intent are important in evaluating the ideas and events that characterized the Nazi campaign in eastern Europe and the Americans' westward expansion, this comparison, like any other historical case study, begs the question concerning the validity (and value) in comparing these events. In this sense, Fascism in Italy under Benito Mussolini may have fundamentally differed from the Nazism of Hitler's Germany, but the similarities and differences between the two cases still have allowed for assessments that reveal important continuities and ruptures between the experiences of these two countries.[17] Similarly, the process of historical comparison may reveal important insights into the processes, beliefs, and actions that have resulted in genocide, whether in Armenia, Cambodia, Rwanda, or in Europe during World War II. For example, the fact that Pol Pot, the leader of the Khmer Rouge in Cambodia, chose to describe "enemies of the Party" as "ugly microbes" certainly brings to mind the Nazi use of the terms "plague" and "bacillus" to describe Jews.[18] In this case, noting the similarity in the process of the dehumanization of one's alleged enemy provides a relevant point of comparison. But equally relevant are the distinctions between a campaign aimed at creating a utopian Communist agrarian paradise by targeting the urban and intellectual political enemies of the revolution in a brutal and massive "reeducation campaign" and the Nazi plans for the creation of a millennial racial empire in which perceived immutable blood traits, not class status, would be the factor determining the difference between life or death. Regarding Jews, reeducation and assimilation were never options for Nazi planners.

Comparing the Nazi East and the American West

In comparing the Nazi campaign in Europe and the process of American westward expansion, it is immediately clear that there are considerable variances between the two. First, the span of chronology of each event is significantly different. The entire process of westward expansion in North America covered a period of several centuries. The period of initial contact between Europeans and the various tribes of the "Americas" had terrible consequences for the indigenous tribes and clans, as expressed in the eyewitness account of Bartolomé de las Casas, who described "the massacres of innocent peoples, the atrocities committed against them, and among other horrific excesses, the way in which towns, provinces, and whole kingdoms have been entirely cleared of their native inhabitants." While de las Casas's writings have been tied to the creation of a "black legend" that focused on Spanish atrocity at the exclusion of French and English actions, the more important issue is not whether his tales were exaggerated, but rather that his account came to dominate public perception and became, in many respects, emblematic of European and Indian interaction.[19] Similarly, the settlement of the original thirteen British colonies, the establishment of the United States, and U.S. policy in the first half of the nineteenth century had significant implications for Indian tribes that experienced the devastating combined consequences of epidemic disease and warfare. Even a focus on the U.S. "conquest" of the Great Plains and the Desert Southwest alone involves a period of four decades, from 1850 to 1890. Yet it is exactly during this time that the United States completed the process described by Elliot West as the "Greater Reconstruction," a term that encompasses not only the reabsorption of the Confederate South but also the process of westward expansion that together completed one national project.[20] In contrast, Nazi plans for the conquest and occupation of eastern Europe began with the blitzkrieg into Poland in September 1939 and ultimately ended with the retreat from the Soviet Union in 1944, a relatively brief chronological period in comparison, but one made all the more horrific by the scale of the slaughter involved.

A second point of contrast includes the scope and the scale of the war in Europe, with millions of soldiers, sailors, and airmen on both sides equipped with modern military technology involved in large-scale conventional battles as well as extensive antipartisan or irregular operations. In the American West, the U.S. Army gradually secured a major technological advantage in arms, transportation, and communication over the various tribes, advantages that the Indians recognized could be overcome only by adopting a style of guerrilla warfare. Likewise, the *total* size of the regular U.S. Army numbered less than 10,000 men between 1800 and 1860 and never more than 28,000 up until the end of the nineteenth century, with the exception of the Civil War years. Furthermore, compared to 200 million Polish and Soviet citizens in 1939, there were approximately 360,000 Indians living in the entire western United States by 1850.[21]

Likewise, the American Indians were not organized into nation states but consisted of tribes, bands, and clans with loose kinship groupings between peoples of related ancestry that also included traditions of great enmity with rival tribes.

If the scale and the scope of Nazi actions in eastern Europe distinguished it from those in the American West, then the nature and objectives of government policy and actions stands as another major difference between the two cases. Nazi administrators pursued a policy with the explicit goal of the physical annihilation of millions, either through direct murder, using an industrialized process of extermination as in the case of the European Jews, or using indirect means, such as mass starvation aimed at the local populations in the areas under German occupation. The core principles of enslavement, exploitation, and extermination guided Nazi actions in the East, and the regime's racial ideology expressly rejected the ability of Slavic "subhumans" or "parasitical" Jews to assimilate into the German *Volksgemeinschaft* (people's community). According to Nazi ideology, the mere existence of these groups, especially the Jews, constituted a mortal threat to the Aryan race. In addition, Hitler envisioned the subjugation of eastern Europe as part of a concept of serial warfare, in which the last military campaign of conquest constituted the stepping stone for the next campaign, a process ultimately aimed at achieving global domination with the intent "to bring about a total demographic and racial reordering of the globe." In this case global conquest envisioned the annihilation of target groups such as the Jews well beyond the existing borders of Nazi Germany, whether in Great Britain, Ireland, or the Middle East.[22]

In contrast, westward expansion was neither the prelude to global conquest nor the precursor for extraterritorial campaigns aimed at the Native populations of the Western Hemisphere. In fact, with the exception of a few limited punitive raids into Mexico, the southern and northern borders of the United States provided safe havens for the tribes of Desert Southwest and Plains Indians throughout the period. Similarly, U.S. policy during westward expansion never envisioned the enslavement of the tribes or their complete physical annihilation. Specific individuals and groups, especially western settlers and frontier newspapers, did advocate the extermination of the Indians, but the policy of assimilation and "civilization" provided the guiding principles of official national policy. In the pursuit of efforts to "civilize" and bring Christianity to the tribes, however, politicians and military leaders were attempting to remake so-called savages and hostiles in the image of nineteenth-century white society. Whether defined as a process of "cultural genocide" or "cultural asphyxiation," the intent was to extinguish the essential elements of Indian culture, beliefs, and way of life.[23] Still, throughout the period of white and Indian contact, the various tribes in the West were not simply passive objects of cultural manipulation, but instead they were actors who resisted, adopted, and adapted to cultural pressure on their own terms.[24]

Imagining the East and the West

Despite the substantive differences between the two cases, there are a number of important similarities. Perhaps the most intriguing similarity between the Nazi East and the American West is that both were in a very real sense "imagined" areas. In the case of the East, Hitler and an army of demographic and racial administrators viewed eastern Europe and the Soviet Union in terms of a magnificent vision of colonial fantasy, a potential German "Garden of Eden" in which a new breed of soldier-farmers would extend not only German territory but also "precious" German blood into the bountiful Eurasian steppe. In Nazi ideology, the German went east as a 'holy warrior' with the dual objective of eliminating the Slavic "subhumans" and propagating the Nordic race in a grandiose colonization program devoted to *Blut und Boden* (blood and soil). The American West also was an imagined area in which "intrepid" farmers, characterized by Thomas Jefferson "as the chosen people of God," would remake the land and refashion American virtue. The West also existed in the minds of eastern reformers as a wild and untamed area peopled by "noble savages" or "ignoble savages," both requiring the powers of civilization and Christianity in order to be "raised up." For missionaries, "American expansionism and Indian salvation thus began to become synonymous." In this critical respect the process of westward expansion embraced the same messianic elements of Nazi colonization and the effacement of ethnic and racial identity, even if the implications for the Native Americans did not involve the corresponding dynamic of physical extermination. Similarly, Frederick Jackson Turner's "frontier thesis" and his vision of the West intersected in part with Nazi utopianism. Turner viewed the conquest of the West as a process by which diverse European immigrants emerged as "Americans." In this respect the frontier provided both a location and a process for "Americanization" and the creation of a U.S. version of the *Volksgemeinschaft*. To be sure, the process was similar if the product was not. Turner praised this process for its promotion of individualism and democracy, both antithetical concepts to Nazi views on the people's community.[25]

Economic considerations provide another factor fundamentally linking Nazi views of the East and American visions of the West. Wendy Lower described the integration of colonial and economic motives in the National Socialist worldview as a merger of "two expansionist currents—one focused on population policies, the other one on economic extraction—centered on eastern Europe." Hitler saw the "black earth" region of eastern Europe as the potential breadbasket for his Thousand Year Reich, a land of abundance that would allow the nation to create a "pearl of settlements" capable of producing a bounteous harvest for the German people. Likewise, the vision of the western "Garden of the World," with its "virgin" and abundant wilderness, existed in the minds of fur trappers, miners, fortune seekers, buffalo hunters, and eventually farmers, who each in turn acquired an area and its resources with a sense of natural entitlement. If the American West was the "golden land" laden with precious minerals, by the mid-nineteenth century, it was the land itself on the Great Plains that offered vast rewards to those who took possession of it. In the words of one historian, "The conflict between the whites and Indians that marked American Indian relations was basically a conflict over land, . . . in the thinking of the settler or of the eastern or western speculator in western lands; they saw the rich lands of the Indians and they wanted them."[26]

Spatial elements and the delimitation of space also serve as fitting points of comparison. The area covered in both Hitler's vision of eastern conquest and the American desire for westward expansion encompassed vast landscapes and millions of square miles. The use of these spaces for agricultural and resource exploitation provides one similarity, while the creation of restricted spaces, as in the case of the Lublin Reservation and the Polish General Government in eastern Europe and the Indian reservations and agencies in the West, provides another. Although the nature of political control and the specific policies of these regions were widely disparate, the concept of isolation and the objective of transformation inherent in their creation were similar. Finally, the spaces in both cases were scenes of frequent conflict and abject brutality, areas where force and coercion were ever present and where acts of atrocity and mass murder often dominated the relationship between the conquerors and conquered.

The comparison between the two national projects also offers insights into a contemporary historical debate concerning the relative influence between policymaking at the "center" and that at the "periphery."[27] Although this argument heretofore has focused on the Nazi East in an attempt to determine whether the primary source of radicalization for the genocide of the Jews emerged on the ground from administrators in the occupied territories or came directly from party and governmental institutions in the Reich capital, the example of the American West offers an additional case for evaluating this dynamic. In other words, an empirical examination of these two cases can help establish the role and importance played by political power centers in Berlin and Washington, D.C., on the actual conduct of political and military policies versus the degree of power and independence enjoyed by local and regional authorities operating in the East and the West, respectively.

Comparing Conquest and Genocide

Without doubt, Hitler, if not Nazi bureaucrats, believed that the U.S. conquest of western North America and the displacement and killing of the indigenous population provided a historical precedent for his own plans in eastern Europe. Equally clear is that both cases fused a sense of national purpose with racial stereotypes of the native populations, stereotypes that helped promote the processes of exclusion, expropriation, and killing. The purpose of this book is to offer a comparison between these two national projects that examines not only the rhetoric and pronouncements associated with each but also evaluates the reality of the application of policy and ideology as implemented "on the ground."

An analysis of Nazi goals in the occupied East with the course of westward expansion by the United States requires a comparison of several areas. First, the ideological and philosophical impulses for the concepts of manifest destiny and lebensraum must be examined. What was the intent of each, what was the overarching rationale that guided their implementation, and perhaps most importantly, what were the implicit and explicit consequences for the indigenous populations of these philosophies? In other words, does Frederick Jackson Turner's "frontier thesis" find its counterpart in the Nazi's grandiose resettlement scheme, the *Generalplan Ost* (General Plan East)? Likewise, how were the visions for both of these projects communicated to the public audiences of Germany and the United States? What was the language of conquest for each case, and where was this language to be found? Finally, what was the role of the media in this process, and how did propaganda efforts influence public perception?

Second, the role of government administrators and political leaders provides an additional and important perspective for comparing both projects. How was policy formulated in each, and what were the explicit and implicit assumptions made to support the policy and its eventual implementation? What was the nature of political and popular discourse and rhetoric used to promote and justify conquest and expansion? Likewise, it is crucial to examine the language used and the role of semantics and euphemisms employed in the United States and Germany. Did the popular perception and description of the Native American tribes as "savages" and "barbarians" find a valid counterpoint in the description of Slavs and Jews as *Untermenschen* (subhumans)? Additionally, how did individual political leaders influence the course of governmental policy?

Third, it is essential to examine the goals and objectives of political and military leaders at the strategic, operational, and tactical levels. In this respect, the administrative policies of senior political decision makers and the operational strategies of military leaders provide a critical framework for comparing the nature of warfare and governance in these cases. The key players in the occupied East included the Nazi Party administration, specifically the *Gauleiter* (district leaders); the leadership of the SS and police complex; and Wehrmacht leaders, each of whom established and enforced Nazi rule. In contrast, it was the civilian leadership of the Bureau of Indian Affairs, specifically Indian superintendents and agents, and military commanders in the western departments who drafted and implemented policies and guidance that set the tone for relations with the various Indian tribes.

Fourth, annihilation or genocide, no matter how defined or conceived, occurred at the local level, and mass murder required the availability and participation of individuals who proved willing to kill indigenous peoples in support of a regime's or administration's plans. Under National Socialism, these forces included units of the SS and the police specifically tailored for mass murder, including Heinrich Himmler's *Einsatzgruppen* (special-mission units, or death squads) and police battalions, ethnic German and local auxiliaries, and Wehrmacht forces. In the case of the American West, U.S. Army units, state militias, local volunteers, and vigilantes provided the manpower for coercion and killing in the implementation of government policy. The specific roles and missions given to these forces and the individual motivations for their actions provide essential points of comparison between these various groups at the local level, but they also provide the reader with more profound and important insights at the macro level. The answers to these questions provide a critical point of comparison in any analysis between the "wild East" and the "wild, wild West."

As the opening quotation shows, Hitler made a specific comparison between his own genocidal project and what he believed had happened during the course of American westward expansion. The key question, however, is what does a comparison between the political philosophies, racial beliefs, economic factors, government policies, and military strategies that framed the dynamic of American expansion between 1850 and 1890 and the Nazi war of conquest in eastern Europe between 1939 and 1945 reveal about each of these national projects. In the end, the conquest of the West and the National Socialist *Drang nach Osten* (drive to the east) were both immense national projects that required the allocation of vast resources. Likewise, each involved the use of military force in support of political, economic, and racial objectives. The process of looking at each separately and then comparing them provides a number of insights into the use or misuse of state power and the methods by which concepts of nation building and the quest for empire influenced those who implemented them and those who resisted. The similarities and differences in these two processes also provide a framework for understanding the significance of each event in a broader historical perspective, a view that discloses similarity and uniqueness, ultimately revealing the importance of both.

CHAPTER 1

VISIONS OF CONQUEST

MANIFEST DESTINY AND LEBENSRAUM

Manifest destiny and lebensraum have emerged as the historical catchphrases designed to encapsulate a perceived zeitgeist, or "spirit of the time." Both philosophies encompassed the concepts of conquest and expansion and began as conceptual expressions and imaginings of a particular place and time in history. The historian Elliot West described the American view of westward expansion in the context of "overarching stories" that depict the relationship of people to their environment and "become guides and encouragements for living out a newly dreamed existence." For the conquerors, such visions justify possession and serve as evidence that "they have been summoned by fate or history or God in their rightful homes." In the case of Nazi Germany, Hitler authored, if not adopted, his own sense of divine mission in lebensraum from the discourse and ideas of right-wing and conservative groups developed at the turn of the nineteenth century. He embraced the imperialistic ambitions inherent in this concept, which became "the sine qua non of German foreign policy" under the Third Reich. The führer preached a gospel of "national salvation" that depended on "the 'removal' of the Jews and the acquisition of 'living space' in the east." In fact, this idea of a racialized living space to the east became one of the fundamental pillars of Hitler's worldview and an essential planning factor in his war against Poland in 1939 and the subsequent invasion of the Soviet Union in 1941.[1]

The American West and the Nazi East were also "contested spaces." In the case of the former, intertribal warfare both predated and accompanied the efforts of American westward expansion. For example, the Comanches did not earn the title of "Lords of the Southern Plains" merely for their prowess on horseback but, more importantly, as a result of their political and military organization, which enabled them to create an "empire" on the southern plains, to dominate other tribes, and to oppose effectively white settlement on their lands until the 1870s.[2] Likewise, the Apaches and other tribes of the Desert Southwest successfully contested control over this region from the period of Spanish colonial rule to well after its cession to the United States in the wake of the Mexican-American War (1846–48). Finally, the Sioux and the Northern Cheyennes exerted political and military power throughout the northern plains that forced the abandonment of the forts along the Bozeman Trail and limited federal authority over the area until the Great Sioux War of 1876–77.

In the minds of Nazi bureaucrats, eastern Europe also represented a contested space. The self-proclaimed ideologue of the Nazi Party, Alfred Rosenberg, a "Baltic German," constructed a worldview that glorified a "drive to the east" (*Drang nach Osten*) anchored in the historical legacy of the economic expansion of German influence by the Hanseatic League in the Baltics and the military conquests of the Order of the Teutonic Knights. Similarly, Reich Leader of the SS Heinrich Himmler saw the East in terms of an ancient German birthright epitomized by the Teutonic Knights and their campaign into Poland and eastern Europe in the fourteenth century. Referencing the knights, Himmler declared, "It is my firm intention to appropriate from it all that was good about this order: bravery, extraordinary loyalty to a revered idea, sound organization, riding out into far countries, riding out into the east." If a group of medieval knights excited the minds of National Socialists for an eastern empire, the experience of the German occupation of the region during World War I provided a more recent claim and a powerful influence. During occupation duty, millions of German soldiers experienced a "fundamental transformation[,] with far-reaching cultural and political consequences." According to one historian, these men experienced a "sweeping antipathy" that combined "ambitions for colonization" and a determination to "overcome the *Unkultur* [lack of culture] of the conquered lands and peoples."[3] For these men and their Nazi epigones, especially Hitler, the East was less a contested space than an entitlement for the expansion of German *Kultur* in the form of the sword and the plowshare.

In both the Nazi East and the American West, the process for control of the land and its resources involved a struggle between those seeking to supplant existing groups or societies and those currently occupying these lands. In the case of the East, this process involved a plan of military conquest and an army of party and SS bureaucrats with visions of establishing a Nazi agrarian colony, with the indigenous peoples either reduced to the status of slaves or eliminated. In the case of the American West, frontiersmen, fortune hunters, and white settlers represented the vanguard of occupation. But this *"Drang nach Westen"* (push to the west) and the efforts aimed at constructing transcontinental railroads and telegraph networks led to a vast expansion of federal authority into these areas, introducing the government and specifically the U.S. Army as major actors in the struggle for control over these spaces. It was this national power that most threatened the Indian tribes' control over the Great Plains and the Desert Southwest in the decades after 1850. Both the Nazi vision of the East and the American popular image of the West may have been illusions, but the battle for control of these regions was a very real process. Similarly, it was less important that the ideas, concepts, and images were flawed and imperfect than that they created a perception that provided the fundamental rationale for conquest.

Imagining the "American" West

The term "manifest destiny" was coined by John O'Sullivan in 1845 and referred in part to two intertwined Jacksonian ideals: the concept of American exceptionalism and the necessity for territorial expansion. By the 1840s, these two notions coalesced in the policies of two generations of American political leaders who, in the words of one historian, "had by then developed an exceptionalist imperial ideology to justify the nation's territorial and commercial aggrandizement." Already in 1811, John Quincy Adams, while serving as an envoy in Russia, sent a letter to his father that outlined an imperial and messianic vision for future U.S. expansion: "The whole continent of North America appears to be *destined by Divine Providence* to be peopled by one *nation*, speaking one language, professing one general system of religious and political principles." The future president's sentiments would find renewed expression more than three decades later in the rhetoric that preceded the war with Mexico. In an anti-Mexican polemic in support of the annexation of Texas and the independence of California in 1845, O'Sullivan accused foreign powers of "thwarting our policy and hampering our power, limiting our greatness and checking the fulfillment of our manifest destiny to overspread the continent allotted by Providence for the free development of our yearly multiplying millions." O'Sullivan thus coined a phrase that became a symbol and justification of American expansion over the course of the next five decades, a phrase that in many respects expressed the concept of nineteenth-century progressivism and came to embody a messianic sense of "Mission" to advance "the enduring values of American civilization."[4]

Ironically, it was a British observer and not an American historian who most clearly explicated the essential elements of westward expansion. Francis Joseph Grund argued: "It appears then that the universal disposition of Americans to emigrate to the western wilderness, in order to enlarge their dominion over inanimate nature, is the actual result of an expansive power which is inherent in them, and which by continually agitating all classes of society is constantly throwing a large portion of the whole population on the extreme confines of the State, in order to gain space for its development. Hardly is a new State or Territory formed before the same principle manifests itself again and gives rise to a further emigration; and so is it destined to go on until a physical barrier must finally obstruct its progress."[5]

From the perspective of the 1840s, the expansion of a domestic American empire had become a "two-front war" for the Indian tribes as white settlers pushed westward across the Mississippi and Missouri Rivers and inland from the Pacific coast. During this process, emerging technology in the form of railroads and the telegraph would serve as sinews, pathways, and neural nets binding these two fronts and leading to an inexorable increase in pressure during the coming decades. In this period it was not the miniscule U.S. Army and its far-flung systems of forts that provided the impetus for expansion, but rather it was the "pioneers, not statesmen or soldiers, [who] conquered land for the United States; technological innovation, not force, would bind the expansive empire into a cohesive whole." In fact, the U.S. Army often came into greater conflict with frontiersmen than with Indian tribes during the first half of the nineteenth century, confrontations in many cases precipitated by the actions of white civilians against the Indians. In 1853 then–Brevet Captain Ulysses S. Grant shared the following sentiment with his wife: "It is really my opinion that the whole race [Native Americans] would be harmless and peaceable if they were not put upon by the whites."[6]

Grant's observation points to an important aspect of white-and-Indian relations, especially by the late 1850s. The passage of a quarter million white settlers across the Overland Trail en route to the Pacific coast combined with the fur trade between the two groups had "increasingly entangled" the narratives of both cultures in a reciprocal, if unequal, relationship. Elliot West has argued that, despite the illusions held by specific settlers, by 1857 "no clean frontier existed between ways of life" of the two cultures. During this period, there were in fact vast areas of contested space in the West and the Southwest, especially given the small size of the frontier army and the inability of the federal government to exercise authority in areas controlled by the various Indian tribes or groups of white settlers.[7] At this time the Comanches, with some 20,000 members and 4,000 warriors, represented a powerful force on the southern plains, one capable of more than matching the small army units spread throughout the region.[8] Despite the absence of capability, the vision of American expansion and the rhetoric of growth was not found wanting.

William Gilpin, propagandist, politician, ardent advocate of western expansion, and the first governor of Colorado Territory, embodied the standard of American manifest destiny in the antebellum period. He prophesied, "The untransacted destiny of the American people is to subdue the continent . . . to cause a stagnant people to be reborn—to perfect science—to emblazon history with the conquest of peace . . . and to shed blessings around the world!"[9] Gilpin's words provided a messianic framework to the process of expansion and explicitly sanctified "the conquest of peace" in the mission to reshape the West and its inhabitants into a nineteenth-century equivalent of a "New World Order." For him and other prophets of westward expansion, Native Americans were objects to be reshaped and remolded into the image of an existing social order. This process admitted of three possible outcomes for the tribes: (1) the abandonment of Native customs and practices and the embrace of Christian civilization; (2) removal and isolation to areas reserved for the tribes; or (3) subjugation and extermination should the first two outcomes prove unrealizable. To be sure, all three initiatives found expression in government policy over the course of the century.

Politicians responded to the rising tide of public opinion favoring U.S. expansionism, and while President James K. Polk emerged as the primary instigator of war with Mexico and the "agent of

Manifest Destiny," other leaders joined the chorus. From the floor of the Congress in 1845, Illinois Republican John Wentworth described a continental vision of a U.S. empire stretching from Nova Scotia to Cuba, Mexico, and even to Patagonia. Stephen Douglas echoed this sentiment in his promise to "blot out the lines on the map which now marked our national boundaries on this continent, and make the area of liberty as broad as the continent itself." Some five decades later, in the shadow of war with Spain, President William McKinley argued: "We need Hawaii just as much and a good deal more than we did California. It is manifest destiny."[10]

In the period between the annexation of Texas and the War of 1898, the concept of manifest destiny found multiple incarnations.[11] In the cases of the Republic of Texas and Oregon Territory, the term became focused primarily on realist political arguments for territorial expansion and the growth of U.S. political power. In the case of the former, President Polk exclaimed, "a glance at the map was enough to convince one that sooner or later the United States must extend to the Rio Grande." In fact, manifest destiny formed a key pillar for validating wars against Mexico in 1846 and Spain in 1898, both conflicts aimed at the defeat of foreign powers and the acquisition of territory. Racial thinking also was implicit in the concept and its multifarious expressions in the latter half of the nineteenth century. The historian Julius Pratt highlighted the dual nature of manifest destiny in the 1840s, with its "expression of a half blind faith in the superior virility of the American race and the superior beneficence of American political institutions." Furthermore, he traced the influence of Charles Darwin's theories in the latter half of the century that led propagandists to utilize the lexicon of natural selection and survival of the fittest as justification for Anglo-Saxon superiority and global dominance. Often, racialized thinking combined economic justification as in the war with Mexico, in which Mexican territory would "pass from its currently shiftless residents to hard working white people better able to husband their resources." Yet the conquest of the American West between 1850 and 1890 ultimately centered on the issue of economics, not race, and the expansion of U.S. power across the continent occurred as a result of a combination of the sword, the plow, and the rail. In the case of the last, General William T. Sherman, upon his retirement from the army in 1883, reflected, "the four great transcontinental railways, which have in my judgment done more for the subjugation and civilization of the Indians than all other causes combined, and have made possible the utilization of the vast area of pasture lands and mineral regions which before were almost inaccessible, for my agency in which I feel as much pride as for my share in any of the battles in which I took part."[12]

The railroad acted as both a metaphor and an agent of American conquest in the West. In the former role, gleaming coal-fired locomotives, or "steel horses," represented one of the singular accomplishments of the Industrial Revolution and symbolized the march of progress and modernity in American popular imagination. In the latter role, the conquest of the West and the consolidation of American empire depended on the completion of these transportation lines, which would link the producers of agricultural and mineral resources to national and international markets. The enormous capital investment required for railroad development led to the demand for federal subsidies and the involvement of the government in the expansion of the rail networks in the 1860s. This inevitably resulted in the extension and exercise of federal power in the West, authority that found its expression in the use of army engineers in the laying of these lines and the employment of army units to protect their construction.[13] By 1880, the railroads emerged not only as engines for economic growth but also as instruments for consolidating physical control of the West. In his annual report to the secretary of war, General Philip Sheridan observed, "Amongst our strongest allies in the march of civilization upon the frontier, are the various railway companies who are now constructing their new lines with great rapidity."[14]

Justifying Conquest

Frederick Jackson Turner became the most identifiable and avid proponent of American westward expansion based on an essay entitled "The Significance of the Frontier in American History," delivered at a meeting of the American Historical Association in Chicago in 1893. In it the historian argued: "American social development has been continually beginning over again on the frontier. This perennial rebirth, this fluidity of American life, this expansion westward with its new opportunities, its continuous touch with the simplicity of primitive society, furnish the forces dominating the

American character. The true point of view in the history of this nation is not the Atlantic coast, it is the Great West." For him, the arc of American history and the western frontier constituted "the meeting point between savagery and civilization." In the 130 years since its promulgation, Turner and his thesis has been repeatedly called to the bar of history, and the resulting judgments have resulted in numerous indictments against the man and his theory. In one key respect, however, the mindset and the vision that underpinned Turner's "frontier thesis," despite its implications for the Native peoples, reflect a spirit of the times and popular sentiment that provide insights into the methods by which the conquest of the American West was envisioned and legitimized at the time.[15]

Propaganda in the West

Paradoxically, as Turner addressed his academic colleagues in Chicago in 1893, his evolving "frontier thesis" did not constitute a blueprint for envisioned conquest, but rather served as a post-hoc justification of westward expansion. In fact, "the last Indian war," a campaign immortalized in Chief Joseph's famous comment "I will fight no more forever," or more literally "From where the sun now stands, I will fight no more," had ended in 1877 with the surrender of the Nez Perce. At the time of Turner's address, the last major confrontation between the army and the so-called Ghost Dancers had taken place almost three years earlier, resulting in the killing of some 200 Sioux men, women, and children at Wounded Knee and the deaths of twenty-five soldiers (see chapter 4).[16] In 1890 Wyoming and Idaho had been admitted to the Union, preceded in 1889 by Washington, Montana, North Dakota, and South Dakota. In this sense, even as he penned his essay, the frontier of Turner's imagining largely had become itself a historical artifact. In order to understand the ideas and concepts that shaped American popular opinion in the West and on the Eastern Seaboard in the period between 1850 and 1890, it is not Turner's essay but the role of the media; the manifestations of popular culture, including dime-store novels; and traveling exhibitions that provide insights into the ways in which the West was imagined and ultimately defined.

Newspapers and the Press

In the process of American westward expansion, the press played a critical role in shaping public opinion and defining popular perceptions of the various contestants involved in the battle for control. By the mid-nineteenth century, the United States emerged as "the world's preeminent newspaper-reading country." Likewise, the presence of a large and literate population, at least of whites and free persons, created a demand for newspapers especially among the urban middle class in the North. By 1860, there were a total of 3,300 separate newspapers in the United States. Horace Greely's weekly *New York Tribune* had a circulation of 200,000 alone, and the "prophet of western growth" used his paper as an influential forum for the promotion of expansion. In this way newspapers became not only a key conduit for transmitting the news but also instruments for shaping public attitudes and opinions. William Randolph Hearst's famous and perhaps apocryphal boast "You supply the pictures and I'll supply the war" certainly exaggerated the power of the press in nineteenth-century America. Yet newspaper owners and editors did aspire to shape public opinion. James Bennett, the owner of the *New York Herald*, declared as his goal, "to impress the whole nation . . . with the same idea at the same time."[17]

In generating sales and shaping public opinion, wars played a key role in nineteenth-century reporting, starting with the Mexican-American War. During the Civil War, reporters or "war correspondents" supplied the nation's appetite for news on the conflict. In the West after 1865, a new generation of journalists was not only writing copy but also using rifles and revolvers alongside army regulars, becoming active participants in battles not only fought on the plains but also in print. Likewise, newspapers played a key role in both the East and the West in shaping and reflecting the debates on the treatment of the tribes. While sensationalism was a defining attribute of the "yellow press" era, reports found in eastern and especially western newspapers often exhibited elements of sensationalism and falsification, with the atrocity story becoming a "standard ingredient of war reporting." Frontier newspapers used such stories to generate sales and support for actions against the tribes by prodding the government for army intervention. Major General George Crook ("Grey Fox" or "Three Stars"), one of the most capable "Indian fighters" in the U.S. Army and an advocate for Indian rights, remarked on the role of sensationalism in the western press. Discussing the role of the media, Crook observed: "It is too often the case that border newspapers . . . disseminate all sorts of exaggerations and falsehoods about the Indians, which are copied in papers of high character and wide circulation, in other parts of the country, while the Indians' side in the case is rarely ever heard. . . . Then when the outbreak does come public attention is turned to the Indians, their crimes and atrocities are alone condemned, while the persons whose injustice has driven them to this course escape scot-free and are the loudest in their denunciations."[18]

Crook's observation points to two key points with respect to the role of journalism in the nineteenth century. First, it was common practice by newspapers to reprint entire articles from other papers. In fact, editors had reciprocal subscriptions and used these issues as additional sources for articles. As a result, sensational or fabricated stories from one source might be reproduced in a number of other newspapers throughout the country. Second, editors and reporters on the frontier and in the West were often guilty of advocacy rather than objective reporting, often calling for the most extreme actions against the tribes and using exterminatory language. According to James Mueller, such rhetoric must be put into context since "calls for extermination in newspapers were not always racially based but rather can be better understood as a continuation of the hard war attitudes formed during the Civil War." With respect to the accuracy of their reporting, one historian observed, "At their most objective, editors tended to sift through reasonable truths to pull out the one that fit most snugly their local needs."[19]

This practice of favoring advocacy over objectivity also included press attacks and smear campaigns aimed at army officers and politicians who acknowledged the justified grievances of the Indians or who favored policies of negotiation and reconciliation. For example, Colonel Benjamin Grierson, the commander of the Tenth Cavalry (a famed unit of Buffalo soldiers), was not only a supporter of the military abilities of black troops but also argued that the government's failure to fulfill obligations to the Indians was the primary cause for conflict and for Indians deserting the reservation. His position on Indian affairs led Grierson to be "heartily abused" in the local press, especially by those newspapermen "who preached extermination." Similarly, when Vincent Colyer, the secretary of the Board of Indian Commissioners, arrived in Arizona Territory in 1871 to make peace with the Apaches in the wake of the Camp Grant Massacre, a vigilante action that resulted in the deaths of 150 Apache men, women, and children, the local press pilloried his mission "to mesmerize the Apaches into peace" and ridiculed him as "Vincent the Good." The *Arizona Star* described President Ulysses Grant's envoy as a "hypocrite, and accessory before the fact to murder," while the *Arizona Miner* labeled Colyer an "egregious ass" and a "self-conceited idiot." The use of such vitriolic hyperbole aimed at members of a peace commission provides an indication of western-press attitudes and offers implicit evidence of the feelings of the reading public. Likewise, it was not coincidental that Geronimo, when negotiating his final surrender in 1886, remarked that his previous breakouts from the reservation were the result of "bad talk" and "stories in the newspapers that I am [was] to be hanged."[20]

Not all western papers took such a hard line, and there are examples of editors who took a stand in favor of the tribes. Thomas H. Tibbles, for example, an assistant editor at the *Omaha Herald*, used the paper as platform to advocate on behalf of a small group of Ponca Indians who had left Indian Territory in 1879, the year after their forced resettlement there resulting from a federal-government error that transferred their promised reservation on the Missouri River to the Sioux. Tibbles successfully mobilized church officials and prominent citizens within the community and gained support for the cause in the East from groups such as the Boston Indian Citizenship Committee. Two Omaha lawyers filed a writ of habeas corpus on behalf of the Poncas to force their release from military custody and to prevent their return to Indian Territory. As commander of the region, General Crook openly sympathized with the Poncas and described orders to return them as a "disagreeable duty."[21] In a landmark decision, U.S. District Court judge Elmer S. Dundy heard the case, *Standing Bear v. Crook*, and ruled in favor of the displaced tribe. The judge ruled that "an Indian is a 'person' within the meaning of the laws of the United States, and has, therefore, the right to sue out a writ of habeas corpus in a federal court."[22] The government later agreed to indemnify the Poncas for their losses during the forced resettlement and gave the tribe the option to remain in Indian Territory or to return to their former reservation.

The actions of Tibbles and the *Omaha Herald* on behalf of the Poncas offers an exception to the rule in the case of frontier newspapers. The controversy, however, raises a key point with respect to a divided media message. Prior to the Civil War, sectional rivalries involving the question of slavery found their most bitter expressions in the war of words between northern and southern newspapers. In similar fashion, proposals related to the treatment of the Indians split along a divide between the major newspapers of the Eastern Seaboard and their smaller media competitors in the West. As part of a larger reform effort aimed at promoting the rights of the tribes, the Women's National Indian Association emerged as "one of the most active and influential of the Indian-rights groups during the 1880s." In promoting the goals of education, civil rights, civilization, and full citizenship, the association printed various types of literature, including a monthly paper, *The Indian's Friend*, to record current legislation related to the Natives and to promote the group's activities. Amelia Quinton and Mary Bonner formed the association in 1879 partly due to reports in the eastern press concerning the unjust treatment of the tribes. Quinton described the group's goal of bringing "legal status" and "protection of law" to the Indians through "missionary activity." As she openly admitted, the association's objectives focused not only on the just treatment of Indians but also on their conversion to Christianity and the effacement of their previous cultural, or "barbarian," identity.[23]

The depiction of Indians as "savages," "treacherous," and "warlike" are recurrent themes in the newspaper reporting during the period. Likewise, the use of the term "extermination" appears frequently, applied to either a proposed solution to the "Indian problem" or attributed to Indian intentions with respect to white settlers. For example, the *New York Herald* reported on an Indian uprising in the Pacific Northwest in May 1856, declaring that "tribes of Indians have formed an alliance for the extermination, as they say, of the whites." Two months later a letter to the editor from a correspondent in Oregon alleged that settlers had been "cruelly butchered" by the tribes and argued that "extermination, however, unchristian-like it may appear, seems to be the only resort left for the protection of life and property." Almost a decade later another correspondent raised the specter of extirpation in the wake of the conflict on the plains in 1865. Describing a battle with Northern Plains Indians in July, the correspondent declared: "This was, therefore, in all probability, the first of a series of fights, that will result in the extermination of that race in the limits of the United States Territories—the first combat of an Indian war that will prove the last we will be troubled with." Furthermore, he opined that the Indian "has accomplished his part in the development of one portion of this continent" and needed to make way for others, including white settlers and freed slaves. In another example, a report from Nevada City, California, appeared in the *Boston Daily Advertiser* on August 28, 1865, in which the correspondent remarked on his coach driver's solution to the "Indian problem," calling for the use of unpaid volunteers to punish the Natives into "submission or extermination" at the cost of the plunder from their efforts. Such remarks certainly reflected the vox populi of many western settlers.[24]

The role of some western newspapers in advocating extermination is exemplified by a story that appeared in the *Idaho Tri-Weekly Statesman* on June 14, 1866. The article began with a transcript of a letter sent by the governor of Idaho Territory, Caleb Lyon, to the commissioner of Indian affairs in which Lyon alleged that a massacre of sixteen Lo Indians had been abetted by a newspaper editorial, which he quoted as stating: "We long to see this vile race exterminated. Every man who kills an Indian is a public benefactor." The newspaper's editor, James S. Reynolds, responded to Governor Lyon's accusations by calling the quotes "a forgery in every sentence and sentiment." Reynolds then acknowledged: "We have advocated the extermination of the Indians occupying all that large section of country known to be inhabited by hostile savages, as the only means of bringing them to peaceable terms. We entertain that opinion in common with all the people of this Territory."[25] With this admission, the editor concluded with the hope that the newspapers in Washington, D.C., and New York City that published Lyon's charges would also publish his response.

Reynolds's reply offers several insights into the larger issues of newspaper reporting in this period with respect to the Indians. First, western papers routinely proposed annihilation and extermination as the preferred solution for dealing with Indians. Second, this sentiment did not simply originate in the minds of the editors but was a reflection of the thoughts of many white settlers, who sought to displace the Natives from their lands in support of their own economic imperatives. Finally, Reynolds's last comment demonstrates a perception in the West that eastern newspapers were biased. Ironically, his own words provided a more telling indictment than any story that might appear in eastern journals. In this respect, however, Reynolds was partially correct since the core of political support for the Indians was found in the major media centers of the East, especially in New York, Boston, and Washington, D.C. Thus, like the sectional divide between northern and southern papers prior to the Civil War, an East-West divide emerged in the 1860s with respect to print reporting and proposals for dealing with the tribes.[26] In one telling example, the *New York Herald* published a story in 1867 that argued against "exterminating" the Indians and instead for "emancipating them, like the negroes, from political disabilities, and thus merging them into the great common nationality of United States citizens."[27]

Despite favoring the assimilation of the Indians through Christianization and civilization, eastern papers provided a forum in which the rhetoric of extermination found frequent usage, especially at times of increased tensions between the tribes and the federal government. During the Great Sioux War (1876–77), a conflict that witnessed the decimation of the Seventh Cavalry under George Custer, the issue of extermination or submission constituted an ongoing debate. For example, Senator John A. Logan (R-Illinois) argued in opposition to an amendment to transfer the Indian Bureau from the Department of Interior to the War Department in June 1876. The *National Republican* reported: "He [Logan] held that the work of humanizing and civilizing the Indians would be practically abandoned by transferring the care of the Indians to the War Department. It would signify a change from a peace policy to a war policy, . . . [and] meant war to the very extermination of the Indians." Ironically, this story appeared only four days before Custer met his fate at Little Bighorn, a battle that would reignite the calls for extermination. The *Memphis Daily Appeal* carried a story from Chicago on August 26, 1876, that detailed the travel of a peace commission, including Bishop Henry Whipple, a longtime reformer and advocate for Indian rights, to meet with the Sioux. Operating under the authority of the Department of the Interior, the commission was instructed to inform the Sioux to return to their reservations and to "stop their depredations" or "submit to extermination." Newspapers associated with religious denominations also entered into this discussion. For example, the *Morning Star and Catholic Messenger* ran a story in November 1876 calling for support to Catholic missionaries working with the Indians. It noted that the "only" expectation for current government policy was for the "extermination" of the Natives and called on the readership to donate three cents a month and pray the Ave Maria "to take up defence of our poor Catholic Indians."[28]

Despite the passions engendered by the loss of Custer and the Seventh Cavalry, newspapers such as the *New York Herald* continued to advocate against extermination. In a front-page story entitled "The Indian Question," later picked up by the *Iola Register* in Kansas, the reporter argued, "The hostile Indians cannot be exterminated unless they be slain regularly in battle, for troops set at the business of murdering prisoners and slaughtering women and children would be only fit for extermination themselves." He continued, "The war is our own breeding, and we can dispose of the hostile savages only by capturing and compelling them to cease to be vagabonds, take claims, go to work and become self-supporting." During the last of the Apache Wars against Geronimo and his band, the *Dallas Morning News* carried a story in its issue of June 20, 1886, with a dateline from Tombstone, Arizona. In a story entitled "A War of Extermination Inaugurated—Latest from the Front," a correspondent remarked that an army force under the command of Captain Henry Lawton had enlisted Yague Indians as scouts for the campaign against the Apache leader. The report did not quote Lawton directly but stated, "he will take no prisoners when the Indians are overtaken. Neither men, women, or children will be spared." Interestingly, Lawton in a letter to his wife on August 5, 1886, remarked on the arrival of Lieutenant Charles Gatewood, a leader of Apache scouts, whose mission was to contact Geronimo's band and "offer them a chance to surrender." He also commented, "I have great hopes of winding up the war soon."[29] In fact, one month after Lawton wrote this letter, Geronimo and his small band surrendered to Brigadier General Nelson A. Miles, thus ending the Apache Wars.

The Western Dime Novel

While newspapers played a major role in shaping public opinion about the West, it was the dime novel, a genre born during the process of westward expansion, that both reflected and created popular perceptions of the American West. The dime novel first emerged in the 1840s but only experienced major popular success in the 1860s. Newspaper serials represented the first incarnations of these novels, but it was the emergence of technological innovations in printing and publishing in 1860 that allowed for westerns to be marketed to a mass audience. Based in Buffalo, New York, Beadle Publishing became the standard bearer for the new genre and dominated the field until the establishment of Street and Smith Publishers in 1889. Andrew C. Wheeler, a New York theater critic, reflecting on the influence of this genre in 1876 wrote, "Thanks to Cooper and Beadle's dime series we are all Indian-mad." He continued: "[T]hrough the progress of settlement in the Far West, and the presence there of the army, . . . almost all of us have a personal interest in the ceaseless struggle with the Indians. Romance and intense personal feeling are thus blent [sic] as they, perhaps, never have been."[30]

Although not focused entirely on western themes, the mass market was dominated by the western and the detective novel. In fact, one of Beadle's first publications, *Seth Jones; or The Captives of the Frontier* (1860), became a bestseller, with a half-million copies sold. During the U.S. Civil War, soldiers became the primary readers of these action stories, and the company sold a total of four million books.[31]

The dominant theme of western novels in the 1860s involved the clash between wilderness and civilization, with a plot centered on the hero's role in "resolving conflict between the townspeople and the villains, usually by participating in a sequence of capture, flight, and pursuit." The publishers played a key role in creating a formulaic approach to these stories, while authors were expected to churn out prose to meet these expectations. In the case of *Seth Jones*, the protagonist is portrayed on the front cover as a coonskin-cap-wearing frontiersman replete with deerskin clothing, powder horn, and the ubiquitous musket. In this story Jones sets out to rescue a settler's daughter taken captive by Indians, joined in his quest by her father, her fiancé, and an Indian fighter determined to avenge the massacre of his family. In addition to the formulaic nature of the stories, Indians constitute the principal villains in many of the earlier novels, with occasional white villains who are "heavily disguised" as Indians until the end of the story. After the Civil War, however, additional bad guys emerged who reflected the sectional nature of the conflict, including Kansas-Missouri border ruffians and white outlaws.[32]

In one respect the novels reflected an accurate view of life in the West as violence formed a key constituent of the narrative, with as many as twenty deaths not being unusual in a story. For example, one hero was described as "honest and upright. . . . He was brave, and had shot two or three in brawls, but he was not regarded as quarrelsome." In contrast, sexual violence conforming to the Victorian standards of the time was largely absent, even if the premise of female captives undoubtedly raised this issue in the mind of the reader. Still, this imagery was explicitly included in some issues of the *Deadwood Dick* series in the late 1870s, with a heroine bound to a whipping post, naked from the waist up, and bleeding from whip marks as she is rescued from Indian captivity.[33]

In contrast to James Fenimore Cooper's depictions of the "noble savage" and a protagonist who finds himself caught between the irreconcilable worlds of the "wild" frontier and the "cultured" settlements, the characters in the majority of the dime novels were stereotypical.[34] The rejection of Cooper's romanticized view may be explained in part by the perceptions of army officers and their wives, who embarrassedly dismissed this naïve perspective after their initial encounters with the tribes. Likewise, the depiction of Indians as "villains" in the 1860s corresponded with the escalations in conflicts with whites due to increasing numbers of settlers flooding into the West and encroaching upon tribal lands.[35] In this respect sensational newspaper accounts of actual and alleged Indian depredations provided the fuel for the popular perception of the tribes as savage and treacherous, a perfect foil to the virtuous and courageous heroes of these books. Interestingly, one of the most recognized protagonists of the dime-novel era was not a fictional character but a real-life frontiersman, William "Buffalo Bill" Cody.

In a series of western novels at the start of the 1870s, Ned Buntline used Cody and "Wild Bill" Hickock as the protagonists in a standard storyline of killing the bad guys and rescuing a damsel from Indian captivity.[36] Serving as friend and sidekick to Cody, Buntline described Hickock as "a veritable terror to bad men on the border." Likewise, the duo's exploits included frequent clashes with Indians, as exemplified in the following passage:

> There was a wild, fierce yell, such as only the Sioux throats could utter, as they leaped to their feet and made a dash toward him. Quick as was their movement, Bill had gained his feet ere the red devils gained the thicket. There was no time to use his Winchester, but the two six-shooters leaped from his belt, and the scout was soon surrounded by a sheet of flame as his deadly revolvers vomited leaden hail into the scarlet foe.[37]

The purple prose of this description offers a perfect illustration of the style and content of the thousands of western dime novels that flooded eastern markets with millions of copies between 1860 and 1890. By the end of this period, the western-fiction genre had developed a collection of stereotype characters including the intrepid scout, the murderous Indian, the deceitful Mexican, the hanging judge, the quick-handed sheriff, and the daring outlaw, among others.[38]

In the end the propagandistic effects of the dime novels appears to have been circumscribed, with the genre serving more as escapist literature for eastern men and boys interested in a vicarious adventure. Additionally, the romanticized visions of duty on the frontier in these novels influenced some young men to join the army. The general depiction of Indians as treacherous, savage, and murderous in one sense provided the reading public with an implicit justification for the process of confining the tribes to reservations and "civilizing" them. Likewise, characters such as Daring Dick the Apache Killer and Bloody Nathan were individuals whose reputations rested on their prowess at killing Indians. In the case of the latter, Robert Bird's aptly named Nathan Slaughter was an archetype of the "Indian hater" whose literary killings were justified by "the ferocious example of the red man." The formulaic nature of these works, matched by the low quality of the paper used to produce them, serve as perfect metaphors for novels designed as cheap and disposal instruments of popular culture. But a shift in the genre's focus occurred near the end of the nineteenth century with the portrayal of the West as a "virile, healthy society," a representation that in many respects reflected the essential elements of Turner's frontier thesis.[39] In this case, the genre merely reflected popular beliefs instead of created them. By 1900, the western genre had become largely a relic for hack writers and pulp fiction, though the "Old West" by now had passed into memory and nostalgia, becoming more of an imagined space than ever before.

"The Greatest Show on Earth?"

While dime novels provided the medium for introducing generations of Americans to the West, Buffalo Bill's Wild West shows, complete with live fire and authentic Indian actors, became not only a national but also an international sensation on stages and fairgrounds around the world, productions that "dominated public entertainment" in the last three decades of the nineteenth century. The idea for the show came from Buntline, the dime-store novelist and popularizer of the Buffalo Bill legend. The initial play, "The Scouts of the Prairie," written and rehearsed by Buntline in the space of four hours, opened in Chicago in December 1872, with a group of hastily enlisted hotel employees playing the roles of "real Indians" accompanied by Buffalo Bill, who forgot his lines and had to ad lib his performance. Despite the amateurish start, the *Evening Journal* gave the show a favorable notice. "Nixon's Amphitheatre was last night the scene of a most extraordinary character," its reviewer wrote, "not less than 2,500 boys and young men crowded the amphitheatre to catch a glimpse of their heroes." The reviewer for the *Times* proved much less favorable, commenting, "Such a combination of incongruous drama, execrable acting, renowned performers, mixed audience, intolerable stench, scalping, blood and thunder, is not likely to be vouchsafed to a city for a second time—even Chicago."[40]

The reviewer for the *Evening Journal* unknowingly pinpointed the reason for the popularity of the play despite its manifold failings. An audience of young men and boys came to be entertained, to partake vicariously in the adventure of a true-life hero and witness his skill with a rifle and revolver, and to enjoy the thrill of an exotic romance, not to be morally uplifted or intellectually challenged. The initial play, a melodrama, also highlighted the ambiguity associated with the portrayal of Indians. Its alternate title was "Red Deviltry as It Is," but Dove Eye, a beautiful Indian maiden, was a central figure in the plot, a late eighteenth-century Pocahontas desired by cowboy and audience alike.

From its modest opening at a Chicago theater, Buffalo Bill's stage show maintained a profitable and popular run over the course of the next decade before expanding into a western extravaganza, a mix of rodeo and frontier fantasy, replete with steer riding, buffalo herds, simulated battles with authentic Indians, and even a stagecoach attack. Opening in Omaha in May 1883, the Wild West, Rocky Mountain, and Prairie Exhibition became a smash hit and an "instant national mania" that would entertain crowds around the world for the following three decades. One famous spectator, Samuel Clemens, better known as Mark Twain, wrote Cody a letter in 1885 in which he remarked: "I have now seen your Wild West show two days in succession, enjoyed it thoroughly. It brought back to me the breezy, wild life of the Rocky mountains, and stirred me like a war song. The show is genuine, cowboys, vaqueros, Indians, stage-coach, costumes, the same as I saw on the frontier years ago." The inclusion of Chief Sitting Bull to the entourage in 1885, less than a decade after Custer's fall at Little Bighorn, provided another major public draw; the Sioux leader was greeted with derision by U.S. crowds and adulation by Canadian spectators during his one season with the show. Despite Twain's praise and Sitting Bull's short stint, the Wild West Show increasingly "made little attempt at authenticity" and became a source of "entertainment and nothing else."[41]

As the show toured European capitals to crowned heads and overflow crowds in the late 1880s, it was as a caricature and not as a representation of the American West. In Germany the troupe of over two hundred cowboys and Indians created a "sensation" throughout the country between April 1890 and May 1891 as "people waited by the thousands to welcome the participants as they arrived in each city." In fact, it is possible that a German fiction writer, Karl May, a man who never visited the West, attended the show while it toured in the summer of 1890 and was himself affected by the wave of "Indianthusiasm" that swept the country. Perhaps not coincidentally, his most famous western-fiction series, *Winnetou*, appeared in 1893.[42] May was the writer whose fictional accounts of cowboys and Indians were "devoured" by Hitler as a boy and served as the future führer's primary source of information on the American West.[43] Ironically, one of the most lasting vestiges of Buffalo Bill's Wild West Show may have been its transmission of images from an imaginative writer to an enraptured young Austrian boy at the turn of the century.[44]

Imagining the Nazi East

In contrast to the amorphous nature and varied impulses that catalyzed American expansion, the idea of lebensraum emerged primarily from the vision of one individual, Adolf Hitler. In his formulation of "living space," Hitler borrowed from the theory of geopolitics, including and specifically from the ideas of Karl Haushofer. For Hitler, the East was not a "geographic" region, but instead a *blutsmäßigbedingter Begriff* (blood-based concept). Similarly, in the writings of Haushofer and other geopoliticians of the "German school," the state was seen not only as an "organism subject to biological laws" but also as an entity with the inherent right to expand beyond its existing borders. Haushofer and his acolytes framed this process in Social Darwinist terms as the expansion or decay of the state. As such, geopolitical theory posited war as the "natural state of man" and provided the "rationalization for German racism." Haushofer's ideas resonated with Hitler and found expression in the Nazi worldview, a perspective that elevated race to the supreme element of spatial politics.[45]

In his formulation of a German living space in the East, Hitler was equal parts prophet, propagandist, and racial theorist. Already in 1925 in *Mein Kampf* (*My Struggle*), Hitler made an explicit connection between Nazi racial imperatives and German expansion. He described "the essence of the foreign policy" within a *volkisch* state as "guaranteeing the existence . . . of the race . . . by establishing between the number and growth of the population, on the one hand, and the size and value of the soil and territory, on the other hand, a viable, natural relationship." Hitler labeled Germany's present territorial size as "ridiculous" for a country aspiring to world-power status and consequently called for an effort "to eliminate the discrepancy between our [Germany's] population and our area."[46] Tellingly, he rejected the idea for a restoration of the pre–World War I borders but demanded instead an extension of the "German nation [and] the soil and territory to which it is entitled on this earth." He also extolled expansion as a type of "national sacrifice" to be achieved by "a triumphant sword," though only at the cost of German blood.[47]

In his writings Hitler made reference to the Teutonic Knights of the fourteenth century and warned, "But if we talk about new soil and territory in Europe today, we can think primarily only of Russian and its vassal border states." His choice of the Soviet Union was not coincidental but reflected his own racial and anti-Semitic philosophy. He contended that Russia had fallen under "the yoke of the Jews" and was now ready for collapse in the face of a "new Alexandrian campaign" in which the sword would provide new lands for "the industrious labor of the German plow."[48]

Hitler had clearly formulated his thoughts on the question of living space by 1925, yet he provided a more detailed discussion of this topic in 1928 as he composed the manuscript for his so-called *Second Book*. This second manifesto was dominated by the themes of lebensraum, military conquest, anti-Semitism, and the requisite need for German expansion in the East. In it Hitler asserted that "a people's entire struggle for survival in reality consists only of securing the necessary territory and land." From this perspective, expansion offered a binary choice between either the survival or the death of a state and its people and forms a "heroic act." As a result, war and sacrifice were elevated to the status of virtues, even moral obligations, with expansion tied to "ethnic and racial perceptions." Hitler elaborated on the issue of racial considerations with respect to conquest in the East: "The ethnic state, in contrast, could under absolutely no circumstances annex Poles with the intention of turning them into Germans one day. It would instead have to decide either to isolate these alien racial elements in order to prevent the repeated contamination of one's people's blood, or it would have to immediately remove them entirely, transferring the land and territory that thus became free to members of one's own ethnic community."[49] In other words, "isolation" and "removal" of dangerous contaminants, however defined, and not assimilation provided the crucial element of his plans for the peoples of eastern Europe.

In expounding on his vision of a German East, Hitler repeatedly referred to his own belief in the inextricable relationship between Judaism and Bolshevism. He also emphasized the essential racial differences between Nordic and Slavic peoples, going so far as to identify "an infinite chasm" between the two peoples, one that prevented any chance of cooperation but rather demanded a competition between them for available resources. Ultimately, Hitler advocated a "policy of space . . . [that] turns away from all international industrial and international trade policy attempts and instead concentrates all of its strength on marking out a way of life for our people through the allocation of adequate Lebensraum for the next hundred years . . . by forming a decisive power on land."[50]

The "decisive power" Hitler advocated was not merely a means to conquest in the East but also a mechanism for *Weltherrschaft* (global domination), a point he made to an audience of students and faculty members at Erlangen in 1930. Indeed, he ultimately envisioned "a world in which there would be not three or four great powers with attendant empires, but one: Germany." In this sense the war in the East was merely one way station, albeit a critical one, in a larger plan of conquest and genocide in which "the Nazi regime would not have settled down after a victory over the allies and the conclusion of the Holocaust but carried on drawing social elixir from destroying other peoples" in an orgy of "serial genocide."[51]

If Hitler's ambition and vision exceeded his grasp in 1930, such was not the case after he became chancellor on January 30, 1933. Already in February he informed Wehrmacht leaders of his plans for German expansion and underscored the need "for the conquest and ruthless Germanization of new living space in the East." If the belief in American exceptionalism had buttressed the arguments for westward expansion, lebensraum offered the belief in German racial superiority as the fundamental justification for the conquest of the East. The fact that Germany did not possess the economic and military means to achieve this vision at the time provided the rationale for Hitler's massive rearmament plans, with the ultimate goal of first continental and later world hegemony.[52]

As a foreign-policy goal, hegemony could only be accomplished through war and conquest. In *Mein Kampf* Hitler claimed that "[s]tate frontiers are man-made and can be altered." He then underlined the necessity for war and conquest by recognizing that "only the might of a triumphant sword will in the future assign us territory, and with it life for our nation." In addition to military might, the subjugation of the East would require a vast expanse of superhighways and railroads to facilitate German settlement and to assure control over these areas. Hitler repeatedly referred to this transportation system and described it as the "essential prerequisite for the domination and economic exploitation" of the East. The manpower for the construction of the "Führer's Roads" would come for the most part from the massive use of forced and slave laborers, to include prisoners of war and Jews, a precedent set already in 1940 with the use of thousands of such workers in the building of a superhighway between Frankfurt an der Oder and the captured Polish city of Posen. The practice of using Jews as slave laborers continued after the invasion of the Soviet Union in June 1941, with the explicit intention of not only exploiting their labor but also of achieving the additional objective of *Vernichtung durch Arbeit* (annihilation through work).[53] In this sense road and rail projects became not only means of extending German control over the conquered areas but also tools for achieving mass extermination under the "triumphant sword."

The sword was an apt symbol for Nazi plans in the East, but the military preparations for war with Poland, already begun in March 1939, were augmented by one of the most extensive and ambitious propaganda machines of the twentieth century.[54] Nazi propaganda efforts during the Third Reich were aimed at gaining support for the regime and for shaping German popular opinion of the führer, the party, and especially the enemies of National Socialism.

Propaganda in the Third Reich

Hitler described propaganda as a form of "art," one that revealed its full importance to him during the crucible of World War I. To him, propaganda was not an instrument for influencing the opinion of the educated elites, but rather it served as the critical means for shaping the views of the masses. He declared: "All propaganda has to be popular and has to adapt its spiritual level to the perception of the least intelligent of those towards whom it intends to direct itself. Therefore its spiritual level has to be screwed the lower, the greater the mass of people which one wants to attract." Furthermore, he contended, "all effective propaganda has to limit itself only to a very few points and to use them like slogans until even the very last man is able to imagine what is intended by such a word." Hitler's epiphany concerning the role and importance of propaganda found expression in the Nazi Party's use of a variety of media, including newsprint, posters, radio, and even airplanes for campaigning prior to 1933. In this sense Hitler devoted considerable attention to the formulation of his party's propaganda prior to becoming chancellor.[55] Afterward, it became a state-sponsored and state-directed activity, a fact clearly underlined by his creation of the Ministry for Popular Enlightenment and Propaganda under the direction of one of his most faithful and infamous paladins, Joseph Goebbels.

For his part, Goebbels proved adept at the task and confident in his ability to demonstrate "what one can do with the state apparatus when one knows how to use it." In March 1933 Goebbels took control of the newly created ministry, one that included departments for the press, radio, theater, film, and propaganda. It not only reigned over the instruments of popular culture in the Third Reich but the avenues of information and high culture as well. Goebbels framed his mission in martial terms as a battle for the minds and souls of the German people. Referring to World War I, he remarked, "We did not lose the war because our artillery gave out but because the weapons of minds did not fire."[56] The allusion to war was a fitting one since the period between 1933 and 1939 served as a prelude to conflict during which the Propaganda Ministry focused a great deal of effort in promoting a "military spirit" and martial identity among Germans, an effort characterized by the explosion of uniforms throughout the Reich as state and party organizations outfitted themselves with badges, belts, and sidearms etched with slogans of loyalty and sacrifice.

The outbreak of the war in September 1939 intensified the propaganda campaign among the German people. Over the course of the war, this onslaught focused on mobilizing popular support for the conflict and was characterized by three strategies. One overarching strategy offered the vision of national expansion, which could only be achieved by force of arms. In the period between 1939 and 1941, the ministry's efforts framed the campaigns against Poland, France, England, and the Soviet Union as preemptive actions taken in the face of the aggressive intentions of Germany's neighbors. Between 1942 and 1945, Nazi propaganda created the specter of "barbarous Bolshevik hordes" and cast Germany as the last bulwark for saving European civilization.[57]

While newspapers and print media played an important role, the radio became the central medium for the regime and its efforts to shape German public opinion. Goebbels described this relatively nascent technology as "by nature authoritarian" and an instrument that "automatically offers itself to the Total State." The production of an affordable *Volksempfänger* (people's radio) and the placing of "Reich loudspeaker columns" on street corners and in public squares throughout Germany were two key initiatives aimed at putting all Germans within the regime's oratorical reach. Likewise, Hitler's carefully orchestrated broadcasts emphasized national redemption and revival, using religious and mystical imagery that left many listeners enthralled and exultant. Openly declaring his intentions with respect to radio, Goebbels exclaimed, "We make no bones about it: the radio belongs to us, to no one else!" He continued, "And we will place the radio at the service of our idea, and no other idea shall be expressed through it."[58]

War Propaganda and the Party Line

The invasion of Poland provided the opportunity to realize the goals of avenging German honor for the loss of the Great War and beginning the process of national expansion on the road to achieving lebensraum for a millennial empire. In the months preceding the outbreak of war, the Propaganda Ministry initiated an "orchestrated" campaign that emphasized and made effective use of existing anti-Slavic prejudices. Stories and rumors of atrocities were used to generate support for retribution against the Poles. A report by the German Social Democratic Party detailed the effectiveness of this campaign: "An action against Poland would be greeted by the overwhelming mass of the people. . . . The Poles are enormously hated among the masses for what they did at the end of the [Great] War." One of the major themes of Nazi propaganda in the first weeks of fighting repudiated the "shame" of Versailles and German humiliation in November 1918 by explicitly stating that such events would never be allowed to occur again. Nazi propaganda also focused the blame for the war on the "English plutocracy" and the "English-Jewish international war clique." In a directive of September 17, 1939, Goebbels emphasized, "It is essential to represent the English plutocracy as the true warmongers and to incite the whole nation to a holy rage."[59]

The creation of a "holy rage" during the invasion of Poland included a dedicated campaign to highlight real and alleged atrocities committed against ethnic Germans there, an effort that "contributed immensely to inciting venomous antagonism towards the Poles." The actions of German forces operating in Poland evolved due to a number of factors, not least of which were historical stereotypes, personal biases, and wartime propaganda, most importantly the representations of their enemies imparted by party and military leaders, whether through ideological instruction and professional publications or via directives and orders. In addition, newly formed Wehrmacht propaganda units, designed to document German martial skill and to stigmatize the enemy, accompanied combat forces into Poland and created a *novum* in warfare.[60]

The Nazi campaign in the East, like the Indian Wars, was not relegated to combat actions but also included a war of words aimed at putative enemies. The SS weekly newspaper the *Black Corps* constituted an important venue for propagating the SS ethic and the Nazi worldview among Himmler's political soldiers and within the public at large. Published between 1935 and 1945, with a maximum circulation of 750,000 copies, the paper "had a strong impact on the public" and was described as the "most extraordinary and most widely feared organ of the National Socialist press." Within the police, many units subscribed to the publication for the purpose of incorporating it into their ideological-training program. An order of October 1939 directed the distribution of free copies among their ranks and detailed plans for finishing the construction of public display cases specifically for the *Black Corps* within police stations.⁶¹ It is important to note that for Germans in this period, the use of such display cases was extremely important since numerous readers unable or unwilling to spend their money on newspapers regularly stopped to read them at these sites.

Throughout its publication, Himmler maintained a deep personal interest and helped frame the major themes presented in the *Black Corps*. Anti-Bolshevism and Nazi racism constituted two topics that dominated the pages of almost every issue. In the case of the latter, "nearly every issue and, so it seemed, every article had some reference to race." The paper's anti-Semitic message found expression in a two-part piece entitled "The Plague of Vienna," a pictorial depiction of the "Jewish ghetto" in Vienna designed to "evoke revulsion and disgust from the readers." In another example, an article entitled "Money out the Window" compared the costs of a program to build low-cost housing for newlyweds with the "waste" of almost a million reichsmarks associated with the housing of the mentally and physically handicapped in Breslau.⁶²

With the invasion of Poland and especially after the attack on the Soviet Union, the image of the "dirty" Jew became a standard trope in the pages of the *Black Corps*, and the themes of anti-Semitism and anti-Bolshevism merged into an inseparable whole. Although the editors made no direct mention of the "Final Solution," the use of terms such as "annihilation" and "extermination" in reference to the Jews established an explicit image for the reader. With respect to the SS and the police, stories concerning their cooperation in bringing "order" to Poland as well as articles on the actions of these units in antipartisan operations against "bandits" and "Bolsheviks" intimated at the prosecution of the racial war in the East.⁶³ For most readers among the policemen who had served in the East or who had colleagues and friends there, the real meaning of these terms and their connection could hardly be missed.

War and Popular Literature

The outbreak of hostilities in 1939 engendered a veritable flood of popular literature describing the role of German military and police forces in the various theaters of war. These stories had their forerunners in the youth-war literature of the Great War that had "encouraged violent fantasies about soldiering and national greatness." These book and magazine accounts of World War I and World War II were analogous to the western dime-store novels in that they were aimed at the public, especially young readers. Works such as *The Heroic Battle for Narvik* and the *Battle for Norway* used operational accounts and eyewitness reports, interspersed with propaganda and war paroles, to justify these campaigns and to laud German military prowess. In this respect the attack on Norway was characterized not as aggression against the Norwegian state, but rather as a blow aimed at England and the threat posed by the British blockade, a point made explicit in the *Battle for Norway*'s subtitle, *Reports and Pictures of the War against England*. In contrast, Rolf Bathe's *The Eighteen Day Campaign*, using military situation reports, purported to provide a chronicle of Wehrmacht operations against Poland. Already in his foreword, however, Bathe made use of National Socialist talking points in his declaration that the war was being "fought for German freedom and living space (*Lebensraum*) and to free ethnic Germans in the East from the murdering hands of white hot Polish chauvinism." Citing British attempts to encircle Germany, alleged Polish border violations, and atrocities against ethnic Germans in Poland, Bathe characterized the invasion as a justified response to "a campaign of annihilation against defenseless [Germans]." In the end, it was not alleged Polish perfidy that triumphed, but a "young National Socialist Wehrmacht," an army reborn and imbued with the "spirit of uncompromising effort and a self-evident commitment to duty."[64]

In a totalitarian state with an official propaganda apparatus, messages of conquest and racial hegemony were a central element of governance. The Wehrmacht was not the only military arm used as an instrument to transmit such messages. A popularized account of police activities published shortly after the conclusion of the campaign in Poland, *Mounted Police in Poland*, exemplified the technique of conjoining racial stereotypes with criminal activity. One officer, Helmuth Koschorke, described the activities of the mounted police forces during the invasion by conflating the image of the "Asian" other with the Poles. Additionally, he emphasized the "criminal" nature of their opposition to occupation and portrayed Poles as indolent, shifty, dishonest, malicious, and drunken. Koschorke also described police efforts to hunt down "snipers" and "marauders" in order to reestablish "order" and the use of the police units for "suppressing . . . flare ups of guerrilla warfare [Bandenkrieg] with an iron fist." Later he quoted one officer instructing his men on the unit's mission involving the "cleansing" of "murderous arsonists" and "the rendering harmless" of "murderous scoundrels."[65] His choice of expressions provided perfect examples of the use of euphemistic language to disguise actions and of the way in which the "object" of the action was delegitimized. Indeed, one might expect the use of both devices in a popularized account aimed at the general public.

Koschorke focused specifically on reinforcing racial prejudices with respect to the Slavic stereotype of the Roman Catholic Pole. Likewise, clerics are depicted as hypocritical prevaricators who used their positions and their churches as cover for murderous acts aimed at the ethnic German population or the occupying German forces.[66] Noticeably absent from this account is a discussion of Poland's large Jewish population, a fact in part explained by Koschorke's publication of a second work in 1941, *The Police Intervenes!* In this book he adopted the style of a diarist to track the progress of German campaigns in 1939 and 1940.

In addition to his emphasis on the military tasks of the police in Poland and his description of officers serving "shoulder-to-shoulder" with the Waffen SS and the Wehrmacht, Koschorke gave full vent to the crudest expressions of anti-Semitism. Similar to his earlier book, with its thick portrayal of Slavic prejudice, this one employed the strongest form of racial caricature in its depiction of Polish Jewry. In a literary sleight of hand, Koschorke indicted both the Jews and the Polish aristocracy ostensibly in the words of a simple Polish peasant, who is quoted as saying that he does not care who rules the country as long it is neither of these two groups. In a subsequent entry he described a small town near Radom as a "nest of Jews" and later detailed his own reaction to his own encounters with Polish Jews: "When I think back on the last two days, I become nauseous. Jews, Jews and again more Jews. We rounded up hundreds and hundreds of the most abominable examples."[67]

The Role of Film

In his study of propaganda, Hilmar Hoffmann asserted, "Film was doubtless the most influential among the mass media in the Third

Reich." The words of the Nazi director Fritz Hippler support this contention. Discussing the influence of movies, Hippler remarked, "film has a particularly forceful and lasting psychological and propagandistic impact because of its effect not on the intellect, but principally on the emotions and the visual sense. . . . [F]ilm can exercise an influence on society that is more enduring than that achieved by church or school or, for that matter, literature, the press or radio." Without doubt, Goebbels and his Propaganda Ministry made extensive use of cinema as a means to influence German public opinion. After the start of the war, film was used to portray the heroic exploits of German soldiers, sailors, and airmen on the one hand, and as a vehicle for identifying the Reich's enemies on the other.[68]

The Nazi cinematic campaign aimed against the Jews experienced its most profound success in 1940 with the release of two widely distributed anti-Semitic productions, *The Jew Süß* and *The Eternal Jew*. In the former, Ferdinand Marian, a popular German actor, portrayed the fictional Jew Süß, a greedy, power-hungry, and sinister adviser to Duke Karl Alexander of Württemberg in the eighteenth century. The story details Süß's rise to power by his manipulation of the duke's financial situation. By the end of the film, Süß has essentially taken control of the kingdom's affairs and, assisted by Jewish accessories, is exploiting the citizens through taxes and tolls. In addition, Süß is portrayed in the classic anti-Semitic role of "Jewish molester and pornographer" in his pursuit of the chaste and decidedly Aryan Dorothea Sturm (Kristina Söderbaum). In the end he rapes Sturm after attempting to blackmail her for sex in exchange for the release of her imprisoned fiancée. Her subsequent suicide catalyzes a revolt that leads to the fall of Süß and the death by heart attack of the hapless duke. The movie ends with Süß begging for his life to no avail and the pronouncement, "Herewith, the Jew ban is in force for all of Württemberg."[69]

The Jew Süß was screened throughout occupied Europe to over 20 million people between 1940 and 1943. While gauging its reception is difficult, it appeared to have achieved its intended purpose among some viewers. Bruno Manz, then a nineteen-year-old soldier, later remembered his reaction: "It persuaded me to believe the old *Stürmer* canard that the Jews were trying to subjugate the German people by debauching their women." He continued: "Indeed, it convinced me that the alleged Jewish conspiracy was much more than a purely political plot. . . . [I]t now appeared a systematic attempt to destroy the Aryan race by defiling their women and 'polluting' their blood." Other viewers had similar reactions, and in some cases the screening of the movie promoted violent attacks on Jews, including one incident where a group of moviegoers ripped the beard from one man in Budapest. Similarly, after viewing the film, SS guards at the Sachsenhausen concentration camp conducted a roll call of the Jewish prisoners and proceeded to beat them in retribution for Süß's alleged sins against the German people. Himmler liked the film so much that he ordered that it be seen by the "entire SS and police" as a part of ideological instruction, a process whereby fiction became transformed into historical fact for the Reich's political soldiers.[70]

Perhaps the most notorious example of Nazi anti-Semitic films can be found in Fritz Hippler's *The Eternal Jew* (1940). Hippler, a member of the SS, was described as "the most eager and unscrupulous among Goebbels's film experts who knew how to arrange the most disparate clips and most antagonistic arguments into a triumph of dialectical destructiveness." Employing a documentary style, Hippler and a team of cameramen filmed Polish Jews after the German occupation in 1939. Adopting a false tone of objectivity, the narrator comments, "No Jew was forced into any kind of action or position during the shooting . . . , and [we] tried to shoot in moments when they were unaware of the camera's presence." The film crew's selections were far from random. Hippler used archetypes and played upon popular caricature to display Polish Jews as a pestilence and a "race of parasites." One of the most insidious comparisons in the history of cinema appears with the juxtaposition of Polish Jews with hordes of rats. At this point the narrator declares: "Comparable with the Jewish wanderings through history are the mass migrations of an equally restive animal, the rat. . . . Wherever rats appear they bring ruin, they ravage human property and foodstuffs. In this way they spread disease: plague, leprosy, typhoid, cholera, dysentery, . . . no different from the Jews among mankind!"[71] The use of such imagery was designed to evoke fears of "plague" and "epidemic" while justifying the use of extermination and annihilation to "cleanse" Europe from these imagined dangers. In this case, terms such as "extermination" and "annihilation" used in conjunction with fighting a Jewish or Bolshevist "pestilence" provided the perfect linguistic complement to this biologically prescribed threat.

The portrayal of the Jews as a deadly and foreign pathogen within the German body was not new. Hitler made use of this disease simile in a meeting with the Hungarian regent, Admiral Nikolaus Horthy, in April 1943: "They [the Jews] would have to be treated like tuberculosis bacilli from which a healthy body could become infected.... Why should the beasts that want to bring us Bolshevism be spared?" The successful conflation of Jews with disease was not limited to film screens and Hitler's monologues, as demonstrated by an article in a police magazine in January 1, 1940, that remarked on the "cleaning up" taking place in Poland, a process aimed at "bacillus" and "caftan wearers" (that is, Jews).[72]

The Eternal Jew, like *The Jew Süß*, catalyzed acts of violence against Jews throughout Germany and eastern Europe. But the larger effect of such films on shaping public opinion and conditioning the population to apocalyptic measures in dealing with this alleged threat had the most profound ramifications. Hoffmann argued: "It is no coincidence that the machinery of genocide was set in motion at the same time that this 'documentary' justification of mass murder was released.... Cinematographic instruments that worked so insidiously and manipulated the consciousness of the masses as effectively as possible secured a consenting silence on a massive scale."[73] The Nazi success in using films to transmit and promote anti-Semitic stereotypes found renewed expression after the invasion of the Soviet Union in June 1941.

The attack on Russia resulted in a concerted effort by Goebbels and his ministry to frame the conflict in the East as an apocalyptic struggle between two diametrically opposed ideologies, a position Hitler made repeatedly in his preinvasion meetings with Wehrmacht generals. In the words of one historian: "The official version sought to legitimize the Russian campaign by presenting the war in the East as a life-or-death struggle pitting Germany, Europe, perhaps the entire white race against those 'Asiatic subhumans' who, like their Mongol, Avar, and Hun ancestors, were once again making plans to install themselves as slave masters of the West." German artists adapted this theme in stylized depictions of Teutonic Knights battling against "hordes from the East." Nazi propaganda not only portrayed the invasion as a battle against Communist-inspired Asiatic hordes but also as the result of a "Jewish swindle" in which "the Jews have driven the peoples of the Soviet Union into this unspeakable situation through their devilish system of Bolshevism." In order to unmask this "swindle," Goebbels called for a "hard-hitting campaign of enlightenment" using words and photographs to contrast the "inhuman conditions of the Soviet Union" with the high cultural level and the healthy joy in life" enjoyed by Germans.[74]

The Wehrmacht's offensive was accompanied by a propaganda assault on Bolshevism that incorporated every media, including cinema. Two Nazi propaganda films released after the attack offer insights into the ways in which the Propaganda Ministry sought to manipulate public opinion to support the campaign by raising the fears of a "Jewish Bolshevist" menace to German society. In a radio address on the opening day of the invasion, Goebbels identified "the Jew, through his demonic system of bolshevism," as an existential threat to the German people. Similarly, *The Soviet Paradise*, released in 1942, began with a commentary describing "the gray misery of the collective farm, . . . where the Soviet peasant lives as a slave." According to the film, the source of this misery could be found in "the disastrous results of twenty years of a bloody regime run by a Jewish-Bolshevik terror clique." Goebbels also raised the specter of the "bestial hordes" of the East intent on overwhelming European civilization. Likewise, *The Soviet Paradise* adopted the imagery of the "bestial" by its use of coded language such as "caked in filth," "unkempt," and "enslaved."[75]

A second film released in 1943, *In the Katyn Forest*, used the filmic device of a documentary to camouflage the more overt propagandistic elements of the production. The discovery of a mass grave in Poland near the town of Katyn, where members of the Soviet Secret Police had murdered thousands of Polish military officers, provided the pretext for making the picture. By using images of disinterred corpses along with "interviews," the film sought to blame both the Communists and the Jews for the massacre. The narrator describes Bolshevism as "a Jewish organization for the extermination of the intelligentsia and the culture of Europe and the world."[76] The piles of Polish corpses flickering across the screens of German cinemas, however, were dwarfed by the mountains of Jewish and Slavic victims of the war in the East. By this time millions of Jews, Poles, and Soviet citizens had perished at the hands of German executioners, acts of mass murder that had been prepared and facilitated in part by an enormous Nazi propagandistic onslaught.

Comparing the Nazi East and the American West

Undoubtedly, Hitler in his own writings and statements used the process of American westward expansion as a point of comparison for his own ideas on lebensraum and his designs in the East. Ironically, Turner's frontier thesis reflected in part the American's reading of the work of Friedrich Ratzel, a nineteenth-century German political geographer. In turn, Ratzel's ideas, like those of Haushofer, were used by Hitler in formulating his own views on a German empire in the East.[77] Although both lebensraum and manifest destiny expressed the necessity for expansion and posited an inherent right to the conquest of areas inhabited by other peoples, the ultimate rationale for each of these national projects was different in one vital respect. The purpose of lebensraum focused not only on the material and geographical dispossession of the Slavic population but also on the planned racial restructuring of the East through a process of large-scale physical extermination. According to Nazi ideology, the region would be "cleansed" of millions of its inferior peoples and replaced by a new race of Aryan soldier-farmers. Likewise, the conquest of the East was merely one step in a fantastic plan for global domination, a plan that encompassed not only serial warfare but also serial genocide. Although economic calculation played a key role in this scheme, racial considerations provided the fundamental justification for acts of conquest and annihilation. In contrast, manifest destiny emerged as a propagandistic slogan within the U.S. media designed to promote territorial expansion within the continent as both an American divine right and an economic imperative. Although this philosophy undoubtedly held significant implications for the tribes occupying western lands, the governmental policies that underpinned this expansionary effort never embraced the large-scale extermination of Native peoples in a physical sense, but rather their pacification and the effacement of their ethnic and cultural identity through a process of disappropriation, isolation, and eventual assimilation. In this national project the economic incentives of land and resources provided the primary rationale for supplanting the established tribes.

The role of propaganda in each of these national efforts offers an additional point for comparison. In the case of Nazism, lebensraum may have found expression in the mind and writings of Hitler, but it was his ability to translate these ideas into specific government policies of occupation and subjugation that proved most significant. These were formulated at the highest levels of Nazi government and supported by a state-sanctioned and state-controlled media apparatus specifically designed to promote these ideas among the German population. The use of mass communication and instruments of mass influence, including the radio, print, and film, provided potent mechanisms for spreading these messages in a totalitarian society.

In contrast, the prophets of manifest destiny began selling their ideas in the penny press and in the pages of pamphlets and newspapers aimed at influencing popular opinion and, by extension, the politicians who represented the American public. In a democratic state, however, manifest destiny was a contested idea as witnessed by the northern Whig opposition to "Mr. Polk's War" and that party's resistance to the annexation of large areas of the Southwest. Likewise, politicians and private citizens were free to raise their voices in protest to this "wicked war." In the end, manifest destiny was not a coherent idea but a slogan that would be reinvented, repackaged, and resold to the American public in the six decades between 1839 and 1898. In the case of the War of 1898 with Spain, it was again a point of political and social contestation as witnessed in the words of William Graham Sumner, a Yale sociologist and prominent intellectual, who argued: "Expansionism and imperialism are nothing but the old philosophies of national prosperity which have brought Spain to where she now is Those philosophies appeal to national vanity and national cupidity. . . . They are delusions, and they will lead us to ruin unless we are hard-headed enough to resist them."[78] William Randolph Hearst and his media empire may have helped "furnish" the war, but his was a private voice and did not guarantee hegemony for his ideas. Though the voices in favor of American expansionism eventually triumphed, it was only in the wake of a public and political contest.

The concepts of lebensraum and manifest destiny also differed in another critical respect. Nazi ideology portrayed the German "push to the East" as a racial and national imperative that literally involved the survival of the state. This idea was a natural extension of the embrace of Social Darwinism within the National Socialist worldview. In this case the struggle of individual peoples and races for dominance over competing and adversarial races formed the larger context of a view in which individual species fought to maintain their place within a given ecosystem. Under such a system, it was the "triumphant sword" that would reign supreme. In comparison, manifest destiny did not posit competition for territory in apocalyptic terms, but rather in messianic terms. A belief in American exceptionalism and a sense of mission provided the rationale for expansion into the West. The twin pillars of Christianization and civilization, along with the rifle and the plow, served as the instruments for the assimilation of the "savage" Indians. Indeed, the broad trajectory of U.S. government policy after the 1850s, and especially after 1869, focused on methods devoted to the integration of the tribes into U.S. society. In a real sense these policies reflected the colonial mentality expressed in Rudyard Kipling's concept of the "white man's burden." It was a process that was intended to deprive the Indians of their cultural way of life but not their physical existence. In the case of westward expansion, the president, Congress, and the public each played a role in determining the course of federal policy and selecting the instruments involved in the effacement of Indian identity.

CHAPTER 2

NATIONAL POLICIES OF RACE AND SPACE

National policies establish objectives for government bureaucracies and create the framework for aligning higher-level political goals with the specific guidelines, procedures, statutes, and laws designed to attain them. In the case of the Nazi East and the American West, government and party bureaucracies played a critical role in framing policy objectives for areas targeted for conquest. Likewise, individuals and organizations in these areas played a key role in the implementation and exercise of authority. The analysis of these policies, objectives, and actors provides a point of reference for analyzing specific initiatives as well as the nature of rhetoric and the trajectory of governmental and political policy in both regions. It also allows for the assessment of the roles of local government and of national agencies involved in the direct organization and management of conquered areas as well as the nature of day-to-day administration. This comparison provides important insights into the relative influence of the national government (the center) versus local actors (the periphery) in formulating and implementing policies on the ground.

The categories of race and space form key criteria within the literature of comparative genocide studies for evaluating historical cases. Their examination is often tied to the concept of "colonial genocide," a model used to study the treatment of aboriginal peoples in Australia and the Americas, European imperialist expansion into and subjugation of Africa, and the Nazi conquest of eastern Europe and the western Soviet Union. Without doubt, a comparison of the racial and economic beliefs and policies underpinning the German campaign of conquest in the East with the racial and economic assumptions providing the framework for U.S. governmental policy in the West offers important insights. It also highlights the complexity involved when attempting to detangle racial and economic motives in the process of conquest.

In the case of Hitler's war in the East, racial considerations provided the primary justification for launching a war of extermination and enslavement against the native populations of eastern Europe. In fact, Hitler lectured his military leaders on March 30, 1941, about just such a war of extermination and the "massive demographic revolution" it entailed.[1] It was ultimately on the grounds of racial superiority and under the tenets of Social Darwinism that German civilian bureaucrats and military leaders agreed on the necessity for the elimination of millions of inhabitants through direct and indirect murder *in advance* of the invasion. Similarly, racial ideology framed the spatial aspects in the planning for conquest, though "space" also provided the necessary prerequisite for economic exploitation. In this respect the captured lands were designed to serve as the new agricultural heartland of the Third Reich, an area that would be dominated by martial settlements in which German farmers ruled with the rifle and the plow. Above all, racial beliefs and Nazi ideology formed the bedrock upon which the eastern policy was based.

The trajectory of American westward expansion also embraced racial precepts along with concepts of spatial conquest, yet it was the desire for space and economic exploitation that provided the fundamental justification for U.S. policies of conquest and expansion into the areas under Indian control. It should be noted that this involved a contest not only with Native tribes but also with other nations, including Spain, Great Britain, Russia, and Mexico. In the case of the last, the war of 1846 clearly revealed U.S. attitudes of racial superiority, which in many cases may have contributed to atrocities against enemy soldiers and civilians alike. In regard to the Indians, the racial elements of westward expansion certainly included a belief in their inferiority as "uncivilized" and "savage" peoples, but eventual acculturation and assimilation, not physical annihilation, constituted the primary goal of U.S. governmental policy.[2] Despite the rhetoric of extermination found in the frontier newspapers circulating among white settlers and discussed by some military officers, an intentional policy for the physical annihilation of the Native populations on racial grounds or characteristics was missing. This absence of plans for physical extermination did not preclude the desire for the cultural obliteration of tribal customs, beliefs, and societies in a premeditated process of "civilizing" the Indians by the cross and the till. Still, economic imperatives and the desire for land and resources provided the primary impetus for expansion and conquest in the West. It was the desire of white farmers, land speculators, gold seekers, and a host of associated business interests that provided the motive force for encroaching upon Indian lands and consequent acts of concentration and dispossession. In the end, the desire for space and its associated economic advantages provided the primary rationale for westward expansion.

U.S. Policy and the Indians

If the history of U.S. policy with respect to the Indians is replete with broken promises, coercive measures, and negotiations conducted in bad faith, it is equally clear that formal laws shaped and occasionally limited the acquisition of Indian lands by white settlers and the government. Acquisition of these lands proved to be a function of both law and power, and the relative weights of these factors varied over time. The legal scholar Stuart Banner argued: "Whites always acquired Indian land within a legal framework of their own construction. Law was always present, but so was power. The more powerful whites became relative to Indians, the more they were able to mold the legal system to produce outcomes in their favor."[3] Although the scales of justice were tilted in favor of settlers, federal policy could not completely ignore the rule of law or the appearance of due process in its dealings with the tribes.

While an increasingly unequal contest between law and power characterized the development of Indian relations between the seventeenth and late nineteenth centuries, this tension remained an important and perennial aspect of U.S. government policy over the course of the Republic's first century. During the first session of Congress in 1789, four of the first thirteen statutes enacted by the fledgling legislature related to Indian affairs. Eight decades later President Ulysses S. Grant would make a "peace policy" with the tribes of the West a key issue of his administrations between 1869 and 1877. In his inaugural address the former commander of Union forces during the Civil War promised "careful study" of the proper treatment of the "original occupants of the land" and offered his support for "any course towards them that tends to their civilization, Christianization, and ultimate citizenship."[4]

Certainly, the rhetoric of U.S. policy from the early days of the Republic offered a vision of Indian relations based on good faith and mutual respect. In fact, one of the initial thirteen statutes passed by the First Congress incorporated the statement from the Northwest Ordinance of 1787 that "[t]he utmost good faith shall always be observed towards the Indians; their land and property shall never be taken from them without their consent; and in their property, rights, and liberty, they never shall be invaded or disturbed, unless in just and lawful wars authorized by Congress." The measure went even further by promising "laws founded in justice and humanity shall from, time to time be made, for preventing wrongs being done to them, and for preserving peace and friendship with them." The lack of political or military resolve to enforce such pronouncements on a consistent basis, however, exposed the disconnect between words and action. Still, much of this rhetoric found continued expression in the formulation of treaties throughout the nineteenth century and in the actions of eastern reformers and reform groups seeking to protect Indian rights either by "civilizing" them or by isolating them from the effects of modernity and proto-industrialization.[5]

Removal and Dispute

In many respects the administration of Thomas Jefferson established the framework for the government's approach for dealing with the Native tribes, a structure that formed the basis of later efforts as well. Initially, Jefferson believed that Indians could be assimilated and ultimately "blended together" in white society through intermarriage. Furthermore, he saw the process of farming and agricultural development among the tribes as the path to incorporation in the "American project." In his annual message to Congress in 1803, Jefferson stated, "With many of the other Indian tribes improvements in agriculture and household manufacture are advancing, and with all our peace and friendship are established on grounds much firmer than heretofore." In fact, the president argued that the adoption of agricultural practices by the Indians was "essential in their preservation." He also argued that "commerce" was a "more effectual, economical, and humane instrument for preserving peace and good neighborhood" with the tribes than "an augmentation of military force." Ultimately, Jefferson began to doubt the possibility of full integration and, in the wake of the Louisiana Purchase, received authority from Congress "to stipulate" with any tribes wishing to trade their eastern territory for lands west of the Mississippi River, thus establishing a legal precedent for "voluntary removal."⁶

The actual or perceived requirement on the part of the government for embarking upon the process of negotiation to effect mutual agreement and treaties is an important aspect of the process of westward expansion. Similarly, the Indian tribes refused to accept the role of passive victims in the face of broken treaties or arbitrary laws, taking recourse to the courts or threatening reprisals or other acts of physical force. In the case of the former, the planned expropriation of Cherokee land by the state of Georgia resulted in an extended legal battle involving the Cherokees, the federal government, and the state government. In this instance the success of the Indians in cultivating their lands, some five million acres, aroused the avarice of federal and local officials, who offered a swap of these improved holdings with territory west of the Mississippi. When U.S. officials proved unable to garner Cherokee agreement with such an exchange, the Georgia legislature introduced a series of statutes designed to establish sovereignty over the Cherokees that culminated with the seizure of all of their lands in 1830.⁷

The dispute eventually reached the U.S. Supreme Court and resulted in the landmark case *Cherokee Nation v. Georgia* in 1831. Writing for the majority, Chief Justice John Marshall expressed sympathy for the plaintiffs by remarking, "A people once numerous, powerful, and truly independent, found by our ancestors in the quiet and uncontrolled possession of an ample domain, gradually sinking beneath our superior policy, our arts and our arms, have yielded their lands by successive treaties, each of which contains a solemn guarantee of the residue, until they retain no more of their formerly extensive territory than is deemed necessary to their comfortable subsistence." Despite this, Marshall denied the injunction sought by the Cherokees on the grounds that the tribe did not have standing in the dispute as a "foreign nation," but rather constituted a "domestic dependent nation . . . in a state of pupilage" to the United States. Interestingly, the three justices writing in the minority agreed that the Cherokees were a foreign nation, argued for the jurisdiction of the court, and sided with the tribe.⁸

In a subsequent case in 1832, *Worcester v. Georgia*, the court sided with the plaintiff, Samuel Worcester, a missionary to the Cherokees, who was convicted and imprisoned by Georgia for not securing a license to live among the Indians. The court not only ruled Worcester's imprisonment in error but also stated in the opinion: "The Cherokee nation, then, is a distinct community, occupying its own territory, with boundaries accurately described, in which the laws of Georgia can have no force, and which the citizens of Georgia have no right to enter but with the assent of the Cherokees themselves, or in conformity with treaties and with the acts of Congress. The whole intercourse between the United States and this nation is, by our Constitution and laws, vested in the Government of the United States." In the end, the judiciary could rule in favor of the Indians in specific cases related to persons and property, but the power to enforce broader policies remained with Congress and the president. In the case of the latter, Andrew Jackson repeatedly supported the rights of individual states, including Georgia, to exercise authority over the tribes and refused to use federal power to enforce the rulings of the courts. His primary objective involved the removal of the Indians and the appropriation of their lands on economic grounds. The leading advocate of removal, Jackson framed the issue as a question between "removal and settlement" west of the Mississippi or "perhaps utter annihilation."[9]

Despite Jackson's unreserved support, the Removal Act of 1830 passed the House of Representatives by only five votes. Still, the law perfectly illustrated the imbalance in power between the government and the tribes. The key provision of the act involved the congressional allocation of funds for the movement of the eastern tribes, appropriations that paved the way for the displacement of the so-called Five Civilized Tribes. This precedent of removal and isolation formed the linchpin of U.S. policy for most of the century, even if "the national government had failed to allocate the resources necessary to make the removal and reservation policies live up to the lofty promises of American officials."[10]

The Removal Act eventually led to the suffering and death endured during the "Trail of Tears," a forced migration supervised, if not endorsed, by U.S. Army officers and resulting in the deaths of as many as 4,000 Cherokees. In this case the failure of actions to match government rhetoric had catastrophic consequences for those Indians forced to take the journey even if "the principal responsibility for the mass hardship and death . . . lay with the priorities of removal policy rather than the means employed to execute it."[11] Although President Jackson argued that the trek "placed [the Indians] beyond the reach of injury and oppression," the loss of life and brutal conditions of the journey highlighted the ever-widening disparity of power in the relationship between Indians and whites in the eastern United States.[12]

Over the course of the 1830s and 1840s, eastern tribes, including the Choctaws, Creeks, Chickasaws, Cherokees, and Seminoles, ceded some 100 million acres in the East for 32 million acres in the West and pledges of $68 million in annuity payments.[13] One of the key lessons from the circumstances of the Cherokees, one of the most outwardly assimilated tribes in American society, was that motives of economic exploitation could supersede the stated objectives of assimilation. In other words, the desire for space trumped the element of race in the dispossession of the eastern tribes, which is not to say that race was not a factor, only that it proved to be a lesser motive. For his part, President Jackson justified the appropriation of Indian lands under the pretext of racial superiority. In his message to Congress in 1833, he claimed: "They [the tribes] have neither the intelligence, the industry, the moral habits, nor the desire of improvement which are essential to any favorable change in their condition. Established in the midst of another and a superior race, and without appreciating the causes of their inferiority or seeking to control them, they must necessarily yield to the force of circumstances and ere long disappear." Despite Jackson's apocalyptic imagery and his racist sentiment, Richard White observed, "[r]acism did not dominate Indian policy until the twentieth century. Until then, reformers effectively argued that Indians were inferior to whites not because their innate capacities were different, but because they, like children, were still advancing up 'the ladder of civilization.'"[14] Although the western frontier, especially in the Southwest, remained a "cultural crossroads" in which race and kinship were subject to negotiation, the tribes faced a stark choice during most of the nineteenth century between embracing the "law of civilized progress" by adopting "white ways" or facing "the prospect of extinction."[15]

Throughout the 1830s, federal Indian policy displayed a continuing dichotomy between the rhetoric of peaceful coexistence and guardianship and the practical application of such methods as removal. In one respect the House Committee on Indian Affairs fully recognized the failure of the government to "meet the just expectations of the country in the fulfillment of its proper and assumed obligations to the Indian tribes." The committee's report continued,

"Yet, so manifestly defective and inadequate is our present system, that an immediate revision seems imperiously demanded." The resulting Indian Trade and Intercourse Act of 1834 included provisions aimed at protecting Indians from unscrupulous traders and profiteers by requiring that merchants obtain a license and restating prohibitions of the sale of alcohol. In the case of the former, the House committee recognized that "the Indians do not meet the traders on equal terms and no doubt have much reason to complain of fraud and imposition."[16]

Until 1849, the responsibility for the enforcement of federal measures designed to monitor Native behavior and to control the interaction between whites and the tribes resided with the assigned Indian agents and ultimately the War Department. For this purpose, a scattering of military forts ranged from north to south in a line stretching from Louisiana into Minnesota along the inaptly named "Permanent Indian Frontier." The forts and the boundary they ostensibly maintained acted less as obstacles to white settlement and movement westward and more as observation posts and waypoints leading into the interior of the American West. So long as the number of settlers and fortune seekers remained low, this system worked to limit potential conflict. But the annexation of Texas, combined with the outbreak of the Mexican-American War, signaled a vast expansion of American empire, with significant implications for the lives of the Northern and Southern Plains Indians and the tribes of the Southwest.

Expanding an American Empire

The war with Mexico and the subsequent Treaty of Guadalupe Hidalgo (1848) resulted in the U.S. acquisition of a half million square miles, including all or parts of ten modern-day states. The incorporation of these new territories into the United States not only portended a vast expansion of federal power but also an enormous growth in the number of Indian tribes under U.S. jurisdiction. It also brought with it the challenge of first controlling, and later protecting, white settlement in areas largely under Indian control. One historian described the military challenges of territorial expansion: "At the end of the conflict with Mexico, the army undertook an old mission on frontiers new to the United States: occupying territory; suppressing American Indian resistance; [and] keeping the peace among feuding Indians, Hispanos, and Anglos; . . . contests [that] often erupted in violence that sucked the army into riot duty and bloody war."[17] Despite the expansion into the West and the significant increase in responsibilities for the U.S. Army, Congress transferred responsibility over the Bureau of Indian Affairs to the newly formed Department of the Interior in March 1849 over the protestations of the War Department. Over the next four decades, this reallocation of authority would serve as a major source of complaint within the army and among its officers.

The Indian Bureau exercised its authority through a system of superintendents and agents. These men were political appointees who served as the representatives of the federal government and decided such issues as the disbursement of annuity payments and the allocation of goods and firearms. The primary complaints associated with the civilian management of Indian policy were institutionalized corruption and a "system of graft" that accompanied the political spoils system. Without doubt, some corrupt agents lined their pockets by shortchanging Indians and entering into "sweetheart deals" with traders. But if soldiers bemoaned the corruption of the "Indian Ring" and the agents' reputed unwillingness to enforce discipline, the civilian agents castigated the army for its perceived overreliance on the use of military force and the use of punishment in dealing with the tribes.[18] These stereotypes contained more than a grain of truth and reflected the different organizational cultures and value systems. In fact, the clash of cultures between the Department of the Interior and the War Department would constitute a recurrent theme between 1850 and 1890.

With the expansion of American empire came not only internal governmental conflict but also a renewed emphasis on the implementation of a reservation system as a means for dealing with the problems caused by increasing white and Indian interaction. Reservations served two complimentary functions in the eyes of the government officials tasked with establishing them. First, each was designed to create "an island of Indian territory within a sea of white settlement." The enforced separation of the tribes and the controlled access by whites to the reservation was intended to prevent the misunderstandings and incidents that so frequently escalated into acts of violence or even war, though they also became a means for isolating the Indians. Second, the reservation as a controlled environment corresponded with the goal of assimilating the tribes into white society. Luke Lea, the commissioner of Indian affairs, made this point explicit when stating that the goal of the reservation system involved the "ultimate incorporation [of the Indian tribes] into the great body of our citizen population." In the words of Richard White, "The reservation was not supposed to be just a place where Indians adopted elements of white belief systems and technology; the reservation was, above all, supposed to be a place where Indians were to be individualized and detribalized." Although federal policy did not aim at the physical extermination of the Indians, it did seek to achieve the extinction of their cultural practices, beliefs, and ultimately their ethnic identity. Yet the government's repeated failure throughout the West, from the San Carlos Reservation to the Rosebud Reservation, to consistently meet treaty obligations with respect to annuities, facilities, and provisions constituted a major policy failure and served as a flashpoint for conflict.[19] Whether this failure was the function of corruption, mismanagement, or congressional parsimony, it often had catastrophic consequences for the people living on the reservations. In the end, policies aimed at assimilation and acculturation could only be successful if the tribes acquiesced and the government provided the promised goods and annuities to sustain them during this transformation.

Education for Assimilation or Extinction?

Education and the creation of schools for Indian youth provided another instrument used by the federal government aimed at assimilation, detribalization, and creating economic self-sufficiency. Thomas L. McKenney, superintendent of Indian trade between 1816 and 1822, became the primary advocate for the creation of a national school system for the Indians in an effort to convert them from nomadic hunters to farmers and "anchor" them to the soil. McKenney, like many of his peers, brought an evangelical zeal to his mission and tied his educational efforts to the "salvation" of the Indians. The schools' proposed curriculum focused on the teaching of basic English-language and math skills as well as the tenets of agriculture. Yet there were only fifty-two schools with a mere 1,512 students by 1830. Despite the small number, "the goal of civilizing and Christianizing the Indians [through schooling and education] remained an important element in government policy well into the twentieth century."[20]

In the 1840s Commissioner of Indian Affairs T. Hartley Crawford emphasized the value of education as a means for assimilation. In response to critics, Crawford asserted, "It is proved, I think, conclusively that it [the Indian race] is in no respect inferior to our own race, except in being less fortunately circumstanced." He continued, "As great an aptitude for learning the letters, the pursuits, and arts of civilized life is evident; if their progress is slow, so had it been with us and with masses of men in all nations and ages."[21] In Crawford's view it was not racial characteristics or mental capacity, but the lack of opportunity that prevented the tribes from assuming their rightful place in "civilized" society, a process that time and education would eventually ensure.

Protestant denominations took the leading role in educational efforts and focused on teaching English-language and vocational skills related to agriculture. Additionally, they emphasized teaching Indian youths, both girls and boys, in the West versus sending students to schools in the East. By 1849, Commissioner of Indian Affairs Orlando Brown confidently asserted, "The dark clouds of ignorance and superstition in which these people have so long been enveloped seem at length in the case of many of them to be breaking away, and the light of Christianity and general knowledge to be dawning upon their moral and intellectual darkness."[22] In this case Brown's optimistic assessment reflected the aspirations for the program rather than the reality of the situation.

The commissioner of Indian affairs in his annual report of 1875 noted that the number of Indian children attending schools had reached 10,598. Despite this number, he observed, "The school-reports do not show a gain in education equal to that shown in the products of labor." The disparity between education and "products of labor" was a direct result of the focus of the curricula. For example, schools in Kansas and Indian Territory were "in every sense industrial schools" that taught "every kind of manual labor" to Indian boys, while Indian girls received training in homemaking skills such as cooking, sewing, and housekeeping. The ultimate goal involved a process of cultural conversion. Mary Todd, the head of a school for Indian girls, made this point explicit in her contention that "[t]he education of the Indian girl means the uplifting of the tribes in every way, and yet it means also and soon, the losing of the races of red men from off the face of the earth."[23]

By 1890, it was an "army of Christian school-teachers" and the concept of the common school, a centerpiece of the Progressive Era, that would lead the charge in transforming the Native tribes of the West by concentrating on "civilizing" Indian youth. Reformers believed that this pedagogical offensive would slowly but inextricably result in the assimilation of the tribes. Merrill Gates, a leader in the Indian reform movement, predicted: "We are going to conquer barbarism, but we are going to do it by getting at the barbarism one by one. . . . We are going to conquer the Indians by a standing army of school-teachers, armed with ideas, winning victories by industrial training, and by the gospel of love and the gospel of work."[24]

The boarding school, whether on or off the reservation, became the primary battleground for the "hearts, minds, and souls" of Indian children. The use of the term "battleground" proved apt as many of the schools, like the Sherman Institute and the Carlisle School in Pennsylvania, created a military atmosphere in order to promote the process of assimilation and acculturation, a process that involved short haircuts for boys, the wearing of uniforms, marching, and the enforcement of strict discipline for boys and girls alike. For Thomas Jefferson Morgan, the commissioner of Indian affairs from 1889 to 1893, the schools were to serve as sites to imbue "a sense of independence, self-reliance, and self-respect" among the students. Morgan argued: "Education should seek the disintegration of the tribes, and not their segregation. . . . In short, public schools should do for them what they are so successfully doing for all other races in this country,—assimilate them."[25]

For Morgan and other reformers, the effectiveness of education could best be guaranteed by the creation of off-reservation boarding schools and mandated compulsory attendance. Regarding location, assimilationists contended that "the task of 'civilizing' Indian children would be easier and lapses into tribal ways less likely if students stayed away from their homes and relatives until their education was complete." For their part, many tribal leaders feared for the health of children sent to off-reservation sites, where in the words of one Sioux leader, "the breath of the earth rises up and poisons our children." Ultimately, the passage of a compulsory-attendance law by Congress in 1891 was intended to address the issue by allowing for attendance at either reservation schools or boarding schools.[26]

If boarding schools were not made mandatory, this did not prevent some government officials from applying forms of compulsion, including the withholding of rations and annuities, to force parents to send their children away.[27] In the end, education was seen as the mechanism for creating self-sufficient wage laborers and ultimately "Americans" by effacing tribal culture and identity.

Imagining the Reservation

If education served as the means of "enlightenment" among young girls and boys, then the reservation was conceived as a pivotal location for effecting this transformation among the Indians as a whole. In fact, the reservation system emerged as the central element of federal Indian policy between 1840 and the 1890. Initially, white reformers and "friends of the Indians" viewed the reservations as the necessary and viable alternative for promoting acculturation while "protecting" the Indians from the corrupting influences of less desirable elements of white society. For its part, the army, despite its small size and being "undermined" by congressional parsimony, was expected to garrison military posts on the perimeter of the reservation areas. From these the troops were expected to prevent unauthorized interactions, such as the sale of liquor, and to provide the armed force necessary to quell any disturbances or to pursue Indians who left the reservation for whatever reason, including raiding forays, hunting parties, or attempts to return to ancestral homelands.[28]

Establishing forts near reservations and in Indian country allowed the federal government to exert influence on both the tribes and nearby white settlers. But despite the prohibitions on white settlement, encroachment on Indian lands became a perennial problem, and the government repeatedly demonstrated a lack of ability or will to strictly enforce the Trade and Intercourse Acts. One historian described such acquiescence in this process: "The policy of the United States was based on an assumption that white settlement should advance and the Indians withdraw. The federal government was interested primarily in seeing that this process was as free of disorder and injustice as possible. It meant to restrain and govern the advance of the whites, not to prevent it forever."[29] The growing demand for land generated its own political and economic imperatives, a process that once again highlighted the growing imbalance between law and power in the West.

As white civilization advanced into the West, the construction of roads through Indian lands emerged as a major source of conflict. In his annual report to Congress in 1851, Commissioner Lea remarked on the recent purchase of lands from the Sioux in order to establish an overland route to the Pacific. Lea observed that the agreement allowed "for the spread of our population westward.... [as] the only practicable means of saving the border tribes from extinction." He continued, "Without it, in a few years, they will be forced to abandon their present possessions to an emigrating population, and be driven forth to perish on the plains."[30] Lea's remarks highlight the paradox facing the Indian Bureau by the middle of the nineteenth century, as the advance of white settlement increasingly threatened the maintenance and survival of Native customs and society.

By the 1870s, the growth of the railroads had turned Lea's concern on its head as nineteenth-century Americans embraced the "steel horses" as the "epitome of modernity" and the "great civilizer of modern times."[31] The roads and rails that began to reach across the plains not only encouraged white transit and settlement, with all the attendant problems, but also pierced traditional hunting grounds and contributed to the escalating existential crisis of the tribes. The consequences of this expansion were not lost on the Indian Bureau, but they were most profoundly felt by the tribes themselves. Likewise, it was the creation of a series of forts along the Bozeman Trail in 1866 that brought tensions between the Northern Plains Indians and the federal government to a boiling point.

Disaster and Negotiation

The complete annihilation of an eighty-man force under Captain William Fetterman by Northern Plains Indians near Fort Phil Kearny along the Bozeman Trail in December 1866 (see chapter 4) once again forced the issue of Indian affairs into the political spotlight. The attack resulted directly from the anger among the Indians, especially the Sioux under Red Cloud, at the building of forts within their sacred territory. In the wake of the engagement, the largest loss of U.S. troops in the Trans-Mississippi West until the Battle of Little Bighorn (1876), newspapers published sensational and often-fabricated stories of the attack. Western editors used the debacle to renew calls for the extermination of the Indians. In contrast, the Bureau of Indian Affairs publicly placed the blame for the incident on the fort's commander, Colonel Henry Carrington. The commissioner issued a statement that the Indians had been "provoked" into attacking, and he questioned Carrington's estimate about the number of warriors involved in the fighting. In an unusual preface to the commissioner's annual report in 1868, the secretary of the interior asserted that a "costly Indian war, with all its horrors, would have been avoided" if only Congress had allocated sufficient appropriations for the care of the tribes. For its part, the War Department used the disaster to reopen the debate over the authority for dealing with the Indians by once again demanding the transfer of the Indian Bureau from the Department of the Interior, a measure that would allow the army unfettered access to the reservations. Lieutenant General William T. Sherman, as commanding general of the Military Division of the Missouri, within which the massacre occurred, declared, "We must act with vindictive earnestness against the Sioux, even to their extermination, men, women, and children."[32] Once again, a senior army leader raised the specter of annihilation. But the rhetoric of extermination soon was replaced by a renewed effort at negotiation with the tribes of the northern plains.

Sherman was not alone in his calls for action instead of negotiation. Some frontier newspapers initially joined the chorus for military operations. For example, the *Omaha Weekly Herald* published an editorial on May 8, 1868, that contended: "We believe in the wisdom of making peace and removing Indians to far reservations. But why sit idly by and talk of peace whilst your neighbor and friends are being murdered by these red devils? Why not declare war and wage it? We are for war, if we cannot have peace, because that is the only alternative." Two weeks later, after news that an agreement with Red Cloud and the Sioux had been reached, the *Weekly Herald* reversed course and proclaimed: "It has been the White Man, and not the Red Man, who has violated agreements under which the former has nearly crushed the latter out of existence. We are, as we have been, for peace with these savages." Despite voicing concern, a number of other frontier newspapers ultimately chose to support the commission and the Fort Laramie Treaty since peace proved preferable to war; several also noted the responsibility of Colonel

John Chivington and the Sand Creek Massacre (see chapter 4) as the cause of the current conflict.[33]

While senior army leaders felt bitterness at the humiliation of a forced withdrawal, plans for a campaign to "punish" the Sioux were abandoned in favor of the Department of the Interior's peace initiative. Sherman, however, did approve a punitive expedition in Kansas in the spring of 1867 aimed at stopping Indian "depredations" in that state. Under the command of Major General Winfield S. Hancock, a hero of the Battle of Gettysburg, the campaign's objective was to end attacks along the westward travel routes. Hancock's statement that he "was prepared for war" and that "no insolence" was to be tolerated from the Indians created an unstable and explosive environment among the southern-plains tribes, for whom the memories of the Sand Creek Massacre of 1864 were still vivid. If Hancock was looking for a fight, he got what he wanted. The initial isolated attacks of the spring multiplied into numerous incidents and skirmishes in Kansas and Colorado by the summer as "Indian warriors ran wild on the Arkansas, Smoky Hill, and Platte [Rivers]."[34]

In the end, the results of the campaign, including the destruction of an abandoned encampment of over 250 lodges at Pawnee Fork in April and a largely fruitless and exhausting chase of the tribes by a force under Lieutenant Colonel George A. Custer, proved inconclusive. By the summer of 1867, the question was whether the army's actions had generated the "war" that they professed to want to avoid. A peace commission appointed by Congress in June received the task of determining and removing the causes of the conflict, securing the frontier settlements and the railroads, and initiating a plan for "civilizing the Indians." Once again federal policy favored negotiation in the wake of indecisive military operations and focused on a solution aimed at "collecting the Indians on reservations."[35]

The new commissioner of Indian affairs, Nathaniel Taylor, a former Methodist minister, headed the commission to negotiate with the Plains Indians. Congress tasked them to "remove all just causes of complaint on their [the Indians'] part, and at the same time establish security for person [sic] and property along the . . . thoroughfares of travel to the western Territories, and such as will most likely insure civilization for the Indians and peace and safety for the whites." Ironically, the senior military member of the Peace Commission was none other than General Sherman, who now seemed willing to modify his calls for annihilation in favor of a more pragmatic approach to resolving the conflict, stating publicly after his appointment, "It makes little difference whether they be coaxed out by Indian commissioners or killed."[36]

As head of the commission, Taylor began negotiations with the Plains Indians in pursuit of "the hitherto untried policy in connection with Indians, of endeavoring to conquer by kindness." Although the policy of "conquering by kindness" placed a premium on negotiation versus punishment or military coercion, it was nonetheless a policy aimed at conquest and that reserved the right to use military force if negotiations failed. In the end, the commission's objectives complimented the goal sought by religious reformers from the early days of white contact of bringing the "virtues" of civilization and Christianity to the Indians. In his memoir Sherman focused on the practical aspects rather than the spiritual aspects of the talks: "We all agreed that the nomad Indians should be removed from the vicinity of the two great railroads then in rapid construction, and be localized on one or other of the two great reservations south of Kansas and north of Nebraska; that agreements not treaties, should be made for their liberal maintenance as to food, clothing, schools, and farming implements for ten years, during which time we believed that these Indians should become self-supporting." With all sides ready to end the conflict, the Treaty of Medicine Lodge Creek was signed by representatives of all the major tribes (Cheyenne, Arapaho, Kiowa, Comanche, and Kiowa-Apache) and the Peace Commission on October 28, 1867. The agreement, intended to turn the Indians into "happy farmers," temporarily reestablished peace along the travel routes of the southern plains and created two large reservations in western Indian Territory, promised rations and farm equipment, and guaranteed no white settlement.[37]

In the new year Taylor's commission extended its efforts to offer the "olive-branch or flag of truce" to the tribes of the northern plains. It achieved its initial goal by negotiating a treaty at Fort Laramie in April 1868 with a number of the northern-plains tribes. This agreement included the creation of districts set aside exclusively for the Indians to promote agriculture and domestic manufactures, in many respects simply a reformulation of existing reservation policy. For example, a treaty signed with several tribes, including one with the Northern Cheyennes and Arapahos, on May 10, 1868, provided incentives to include specific land grants and agricultural equipment for individuals who chose to pursue farming. The major concession achieved from the Indians' perspective involved the federal government's agreement to abandon the contentious forts along the Bozeman Trail and the creation of a Sioux reserve west of the Missouri in Dakota Territory. After the army evacuated these posts, Red Cloud and his warriors watched them burn to the ground, thus suspending, though not ending, one chapter in the process of westward expansion. In his retrospective on the treaty, Sherman noted a different achievement of the commission that proved much less salutary not only for Red Cloud but also for all the Plains Indians. He asserted that the Peace Commission laid the foundation for the great Pacific railroads, "which, for better or worse, have settled the fate of the buffalo and Indian forever."[38]

The government's reaction to the Fetterman disaster and subsequent incidents of conflict across the Great Plains illustrates several key points concerning U.S. policy in the West. First, civilian leaders within Congress and the Department of the Interior often held the upper hand over the War Department and the military in the formulation of Indian policy. Second, the creation of reservations intended to isolate the tribes during this process of assimilation and turn them into farmers remained the primary objective of reformers. Third, the ultimate goal of these policies was not the intended physical annihilation of the tribes, but the voluntary renunciation of their cultural identity and acceptance of white values. In this sense "Indians would 'exchange' some of their lands for the time and material resources necessary to being assimilating into the dominant society." Additionally, these plans assumed that the federal government would meet its obligations in providing goods and annuities as promised. Finally, despite the reformers' efforts, the War Department and senior army leaders remained ready to implement "a sharp and severe war policy" against those tribes that resisted this process.[39] Ironically, it would be a former army leader, famed for his conduct in the nation's bloodiest war, who would launch the most concentrated Indian peace offensive of the nineteenth century.

The "Peace Policy"

On February 25, 1869, the *Boston Advertiser* led with a front-page story concerning President-elect Ulysses S. Grant's plans for dealing with the Indians under his administration. According to the account, Grant intended to pursue a "peace policy" and to make use of prominent members of the Society of Friends, or Quakers, a group that had been championing a policy change toward the tribes since 1866 as the primary intermediaries of this "new" approach. In truth, this peace policy proved more of a philosophical orientation than a formal program since military force remained a ready instrument when negotiation and moral suasion failed to achieve government objectives. For his part, Grant promised that "all Indians who are disposed to peace will find that the policy of the new Administration is a peace policy." He chose the Quakers based on their history of peaceful relations with the Indians in colonial America and "their opposition to all strife, violence, and war, . . . and their strict integrity and fair dealings." If the continued goal of federal Indian policy involved bringing them into the fold of "civilization" and "Christianity," then the choice of religious men as Indian agents seemed to offer a "heaven sent" solution, even if the policy raised some thorny constitutional issues concerning the separation of church and state. In reality, Grant's plan limited the Quaker agents to reservations located in eastern Nebraska, and he made extensive use of military officers as agents for the nontreaty tribes. His appointment of a former military aide-de-camp and confidante, Ely S. Parker, a Tonawanda Seneca chief, as commissioner of Indian affairs seemed to reflect a genuine desire to open a new chapter in Indian-white relations and to continue efforts at "conquest by kindness."[40]

In the handwritten draft of his inaugural address, Grant promised to rebuild a "prostrate commerce" and to promote industry by restoring "national pride" and joining all geographical, political, and religious groups in this "common sentiment." His appeal to a nation in the process of recovering from the charnel house of the Civil War also included the promise to make a "careful study" of the "proper treatment" of the Indians and to promote their "civilization, Christianization, and ultimate citizenship."[41] The cataclysmic intersectional conflict had absorbed the nation's focus for over four years and had cost the nation dearly in blood and treasure, but the end of that war allowed the administration and the nation to shift their attention to the West. In fact, many demobilized Civil War soldiers made their way westward to start a new life and to take advantage of lands made available by the Homestead Act of 1862.[42]

If Grant's inaugural remarks touched only briefly on Indian affairs, his first address to Congress in December 1869 developed the issue in more detail. In this speech the president described the history of the government's Indian relations as "one of embarrassment and expense" accompanied by "murders and wars." Furthermore, he stated, based on his own experience on the frontier, neither legislation nor the actions of white settlers were "blameless for these hostilities." He noted that past mistakes could not be "undone" and outlined his "new policy towards these wards of the nation." Grant also defended his selection of military men as being superior choices compared to civilian political appointees as Indian agents, arguing that army officers served for life and not at the discretion of a political administration. More importantly, he asserted that such men had a personal interest in living at peace with the Indians and "in establishing a permanent peace to this end." In line with this objective, Grant had previously appointed sixty-eight officers to serve as Indian agents or superintendents on May 7, 1869, detaching them from the War Department and placing them under the authority of the commissioner of Indian affairs.[43]

In his remarks Grant also acknowledged that the extension of the railroads into the West was "rapidly bringing civilized settlements in contact with all the tribes of indians." Although he recognized that this process brought tremendous friction and potential for conflict, he rejected any solution aimed at the physical annihilation of the tribes: "A system which looks to the extinction of a race is too horrible for a nation to adopt without entailing upon itself the wrath of all Christendom, and without engendering in the citizen a disregard for human life, and the rights of others, dangerous to society."[44] The only solution in the president's mind involved the creation of large-scale reservations as rapidly as possible and the assurance to the tribes of "absolute protection."

Grant's address clearly outlined the key points of federal policy. First and foremost, the continued expansion of American power and settlement into the West was a foregone conclusion, a process that could not be stopped. Second, the president recognized that this process had profound implications for the western Indian tribes, but he categorically rejected any solution based on the concept of physical extermination. Grant's sentiment in this case reflected those of the many reform groups that waged a "campaign specifically at saving a race from earthly extinction." Finally, only one viable option remained, the confinement and isolation of the various tribes within the confines of reservations. The president's policy in this respect followed a strategy described by General Sherman as "peace within [the reservation], war without."[45] In short, the ultimate success of Grant's plan rested on the ability of the government to meet its obligations to the tribes and on the willingness of the tribes to remain within the lands allotted to them by the government.

Agents and Missionaries

For the humanitarians involved in the framing of the peace policy, the essential elements of the plan included the creation of a reservation system, the education and Christianization of the Indians, and the assimilation of the tribes into the economic and social system, including citizenship, a process intended to be "accomplished without bloodshed." But Grant's policy endured a major test in January 1870 when units of the Second Cavalry under Major Eugene Baker attacked a Piegan encampment in Montana and killed at least 173 people, overwhelmingly women and children (see chapter 4). Public outcry in the East led to calls for a congressional investigation and torpedoed Grant's plans for the transfer of Indian affairs to the War Department. The incident also resulted in a statute barring officers from serving in civil positions, effectively ending the practice of military men serving as Indian agents. One of the immediate effects of this prohibition was the administration's decision to open these positions to members of other religious denominations. By 1872, there were thirteen denominations in control of seventy-three agencies with responsibility for almost 240,000 Indians. Commissioner Parker framed the missionaries' goal as directing the Natives "toward that healthy Christian civilization in which are embraced the elements of material wealth and intellectual and moral development."[46]

The deployment of an army of missionaries onto the reservations was the second part of a one-two evangelical punch pursued by the Grant administration. The earlier establishment of the ten-person Board of Indian Commissioners, composed of individuals selected for their "intelligence and philanthropy," in 1869 was intended to assist the secretary of the interior in the disbursement of tribal appropriations. The first board members believed that the

Indians "had been made suspicious, revengeful, and cruel by the treatment they had received from the whites." Displaying a complete lack of understanding for the diversity of Indian cultures, they advocated the consolidation of all the tribes on contiguous pieces of land in a great reservation that would one day become a state in the Union, one in which the ethnic and cultural identities of its inhabitants had ceased to exist. Board members professed, "The religion of our blessed Savior is believed to be the most effective agent for the civilization of any people."[47] These arbiters of Grant's peace policy prophesied a gospel of spiritual conquest and cultural transformation.

The attempts at reshaping or effacing Indian culture involved the use of both power and law. The peace policy attempted to employ moral suasion as the mechanism for effecting change and to deemphasize the use of military force or physical coercion. From a legal perspective, however, the decision by Congress in 1871 to end the process of treaty making between the government and the tribes proved to be important more for its symbolic rather than practical value. This move essentially supported the position of those who viewed the Natives as wards of the state or government dependents. In a practical sense the government still negotiated "treaty substitutes" with the tribes, a process that allowed both houses of Congress a voice, and a vote, in the negotiations. The symbolic effect of the legislation, however, proved more profound as it reinforced the idea that Indians were, in the words of Commissioner Parker, "helpless and ignorant wards," people to be acted upon but without the power or right to act on their own. In truth, the very fact that the government was required to enter into negotiations provided the tribes with legal and political leverage even if the creation and realization of these agreements often served the government's seemingly unquenchable thirst for land. Yet it was equally clear that the "trajectory of power" for the tribes was in continuing decline relative to that of the federal government, a process that would accelerate throughout the remainder of the century.[48]

In his third address to Congress in December 1872, President Grant reflected on the "beneficial results" achieved in the pursuit of his peace policy. Nevertheless, he did remark on the increasing number of disturbances between white settlers and Natives as a result of "the encroachment of civilization upon the Indian reservations and hunting grounds." He predicted that this tension would continue to exist "until each race appreciates that the other has rights which must be respected." Despite this recognition, Grant reiterated his intent "to collect the indians as rapidly as possible on reservations, and as far as practicable within what is known as the Indian Territory and to teach them the arts of civilization and self support." He warned, however, that those Indians "found off their reservations and endangering the peace and safety of the whites . . . will continue to be punished."[49]

Francis A. Walker, Parker's successor as commissioner of Indian affairs, echoed the president's sentiment by asserting, "the Indians should be made as comfortable on, and as uncomfortable off, their reservations as it was in the power of the Government to make them." Grant's speech and Walker's remarks once again highlighted a policy that was based on the isolation of the Indians and the threat of force should the tribes or any individuals choose to leave these areas. In contrast to Grant's optimism, many settlers in the West viewed the peace policy in wholly different terms. For example, a story that appeared on the front page of the *Dallas Weekly Herald* in December 1871 warned that "Grant will be enabled to witness the impoverishment and extermination of the bordermen." The correspondent continued, "It [the peace policy] has resulted so far in furnishing the Indians with the implements of their more civilized neighbors, with which to carry on savage warfare and robbery."[50]

An Indian Alcatraz?

If the concepts of physical isolation and coercion underpinned Grant's speech in 1872, these ideas also found expression in the media. In July 1874, Sheridan, then commander of the Military District of Missouri, received a letter from the editor of the *Gem of the West*, a newspaper based in Chicago, with perhaps the most bizarre Indian-policy proposal from the period. The editor, C. Augustus Haviland, in a handwritten note asked the general if the army had considered the transfer of Indians to islands "where they can be guarded by gunboats." Haviland argued that his plan was "feasible" and asked Sheridan for his views on the subject. In addition to his letter, the editor enclosed a copy of an article on the subject that he authored for the *Gem of the West*. Entitled "The Indians: How to Protect Them and Ourselves," it argued that attempts to make "civilized beings" of the Indians had failed and that those seeking to make "a home and fortune in the Far West" were dissuaded by tales of "the Scalping Knife and Tomahawk" and the "butchering" and "murder" of frontier settlers. Haviland rhetorically asked: "Shall we sit idly by and let our brothers and friends be murdered thus? We answer no, NO, a thousand times NO!"[51]

According to Haviland, the "only" solution in dealing with the Indians as "wards of a nation" was to place them on islands in the Great Lakes and off the coast of Maine and California, where they would be "entirely isolated from every other race of beings." He concluded, "There is no other way in which we can protect our frontier settlers, and make the vast agricultural and mining region of the Far West attractive for our Yankee brothers."[52] Significantly, the article failed to mention the use of gunboats and the effective imprisonment of the tribes on these islands. The concept essentially called for the complete isolation of the Indians from white society and the use of the military to enforce it. There is no record of Sheridan's response to the letter or the proposal, but it is interesting to note that Haviland's scheme was based primarily on economic considerations.

Haviland's letter to Sheridan came at a critical time in Indian relations as a series of violent encounters between the two groups began to call the peace policy into doubt. On April 11, 1873, Good Friday, a group of Modocs in California had killed and mutilated a group of peace commissioners trying to negotiate the relocation of the tribe to another reservation away from their ancestral homes. The fact that the attack involved the killing of Brigadier General Edward S. Canby, commander of the Department of Columbia, under a flag of truce inflamed public opinion. The incident again revealed a sectional media divide as "Western editors called for blood and blamed the Peace Policy," while eastern papers generally defended Grant's efforts. During an interview with reporters, Vice President Henry Wilson supported the "extermination" of the Modoc but still advocated for maintaining the peace policy. The eventual punishment for the small tribe included five death sentences for the alleged ringleaders and the transfer of the remaining 153 Modocs to Indian Territory and their forced merger into other tribes. Secretary of the Interior Columbus Delano described the act paradoxically as a "humane punishment" that inflicted the "severest penalty" by "extinguishing their [the Modocs] so-called national existence."[53] In this view the effacement of Modoc culture and not physical extermination provided the "humane" punishment.

Despite public calls for revenge, the Board of Indian Commissioners published an account of the events that placed the blame for the violence on frontier settlers, speculators, and the Indian Ring. In New York a special meeting of the commission, headed by Peter Cooper, convened to "protest the slaughter of Indians by 'lawless' men." Likewise, the newly established American Indian Aid Association admitted that the killing of the peace commissioners was a treacherous act but saw the Modoc response as a form of self-defense.[54] If this incident caused the peace policy to teeter, then it was a widespread series of raids and attacks by Comanche, Kiowa, and Southern Cheyenne warriors in the summer of 1874 that led to the ultimate demise of Grant's policy.

The start of the "Red River War" signaled the death knell for the peace policy as first the southern plains and then the northern plains erupted into hostilities. In truth, Grant's policy had never signified true peace, as the president had himself admitted in his address to Congress in 1872. The attempts to "conquer by kindness" had always assumed the potential need to "chastise" or "punish" those who refused to submit to "benevolent subjugation." Still, the fundamental trajectory of federal Indian policy demonstrates that, while the rhetoric of extermination and annihilation existed within western circles and among some members of the army, it was negotiation and moral suasion that formed the principal thrust of official activity, even if the use of military force remained a viable option as demonstrated by the Piegan Massacre and the Modoc War.

By the early 1880s, with the process of removal complete and the threat of credible opposition essentially absent, the focus of Indian policy shifted to the effacement of tribal identity and their complete assimilation into white society. In the words of Senator John Logan to Sitting Bull: "[Y]ou have no following, no power, no control, and no right to any control. You are on an Indian reservation merely at the suffrance of the government. . . . The government feeds and clothes and educates your children now, and desires to teach you to become farmers, and to civilize you, and make you as white men."[55] This statement reflects in great part the increase in federal power achieved during the previous decades with the defeat of the Comanches and the Sioux on the southern and northern plains. By the end of the 1880s, however, supporters of Indian reform viewed the reservations not as a tool for assimilation, but rather as an obstacle.

The reservation provided for the continuation of the tribal system and the perpetuation of tribal identity while the government's rationing system, despite its many flaws, was seen as "instilling an attitude of dependency." This belief led reformers to champion the concept of "severalty" and to efforts to partition the reservations into individual homesteads for Indians, selling "surplus" land to white settlers, with the proceeds from these sales held by the Treasury for the "education and civilization" of the tribes. The General Allotment Act of 1887, or the Dawes Act, was passed by Congress with the expectation that "this law, if faithfully and honestly administered, will . . . solve the Indian problem and be the means ultimately of elevating the Indian to the high plane of American citizenship." Reminiscent of the Jeffersonian ideal, supporters of the measure argued that by becoming farmers, Natives would "acquire the habits and virtues associated with private property and possessive individualism." One congressman, much less idealistically, described the bill as the means for the Indians to abandon "the scalping knife and give to them the pruning hook."[56]

Despite the rhetoric that accompanied its passage, such as "the most important step forward ever taken by the national Government in its methods of dealing with the Indians" and "the only escape open to these people from the dire alternative of impending extirpation," the Dawes Act ultimately failed in its objective to turn unwilling or unprepared Indians into farmers, absent suitable farmland and the necessary motivation, training, and equipment. Even worse for the tribes was the loss of 60 million acres of "excess" lands after the process of allotment, representing over 40 percent of existing tribal holdings at the time.[57]

The policies of race and space that governed westward expansion embraced a broad range of initiatives and included a diverse range of governmental and private actors. In the case of the government, the use of violence and direct coercion ranged from individual acts of massacre and atrocity and the employment of the army in campaigns to "pursue and punish" to policies designed to subsume tribal identity through religious conversion, adoption, education, and vocational training. Regarding the issue of space, frontiersmen, speculators, government officials, missionaries, and eastern reformers and philanthropists, depending upon their specific economic or political interests, set about the task of eliminating tribal identity through a range of measures that involved the transfer of lands, the creation of reservations, and the promotion of agrarianism. Significantly, by the start of the 1880s, these acts of expropriation proceeded largely under the guise of legality since "talk of a military solution seemed increasingly inhumane to everyone except the most virulent Indian-hater." Even if physical extermination was never a viable or desired objective for either those who formulated Indian policy or those who sought to enforce it, the rhetoric of annihilation was constantly invoked by both frontiersmen and policymakers who, like Secretary of the Interior Lucius Q. Lamar, asserted that the "only alternative now presented to the American Indian race is speedy entrance into the pale of American civilization, or absolute extinction."[58]

For the European Jews, however, there was no access into the "pale of German civilization," and Nazi policymakers envisioning a new empire in the East matched their rhetoric of annihilation with lethal deliberations and murderous deeds.

Nazi Policy in the East

During the Third Reich, the dominant thrust of National Socialist ideology revolved around the two ideas of race and space: "Racial vitality and spatial expansion were directly related." In the case of the former, the concept of anti-Semitism, based on a corruption of Social Darwinism and the idea of the survival of the fittest, constituted the central pillar of the Nazi worldview; Hitler blamed the defeat in World War I on the "Jews and their Marxist fighting organization," which had stabbed the German people in the back. His conflation of the Jews with Bolshevism provided the foundation upon which the genocide of the Jews would be built. In the case of space, Hitler repeatedly advocated "the adjustment of space to population by the conquest of additional land areas whose native population would be expelled or exterminated, not assimilated."[59]

One of the unavoidable implications of this ideology included a German population steeled to the hard realities of war and the requirement for conquest. On May 23, 1939, Hitler informed senior military leaders that he intended to order an attack on Poland "at the first suitable opportunity." German expansion was necessary to solve "economic problems," he asserted: "Living space proportionate to the greatness of the State is fundamental to every Power. . . . The alternatives are rise or decline."[60] Although emphasizing the economic rationale for conquest, Hitler's words "rise or decline" reflected his own racial beliefs in the inevitability of conflict between Aryans and Slavs as well as the principles of Social Darwinism that framed his policies for the East.

On August 22, Hitler again met with his senior military commanders to share his final instructions for the impending invasion. He told them that the time for dealing with Poland had come and that Germany was faced with a decision of "striking or of certain annihilation sooner or later." Later that day he emphasized the importance he attached to the "destruction of Poland." He then exhorted the assembled Wehrmacht leaders: "Close your hearts to pity. Act brutally. Eighty million people must obtain what is their right. Their existence must be made secure. The stronger man is right. The greatest harshness [is demanded]." During the meeting, the chief of the German General Staff, General Franz Halder, recorded Hitler's order to "have no pity" and for German forces to act with "the greatest brutality and without mercy." He also documented the führer's statement that the campaign involved "the physical annihilation of the Polish population."[61]

Conquest and Occupation in Poland

The invasion of Poland on September 1, 1939, provided Hitler with the war he so desperately desired and the opportunity to test a rearmed and remade Wehrmacht. The capitulation of Warsaw on September 27 signaled the end of the Polish state and initiated both a genocidal process and the absorption of the occupied territory. The plan for the dismemberment of Poland included the annexation of western parts of the country to the Third Reich and the creation of the "General Government" in the eastern half. The latter area, under the control of Nazi administrator Hans Frank, was intended as a German "fiefdom" and a type of reservation or dumping ground for Poles and Jews who would be expelled from areas to the west. In contrast, the regions incorporated into Germany were intended to serve as an "eastern wall of flesh and blood." In his inaugural address on November 5, Arthur Greiser, the newly appointed Nazi *Gauleiter* (district leader) for the incorporated area known as the Warthegau, proclaimed his objective for the region: "We must ensure that here in the Warthegau [we] erect an eastern wall of living human beings with vigilant minds and loyal hearts, ready to seize the plow with strong fists and once again make the mark of decent German [farmers] on the land."[62]

In a meeting on October 17, Hitler sketched the outlines of his policy for the occupied areas to a group of senior Nazi administrators, including Frank and Reich Leader of the SS Heinrich Himmler. The führer stated that German rule in the General Government would provide the opportunity to "purify" the Reich of "Jews and Polacks." In this area Poles would be deprived of administrative authority, would lose access to secondary education, and would exist at a mere subsistence level as a source of slave labor, while Jews would be concentrated in ghettos. The territory of the General Government would be exploited for the economic benefit of the Reich. In an earlier meeting Hitler had expressly rejected the concept of any assimilation of the Poles and told Minister of Propaganda Josef Goebbels that the goal was "annihilatory."[63]

If annihilation was the goal, Hitler's selection of Himmler on October 7, 1939, as the "Reich Commissioner for the Strengthening of German Nationality," charged with the Germanization of the annexed territories, proved an apt choice. The policy guidelines given to the Reich commissioner included: (1) the repatriation of ethnic Germans from the Soviet Union and their resettlement in the Reich; (2) the elimination of any "harmful influence" posed by "ethnically alien sections of the population"; and (3) the creation of new settlements composed of the returning ethnic Germans. As a district leader, Greiser's objectives fell into perfect alignment with those given to Himmler. Greiser publically declared, "Our long term goal should be to become a model Gau [i.e., district] of the Greater German Reich, that in large measure guarantees the food supply for Great Germany, that affords protection against Polish and Jewish invasion, . . . [a]nd [that understands that] the most important task before our eyes is to the settlement of this land with people who will later know the term 'Polish' as an historical memory."[64] In short, his long-term objectives included a massive program of resettlement, exploitation, ethnic cleansing, and mass murder.

A short description of the policies pursued in the Warthegau offers a telling snapshot of the nature of Nazi local rule. With respect to resettlement measures, only some 17,000 of the district's

4.2 million Christian Poles possessed the racial characteristics that made them possible candidates for Germanization. In many cases those not deemed worthy of consideration were forced from their farms and homes and sent to the General Government. The deportations of ethnic Poles was critical in order to make room for ethnic German settlers, a number that totaled 290,000 in the first two years of the occupation and eventually reached 536,951. With respect to exploitation, Greiser provided some 450,000 Polish forced or slave laborers for duties in Germany and other occupied areas, including the transfer of almost 4,000 entire families to work as field hands in France. Finally, the Warthegau proved a key site for the conduct of the mass murder of the mentally ill, Sinti and Roma ("Gypsies"), and especially the Jews, of whom an estimated 150,000 were murdered in the death camp at Chełmno alone by March 1943. In fact, Greiser is recognized as having initiated the first mass gassings of Jews.[65]

Ghettoization

The initial creation of ghettos in occupied Poland served the purpose of concentrating Jews with the intent of expropriating their property and wealth before using them as forced laborers at a time when mass emigration was still a possible alternative.[66] Likewise, the ghetto as an institution reflected the belief in the need to isolate Jews as potential carriers of disease, a rationale used by the military commander in Warsaw to "quarantine" them within a closed section of the city. The sheer size of some ghettos in the East almost staggers the imagination. In the case of the Warsaw ghetto, the largest of all, 445,000 people lived in an area of some 2 square miles at an average of 7.2 persons per available *room*, while 144,000 persons were crowded into a 1.6-square-mile area in the city of Łódź. Nazi administrators intended that mass death would result from confining large numbers of Jews in close quarters with little food and water, unheated housing, and poor sanitation facilities. By the winter of 1941, epidemics raced through the Warsaw ghetto as supplies of food were exhausted and sewage pipes froze, leading to the dumping of human waste into streets and courtyards.[67]

Chaim Kaplan, a prisoner in the Warsaw ghetto, recorded its deteriorating state and that of its inhabitants in his diary on November 10, 1941: "This is our third winter under the Nazi regime and our second within the ghetto. Contagious diseases and especially typhus continue to take their toll. There is not a family which has not lost one or even several of its members." By March 1942, Nazi propaganda trumpeted the deaths of 5,000 Jews per month in Warsaw and reported on alleged cases of cannibalism. Over the course of the ghettos' existence, an estimated 33,000 Jews perished in Warsaw while another 45,000 died in Łódź. By the end of 1941, as plans were developed for the murder of all European Jews, the Polish ghettos served as holding areas and way stations in preparation for extermination. In fact, one SS leader remarked: "The establishment of the ghetto is naturally only an interim measure. When and how the ghetto and the city of Łódź will be purged of Jews is something I reserve for my exclusive decision. In any case, however, the final aim will be to burn this fraternity of pestilence to the end."[68]

Life and Death in the General Government

These deadly draconian policies for the demographic restructuring of Poland found their most hellish manifestation in the General Government under Frank. In one respect the General Government typified the anarchy and political infighting of Nazi rule in the East. As governor general, Frank was in theoretical control of the entire administration, but in reality he was locked in a contest with Himmler's SS and police forces for control of occupation policy. Likewise, his four Nazi district leaders and forty county leaders regarded their areas as personal fiefs and gave "priority to local needs at the expense of the criteria laid down by the central government." Additionally, Frank found himself trapped between two competing goals. On the one hand, Hitler's order for the economic exploitation of the area implied a certain level of organization, stability, and support for the inhabitants. On the other hand, the führer's stated desire for the annihilation of the Polish people, in particular the Jews, created a dynamic that, if pursued to its logical extreme, would effectively result in the collapse of Frank's ability to rule. In contrast, Himmler faced no such dilemma, for his SS and police forces were the primary agents for genocide, a mission he openly referred to in a later speech to SS leaders.[69]

In the first months of 1940, German policy in Poland attempted to reconcile economic imperatives and racial ideology. In a meeting with his staff on January 19, Frank indicated that the "decisive point" at that time involved the rebuilding of Poland's productive capability and an end to the plundering of the country. He offered some suggestions for encouraging labor but warned that he would not hesitate to take "the most draconian action" in cases where performance failed to meet German expectations. One ongoing case of "draconian action" involved the creation of the "Lublin Reservation," a roughly three-hundred-square-mile area near that city intended as a dumping ground for European Jews. Frank's deputy, Arthur Seyß-Inquart, remarked that the area known for its "swampy nature, can ... serve as a reservation for the Jews, and this action may cause a considerable decimation of the Jews."[70] In short, the plan's primary objective focused on the extermination of the Polish Jews through disease and neglect. As these masses arrived in early 1940, they found no available housing or infrastructure to support them. The terrible conditions and the threat of epidemics caught the attention of the foreign press and led to the cancelation of the plan by Nazi leaders at the end of March.

The tug-of-war between economic and racial imperatives once again came to the fore during a meeting of the Reich Defense Committee on March 2. At this meeting Frank addressed his most recent policy guidance from Hitler, which once again included the concept of a reservation. He stated, "The Führer has *for the time being* declared that this country will be a reservation for the Poles, ... [and] we have the tremendous responsibility of ensuring this area remains firmly under German control, that the Poles' backbone is permanently broken and that there is never again the slightest resistance to German Reich policy from this area." Frank continued: "This task cannot be fulfilled through a gigantic extermination programme in which people are so to speak, mowed down. We cannot after all kill 14,000,000 Poles."[71] The most interesting aspect of this statement is not the contention that one could not kill fourteen million Poles, but rather that by making such an assertion, it is clear that this option had at some point been considered.

It was the German invasion of France that opened the door for annihilatory practice in the General Government. In a meeting with SS and police officials on May 30, 1940, Frank argued that with the eyes of the world focused to the west, it was time for action in the East. He informed his listeners that he had received the following instructions from Hitler: "We must liquidate those people whom we have discovered form the leadership in Poland; all those who follow in their footsteps must be arrested and then got rid of after an appropriate period." Frank admitted that this "extraordinary pacification action" (AB-Aktion) would "cost some thousands of Poles their lives." In truth, police units already had murdered hundreds if not thousands of Poles in the early months of 1940. In the town of Konski alone, uniformed policemen killed 257 Poles in a nine-day period from March 31 to April 8. The start of the French campaign in June was swiftly followed by a new wave of arrests and murders. General Franz Halder provided one indication of the success of Frank's general pacification campaign in his diary entry of August 27, 1940, noting, "A new wave of liquidation of intellectuals and Jews is on in the East."[72]

Nazi policy in the General Government followed a pattern that would be repeated later in the Soviet Union. In the words of the German historian Thomas Sandkühler: "The German occupation policy in the General Government represented . . . 'the purest example of National Socialist occupation administration.'" He continued: "It [this administration] was characterized by the radical suppression and exploitation of lesser peoples (Fremdvölkischen), a graduated racial hierarchy, [and] far-reaching demographic and social changes [accomplished] through terror, deportations, and genocide."[73] In short, the General Government became a type of laboratory for testing and validating the full range of racial policies aimed at subjugating, exploiting, and eventually eliminating its unfortunate inhabitants.

In a meeting with Frank on October 2, 1940, Hitler once again emphasized his commitment to annihilation and the exploitation of Polish forced labor. The führer reiterated his earlier order that "all the representatives of the Polish intelligentsia must be murdered." He continued: "That sounds cruel but it is the law of life. The General Government is a Polish Reservation, a great Polish labour camp."[74] In the spring of 1940, however, Nazi leaders, including Hitler, still pondered mass deportation as a possible alternative to annihilation.

The Madagascar Plan

The consideration of a large-scale plan for deporting the European Jews to the island of Madagascar off the southeast coast of Africa again underlines the leading role of Himmler and the SS in Nazi

Jewish policy. In a policy memorandum of May 15, 1940, composed for Hitler's consideration, Himmler raised the "possibility of a large-scale emigration of all Jews to Africa or to some colony." In fact, he suggested that such a policy might even be extended to other ethnic groups, including Ukrainians and Poles. The idea of sending European Jews to Madagascar was not new, the concept having circulated in European anti-Semitic circles since the 1880s. SS planners had examined the idea prior to the start of the war, and in November 1938 Hitler had endorsed the idea of creating a Jewish reservation on the island. This plan, though, should not be confused with a "peaceful" or nonviolent solution to the "Jewish problem" since Himmler's SS was to be in control of the proposed "reservation."[75] In short, Madagascar, without regard for its native inhabitants, would become the site for a gigantic Jewish ghetto or concentration camp under SS control. In any event, British control of the seas made the idea impractical, and the visions or delusions related to the scheme had to be abandoned.

Laying the Foundations for a War of Annihilation

By the summer of 1940, Hitler's focus was on the conduct of the war and plans for a potential attack on the Soviet Union. After a series of meetings in November with the Soviet foreign minister, Vyacheslav Molotov, it was clear that the current "marriage of convenience" between the two powers was headed for a nasty divorce. By the end of the year, Hitler, as he had advocated in *Mein Kampf* some fifteen years earlier, began to "direct our [Germany's] gaze towards the lands in the east." On December 18, he signed Directive 21, ordering military preparations for a war designed to "crush Soviet Russia in a rapid campaign." The führer thus began down a road that offered the opportunity for realizing his longest held "colonial fantasy" in Europe, the acquisition of living space in the East that would support German power "for the next one hundred years." In January 1941, he once again gathered his generals and told them of the "immeasurable riches" to be gained by German control of Russia.[76]

Despite Hitler's emphasis on the economic advantages of conquering the Soviet Union, his comments during the planning for the invasion demonstrated that racial objectives and mass murder played the dominant role in Nazi designs for occupied Russia.

Indeed, the attack on the Soviet Union offered both the promise of economic autarchy as well as the chance for Germany to grasp "the grail of a new society built upon racial purity and racial domination." During a meeting with Wehrmacht commanders in early March, Hitler highlighted the ideological objectives for the coming operation: "The impending campaign is more than a clash of arms; it also entails a struggle between two ideologies.... The Jewish-Bolshevik intelligentsia, as the oppressor in the past, must be liquidated."[77]

The task of extermination became the primary responsibility of Himmler's SS and police forces, the regime's political soldiers, who had proven their commitment to Nazi racial policies in the occupation of Poland. Later that month Field Marshal Wilhelm Keitel issued Guidelines in Special Fields Concerning Directive Number 21. This document informed field commanders, "On behalf of the Führer, the Reich Leader of the SS [Himmler] assumes special tasks in preparation for the political administration within the army's field of operations that arise from the final, decisive battle between two opposing political systems." In a subsequent meeting with his senior military commanders on March 30, Hitler explicitly commented on the nature of the "special tasks" facing German forces in the Soviet Union. In his journal Halder recorded the führer's description of the coming campaign as a *Vernichtungskampf* (war of annihilation) between two opposing ideologies and noted his instructions for "the extermination of the Bolshevist Commissars and of the Communist intelligentsia."[78]

In conjunction with efforts to prepare the armed forces for "special tasks" in the East, Hitler also limited military jurisdiction by restricting the authority of military courts to examine incidents of criminal offenses involving Soviet citizens. This move essentially deprived civilians of due process and placed their fates in the hands of military and SS field units. On May 13, Keitel issued a decree suspending military jurisdiction for "enemy civilians" committing criminal offenses, thus creating a situation in which Wehrmacht, SS, and police forces literally became judge, jury, and executioner.[79]

As Wehrmacht commanders finalized their operational plans for the invasion of the Soviet Union, Himmler and Reinhard Heydrich, chief of the security police and SD, developed the blueprint for the activities of SS and police forces. In a meeting with Hermann Göring on March 26, Heydrich reported on SS plans for the "solution to the Jewish question" in conjunction with the coming campaign. For his part, Göring expressed his concern that German forces be made aware of the danger posed by Soviet intelligence personnel (GPU), political commissars, and Jews that they might know "who they had to stand against the wall."[80]

On May 6, the Army High Command sent a letter to Himmler, Heydrich, and Chief of the Order Police Kurt Daluege to arrange a meeting between SS and police leaders with the commanders of the army rear areas and those of the army security divisions, presumably to discuss the command relationships, duties, and responsibilities of both sides in the forthcoming campaign.[81] In a final example, the infamous Commissar Order (*Kommissarbefehl*), issued on June 6, 1941, directed the summary execution of Communist functionaries and political commissars serving with the Red Army, including Jews in party and state positions. In sum, these orders and agreements set the stage for Hitler's self-proclaimed war of annihilation.

Furthermore, even as military and SS leaders discussed operational strategy and individual roles and responsibilities, a group of civilian bureaucrats held their own consultations in order to establish economic policy for the eastern territories to support the military operations. During a meeting on May 2, these bureaucrats summarized several of the key points resulting from their discussions. First, it was apparent to them that the only method for supporting the Wehrmacht involved the exploitation of food resources in Russia. They clearly recognized the horrendous consequences of such a policy for the local populace, remarking laconically: "As a result, x million people will doubtlessly starve, if that which is necessary for us is extracted from the land." The essential outlines of the "Hunger Policy" were finalized by May 23 and envisioned the destruction of cities, the extinction of industry, and the deaths of some thirty million people in the winter of 1941–42 alone. The guidelines explicitly detailed the expected results: "Many tens of millions of people in this territory will become superfluous and will die or must emigrate to Siberia. Attempts to rescue the population there from death through starvation by obtaining surpluses from the black earth zone [that is, Ukraine] can only come at the expense of the provisioning of Europe. . . . With regard to this, absolute clarity must reign." In the words of Timothy Snyder, "German intentions were to fight a war of destruction that would transform eastern Europe into an exterminatory agrarian colony."[82]

Taken as whole, these orders, policies, and directives offer several insights into the racial and political beliefs that framed the invasion of the Soviet Union and how the war was intended to be waged. First, as in the case of Poland, ideology and racial hatred provided a foundation for both legitimizing a war of annihilation and justifying the use of mass murder. Second, Hitler's intimate involvement with the planning for the attack highlighted his leading role in establishing the guidelines to be followed during the campaign. Third, the extensive efforts at coordinating the actions of the military with SS and police, with the specific responsibilities assigned to each, points to the close relationship, at least at the levels of senior command, between the soldiers of the Wehrmacht and the Third Reich's political soldiers. Fourth, the steps taken to lift legal obligations and constraints in the campaign in effect gave German soldiers a free pass to engage in criminal behavior without threat of prosecution. Finally, not only military and SS leaders but also civilian bureaucrats played a key role in formulating policy that assumed and accepted millions of deaths as the acceptable price of a Nazi empire in the East. In the end, the policies and orders that preceded the start of Operation Barbarossa paved the way for the murderous activities of German forces in the annihilation of the European Jews and the conduct of a racial war of extermination.

The Nazi Plan for the East

The invasion that began on June 22, 1941, unleashed a lethal maelstrom upon the Red Army and the Soviet people. During the attack and over the course of the occupation, violence, atrocity, mass murder, and a colossal program of economic exploitation emerged as the defining characteristics of German rule. On the eve of the invasion, Himmler, in his role as Reich commissioner for the strengthening of German nationality, was soliciting plans for a vast demographic restructuring of the occupied and incorporated territories, both current and projected. The initial drafts of *Generalplan Ost* (General Plan East) were completed in the summer of 1941 and envisioned a program of Germanization that included the transfer of millions of German agrarian settlers into the conquered lands and the expulsion or elimination of tens of millions of indigenous inhabitants.

For his part, Himmler was pleased with the concept and anticipated the opportunity to present it to Hitler. One historian described Himmler's plan as nothing less than "a timetable for the extinction of the entire population of Eastern Europe." The essential elements of General Plan East included the deportation, enslavement, assimilation, or murder of native populations not only within the occupied Soviet Union but also throughout occupied and incorporated Poland as well. Under the plan, between thirty-one and forty-five million Slavs were to "disappear" from the areas under German occupation. In one version 85 percent of Poles, 75 percent of Belorussians, 65 percent of West Ukrainians, and 50 percent of Czechs were slated for elimination. In separate conversations in October 1941, Hitler rhapsodized on the settlement of the East with five million and subsequently ten million Germans while dryly discussing the need to "dispense with" vast numbers of the native populations. The final version of the plan, completed in 1942, envisioned the settlement of 220,000 families, 220,000 young couples, and an additional 2,000,000 colonists from urban areas within Germany to take the place of the Slavic populations.[83]

Not coincidentally, Wehrmacht and SS veterans were expected to spearhead the Nazi colonization efforts by establishing fortified military settlements throughout the region. These *Wehrbauern* (soldier-farmers) would form a "wall of flesh and blood" capable of settling and defending the eastern frontier. From Himmler's perspective, SS veterans were to provide the leadership for these settlements and constitute a "pioneer aristocracy" in the East in reward for their wartime service. The failure to achieve a rapid victory over the Soviet Union prevented the realization of this plan in Russia. Still, some three thousand veterans received grants for lands in the Warthegau, as did a number of senior army generals and SS leaders. By the summer of 1944, even in the face of the impending collapse of the eastern front, Himmler still rewarded military and SS veterans who had demonstrated "exceptional service" with land grants, farms, and homesteads through the program.[84]

Although SS planners failed to realize the full scope of their grandiose visions to transform the East into a martial agrarian colony—Sparta with fewer Helots—the plans offer several insights into Nazi ambitions and goals for the region. First, the plan to create German colonies ipso facto required expelling or eliminating the native populations. Second, the creation of a Nazi "Garden of Eden" in the East required the construction of major highways, fortifications, and industrial enterprises to link it with the "Old Reich" and provide protection for the German colonizers. Finally, these massive construction efforts led to the creation of camps of slave laborers, upon whose backs and bones the Nazi empire in the East literally was to be built. In a speech to senior SS leaders in the summer of 1942, Himmler explained the need "to fill our camps with slaves, ... with worker slaves, who will build our cities, our villages, our farms without regard to any losses." For the Reich commissioner, the staggering economic costs of the proposed resettlement plan required a slave-labor force numbering in the millions. Here again racial policy and ideological beliefs complemented economic realities as the Jewish and Slavic "worker slaves" were expendable and their labor was itself intended to lead to "natural death" through physical abuse and exhaustion.[85]

Limiting Education and Reproduction

The mass murder of Jews may have been the central plank in Nazi eugenic and social engineering efforts in the East, but it was accompanied by other initiatives aimed at the non-Jewish populations of the region. Hitler described the Slavic peoples as "a mass of born slaves, who feel the need of a master." One of the key eastern initiatives in the planned subjugation of these peoples were efforts at limiting their educational level and keeping them at the "lowest possible level of civilization (*Kulturniveau*)." In the words of one historian, the Nazis "wanted the locals to work, not think." Although recognizing the need for schools in the East, Hitler remarked that their educational goals should be limited to teaching students to recognize traffic signs.[86]

In accordance with the führer's desires, Alfred Rosenberg, the Reich minister for the occupied eastern territories, ordered the abolishment of all schooling above the fourth-grade level. The only exception to be made to this rule would be for local children identified as "racially valuable." To this end, Nazi administrators, under a program designated as the "Hay Action," conducted a "massive kidnapping operation" that stole such children from their parents and placed them with German families. In Ukraine this included seizing children between the ages of ten and eighteen identified either as "criminally suspect or racially valuable." In the case of the former, incarceration in concentration camps and forced-labor battalions constituted their fate.[87]

If limiting the native inhabitants' educational level and practicing eugenic selection constituted aspects of Nazi policy, then an even more important initiative involved limiting the overall size of the indigenous populations. In a conversation in July 1942, Hitler warned of the "danger" posed by the Slavic populations due to the supposed fertility of their women. He asserted, "We must therefore under all circumstances take preventive measures against an increase in the non-German population." In concrete terms these measures involved the denial of vaccinations and immunizations, the extensive use of abortions, and forced sterilizations. In the case of the latter, Hitler, Himmler, and other Nazi administrators promoted and ordered "policies and programs for forced sterilization and abortions in Ukraine."[88] These were population-control measures that complemented mass murder, starvation, and executions.

The Einsatzgruppen in Russia: "Masters of Death"

As in the Polish campaign, einsatzgruppen (special-mission units) were created to follow behind Wehrmacht forces during the invasion of Russia, with responsibility for the elimination of racial and political enemies. When German forces streamed across the Soviet border on June 22, four of these special-mission units, with letter designations A, B, C, and D, followed closely on the heels of the Wehrmacht but were under the direct control of Himmler. Assigned specific geographic areas of responsibility and numbering between 500 and 1,000 men, the einsatzgruppen were composed of a mix of SS and police forces. Operating primarily in small detachments, known as *Einsatzkommandos* and *Sonderkommandos*, these units initially targeted "political functionaries" such as commissars and Communist Party leaders; the term was expanded shortly after the invasion to include Jewish men and eventually Jewish women and children. The presence of the majority of Russian Jewish communities in the "pale of settlement" facilitated their destruction through means from individual executions to the mass shootings of tens of thousands, such as the murder of over 33,000 people at a ravine near the Ukrainian city of Kiev in September 1941 (see chapter 4).[89]

The activities of the einsatzgruppen once again highlight the overall scale and scope of Nazi plans in the East. In one respect, these killing units crossed a major psychological and symbolic threshold in the summer of 1941 with the start of the mass murder of women and children, an order Himmler personally communicated to unit commanders in July. The einsatzgruppen had been designed as "purpose built" instruments for annihilation in support of a racial and ideological agenda aimed not at punishment, but at physical elimination on the frontier of the expanding Reich. After a mere four months into the campaign, these units reported having killed over 250,000 people, the vast majority of them Jews. By the end of 1942, the total number of victims included more than 700,000 Jews, reaching as many as 1,500,000 by the end of the war. As Hitler received reports of the vast scale of SS murders in the East and pondered a mammoth resettlement program, he chose this moment to compare Nazi expansion into the East with the conquest of the American West: "Here in the east a similar process will repeat itself for a second time as in the conquest of America."[90]

The Decision for the Final Solution

Historians have debated Hitler's exact role in orchestrating the events of the "Final Solution to the Jewish Problem." Some ascribed to him a direct role in steering policy toward this goal, while others have argued for a process of "cumulative radicalization" in which the decision for annihilation grew out of ad-hoc processes of bureaucratic improvisation at the local level. Similarly, the exact dating of Hitler's decision to authorize the murder of the entirety of Europe's Jews is a source of considerable debate among Holocaust historians.[91] Regardless of the arguments surrounding the issues of Hitler's intent and timing, the decision to annihilate the Jews could not have been made without the führer's knowledge and approval. Whether this decision occurred with a nod of the head in the euphoria of seemingly imminent victory in the Soviet Union in July 1941 or later that year as a result of bureaucratic plans for the racial and demographic restructuring of the East seems less important than the fact that the political leadership of Nazi Germany and its executive agents, both uniformed and civilian, conceptualized, organized, and implemented plans involving the *systematic* murder of 6 million European Jews, including 1.5 million children.

By the fall of 1941, the pragmatic and logistical issues associated with the murder of the Jews found expression in a November 3 report from Einsatzgruppe C. The report trumpeted the unit's success and recorded the "liquidation" of 75,000 Jews by shooting, though also noting that large-scale mass executions did not provide a "feasible solution of the Jewish problem." Rudolf Höss, the commandant of Auschwitz, described a conversation that he had with Adolf Eichmann, the notorious SS head of Jewish affairs, at the camp in 1941. Höss recalled: "We went on to discuss the extermination process. It transpired that only gas could be considered, because to eliminate the masses that were to be expected by shooting was absolutely impossible and also too hard on the SS men involved, having to shoot women and children."[92]

Himmler recognized the relative inefficiency of mass shootings and the psychic toll that such operations caused even among his political soldiers, but he did not have to search very long or very far for a solution. The operation for the murder of the physically and mentally disabled within Germany, the so-called T-4 Program, authorized by Hitler in 1939, provided the personnel and the template that allowed for testing methods of mass extermination in the East. During the first two years of its operation, the inaptly described "Euthanasia" program aimed at "life unworthy of life" resulted in the murder of some 70,000 men, women, and children, the vast majority Aryan Germans, through a variety of methods that included starvation, lethal injection, and gassing.[93] Likewise, the SS adapted the T-4 Program's gassing technology into "gas vans" to murder Poles in the annexed territories as early as 1939, a technique later employed by the einsatzgruppen after the invasion of the Soviet Union.[94]

After Hitler's decision to deport all German Jews to the East in the fall of 1941, Himmler's SS and police forces began the planning that would lead to the construction of purpose-built extermination centers, or death camps, in occupied Poland. At Chełmno, gas vans served as the means of execution, while the death camps at Bełżec, Sobibor, and Treblinka made use of diesel engines to pump carbon monoxide into sealed rooms to kill Jews. At Auschwitz a new technique involving Zyklon-B (prussic acid) tablets was tested on a group of Soviet POWs in a sealed bunker in September 1941.

The results validated the method and led to gassing Jews, beginning in January 1942. Originally scheduled for December 9, 1941, the infamous meeting at a villa on the Wannsee in Berlin on January 20, 1942, brought together the various branches of the National Socialist bureaucracy to coordinate "all the relevant agencies on the other activities involved in this final solution."[95]

SS General Reinhard Heydrich, the head of the security police and the SD, chaired the meeting at Wannsee and outlined the plans to eliminate the entire European Jewish population "from west to east." As in the case of the Slavic population of the occupied East, the Final Solution involved the use of Jews in labor gangs for large-scale construction projects such as road building. The physical difficulty associated with the work combined with minimal rations was aimed at creating a "natural wastage [that is, death]" among the workers but also included plans for the direct murder of those with "the greatest powers of endurance."[96]

One indication of the scale of Hitler's plan is found in a detailed listing of Jews throughout Europe, including their numbers in England, Ireland, Switzerland, and Spain, areas outside Nazi control. The Wannsee Conference was not a decision-making meeting, but one dedicated to the implementation of a previously approved policy for the physical extermination of all European Jews. Not coincidentally, a mere ten days later on the ninth anniversary of the Nazi "seizure of power," Hitler made a public speech, also carried by German radio, in which he proclaimed: "We are clear that the war can only end either with the extermination of the Aryan peoples or the disappearance of Jewry from Europe. . . . [T]his war will not come to an end as the Jews imagine, with the extermination of the European-Aryan peoples, but that the result of this war will be the annihilation of Jewry."[97]

The formal discussions concerning the Final Solution in early 1942 simply provided another step in a process that had begun with the mass killings of Jewish men, women, and children by SS and police forces in the summer of 1941. Likewise, the decision served to resolve an existing debate within the party and between the Wehrmacht and the SS concerning the economic costs to Germany that would result from policies of extermination. In this sense the Wannsee Conference also represented the triumph of racial ideology over economic considerations, a fact evident in a directive of December 18, 1941, from the Reich Ministry for the Eastern

Territories with the telling remark: "The Jewish question has probably been clarified by now through verbal discussions. Economic considerations are to be regarded as fundamentally irrelevant in the settlement of the problem."[98]

By March 1942, as the process of extermination began to develop momentum with the shipment of Jews from Polish ghettos to the death camps, Propaganda Minister Goebbels recorded his thoughts in a journal entry of March 27: "No sentimentality can be allowed to prevail in these things. If we didn't fend them off, the Jews would annihilate us. It's a life or death struggle between the Aryan race and the Jewish bacillus." He continued: "No other government and no other regime could produce the strength to solve this question generally. Here, too, the Führer is the unswerving champion and spokesman of a radical solution."[99] In one respect Goebbels was right: the decision for complete physical extermination of a target group required the type of commitment that only could come from a criminal regime anchored to a racial ideology and possessed of the means to achieve its malevolent dystopic fantasies.

Comparing the Nazi East and the American West

In comparing the impulses and events that shaped Nazi policy in the East with U.S. policy during the process of westward expansion, a fundamental difference resulting from the racial and ideological precepts of National Socialism is immediately evident. While German and American policymakers both demonstrated the elements of a "colonial mentality" toward the objects of their intended conquest, Hitler and his administrators conceived of the conquest of the East in genocidal terms that involved not only the murder of the European Jews but also the premeditated direct and indirect murder of tens of millions of the region's native populations. In this respect annihilation and extermination proved to be the initial and the ultimate objectives of the war in the East. Certainly, economic motivations also played an important role in Nazi plans for conquest. The "black earth" region was to become the breadbasket of the Third Reich and the home for an army of "farmer-soldiers." In addition, hundreds of thousands if not millions of the people under Nazi control would be put to work building a series of superhighways in the East to support the movement of peoples and goods in the occupied territory. Although these massive construction projects had an economic objective, they also had the racial goal of literally working the construction teams to death. For those lucky enough to survive the backbreaking work and scant rations, death would come in the form of a bullet to the back of the neck as SS and police forces murdered tens of thousands of these slave laborers in 1943 and 1944.[100] In Nazi ideology it was not one's contribution to the Reich but one's race that determined one's fate. With the exception of a "select" few deemed worthy of Germanization, the vast majority of Slavs and all Jews faced a brutal occupation regime built for their exploitation and aimed at their extermination.

In contrast to the Nazi East, federal policies in the American West ostensibly sought the assimilation and acculturation of the Native tribes. Based on the precepts of Christianity and civilization, government policymakers, religious groups, and civilian benefactors attempted to reshape Indian culture, effectively destroying it, by imposing a reflection of their own ideals, beliefs, and morals onto the tribes. In the case of religious reformers, this process was in most cases pursued with "good intentions" and the sincere belief that they were raising the tribes up in a spiritual, moral, and cultural sense. Similarly, those tasked with the enforcement of policy in the West, professional soldiers, "advocated Indian assimilation . . . [and] wanted that end to come through peaceful diplomacy and education, not through war." These views were no doubt influenced by a sense of moral superiority and cultural chauvinism, but the very goal of assimilation assumed that Indians were members of the human race, if only in a more primitive state. This does not mean, however, that acts of atrocity and mass murder did not accompany efforts to "civilize" the tribes, nor does it mean that there were no interest groups or individuals who advocated extermination as the only solution to the "Indian problem." Indeed, throughout the nineteenth century, state and territorial volunteers and frontiersmen embraced "genocidal sentiment" in operations against Natives. Still, the groups advocating extermination proved unable to mobilize effective support for their vision of annihilation, especially within the country's political centers of power in the East.[101]

As SS leaders and Nazi bureaucrats discussed the Final Solution in January 1942, they conceived plans to murder Jews even in areas that remained outside German control. In this respect, despite complaints of Indians seeking refuge in Canada and Mexico and punishment campaigns that crossed the southern border, the physical extermination of every Indian in the Western hemisphere was beyond the imaginings of all but the most fanatical of "Indian haters." Likewise, the enslavement of the Native populations as forced laborers never became an objective of U.S. policy in the case of westward expansion (although the earlier Spanish treatment of tribes in the California missions offers some parallels for comparison). Similarly, the transcontinental railroads had drastic implications for the tribes of the West and were built in part upon the backs of cheap immigrant labor, but they were not precedents for the Nazi superhighways and cannot be compared with the use of slave labor in the East.[102]

In one respect U.S. policy and Nazi policy found a striking similarity. The use of reservations and ghettos in the East and the use of reservations in the American West both served as areas of isolation, albeit for strikingly different objectives. In the case of a Jewish reservation in Poland, Nazi planners envisioned the area as "a punishing environment in which the Jewish race would fail to thrive," while Governor General Frank, the Nazi leader charged with its administration, remarked: "A pleasure finally to physically assault the Jewish race. The more [who] die, the better."[103] Likewise, the Nazi creation of open and, especially, closed ghettos served both pragmatic and ideological objectives. In the case of the former, concentration of Jews allowed for their spoliation and provided an additional opportunity to expropriate their wealth while creating a ready pool of forced labor for further exploitation. In the case of the latter, isolation and concentration reflected a racial prejudice of Jews as carriers of pathogens, their mere presence constituting a danger for epidemics. The semantic linkage of Jews to disease created its own implicit logic for containing this "contagion" and promoted the eventual impulse for the eradication of this "danger."

In contrast to the ghetto, the western reservation was seen as an "alternative to [physical] extinction" and a place in which the transformation of "savages" into civilized Christians would occur. These goals only could be met if the federal government and its agents met their obligations. All too often, however, it was the failure of the government to provide the promised annuities and supplies that led to abysmal conditions and justifiably promoted anger and unrest among the resident tribes. The ostensible rationale for the isolation of the reservation, again in contrast to the ghettos, was to prevent

Native contact with those who would disrupt this process or negatively influence the intended transformation. In this respect, the Indian agent, whether successful or not, was *intended* to serve as a paternalistic figure responsible for the health and welfare of his "wards," a role diametrically opposed to that of the Nazi district leaders in the East.[104] Additionally, reformers sought to use education as tool for civilization on the reservations in an attempt to provide practical instruction in agricultural techniques along with English-language skills to promote the spiritual salvation of the tribes. Likewise, reformers viewed their students, especially those in the boarding schools, as malleable agents of assimilation who would return to the reservation imbued with a mission to change their families and their tribes into the image of white, Christian society. With respect to the education of Slavs, Himmler made Nazi intentions clear in a memorandum of May 15, 1940, in which he declared: "The non-German population of the eastern territories must not receive any education higher than that of an elementary school. . . . The objective of this elementary school must simply be to teach: simple arithmetic up to 500 at the most, how to write one's name, and to teach that it is God's commandment to be obedient to the Germans. . . . I consider it unnecessary to teach reading."[105] If American reformers wanted to teach the Ten Commandments in a process of spiritual and social conversion, Nazi administrators had no such aspirations for the subject peoples under their control.

Although assimilation of the Native tribes was the professed goal of U.S. policy, the process included elements of compulsion, and both economic and physical coercion played a role in the management of the reservations. For example, Indian agents could and did withhold the distribution of annuities, rations, and goods as a form of discipline or in an attempt to influence behavior. Mismanagement and corruption on the part of the Indian Ring, along with the creation of reservations in desolate or barren areas, not only threatened the continued existence of the tribes (as in the case of the Apache reservation at San Carlos) but also effectively isolated them from the rest of American society. Likewise, this separation was enforced by the Indian Bureau's control of the reservations as well as the presence of nearby army forts. In the case of the latter, the soldiers were responsible both for preventing the tribes from leaving their proscribed areas and for precluding white encroachment or unauthorized trade with the Indians. It should be noted, however, that troops required authorization from the Department of the Interior to enter a reservation for the conduct of operations, a fact that many officers found frustrating in the course of "pursue and punish" campaigns.[106] In this respect the comparison between the objectives of military strategy and the conduct of warfare in the American West and the Nazi East provides further insight into the character of U.S. and Nazi policy in their respective areas.

Columns of cavalry, artillery, and supply wagons during the Black Hills Expedition, 1874. The U.S. Army's use of large columns and wagon trains allowed for extended operations, but these forces often lacked the mobility necessary to find and surprise Native warriors in the field. Photograph by W. H. Illingworth. Courtesy National Archives and Records Administration (77-HQ-264-854).

Slaughtered buffalo, 1872. The loss of the buffalo herds proved a crippling blow to the Plains tribes for its physical and spiritual effects on the Indians, denying them a key supply link for supporting their resistance. Courtesy National Archives and Records Administration (79-M-1B-4).

Indians drawing rations at Camp Supply, Indian Territory, on issue day, ca. 1871. The failure of the federal government and Indian agents to provide promised annuities and provisions often proved a decisive factor in the decision by groups of Indians to leave the reservation in search of food or to raid. Courtesy National Archives and Records Administration (165-AI-2).

Looking Glass of the Nez Perce on an Indian pony, 1877. The traditional Indian pony, although smaller than its fodder-dependent army counterpart, often proved superior during extended campaigns due to its ability to maintain itself on native grasses. Courtesy National Archives and Records Administration (111-SC-87744).

Apache scouts at Fort Wingate, New Mexico. The use of Indian scouts and auxiliaries proved critical to the army's success on the Great Plains and in the Desert Southwest. Courtesy National Archives and Records Administration (American Indian Select List no. 164).

Chiricahua Apaches under guard en route to Fort Pickens, Florida, 1886. Geronimo (seated, first row, third from right) conducted a series of masterful guerrilla campaigns in the Desert Southwest that ended with his surrender in 1886 to Brigadier General Nelson A. Miles. Photograph by J. McDonald. Courtesy National Archives and Records Administration (111-SC-82320).

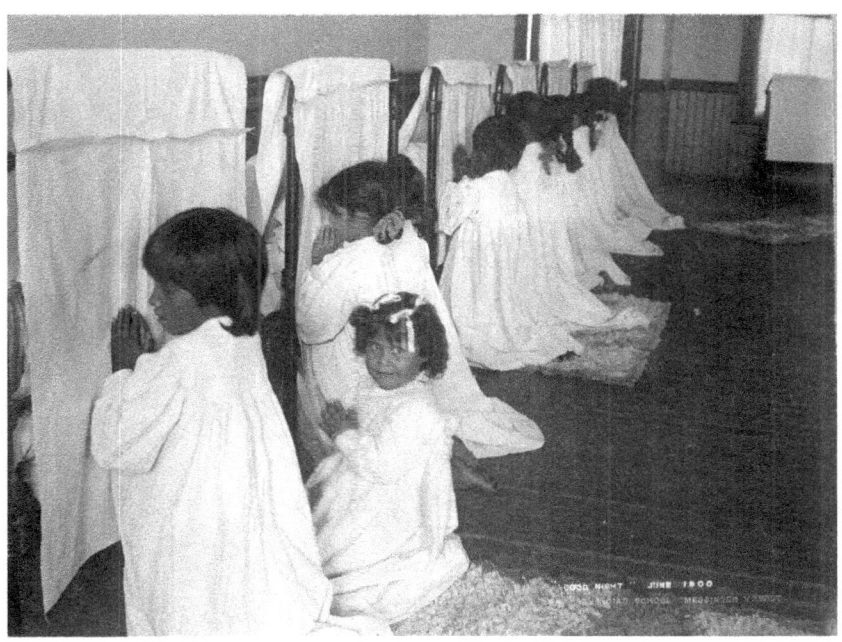

A group of girls praying at the Phoenix Indian School, Arizona, 1900. One aim of the federal government's policy to assimilate Native tribes, especially children, was through a dual process of Christianity and "civilization." Schools, both on and off the reservations, were intended to play a key role in this process. Photograph by Messinger. Courtesy National Archives and Records Administration (American Indian Select List no. 162).

German soldiers marching through a burning Soviet village, ca. 1941. The Wehrmacht, SS, and police forces routinely destroyed entire villages in reprisal campaigns aimed at the local population. U.S. Holocaust Memorial Museum, courtesy Bruce Sadler (no. 65473).

Prisoners at forced labor in the rock quarry at Mauthausen concentration camp, Austria. The National Socialist government made extensive use of slave labor to support the Third Reich economically and as a means of killing political and racial enemies of the state in a policy of "annihilation through labor." U.S. Holocaust Memorial Museum, Archiv der KZ-Gedenkstätte Mauthausen, courtesy Vaclav Berdych (no. 27078).

Jewish children on the streets of the Warsaw ghetto, 1940. The ghettos in the East served as concentration points for European Jews prior to deportation to the killing camps. Disease and starvation took a horrendous toll on the ghettos' inhabitants, especially the young and the old. U.S. Holocaust Memorial Museum, courtesy Interpress, Warsaw (no. 08160).

German forces executing Soviet civilians at a mass grave, 1941. During the campaigns in the East, German forces and their auxiliaries murdered millions of local inhabitants literally "one bullet at a time." U.S. Holocaust Memorial Museum, courtesy National Archives and Records Administration, College Park (no. 89063).

Hungarian Jews on the selection ramp at Auschwitz-Birkenau, Poland, May 1944. This photograph documents the "industrial killing process" of the genocide of the Jews. Those deemed fit for slave labor were sent into the camp, while those deemed unfit were selected for the gas chambers. U.S. Holocaust Memorial Museum, courtesy Yad Vashem, Panstwowe Muzeum Auschwitz-Birkenau w Oswiecimiu (no. 77319).

German police and auxiliaries with a group of Jewish women prior to their execution, 1939–43 (location unknown). This photograph illustrates the process by which German police forces murdered small groups of men, women, and children throughout the occupied East. In many cases the victims faced the added humiliation of having to undress and march naked to the killing sites. U.S. Holocaust Memorial Museum, courtesy of Instytut Pamieci Narodowej, Yad Vashem Photo Archives, YIVO Institute for Jewish Research (no. 43195).

CHAPTER 3

STRATEGY AND WARFARE

In the process of instituting governmental policy, military strategy forms a key element for the attainment of political objectives, especially in cases involving conquest and occupation. The Prussian military theorist Carl von Clausewitz summarized this relationship in his oft-cited assertion, "war is merely the continuation of policy by other means."[1] In short, military strategies should be designed with the intent to attain overarching political goals. In this sense the ultimate intent of the political objective, whether subjugation or annihilation, provides fundamental guidance for the type and the extent of force employed. Similarly, the nature of the government, totalitarian or democratic, combined with the doctrine and capabilities of a country's armed forces are critical in determining how the military will be used against an adversary. In fact, all of these elements combine to determine how military force will be employed.

The Nazi conquests in the East, regardless of their ultimate racial and economic motives, were based on a series of preplanned and organized military campaigns involving massed troop formations operating against the conventional armies of an opposing nation state. In the case of the invasion of the Soviet Union alone, over three million German and Axis troops combined for the opening assaults in June 1941. For their part, senior Wehrmacht leaders envisioned large-scale battles using superior maneuver to encircle the enemy forces and firepower to annihilate them. In fact, the concept of the *Kesselschlacht* (literally, "cauldron battle," battle of annihilation) had formed the ideal for Prussian military leaders since the reign of Frederick the Great. Robert Citino aptly described this "German way of war" as the quest for "a way to fight short, sharp wars that ended rapidly in a decisive battlefield victory, a front-loaded conflict that left the enemy too weak or frightened to consider a second round." The goal of destruction of opposing forces on the battlefield not only borrowed from traditional Prussian and German operational strategy of envelopment and annihilation but also proved fully in consonance with the racial imperatives of the National Socialist regime and its depiction of Slavs as *Untermenschen* (subhumans). In this respect party ideology cut both ways, by denigrating the capabilities of Soviet troops while praising the German soldier as the "pre-eminent weapon [based on] the superior powers of the Nordic fighting man."[2]

In short, military strategy in the East was based on the premise that "racially superior" Germans could achieve the ideal of blitzkrieg, or lightning war, by quickly overpowering their adversary in a series of rapid military campaigns. The six-week campaign in Poland, the rapid defeat of French forces in the West, and the swift conquest of the Balkans seemed to provide both the template and the validation for this concept. In the case of the East, military conquest was to be followed by civil and military occupation designed to exploit these regions and to prepare them for future German settlement. The failure of the Wehrmacht to defeat the Soviet Union in 1941 resulted in a war that involved not only large-scale conventional operations but also smaller-scale guerrilla or partisan battles in the areas under German control. The forces employed to combat these partisan or "bandit" units included regular military forces as well as an array of German and indigenous paramilitary and auxiliary forces, including SS and police units charged with the racial cleansing of the East.

In contrast to Wehrmacht conventional operations in the East, the U.S. Army in the American West faced diverse opponent tribes adept at irregular and guerrilla operations in a variety of climates, from the deserts of the Southwest, to the Great Plains, the forests of the Pacific Northwest, and the mountain ranges of the Continental Divide. The Indians refused to become engaged in the type of set-piece Napoleonic engagements taught to future army officers at West Point and that most typified the Civil War experience. According to one historian, the army lacked a viable "strategic concept" for dealing with the tribes, a shortcoming that reflected "the federal government's failure to define the means through which its general Indian policy was to be implemented." This failure not only prevented the development of a coherent strategy but also placed troops in a reactive posture and a position of tactical disadvantage. Indian methods emphasized the use of relatively small groups of warriors conducting raids against isolated targets of opportunity, such as homesteads, wagon trains, mining settlements, and herds of livestock. The objective of U.S. Army operations, especially during the reservation period, was to "pursue and punish" Indian bands that had abandoned the reservation. The purpose of these centered on the capture or killing of Indians accused of raids and "depredations."[3]

Throughout U.S. history, army strategies for dealing with the tribes contained both elements of annihilation and attrition. In one influential work Russell Weigley has argued, "If the conduct of the Civil War had prepared the United States Army to employ a strategy of annihilation, sometimes with frightful literalness, in its wars against the Indians, the strategy was much in harmony with post–Civil War policy." In contrast, other historians have taken issue with Weigley's use of the paradigms of annihilation and attrition, especially his description of army operations during the Indian Wars as the "annihilation of a people."[4] Certainly, both William T. Sherman and Philip Sheridan had learned the lessons of "hard war" during the sectional conflict and brought such military experience with them to the West. One such lesson involved the use of "punishment" against an opponent. In his memoirs Sherman discussed his objective with respect to the Confederate army: "My aim then was, to whip the rebels, to humble their pride, to follow them to their inmost recesses, and make them fear and dread us. 'Fear of the Lord is the beginning of wisdom.'"[5]

Although Sherman's words evoked the image of biblical retribution, the use of brutal punishment operations against Indian bands by military forces and frontiersman clearly predated the Civil War and included acts such as the destruction of encampments and crops, the killing of women and children, the taking of captives, and the assassination of leaders. Whether or not the Civil War inured officers to mass slaughter and created a strategy of annihilation, decades earlier Major General John Sullivan had led a punishment campaign against the Iroquois in 1779 with the object of a "feed fight" aimed at "the deliberate destruction of crops and villages."[6] Similarly, the campaigns against the Seminoles in Florida in the first half of the nineteenth century provide evidence of operations designed to impoverish the Natives and to destroy their means of subsistence.[7] In fact, campaigns against various tribes prior to 1861, despite individual acts of atrocity and mass killing, incorporated punishment and not complete physical extermination as their primary objective. Still, if complete extermination was not the goal, some army punishment campaigns did seek to eliminate the warriors of a given tribe. For example, in one foray against the Apache in 1862, Brigadier General James Carleton ordered, "The men are to be slain wherever they can be found."[8] The ruthless nature of these military actions faced many Indian survivors with a stark choice between "starvation or submission," and many chose capitulation and removal as the best remaining option.[9]

Addressing the brutality of the Indian Wars, General Sherman highlighted the conflicting demands placed on the army by white settlers and eastern reformers in dealing with the various tribes: "There are two classes of people, one demanding the utter extinction of the Indians, and the other full of love for their conversion to civilization." He continued, "Unfortunately, the army stands between them and gets the cuff from both sides." One method by which officers got the "cuff" from civilians occurred as "predatory frontier citizens ... often took soldiers to court if they attempted to enforce laws intended to protect the Indians and keep the peace." Similarly, it was not regular-army forces in most cases that proved most willing to engage in mass slaughter, but rather state or territorial volunteers, militias, law-enforcement groups such as the Texas Rangers, and civilian vigilantes. Indeed, the precedent for atrocity and mass murder by nonmilitary forces was established as early as the sixteenth century by the actions of frontiersman against Indian noncombatants, a practice that continued into the nineteenth century.[10]

U.S. Army Policy in the West

By the second half of the nineteenth century, the settlement of the West Coast and the acquisition of the Southwest territories ended the illusion that a permanent Indian country could be created to ensure the separation of Natives and whites along a fixed frontier. In recognition of this fact, the United States negotiated the Fort Laramie Treaty in 1851 with the Sioux, Cheyennes, Arapahos, and other tribes to regulate interaction and to establish the boundaries and jurisdiction of each tribe on the northern plains. The agreement called for military posts along the overland trails leading to the West Coast, provided for the payment of annuities, and held individual tribes responsible for acts committed within their territories. Two years later a similar treaty regulated the transit of white settlers along the Santa Fe Trail in the southern plains.[11]

In his annual report of 1857, Secretary of War John B. Floyd argued that the existing strength of the army at 15,764 men was inadequate for guarding and controlling a frontier of 11,000 miles and an area of three million square miles. His main concern was the western frontier bordering the Indian territories. Along with a plea for an increase in the size of the army, Floyd proposed a new strategy involving the creation of a dual line of frontier posts along the western and eastern borders of Indian territory, with an additional line of forts placed alongside the "great lines of intercommunication between the valley of the Mississippi and the Pacific Ocean." The secretary justified this request by stating that "scarcely a week elapses without bringing to us intelligence of some Indian massacre, or outrage more shocking than death." He continued, "it most frequently happens that these acts go unpunished altogether either from the want of troops for pursuit, or from their remoteness from the scenes of slaughter, which renders pursuit useless."[12] Floyd argued that a double line of forts placed near the "Indians usual habitations" would serve as a positive deterrent for raids against white settlements and would allow for "prompt retaliation" upon guilty Indian communities in the event that deterrence failed.

This report raised several issues related to U.S. Army strategy against the Indians. First, it demonstrated the War Department's belief that it was being asked to do too much with too little. Second, it created the perception that, as a result of this manpower shortage, the army was not in a position to deal with Indian raids or attacks against settlers and migrants on the overland trails. Third, it displayed a sense of exasperation in dealing with a foe who chose hit-and-run tactics and whose "only strength lies in a capacity to elude pursuit."[13] The failure of the army to develop a formal doctrine in dealing with the Indians' unique style of warfare reflected either an inability or an unwillingness to foresee the need for this capability. According to one historian, "the Indian troubles that occupied the army year after year called forth a body of essentially orthodox strategies only slightly modified by the special conditions of the police function."[14] In the end, the War Department relied on a general punishment strategy aimed at deterring or when necessary responding to real or perceived Indian outrages.

In the summer of 1857, Colonel Edwin Sumner commanded two companies of the First U.S. Cavalry in a punishment campaign against a group of Cheyennes, the result of a series of minor incidents and misunderstandings during the previous year that had escalated into a larger conflict. Some three hundred Cheyenne warriors chose to engage Sumner's cavalry and a group of Delaware auxiliaries in a battle that resulted in the deaths of two troopers and between four and nine Cheyenne warriors. As the Cheyennes departed the battlefield, Sumner's cavalry pursued and reached an abandoned village some fifteen miles away, where the soldiers helped themselves to dried bison and burned the remaining lodges, foodstuffs, and possessions. Although a seemingly minor operation, Sumner's expedition typified army strategy of the period. Despite the size and technological advantage of his force, the colonel proved unable to draw the Cheyennes into a decisive battle; the destruction of the warriors' logistics base and food reserves proved to be the most significant result of the campaign. While Sumner worried that the Indians had not been "sufficiently punished for the[ir] barbarous outrages," would-be settlers perceived the battle as a harbinger of security on the frontier, prompting a new wave of white settlement into the West and exposing a rapidly vanishing frontier between they and the Natives. In the words of Elliot West: "The Indians' old story was increasingly entangled with that of the whites. . . . A frontier never separated things. It brought things together."[15]

This increasing "entanglement" of Indians and whites in the West faced the U.S. Army with a dilemma. On the one hand, the army existed to protect white settlers from the Indians, but on the other hand, it also was charged with protecting the Indians from the depredations and encroachment of white settlers, speculators, and traders. In the words of Samuel Watson, "Contrary to crude notions of racial conquest, the nation's Indians relations were militarized by restraints on whites as well as aggression against Indians." He continued, "Until agrarian settlement caught up with the national military presence, a large portion of the army's everyday energies was spent . . . to limit friction between white and native by restraining white encroachment in areas as yet unceded by the Indians."[16] In the second half of the nineteenth century, however, the presence of the army served paradoxically as one of the key catalysts for the influx of white settlers into Indian Territory and along the overland trails, a migration that increased the probability of interaction and conflict between the two groups.

By 1865, Alexander McCook, a major general of the volunteers during the Civil War, envisioned only three possible alternatives for dealing with the situation. The first involved the creation of a permanent Indian territory from Kansas to California restricted to the Indian tribes alone. The second called for the creation of Indian reservations in the West, with the army serving as both the guardians and wardens of the tribes placed within them. His final option involved the extermination of the Indians. For his part, McCook discounted the first alternative based on the economic realities and resources present in the western territories. He likewise rejected the third option of annihilation as "so cruel and inhumane that the idea of it cannot be entertained."[17]

McCook's statement raises an important point with respect to army policy. Some historians have pointed to the words and statements of senior military leaders, including U. S. Grant, Sherman, and Sheridan, that advocated acts of extermination or annihilation against specific tribes or the Indians generally as an ethnic group. To be sure, these officers and others used the rhetoric of annihilation on numerous occasions in their personal and official correspondence. But it is equally clear that the physical extermination of the Indians as an ethnic group never became a military goal. For example, while still the commanding general of the army in 1868, Grant vowed to protect emigrant routes in the West "even if the extermination of every Indian tribe was necessary to secure such a result." A year later Grant, now president, in his first annual address to Congress, remarked, "A system which looks towards the extinction of a race is too horrible for a nation to adopt without entailing upon itself the wrath of all Christendom, and without engendering in the citizen a disregard for human life." He continued, "I see no substitute for such a system except in placing all the Indians on large reservations, as rapidly as it can be done, and giving them absolute protections there."[18] Grant's volte-face may be explained in part by the decision to introduce his Peace Policy and a renewed effort to promote the existing reservation system and to extend it to all tribes.

Perhaps no other army leader became more associated with the concept of extermination than Phil Sheridan, a man purported to have said "the only good Indians I ever saw were dead." As commander of the Division of the Missouri, Major General (later Commanding General of the Army) Sheridan became the senior military leader responsible for overseeing army operations against the tribes in the West. He certainly used exterminatory vocabulary in some orders and directives to his field commanders. For example, to Colonel

Ranald Mackenzie regarding a campaign against the Kickapoos on the Mexican border in 1873, Sheridan wrote: "I want you to be bold, enterprising, and at all times full of energy, when you begin, let it be a campaign of annihilation, obliteration, and complete destruction. . . . I think you understand what I want done, and the way you should employ your force." Mackenzie's operation resulted in the killing of nineteen Kickapoos and the capture of forty women and children and sixty-five horses with Texas brands.[19]

In the case of the Kickapoos, orders for "a campaign of annihilation" and "complete destruction" did not translate into killing the entire band. Yet the campaign did expose two important elements in the army's operations. On the one hand, most of the tribes, including the Comanches, the Apaches, and the Sioux, held a distinct advantage over the troops in the field due to their mobility and their intimate knowledge of the local terrain, which often left pursuing forces punching into air. This inability to corner their adversaries was a primary factor for the frontier army's use of surprise morning attacks against Indian villages, in which men, women, and children all became potential victims of indiscriminate fire. In contrast, they as well as the Mexican army were sometimes successful in inflicting significant casualties on male warriors when the tribes engaged in large-scale raiding expeditions, such as those conducted by the Comanches. Additionally, officers repeatedly described warriors, especially young adult males, as the primary culprits for promoting violence among the tribes, and they in turn became the focus of operations. Likewise, many tribes experienced major losses not only at the hands of the army but also during warfare against their Native enemies.[20] While the regular-army units could readily replace their casualties, "the loss of even a few warriors from a large band was a serious matter"; the tribes could not afford to become involved in a battle of attrition with the federal government.[21] On the other hand, a second critical element of these military operations involved the scope and scale of the intended killing. Such campaigns were tactical in nature and focused on specific tribes or even specific clans within tribes and were not reflective of a broader strategy of complete physical annihilation.

Sheridan's history in dealing with the Indians included pre–Civil War service in the Pacific Northwest, and in the immediate years after the war, he attempted to use "persuasive methods" and "to control them [the Indians] through certain men, who, I found had their confidence." The general, like many officers, however, came to believe that persuasion was ineffective and that punishment was necessary. In 1869 Sheridan ordered a subordinate commander to hang any Indians found guilty of murder and to imprison those found guilty of robbery: "The trouble heretofore with Indians has been caused by the absence of all punishment for crimes committed against the settlements. No people, especially those in a wild state, can be expected to behave themselves where there are no laws providing punishment for crime."[22]

In the fall of 1874, Lieutenant General Sheridan met with President Grant, the secretary of war, and the secretary of the interior to propose a new strategy for dealing with potential raids by Sioux operating from the Department of Dakota. Sheridan remarked that the region had been "remarkably quiet during the last year" despite the presence of the "majority of the hostile bands of Sioux." He worried, however, that this relative quiet might induce the Indians to raid in the more plentiful settlements of the Department of Missouri. To preempt such attacks, he proposed the creation of a military post in the Black Hills in order "to better control the Indians making these raids" and to "threaten" both their villages and livestock. An expedition into the Black Hills led by Lieutenant Colonel George Custer earlier that summer had discovered a fertile landscape with extensive timber reserves and reported gold and silver deposits, a finding that led Sheridan to somewhat disingenuously argue for the establishment of the post for the "better control of the Indians." Custer's expedition, along with earlier forays into the Black Hills, constituted a major provocation to the Sioux and played a key role in setting in motion the events that led to the Great Sioux War.[23]

The Red River War (1874–1875)

By the winter of 1874, it was not the Sioux, but rather the tribes of the southern plains that occupied Sheridan's attention. As a result of the government's failure to deliver promised rations combined with the decimation of the southern buffalo herds by white hunters, frustration, starvation, and desperation among the tribes boiled over into open conflict that spring. The uprising seemed to come at a particularly auspicious moment, based on the prophecies of a

Kwahada medicine man, Isatai, who declared that the performance of the Sun Dance held the power to achieve the annihilation of the whites and the rebirth of the buffalo herds.[24] Faced with seemingly inevitable decline in the face of federal power and fueled by Isatai's visions, groups of Comanches, Cheyennes, and Kiowas launched raids against white hunters decimating the buffalo as well as a series of attacks aimed at white settlers in Texas, sparking a large-scale military response.

These strikes led the government to revoke the prohibition of army activities on the reservations. The initial plan for the campaign once again reflected the army's penchant for traditional operations. Sheridan's strategy focused on five converging columns aimed against an estimated 4,800 Indians camped along the headwaters of the Washita River. In his instructions he ordered, "All captured Indians must be treated as prisoners of war and all captured stock regarded as government property." He continued, "All surrenders [sic] must be total and absolute and arms of every description delivered also."[25]

The resulting Red River War demonstrated the ability of the army to pursue the Indians even if the troops proved largely unsuccessful in bringing them to battle. The engagement at Palo Duro Canyon on September 28, 1874, provides one example of the course of the campaign. In this action U.S. forces surprised a large group of Kwahadas, Kiowas, and Cheyennes encamped on the floor of the canyon. The ensuing combat led to the deaths of three Indians, but the major significance involved the soldiers' destruction of over two hundred tipis and hundreds of blankets and robes, the capture of 1,400 horses, and the burning of vast stores of food. Palo Duro Canyon symbolized the "collapse" of the Comanche empire due more to economic factors than to the superiority of the U.S. military.[26] In fact, the army's pursuit of the tribes during the subsequent winter had its intended effect by weakening the Comanches and their allies to the point of surrender, a case in which exhaustion, not annihilation, proved the decisive factor.

Reflecting on the campaign, historian Robert Utley offered this summary: "There were few clashes and little bloodshed, but gradually the exhaustion of the chase, the discomforts of weather and hunger, and, above all, the constant gnawing fear of soldiers storming into their camps at dawn wore them down." By the spring of 1875, all of the tribes had returned to their reservations. A military commission, consisting of five officers, was established to try all Indians suspected of murder, stealing animals, or having killed army personnel. Upon their arrival at Fort Sill, the captured warriors were disarmed, dismounted, and imprisoned in a windowless and roofless icehouse while their women and children were sent to separate camps.[27] Eventually, seventy-four of those designated as "ringleaders" were sent by rail to an old Spanish fortress on the coast of Florida. The end of this conflict signaled the end of fighting on the southern plains and an end to Comanche, Kiowa, Cheyenne, and Arapaho raids into Kansas and Texas.

The Red River War proved an important watershed in army operational strategy. First, the campaign, like Sheridan's actions in 1868 on the Great Plains, once again proved an effective means to harass and weaken Indian resistance at a time of year when food was scarce and adequate lodging most critical.[28] Second, it not only signaled the demise of the Peace Policy but also demonstrated the limits of army objectives. The designation of captured Indians as prisoners of war and the subsequent imprisonment of so-called ringleaders provided a caveat to existing exterminatory rhetoric. The army's response represented a continuation of the existing policy of punishment and coercion rather than annihilation, with the overriding objective involving the confinement of the tribes to reservations. The absence of a premeditated strategy of annihilation does not, however, imply that the army and other military, paramilitary, and vigilante groups were not guilty of acts of atrocity and reprisal against specific tribes.

A Strategy of Indirect Annihilation?

The use of winter campaigning during the Red River War points to a critical issue in the tribal way of life. Although some tribes pursued agrarian activities, the Plains Indians for their part operated in a hunter-gatherer society and depended primarily on the buffalo herds for their existence. The spring and summer hunts were expected to supply not only dried meat for the coming winter but also hides to be used in the construction of lodgings, the making of outer garments, and in trading. The encroachment of increasing numbers of white settlers and their livestock into the West not only threatened the buffalo herds but also the supply of game in general, becoming a key point of conflict between 1830 and 1860. One member of the Southern Cheyennes complained to an army officer in 1845, "The whites have been amongst us, and destroyed our buffalo, antelope, and deer, and have cut down our timber." The loss of game had a significant effect on the tribes, particularly those confined to the reservations and especially during the winter, when hunger became a perennial fact of Indian life. In fact, the Comanche phrase for the period between February and March literally translates as the time "when babies cry for food."[29]

In 1855, one Indian agent reported that the disappearance of the buffalo had forced the southern Plains Indians to slaughter their own horses and mules for meat. The competition for buffalo had two major implications for the Plains Indians and other tribes who relied on this resource. First, the loss of the herds provided a justification for raids on white settlers and emigrant trains to steal horses and cattle. These attacks became a key element of antagonism throughout the period of westward expansion, and minor raids and acts of reprisal often contained the seeds for larger conflicts. Second, the 1870s witnessed an increased commercial demand for buffalo hides that resulted in a dramatic influx of white hunters seeking to make their fortunes. Like the competition for beaver pelts in the previous century, European and American fashion trends created a market that was exploited by whites and Indians alike. This issue became more acute as the buffalo herds of the Great Plains began to decline as early as the 1840s due to the effects of "drought, habitat destruction, competition from exotic species, and introduced diseases." Furthermore, the later organized and systematic slaughter of the buffalo was not solely a function of white hunters but also partially attributable to the "prodigious hunting" efforts of the Indians as well as the continuing influence of disease. Whatever the reasons, the buffalo herds essentially disappeared from the southern plains by 1875 and vanished from the northern plains less than a decade later.[30]

The loss of the bison had enormous implications for the Plains Indians in particular, not only "cut[ting] the heart from the Plains Indian economy" but also profoundly affecting the "cosmology" of Native life. The destruction of the bison also had critical consequences on the ability of the tribes to fight and organize for warfare, a fact recognized by senior army officers. For example, Sheridan addressed the Texas legislature in 1875 to state his opposition to a

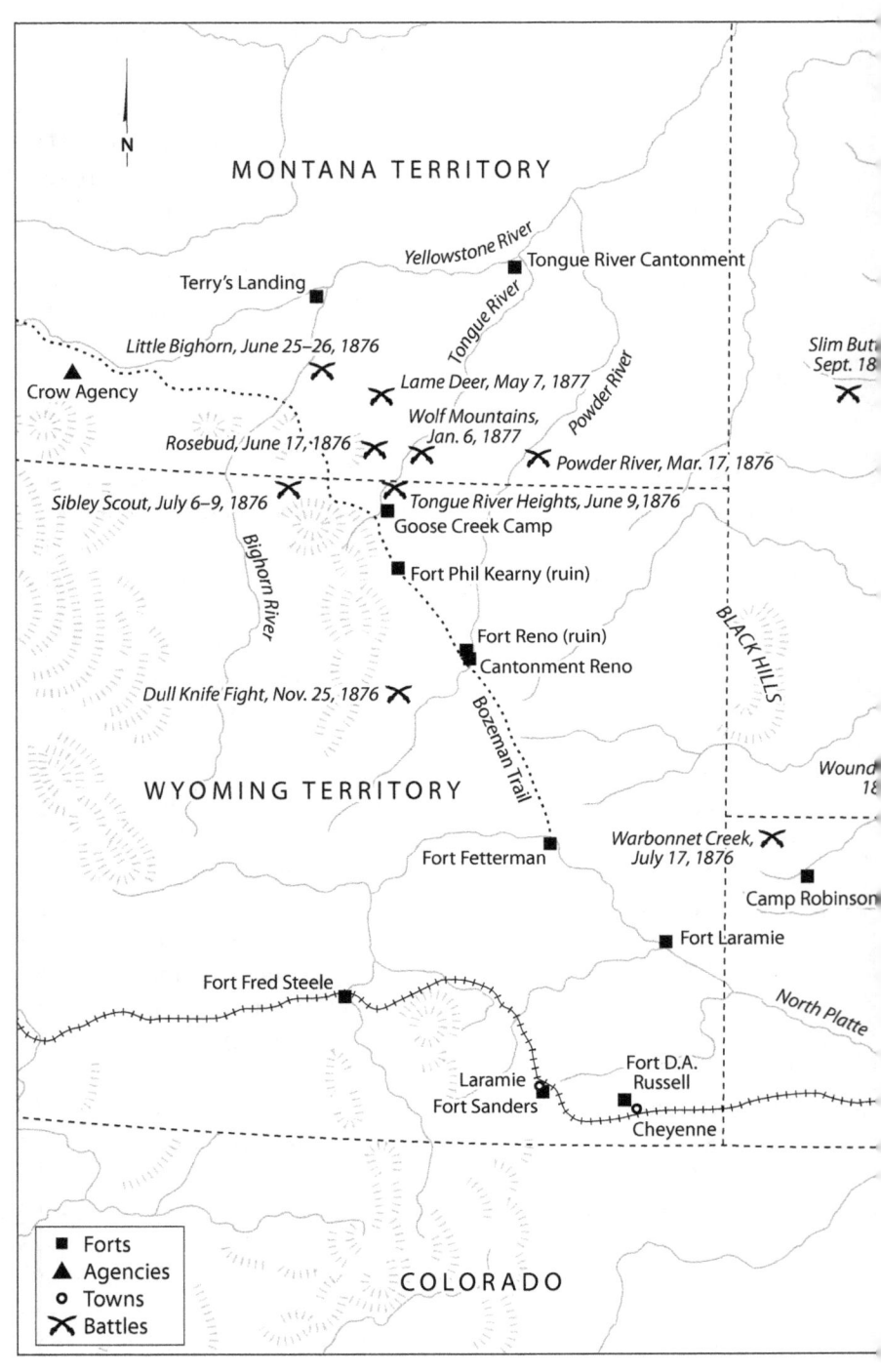

The Great Plains. Map by Bill Nelson. Copyright © 2016 by the University of Oklahoma Press.

bill designed to protect the vanishing buffalo herds. He contended: "These men [the buffalo hunters] have done in the last two years, and will do more in the next years, to settle the vexed Indian question, than the entire regular army has done in the last thirty years . . . , [by] destroying the Indian's commissary; and it is a well-known fact that an army losing its base of supplies is placed at a great disadvantage." Six years later the general repeated this argument: "The destruction of this [northern buffalo] herd would do more to keep the Indians quiet than anything else that could happen."[31]

Sheridan's comments reflected a belief in the military utility of separating an opposing army from its source of provisions, a strategy pursued not only by Union commanders, including Sheridan and George Crook, during the Civil War but also by military leaders throughout the course of human conflict. This strategy that had been pursued during the Sioux Expedition of 1855 had major implications not only for the ability of warriors to fight but also on the entire tight-knit and reciprocally dependent social structure of the tribes themselves.[32] During the reservation period, this strategy was aimed primarily at impoverishment rather than annihilation and reflected the belief that the absence of available sustenance on the plains would tie the Indians to the reservations, prevent their ability to conduct mobile operations, and force them to adopt farming as the only available alternative. One historian has even argued that "the frontier army's well-calculated policy of destroying the buffalo in order to conquer the Plains Indians proved more effective than any other weapon in its arsenal."[33] Although the army may have supported a "scorched earth" campaign against the buffalo, it was commercial and economic interests that drove the demise of the herds, with the unintended if not unwelcome consequences for the Indians as expressed by Sheridan. In any event, at the time when Sheridan was stating his position in 1875, the southern herd had already been decimated, while at the time of his later remark, war had vanquished the tribes of the northern plains and the Great Sioux War was an object of both myth and historical memory.

The Great Sioux War (1876–1877)

The rout and almost complete annihilation of the Seventh Cavalry under Lieutenant Colonel Custer has become an iconic symbol of the

American West and of the contest between whites and Indians for control of the Great Plains. The victory of the Sioux, under the leadership of Sitting Bull, at the Battle of Little Bighorn may have signaled a momentary victory for the Indians, but it came at time when the struggle for the plains was rapidly being decided in favor of the federal government and the constant stream of settlers and fortune seekers who pushed into Wyoming and the Dakotas. At the centennial of U.S. independence, one historian has argued, for most Americans the Indians "were already a thing of nostalgia, mere grist for tabloids and dime novels." In a similar vein Commissioner of Indians Affairs Edward Smith reprinted in his annual report for 1875 a citation from his previous year's report predicting that "except under extraordinary provocation, or in circumstances not at all to be apprehended, it is not probable that as many as five hundred Indian warriors ever again will be mustered at one point for a fight; . . . such an event as a general Indian war can never again occur in the United States."[34]

One clear indication of the decreased level of attention paid to Indian relations in the West is found in the pages of the annual report of Secretary of War William W. Belknap to Congress for 1875. Dated November 22 and consisting of twenty-six typed pages, Belknap's first mention of Indian relations did not occur until page seventeen. Although noting "recent incursions of the reservation Sioux into Northern Nebraska, mostly to steal cattle and horses," he highlighted the successful conclusion of the preceding spring's campaign against the Kiowas, Comanches, and Cheyennes and the Indians' "disarmament and subjection to authority." Returning to a discussion of the Sioux, Belknap admitted that despite the "utmost vigilance," army efforts to prevent unauthorized persons from entering the area had met with "only partial success," but he promised to "use every exertion to prevent [any] collision between white intruders upon the reservation and the Indians occupying it."[35] Despite the recognition of possible conflict in the Black Hills, the growth of federal power appeared sufficient to keep the peace.

The potential for trouble with the Sioux already had been raised in November 1874 by Sheridan in a warning to the headquarters of the army. In this report the general forcefully opposed the Indian Bureau's distribution of arms to the tribes, called for sending more troops into the area, and demanded the creation of a new military post in the Black Hills. These measures, he argued, would "take the hostile backbone out of these unruly savages." Once again Sheridan demonstrated his belief that control of the Indians required a strong hand to threaten and, when necessary, to punish those accused of acts of violence outside of the reservation. Interestingly, he added a point of criticism aimed at the Indian Bureau's policy with respect to the Sioux by questioning the efforts at agrarian reform. Sheridan noted: "The ground cannot be cultivated at the Red Cloud Agency for want of sufficient moisture, which cannot be obtained by irrigation, or the natural conditions of rains. Under this condition, how can we expect any cultivation of the soil, which is the first step in the progress of their civilization after the natural, inborn warlike spirit is taken out of them?"[36] This last comment pointed to a fundamental flaw in the Indian Bureau's plan for "civilizing" the Sioux, a flaw that would become increasingly apparent after the loss of the tribes' traditional hunting grounds.

The discussion of the Sioux and the issue of the Black Hills became a focus of the Grant administration's Indian policy in November 1875. In a series of meetings with civilian and military leaders, including Belknap, the secretary of the interior, Commissioner of Indian Affairs Edward Smith, and Generals Sheridan and Crook, President Grant outlined a change in his Peace Policy that was designed to force the Lakota Sioux and the Northern Cheyennes onto the reservation and into renewed negotiations. The commissioner estimated that some 3,000 "hostile" or "outlaw" Sioux were present in the Dakota Territory in November 1875 and remarked, "It will probably be found necessary to compel the northern non-treaty Sioux, under the leadership of Sitting Bull, . . . to cease marauding and settle down, as the other Sioux have done, at some designated point." The new "get tough" program coordinated between the Department of the Interior and the War Department represented a rare convergence of policy aims. This was due in part to the economic realities associated with public demands to exploit the resources of the Black Hills and the government's desire to force the Sioux out of the unceded territory and onto the reservations, despite treaty requirements "to preserve the integrity of Indian lands."[37]

By February, it was apparent that a large number of nontreaty Sioux had chosen to ignore the summons to the reservation. As a result, Sheridan ordered General Crook, an officer who gained fame for his successful operations against the Apaches in the Southwest, to pursue the Sioux to their winter quarters and force them to submit. Departing from Fort Fetterman on March 1, 1876, with a force of almost 900 men, mostly cavalry, Crook and his command at first found the subzero temperatures and blizzards to be a greater foe than the Indians. In fact, a supporting column under Brigadier General Alfred Terry remained at Fort Abraham Lincoln due to the extreme cold and heavy snow, leaving Crook's force to fight alone. After more than two weeks, Crook's infantry, commanded by Colonel Joseph Reynolds, surprised a group of some 450 Cheyennes, including 150 warriors at their village on the Powder River. The ensuing battle resulted in minimal casualties on both sides, but its major effect was achieved with the destruction of the village, despite the escape of its inhabitants and the soldiers' failure to secure the Indians' pony herd. A Cheyenne woman, Kate Bighead, remembered, "Not many of our people were killed, but our tepees and everything in them were burned." One participant in the fight, Wooden Leg, recalled that upon his return to the camp after the troops had left, he found only one lodge still standing. In this sole remaining tepee was an old blind woman "entirely unharmed," an act that he and his fellow warriors concluded "showed the soldiers had good hearts." In truth, the policy of not killing women and children was based less on "good hearts" and more on the issue of military utility since they could be used as hostages to gain the submission of the warriors. Crook made this point explicit in his orders: "We don't want to kill the Indians. . . . We want to find the village and make the Indians give up their ponies & guns, so that in the future they will have to behave themselves." If submission had been the objective, the general and his force had failed in their winter campaign, the Sioux and Cheyennes easily eluding the mounted regulars. Secretary Belknap subsequently described the operation as "not conclusive or satisfactory."[38]

The Battle of Rosebud Creek

The failure of the winter expedition led Sheridan to draw upon his earlier plan of converging columns that had proved successful in the campaign against the southern Plains Indians the previous year. He outlined the strategy in a telegram to Sherman in which he discussed the objective of disarming and dismounting the tribes, a process that thereafter "would reduce itself to a simple question of feeding them till they learn to raise food for themselves." To achieve this goal, a force of three columns under the command of General

Crook from Fort Fetterman near present-day Douglas, Wyoming; General Terry from Fort Abraham Lincoln near Bismarck, North Dakota; and Colonel John Gibbon from Fort Ellis near Bozeman, Montana; left their bases in late May to converge on the Sioux and Cheyennes located on Rosebud Creek in southeastern Montana.[39]

As Crook's column of 1,000 men, the majority cavalry with some infantry, advanced northward, his aide-de-camp, Lieutenant John G. Bourke, noted his hope that "perhaps the year 1876 would witness the revenge of the horrible scenes of 1866 and '67 and the humiliations of the savages who had participated in the slaughter of our feeble garrisons [namely, Fort Reno and Fort Kearny]."[40] Using Crow Indians as scouts, the column pushed forward until it was ambushed by Sioux and Cheyennes on June 9. Crook gave chase, but the Indians enjoyed the advantage of the high ground and an intimate knowledge of the terrain, leading the regulars in a futile and exhausting pursuit across a series of ridgelines and ravines. Despite not having made contact with either Terry or Gibbon, Crook halted his advance in order to augment his force with an additional two hundred Crow and eighty-six Shoshone warriors. A longtime advocate of the use of Indian scouts, the general remarked, "scouting is the business of their lives," and his reliance on them probably saved his command during the 1876 campaign.[41]

As Crook advanced to meet Crazy Horse and his warriors, past Indian tactics of launching attacks in small groups and melting away into the countryside would be replaced by a large-scale assault of Sioux and Cheyennes as "every hill appeared to be covered with their swarming legions, and up from every ravine, and out of every little vale, more seemed to be coming."[42] In one sense this was the set-piece battle dreamed of by army officers for decades; however, the failure of Sheridan's strategy of convergence left Crook's soldiers and his Indian allies facing a superior enemy force as the battle commenced on June 17. Using the terrain to their advantage, the Indians surprised the column and conducted a series of assaults that at times threatened to cut off units from the larger command. In fact, if not for the actions of the Crow and Shoshone auxiliaries in the initial minutes of combat, Crook's men might have suffered a more devastating fate. One participant, Iron Hawk, described the battle as "all mixed up . . . [with] hard fighting." He also noted, "It was not a finished battle because the night stopped it, but the Wasichus [whites] got whipped anyway, and did not attack our village."[43]

After six hours of fighting, Crazy Horse withdrew his forces, leaving thirteen of his warriors on the field, with nine soldiers killed and twenty-one wounded. Crook's control of the battlefield, however, proved both brief and a pyrrhic victory, the engagement effectively putting his force "out of the campaign."[44] In fact, the battle constituted an operational defeat for Crook, and he withdrew his column to his basecamp at Goose Creek to reorganize and await reinforcements. This unplanned delay would have profound consequences for the Seventh Cavalry to the north.

The Battle of Little Bighorn

The most dramatic act of the Great Sioux War occurred a week later as cavalry forces under George Armstrong Custer moved forward to the Rosebud and on to Little Bighorn in anticipation of an assault on the Sioux-Cheyenne encampment. The plan of attack devised by Terry called for Custer's cavalry to act as the hammer to drive the Indian forces onto the anvil of Gibbon's forces. Lacking knowledge of Crook's engagement of the previous week and expecting a maximum of 800 warriors, Custer was expectant and confident as he moved his 600 men and thirty-five Indian scouts forward on June 22 in search of the encampment. The main concern expressed in the formulation of the plan was "to preclude the possibility of the escape of the Indians to the south or southeast."[45] Once again the opportunity for a set-piece battle presented itself, but it was the decimation of Custer's force and not the destruction of the Sioux camp that resulted. Custer's scouts located the encampment on June 25 and prepared for an attack on the following day in anticipation of linking up with Gibbon's force.

The attack opened with a foray by a battalion of the Seventh Cavalry under Major Marcus Reno into the Indian encampment at Little Bighorn on the twenty-fifth. After setting fire to several lodges, Reno and his soldiers were forced back to a defensive position on a nearby bluff. Reports that Sioux scouts had discovered his presence led to Custer's fateful decision to commence the attack that day, prior to Gibbon's arrival. With Reno's force in retreat and unable to provide support, Custer with the rest of the Seventh Cavalry began an assault on the encampment. Brave Wolf, a Cheyenne participant in the battle, remembered how the number of warriors overwhelmed the soldiers. Despite this fact, he remarked: "It was hard fighting, very hard all the time. I have been in many hard fights, but I never saw such brave men." Red Horse, a Sioux chief, recalled that after driving Reno's force from the village, "the Sioux charged the different soldiers [Custer's force] below and drove them in confusion; these soldiers became foolish, many throwing away their guns and raising their hands, saying, 'Sioux, pity us, take us prisoners.'" Red Horse continued, "The Sioux did not take a single soldier prisoner, but killed all of them; none were left alive for even a few minutes."[46]

While Indian accounts differ in their descriptions of the bravery exhibited by the Seventh Cavalry during the battle, the fight itself was conducted with no quarter and included the widespread mutilation of dead soldiers.[47] The act of scalping, mutilation, and trophy taking played a ritualistic function among many tribes and their white adversaries. In fact, Cameron Strang contends that such practices "were effective attacks because all combatants in the war attached cosmological, social, and personal significances [sic] to human remains." Additionally, not taking prisoners and killing all armed and unarmed male combatants was not unique to the Sioux and Cheyennes but reflected an accepted and recognized practice that also "typically" extended to the killing of all captured adult males by Comanche raiding parties. Much like the case of Sparta, death in combat was preferable to the dishonor of defeat or capture, a standard that prized courage in battle and extended this expectation to one's foe.[48] These practices also reflected existing precedent among the Sioux from earlier engagements, such as the Fetterman Fight in 1866.

Custer's defeat was "one of the most complete disasters in American military annals," with the loss of twelve officers, five civilians, three Indian scouts, and 245 enlisted men. In contrast, Red Horse counted 136 Sioux killed and another 160 wounded. These losses highlight the intensity of the battle and the high cost paid by both sides. In fact, She Walks with Her Shawl, a Sioux woman, remarked: "The Indians did not stage a victory dance that night. They were mourning for their own dead." The casualties suffered by Custer's command were the most since the Civil War and would be the greatest one-day loss sustained by the U.S. Army in the West. The psychological and political effect of the defeat established the "boy general" as a martyr and generated a sense of anger, with public calls for revenge against Sitting Bull, Crazy Horse, and their warriors. A humbled and humiliated high command immediately ordered reinforcements into the area, but the Indians, having won a great victory, chose their traditional tactic of breaking into smaller groups and melting away in the face of Crook's restored force and Terry's plodding column, complete with artillery, ambulances, and supply wagons.[49]

For most of the country, the news of Custer's defeat appeared immediately in the wake of the centennial celebration of U.S. independence; "following closely on the heels of a celebration of the nation's progress, the defeat and killing of a national hero by the Sioux and Cheyenne was a shock to the nation." From the perspective of the press, Little Bighorn was "one of the great news stories of the nineteenth century."[50] Despite the general shock and the anger resulting from the defeat, the *New York Times* counseled caution and even displayed some sympathy for the plight of the Sioux. An editorial on July 7 remarked, "Year after year, the wild Indians have been hemmed in; they fight with no less desperation for that; and, now that we have been defeated in a considerable engagement, defensive tactics must precede the operations necessary for the chastisement of so dangerous and determined a foe." In a similar vein the *Omaha Daily Herald* laid the blame for the conflict on the "illegal occupation of the Black Hills" by white miners but nonetheless called for "a war with the northern Sioux [that] must be prosecuted until they shall be driven into subjection." Another Omaha newspaper, the *Bee*, also argued for a campaign to chastise the tribes: "The massacre of Custer's command teaches us that we have underestimated the strength and fighting qualities of the Indians. . . . To insure the chastisement of these savages the government should organize and put in the field a corps of at least ten thousand volunteers recruited among hardy frontiersmen . . [and] every Indian should be promptly disarmed and dismounted." The paper's suggestion that a group of volunteer frontiersmen would have more success in dealing with the tribes not only reflected a lack of faith in the army but also the widespread belief in the greater efficacy of the "hardline" methods of westerners in dealing with the tribes.[51]

Despite the press response and popular outrage, the Bureau of Indian Affairs still attempted to moderate the military response. In fact, as Jeffrey Ostler has argued, "the Great Sioux War consisted of politics more than battles." Even in the wake of disaster at Little Bighorn, "army officials attempted to lure the Indians into agencies with promises that they would not be punished for wiping out

Custer's men the previous summer."[52] One clear example of the perhaps unexpected restraint shown by the regular army occurred less than a month after Little Bighorn, when the anger and hysteria over Custer's defeat was most extreme.

On July 14, a cavalry force under Colonel Wesley Merritt received word that some 1,000 Cheyennes were planning to leave the Red Cloud Agency in order to join forces with Sitting Bull and Crazy Horse. Merritt's orders were to prevent the Indians from leaving the agency or failing that "to capture or drive them back." Three days later the Fifth Cavalry intercepted a large group of Cheyennes at Warbonnet Creek in Nebraska Territory, and Merritt's force proved successful in turning them back to the agency with "minimal opposition." The encounter witnessed a "duel" between "Buffalo Bill" Cody and Yellow Hand (or Yellow Hair), after which Cody took the "first scalp for Custer," but it concluded with a "bloodless chase" of the remaining Indians back toward the Red Cloud Agency. One Cheyenne participant disputed the story of single combat between Cody and Yellow Hair, but he did note, "The soldiers did not fire upon us, but they kept behind us as we were going back."[53] At a time when passions ran hot and in the wake of a humiliating defeat, the army still proved able to moderate their behavior. Although Sheridan was critical of the carrot-and-stick approach and complained that no Indians had ever left their ancestral homelands without "a fierce strife which disabled and broke them down," he still bowed, even if grudgingly, to the dictates of civilian control.[54]

As the new secretary of war, James D. Cameron, presented his annual report to the president and Congress on November 20, 1876, almost five months after Custer's "Last Stand," he noted the impending conclusion of the campaign against the Sioux as Terry's and Crook's units closed in on the remnants of Sitting Bull's and Crazy Horse's camps. Cameron also mentioned the ongoing success in the "vigorous effort . . . to disarm and dismount the agency Indians." He continued: "[I]f the wild Indians can be compelled by lack of ammunition to submit, and can be concentrated on a few reservations and deprived of their instruments of mischief, it looks indeed as if the 'Indian problem' was approaching a solution, and, as General Sheridan says, 'the Sioux war and all other Indian wars in this country of any magnitude, will be over forever.'"[55]

As the ring of troops slowly closed in on Crazy Horse in the winter of 1876–77 and eventually drove Sitting Bull and his camp northward into Canada, the military efforts to "punish" the Indians of the northern plains focused on disarming and dismounting them after forcing them onto the agencies of the Great Sioux Reservation. The troops conducted a "policy of containment and pursuit" toward the Sioux and Cheyennes, with the objective of shepherding the Indians back to the agencies. By the end of August 1876, Colonel Nelson Miles, an experienced Indian fighter, complained in a letter to his wife about the inability of Crook's and Terry's massive force to intercept and engage the "fugitive" Natives: "After six days march on the trail, the two commands came in here for rest and supplies without seeing an Indian or exchanging a shot, and this is what is called Indian campaigning."[56]

The pursuit during the summer of 1876 proved slow and frustrating for the troops and their commanders alike as the columns followed old trails and attacked into air. One senior officer lamented, "Our stern chase had thus proved a long and fruitless one, and we had no longer even a shifting objective point to move against." Crook's and Terry's forces diverged in late August, which resulted in the lightly provisioned column under the former abandoning its supply train and heading east into Dakota Territory. On September 9, Crook's advance guard fell on a Sioux village at Slim Buttes, capturing a store of much needed supplies, including 5,000 pounds of dried meat and fruit, as well as one hundred ponies. One participant in the two-day battle, Lieutenant Walter Schuyler, described the fight as not "very great" but one that "hurt the Indian's considerably." Crook's forces successfully maintained control of the village in the face of efforts to retake the camp, and especially the ponies, at a cost of three men killed and numerous wounded, while "a large number of [Indian] women and children" died as a result of "undisciplined shooting" by the soldiers. Red Horse remembered the loss of seven Sioux, including four women and an infant, but he noted the most significant consequence of the attack as the loss of "all our lodges, all our buffalo robes, and we had a great many. They took all we had."[57]

As the troops plundered the village for food and clothing, they were reminded of the reason for their operation with the discovery of saddles, equipment, and clothing belonging to the Seventh Cavalry. When Crook's campaign ended in October, he could not point to any major engagements or great successes in bringing his adversary to battle. Schuyler described, however, the primary effect achieved by the operation: "the Sioux, though having lost but one village, have been so kept on the move that they have been unable to lay up the stores of meat, etc., which will be indispensable to them this winter."[58]

The ability of the army to continue operations during the winter of 1876–77 proved to be the key factor in the subjugation of the renegade Sioux and Cheyennes. In late October Crook reached the Red Cloud Agency with his troops and disarmed and dismounted the Sioux bands under Red Leaf and Red Cloud. The general's decision to disarm and dismount only some of the Indian bands drew Sheridan's ire since his instructions pertained to all tribes at the agency. For his part, Sheridan recognized both the physical and psychological significance of dismounting the Sioux in his remark that "a Sioux on foot is a Sioux warrior no longer." Even after his exhausting five-month campaign, Crook argued for keeping up the pressure against Crazy Horse: "The Indians cannot stand a continuous campaign. . . . The best time to strike the Indians is in winter . . . , and then is the time to throw a large force on each band, and crush them all in detail."[59]

The Dull Knife Fight

The subsequent Powder River Expedition went into the field in early November 1876 with the aim of catching the Indian bands in their winter quarters. On November 25, a force under the command of Colonel Mackenzie caught up with a group of Northern Cheyennes under Morning Star (known to the Sioux as Dull Knife) at the Red Fork of the Powder River in Wyoming Territory. Seeking to surprise the village at daybreak, Mackenzie issued orders for his men to surround the camp but not to shoot unless the Cheyennes fired. At dawn the troops, supported by Indian auxiliaries, rushed into the site, initiating a wild firefight as the Cheyenne warriors attempted to gain precious minutes to allow their women and children to flee for the safety of the trees on a nearby ridgeline. After successfully evacuating the village, the warriors maintained harassing fire on the troops in the camp below them while waiting for the cover of darkness to make good their escape. Unfortunately for the Cheyennes, the surprise assault had forced them to run with only the clothes on their back. Mackenzie's men, now in control of the village, plundered the tipis, resulting in at least one case of summary execution as soldiers shot an old Indian woman in order to steal her buffalo robe.[60]

Possessing the village and the Cheyenne ponies but failing to reach agreement with the Indian leaders on surrender terms, Mackenzie ordered the burning of all the tipis along with their contents. Among the plunder taken before the conflagration, the troops again discovered military items taken from Custer's men at Little Bighorn as well as "a buckskin bag containing the right hands of twelve Shoshone babies, and a necklace of human fingers." As the village went up in flames, Mackenzie counted his losses, numbering seven killed and twenty-six wounded compared to an estimated twenty-five Indians dead, many of whom lay on the frozen ground without their scalps. The colonel decided to end his pursuit. For the Cheyennes on the overlooking ridgeline, however, the worst was yet to come as the bitter cold, estimated at thirty degrees below zero, began to take a steady toll on the young and old. Without protection against the elements, eleven infants froze to death that night at their mothers' breasts. Iron Teeth, a Cheyenne mother of five children at the time, recalled the band's ordeal in the wake of the attack: "We wallowed through the mountain snows for several days. We had no lodges, only a few blankets, and there was only a little dry meat food among us. Men died of wounds, women and children froze to death." By forgoing pursuit, Mackenzie had forfeited the opportunity for a decisive victory. Still, the Dull Knife engagement proved a "major disaster" for the Northern Cheyennes and significantly contributed to their eventual surrender.[61]

The Close of the Indian Wars on the Great Plains

As Mackenzie and his men pursued the Northern Cheyennes, the Fifth Infantry, commanded by Colonel Miles, had moved out of its forward operating base at the Tongue River in mid-October in pursuit of Sitting Bull. With winter approaching, Sitting Bull and his Sioux continued to harass army supply columns operating in the Black Hills. But the Indian chief faced a dwindling food supply and, even more worrying, a pressing need for powder and ammunition.[62] In contrast, the colonel had conducted a careful survey of the area using civilian and Indian scouts and had stockpiled supplies in anticipation of a "systematic campaign," a strategy he had pursued with success against the tribes of the southern plains in 1875. Writing later, Miles explained his plan: "My opinion was that the only way to make the country tenable for us was to render it untenable for the Indians. . . . [W]e, with all our better appliances could be so equipped as to not only exist in tents, but also to move under all circumstances."[63]

Miles's plan ironically mirrored the tactic of the Plains Indians in hunting antelope—chasing the quarry until it was exhausted and could no longer run. The Fifth Infantry moved out of their bivouac on October 19 with a good plan, but the question remained as to whether they would be fast enough to catch their intended quarry. A day later Miles sat under a flag of truce with Sitting Bull and other Sioux chiefs, but two days of negotiations failed to bring an agreement for the surrender of the Indians, and both sides prepared for battle, with Custer's defeat fresh in the minds of the troops. The resulting daylong Battle of Cedar Creek on October 21 proved inconclusive, resulting in only two wounded soldiers and an estimated five Sioux casualties, though the fighting provided critical time for Sitting Bull's camp to flee from the advancing army. As Miles gave chase, his men again found discarded remnants from the Seventh Cavalry in the wake of the retreating Sioux.[64]

From this point on, Miles intensified his pursuit of Sitting Bull's band and other nonagency Sioux in an effort to keep them on the move throughout the winter. At his headquarters in Chicago, Sheridan offered his support to this strategy and informed Sherman that despite "some disasters, much labor, and considerable expense . . . , there is a fair prospect of the complete settlement by the defeat and surrender of all the hostile Indians, with their arms, ponies, men, women, and children, before the winter is over." Sherman telegraphed Sheridan to praise Miles's campaign, adding, "I hope he [Miles] will crown his success by capturing or killing Sitting Bull and his remnant of outlaws." His wish for capturing Sitting Bull came close to being realized when a unit of the Fifth Infantry under the command of Lieutenant Frank Baldwin discovered and surprised the Sioux chief's encampment at Ash Creek on December 23. Baldwin's assault initiated a skirmish, during which the camp's women and children made their escape. Although failing to capture Sitting Bull or any of his band, the lieutenant and his men destroyed the camp's 122 lodges and their contents, repeating the scorched-earth policy that was slowly exhausting the Indians' ability to subsist during the brutal northern winter.[65]

The continual pressure exerted by the army's winter campaign eventually convinced the majority of nonagency Sioux to abandon their fight and come onto the reservations by the spring of 1877. Throughout February and March, a constant stream of large and small groups of Sioux and Cheyennes filtered into the agencies to surrender. Finally, on May 6, hungry and running out of ammunition, Crazy Horse reluctantly led his band of 889 men, women, and children and their 2,000 ponies into the Red Cloud Agency and threw down his weapons. Defeated but unbowed, the Sioux chieftain refused an invitation to meet the "Great Father," President Rutherford B. Hayes, in Washington, D.C. After four months at the agency, Crazy Horse fled, only to be captured and later killed under still-disputed circumstances at the Fort Robinson stockade. The surrender of Crazy Horse and Sitting Bull's flight into Canada in May effectively ended the Great Sioux War as well as the Indian Wars on the Great Plains. By July, Sheridan's attention was no longer directed to the West but rather to Chicago, where labor riots led to the deployment of units from the Twenty-Second Infantry to assist civil authorities in quelling the violence.[66]

The Great Sioux War paradoxically witnessed the apotheosis and the nadir of the military power of the Plains Indians. Little Bighorn was an overwhelming tactical victory and achieved short-term operational success, but it failed to translate into long-term strategic success for the Natives. By the mid-1870s, the power of the federal government and the relative strength of the army in terms of manpower, logistics, and technology already had tilted the tide of the contest in favor of white ascendancy on the plains, even if it failed to result in a "completely vanquished foe."[67]

A subsequent campaign between June and October 1877 against the Nez Perce Indians of Idaho Territory, the "last Indian War," demonstrated the final eclipse of the northern tribes as credible threats to white settlement or the process of westward expansion. Although Miles (now a brigadier general) lauded the skill of the Nez Perce warrior as "unequalled in the history of Indian warfare," their skill alone could not compensate for the advantages in firepower, mobility, and communication enjoyed by their army adversaries. In this respect Chief Joseph's famous utterance "From where the sun now stands I will fight no more" provided a fitting epitaph to operations on the northern plains, even as the Apache in the Desert Southwest began their own final stand in the 1880s (see chapter 5).[68]

If the U.S. Army had achieved its goal of the "annihilation of the Indian nations' military power" by 1890, the Wehrmacht embarked upon a campaign in Poland in 1939 and in the Soviet Union in 1941 with clear objectives for the annihilation of military adversary and civilian "enemies" alike.[69]

Wehrmacht Policy in the East

As Nazi Germany's foreign minister, Konstantin von Neurath, negotiated a nonaggression pact with Josef Stalin and his foreign minister, Vyacheslav Molotov, at the end of August 1939, Hitler and his generals were in the final stages of preparing to unleash a military force against Poland created for the express purpose of conquest and exploitation. If France and the western powers had been the führer's initial targets, Hitler then, based on military and political considerations, pragmatically shifted the focus of conquest to Germany's eastern border. In fact, for many Wehrmacht officers and senior leaders, the campaign against Poland was not a war of conquest, but a *Reconquista* aimed at the defeat of an "eternal enemy" and the reacquisition of lands unjustly lost in the "shameful peace of Versailles." If the acquisition of lebensraum in eastern Europe formed a keystone of Hitler's worldview, then the recovery of German lands in Poland was a "critical priority of all German military leaders after 1919. . . . [T]he major line of thinking and planning was directed toward that end."[70]

From an operational perspective, the centerpiece of the campaign into Poland involved the use of highly mobile panzer (armored) divisions designed to encircle enemy forces in the quest for the decisive battle of annihilation, the holy grail of German operational warfare since the Wars of German Unification. During initial planning for the invasion in April 1939, army strategists emphasized the need for surprise coupled with "sudden, heavy blows" in order to quickly destroy Poland's military strength. In fact, the Army High Command's key planning consideration involved the need to defeat Polish forces as quickly as possible in order to shift German forces back to the western border with France.[71]

The Invasion of Poland: A First Step to Genocide

Facing an opponent suffering technological and geographical disadvantages, five German armies poured across the border on September 1, 1939, in a series of concentric drives designed to trap Polish forces and destroy them in detail. By the third day of the offensive, the Wehrmacht already had captured 15,000 Polish prisoners of war (POWs), heralding the birth of blitzkrieg, or lightning war. By the nineteenth, the combined-arms onslaught, using tanks, motorized vehicles, artillery, infantry, and air power, had overwhelmed Polish resistance with the exception of Warsaw. Forces defending the capital surrendered eight days later after enduring a hellish artillery and aerial bombardment that claimed the lives of thousands, if not tens of thousands, of civilians. The mass civilian casualties during the invasion was a defining characteristic of modern industrial warfare, in which the consequences would be borne by combatant and noncombatant alike. In the case of the former, German losses in the campaign included 11,000 killed and 30,000 wounded, while the Polish military counted 65,000 killed, 144,000 wounded, and almost 600,000 taken prisoner.[72]

The major distinguishing feature of Germany's "Campaign of Eighteen Days" was not the speed of victory or the use of combined arms, but rather the introduction of a style of warfare based on racial and ideological precepts. In his examination of the invasion of Poland, Alexander Rossino argued, "perhaps the most decisive change that occurred in the German method of waging war was the morally corrosive influence of National Socialism." He continued, "This influence manifested itself in the deadly racial-political policies that the SS, police, and German army implemented against Poland's civilian population, both Christian and Jewish."[73] This statement raises two fundamental issues. First, it is necessary to analyze how the campaign and the resulting occupation were conducted. Second and equally important, it is essential to examine the array of actors involved with the enforcement of racial policy and by extension acts of atrocity and mass murder.

As the Wehrmacht entered Poland, its mission focused on the defeat of enemy forces and the quelling of opposition to German control. But the army was not the only armed force involved in the war on the ground in the East. Reich Leader of the SS and Chief of the German Police Heinrich Himmler was ultimately responsible for the enforcement and attainment of the Nazi regime's racial objectives, and he controlled a significant number of forces, including the SS, the Security Police, and the Order Police, to achieve them. In fact, Himmler saw his men as "political soldiers" who were expected to work "hand in hand "with the Wehrmacht in the subjugation and rule of the occupied territories. The invasion of Poland not only initiated a campaign of mass killing but also "tested relationships and forged partnerships between organizations that constituted a deadly triad in the East: the SS and police, the Wehrmacht, and indigenous auxiliaries."[74] In fact, one of the unique aspects of the war in the East involved the interaction and complicity of each of these groups in the conduct of mass murder and genocide.

Despite their disadvantages, Polish military forces and even groups of citizens put up significant resistance to the invaders. Many Poles took up arms to oppose Wehrmacht forces, operating alone or in small groups. But these civilians could not hope to engage German forces in conventional combat with any success, so they resorted to hit-and-run attacks or sniping. In response, Wehrmacht generals independently established reprisal policies that ranged from the execution of three to as many as ten Poles for every German killed; on the fourth day of the invasion, one unit had already executed a hundred civilians in reprisals. Commanders in the Eighth Army even issued orders to execute persons found in homes, including women and children, from where suspected shots had been fired.[75]

The participation of Wehrmacht and police forces in the prosecution of pacification and reprisals indicates an important point. The army's almost pathological fear of the actions of civilians and irregulars, tracing from the experience of Prussian forces in France in 1870–71 into World War I, coupled with real and imagined Polish atrocities helped create a situation in which preexisting racial prejudices facilitated atrocity. In the example of the Polish city of Bydgoszcz (Bromberg), pro-Nazi sympathizers among the city's ethnic German population engaged retreating Polish troops. These attacks resulted in retaliatory actions by the Polish army that claimed the lives of over a thousand ethnic Germans, both insurrectionists as well as innocent bystanders.[76]

When German forces reached the city on September 5, "Bromberg's Bloody Sunday" became a symbol of Polish perfidy and provided the pretext for severe retaliation against the Polish inhabitants. Continued sporadic resistance throughout the city and several instances of sniping led the military administration to institute a large-scale pacification operation, resulting in the arrest of several thousand Poles as well as the summary execution of those found with any weapons, including flintlock rifles and bayonets. Military authorities relied heavily on police forces, a precedent that would often be repeated during the invasion of the Soviet Union. During "cleansing actions" by one police battalion in Bromberg, policemen arbitrarily arrested and executed Poles, including 370 persons just in the period September 9–11.[77]

In addition to hostage taking and reprisal executions, Wehrmacht units also resorted to acts of collective punishment by burning down farms or homes in suspect areas. In some cases units took preemptive actions. For example, on September 2, a German officer recorded, "all of the villages [in the vicinity of Albertów] were razed so that there would be no danger of civilians shooting at advancing units." Likewise, the Forty-First Infantry Regiment not only executed every second man in the village of Torzeniec in a reprisal action on the morning of September 2, but its commander also ordered the razing of a neighboring town as the unit advanced. The brutal actions of units in the field were not just supported but endorsed by higher headquarters. General (later Field Marshal) Fedor von Bock issued orders on September 10 authorizing the burning of entire villages and towns in the event that units could not distinguish the specific origin of an attack.[78] Such permission in effect gave units a free hand to destroy entire villages at their own discretion.

Despite Himmler's orders of September 7 that "police units" and not army personnel were responsible for executions, Wehrmacht forces continued to play an active role in the killings. In fact, one of the army's largest victim groups was Polish POWs. Some units simply chose to execute surrendered enemy soldiers instead of taking them prisoner. In one example, after a firefight that resulted in the death of a German captain and fourteen men, the colonel in charge of the unit ordered the 300 captured Polish soldiers to remove their uniforms and then had them shot as insurgents, arguably a case of hot-blooded atrocity. In another case, while being interrogated, a Polish soldier got hold of a weapon and shot his inquisitor. In response, German troops opened fire on and tossed hand grenades into the building containing all of the POWs, setting it aflame and killing all those inside. Most ominously, Jewish soldiers were at greatest risk, separated from other Polish prisoners and routinely subjected to physical abuse and starvation. Required to perform forced labor and to live in separate "ghetto POW camps," an estimated 25,000 Jewish prisoners, some 50 percent of the total captured, perished by early 1940.[79]

In summary, German forces pursued two complementary objectives aimed at the destruction of Poland. First, Wehrmacht forces sought to destroy the Polish military in a series of battles of annihilation. Second, five einsatzgruppen, composed of SS and police forces, followed the army, with orders to combat "enemies of the German people and state in the rear areas behind the fighting troops." In practice, these orders translated into the elimination of the putative racial and political enemies of the Third Reich, including Polish nationalists, members of the Catholic clergy, the nobility, intellectuals, and Jews. Under the codename Operation Tannenberg, Wehrmacht, SS, and police units dealt ruthlessly with cases of actual or perceived resistance, murdering more than 16,000 civilians in September and October 1939 alone. By the beginning of December, the number of victims stood at 50,000 Poles, including some 7,000 Jews.[80]

The invasion of Poland and the murderous actions taken by military, SS, and police forces proved to be a "critical first step" along the path to the genocide of the European Jews and the enormous slaughter inflicted upon the resident peoples of the East, a slaughter that in Poland alone would include 3,000,000 Jews and another 3,000,000 Polish Christians by the end of the war. The initiative shown by these men and their active participation in mass atrocity resulted from anti-Semitic and racial prejudices that had shaped their expectations and also their view of the "enemy." In fact, Christian Hartmann argued that anti-Semitism became a "type of state doctrine (*Staatsdoktrin*)" within the Wehrmacht, finding expression in the actions of specific units and individual soldiers. During the invasion, German soldiers, especially from the lower ranks, humiliated, tortured, and murdered Jews in actions that killed "several thousand." The experience of a Luftwaffe pilot during a stopover in Poland highlights the pernicious effects of these prejudices. After his capture by the British later in the war, the pilot, a Lieutenant Fried, was secretly recorded during a discussion with another POW. Fried revealed: "I once took part in it [the massacre of Jews] myself . . . during the Polish campaign. . . . I had an hour to spare and we went to a kind of barracks and slaughtered 1,500 Jews." He continued:

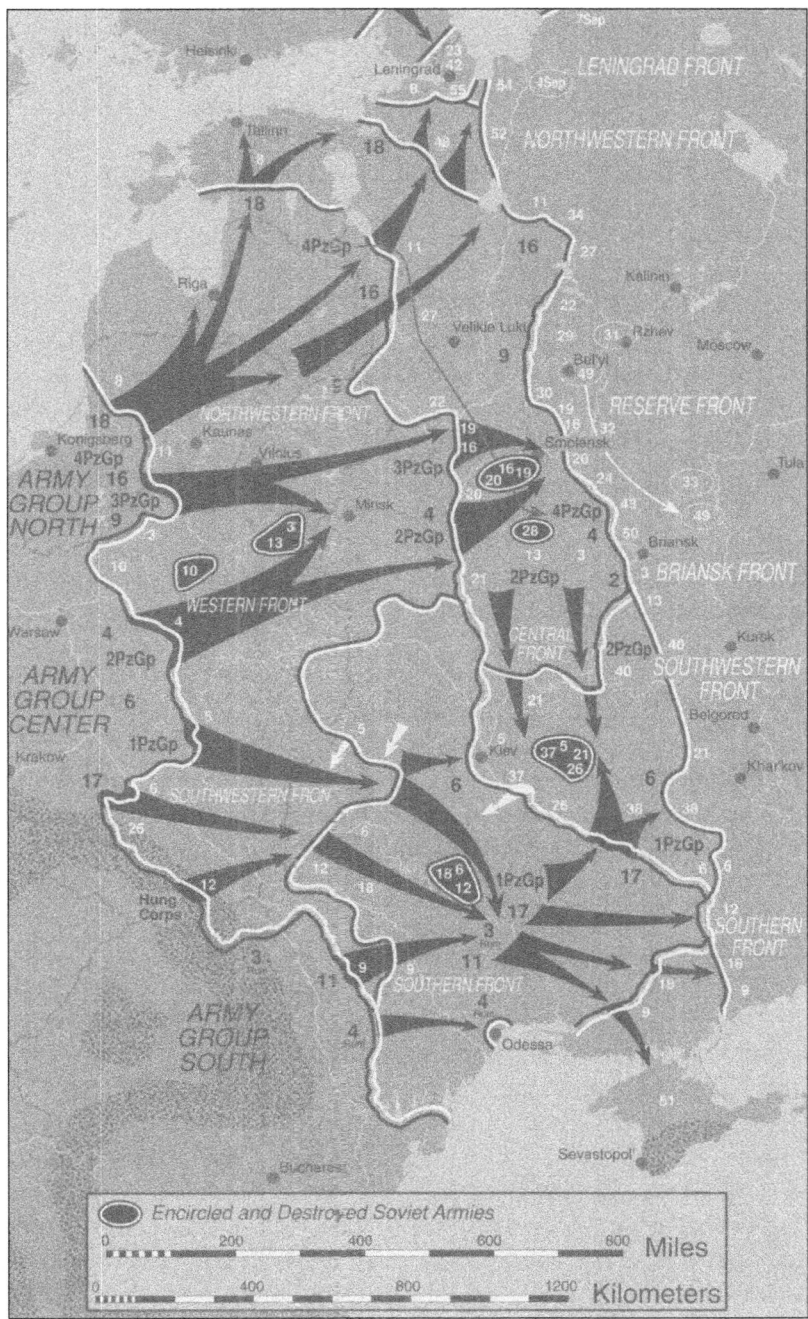

German Military Operations on the Eastern Front, June 22–September 30, 1941. From David M. Glantz and Jonathan House, *When Titans Clashed: How the Red Army Stopped Hitler* (1995), courtesy of the University Press of Kansas.

"There were some twenty men there with tommy-guns. It only took a second, and nobody thought anything about it."[81]

As Fried's stoic account reveals, the Jew and the Pole were not seen as persons who could, with the right guidance, be civilized and incorporated into the German *Volk*. Instead, their very existence threatened the racial purity and the economic survival of the Third Reich, a threat that could only be eliminated by physical extermination. One of the defining characteristics of the campaign in Poland was the "killing rate" of German forces. In a three-month period from September 1 to December 1, German forces killed at least 115,000 Poles, not including collateral civilian casualties as a result of bombing and artillery shelling. Tragically, these losses would pale in comparison to the scale of slaughter inflicted in the first months of operations in the Soviet Union. If the attack on Poland had been a "dress rehearsal" for annihilation, the war in Russia would provide the stage for a sanguinary bravura performance.

Operation Barbarossa: War and Genocide

The planning for the invasion of the Soviet Union far exceeded in scale and resources all of the earlier Wehrmacht campaigns of conquest, a fact recognized by Hitler in a remark to Hermann Göring: "It will be our toughest struggle yet. . . . [F]or the first time we shall be fighting an ideological enemy, and an ideological enemy of fanatical persistence at that." If fanatic resistance was expected from Soviet forces, it still did not change Hitler's opinion that the Russian colossus had "feet of clay" and would crumble quickly in the face of the German onslaught. Indeed, the invasion force of 3,600 tanks, 2,500 aircraft, 600,000 motorized vehicles, and 3,000,000 men was the largest military assembly fielded for a single operation in the history of warfare. Although four armored groups constituted the initial hammer blow, the main striking force consisted of seven infantry armies; the majority of infantrymen would march into Russia accompanied by 750,000 horses to pull artillery and supply wagons, the latter reminiscent of the wagon trains of the American West of the previous century.[82] Divided into three army groups, Army Group Center constituted the main thrust of the invasion, with the objective of moving across central Russia toward Moscow. Army Group South pushed into Ukraine in order to capture the breadbasket of the

Soviet Union and secure the coveted "black earth" country of Nazi colonial fantasy. Finally, Army Group North was to strike through the Baltic states, with the aim of capturing the strategic and symbolic city of Leningrad.

Prior to the invasion, Hitler repeatedly reminded Wehrmacht leaders that this was to be a "war of annihilation," and the army leadership had planned accordingly. Their planning directive described the operational strategy: "During the initial phase the bulk of the Russian Army stationed in western Russia is to be destroyed in a series of daring operations spearheaded by armored thrusts." In short, the armored forces would serve as iron wedges to rapidly penetrate Soviet forward defenses and thrust deep into their rear in order to cut off, encircle, and then destroy the Russian armies.[83] Planners envisioned a campaign that combined the speed and mobility embodied in blitzkrieg with the maneuver and firepower of *Kesselschlacht* to overwhelm Russian forces.

The success of the initial operations by all three army groups appeared to vindicate Hitler's prediction of a rapid campaign and to justify the plan of attack. On July 3, Halder, the army chief of staff, gloated, "It is thus probably no overstatement to say that the Russian campaign has been won in the space of two weeks." His celebration may have been premature, but it was not based on wishful thinking. All along the thousand-mile front, German armor advanced at an astounding pace, the tanks in Army Group Center moving 270 miles toward Moscow in the first week of the invasion, while other forces successfully completed a series of large-scale encirclements that had inflicted "appalling" losses on the Soviets, netting almost two million prisoners by the end of August.[84]

Despite suffering tremendous losses, the Red Army continued to throw men and materiel against the invaders, and by mid-August, the German high command's certainty of a rapid victory began to evaporate. In a journal entry of August 11, Halder worriedly wrote, "The whole situation makes it increasingly plain that we have underestimated the Russian colossus." In point of fact, military intelligence had severely miscalculated the size of the Red Army, the ability of the Soviet state to mobilize reserves, and the technological capability of its weapons systems, especially tanks. In addition to the challenge posed by Soviet forces, Hitler's Wehrmacht, like Napoleon's Grand Armée in 1812, began to experience the limitations imposed by distance and poor transportation networks. For every kilometer that they advanced, German forces lengthened their lines of resupply and increased the difficulties associated with bringing fuel, food, and ammunition forward.[85] In contrast, Soviet lines of supply and movement were shortened with each German thrust.

Between August and September, even as its forces moved toward Leningrad, Moscow, and Kiev, the Army High Command searched for a knockout blow as Hitler shuttled his armored forces from one group to the next. Despite this diversion of units away from the advance on Moscow, the German armies in the south scored a major victory near Kiev in mid-September by capturing 665,000 prisoners, over 3,000 artillery pieces and antitank guns, and almost 900 tanks. At the same time, Army Group North was closing a vise around Leningrad, starting a 900-day siege that would eventually claim the lives of as many as two million Soviet civilians and combatants. By the end of September, Army Group Center prepared for what Hitler and his army planners expected to be the climactic attack on Moscow. On the eve of the offensive, the führer addressed the army in the East in a radio broadcast, exhorting them: "In these 3 1/2 months, my soldiers, the conditions have finally been created for the last colossal stroke, which still, before the onset of winter, should crush this enemy. . . . Today is the beginning of the last great battle of decision in this year." The initial German success in the first two weeks of October seemed to justify Hitler's optimism as the Wehrmacht captured or killed an estimated one million enemy soldiers while suffering 277,000 casualties of their own. Yet these losses combined with overstretched supply lines and fierce Soviet resistance caused the offensive to stall on the outskirts of the Russian capital by the start of December.[86] With the arrival of "General Winter" and a seemingly inexhaustible supply of Soviet manpower, German forces had reached their limit, and a pending counteroffensive seemed to imperil their entire position.

Murder behind the Wire

By the end of the fall of 1941, Soviet forces had suffered an estimated three million casualties and had lost an additional three million soldiers taken captive. The treatment of these POWs provides one of the clearest manifestations of the nature of the war in the East and the exterminatory intent behind it. As discussed previously, the SS and the army had established the precedent for the murder of POWs during the Polish campaign, a practice continued in the Soviet Union. The size of the opposing forces and the massive haul of captured soldiers combined with the ideological context of the invasion led to a campaign of mass murder on an unimaginable scale. Already in mid-July the einsaztgruppen received instructions to conduct a "political monitoring of all inmates" in order to identify and separate Communist Party functionaries and state officials, political commissars, "agitators," and specifically "all Jews." In this respect it is critical to note that the POW camps were under the control and authority of the Wehrmacht, not the SS. The army, however, proved a willing and cooperative partner with the SS, and POW-camp commanders received orders to "work closely" with the murder squads. Although some commandants attempted to limit or stop the operations of the einsatzgruppen, one reliable source estimates that at least 140,000 Soviet prisoners were murdered in this manner, with the overall number probably "considerably higher."[87]

The practice of casual brutality and atrocity was not limited to actions in the prisoner camps as "much documentary evidence" exists revealing a "widespread" practice by German soldiers of summary executions of captured Soviet troops and a policy of no quarter. Already in June 1941, the commander of a regiment of the 299th Infantry Division ordered that "[p]risoners were not to be taken because troops were so bitter about the dishonest fighting style of the enemy." In fact, the practice of summary execution extended to female Soviet soldiers all across the front, women who in the words of one soldier "fought like wild beasts." In total, German forces shot at least a half million Soviet POWs over the course of the war. But it was the premeditated policy of providing minimal rations combined with the overcrowded, unsanitary, and disease-ridden conditions of the camps that led to the decimation of prisoners. A staggering total of 3.3 million Soviet POWs died in German captivity, either as the result of direct murder or as a result of neglect, abuse, starvation, and disease. Although in agreement with the threat posed by "Jewish-Bolshevism," one German soldier and Protestant theologian stationed in one camp expressed in a letter to his wife his distress at the murders committed by the SS and the mass deaths of the prisoners: "It often froze us to our very souls."[88]

Assessing a War of Annihilation

In assessing the scale of slaughter in the East, one might be reminded of the battles of annihilation fought during the Great War some three decades earlier. French losses in the last half of 1914 totaled 955,000 troops, 1,430,000 in 1915, and another 900,000 in 1916. During the Battle of the Somme in 1916, British casualties totaled 415,000 men, with almost 60,000 occurring in a single day, compared to 650,000 German casualties, over a period of some five months. What distinguished the Wehrmacht's strategy and conduct of the war in Russia, then, was not the number of killed and wounded, but rather the objectives and manner of operations. The horrific casualties of World War I occurred in part from the widespread use of lethal technologies, including the machine gun, artillery, and poison gas. They also resulted from a bankrupt tactical and operational imagination that repeatedly led commanders to send thousands of men "over the top" into the face of the murderously efficient weapons of modern warfare. In fact, the trope of the myopic, unimaginative, and inept military leadership found one of its enduring images in the fictional British character Colonel Blimp, who emerged as "a synonym for military or administrative incompetence."[89] In contrast to the ineptitude and criminal lack of imagination displayed by military commanders in World War I, German military and political leaders planned and conducted a premeditated campaign focused on the annihilation of the putative military, political, and racial enemies of the Nazi regime.

The Wehrmacht's complicity in the Nazis' exterminatory objectives can be seen in a number of areas, including its cooperation with the einsatzgruppen, the mass murder of Soviet POWs, its role in "antipartisan" operations, the economic exploitation of the East and the use of slave labor, and finally, the genocide of the Jews and Sinti and Roma (Gypsies). In his study of the Wehrmacht on the eastern front, Dieter Pohl estimated that the frontline German military units participated, directly or indirectly, in the deaths of approximately two million persons, including POWs, Jews, and civilians in "the most brutal occupation regime ... in history."[90]

The brutal nature of this war can be found in the diary and journal entries of the common German soldiers. Only a month into the Russian campaign, one German soldier wrote: "For once sleep as you want, for once eat and drink your fill, for once kill to your heart's content—such are the thoughts that haunt the mind of a man who has long ceased to be a man. That's what our infantry is like at the front in the east." Another's journal also reflected this process of dehumanization: "Our humor was born out of sadism, gallows humor, satire, obscenity, spite, rage, and pranks with corpses. . . . The fact that we were soldiers was sufficient basis for criminality and degradation, for an existence in hell."[91]

In this hell Wehrmacht forces and Himmler's SS and police often cooperated in mass murder. For example, German reports describe the "frictionless cooperation" between einsatzgruppen forces, the military administration, and the police in the massacre of 12,000 Jews at Charkow at the end of 1941. Although the "majority" of Wehrmacht soldiers may have proved reluctant to conduct the mass murder of Jews "on their own initiative," there were "numerous cases" of direct participation in murder by units and individuals. Furthermore, the Army High Command and especially the General Quartermaster Corps played a hitherto underrecognized role in the formulation, planning, and conduct of the war. Dieter Pohl declared, "The importance of the Army High Command has been largely underappreciated with respect to the war of annihilation in the case of mass crimes and the atrocious treatment of the civilians in the East."[92]

The General Quartermaster primarily was responsible for logistics support to units in the field. These "military planners," especially those in Department II—War Administration, played a critical part in the administration of the occupied territories. In fact, Department II, in conjunction with its civil counterpart, the Economic Staff East, proved crucial in formulating policies in the occupied areas dealing with the handling of civilians, the establishment of racial hierarchies, the treatment of POWs, and the coordination of the antipartisan campaign. In other words, Wehrmacht leaders and civilian bureaucrats maintained an active and close working partnership in the design and implementation of ruthless occupational policies that resulted in the direct and indirect mass murder of millions. These policies perfectly reflected Hitler's plans for the East, a sentiment he shared in a private audience with a former member of his SS bodyguard, in which he revealed his plans for a strategy of starvation designed to decimate the Soviet population by the millions.[93]

The German Generals Talk

Shortly after World War II, the distinguished British military historian B. H. Liddell Hart published a work entitled *The German Generals Talk*, which provided the views of the Wehrmacht's "professional" soldiers concerning Hitler's role in formulating strategy. In their criticisms of the führer as a military dilettante or amateur tactician, the generals freely discussed available forces, planning considerations, and operational strategy, but one subject they never addressed was their own participation in the framing and conduct of the war of annihilation in the East.[94] If these generals proved reluctant to speak openly about their role in support of the Reich's racial crusade in the East after the war, such was not the case during the war itself.

In March 1941, General Walther von Brauchitsch, the commander in chief of the army, informed his subordinate commanders that "this struggle [the attack on Russia] is being waged by one race against another, and [must] proceed with the necessary harshness."[95] Two months later General Erich Hoepner, the commander of Armored Group Four, issued the following order to the men under his command:

> [The war against Russia] is the old fight of the Germans against the Slavs, the defense of European culture against the Muscovite-Asiatic flood, the repulsion of Jewish Bolshevism. The goal of this fight must be the destruction of contemporary Russia and therefore must be conducted with enormous violence. Every combat action, in its conception and conduct, must be governed by the iron will to pitiless and complete annihilation of the enemy. In particular there is no mercy for the carriers of the current Russian-Bolshevik system.[96]

These orders originating at the highest levels of the Wehrmacht set the tone for a "war without mercy" founded on the regime's own racial proclamations.

The support by senior military leaders for the regime's racial and ideological objectives found repeated expression in the fall of 1941 as German forces began their assault on Moscow. On October 10, Field Marshal Walter von Reichenau, commander of the Sixth Army, issued the following infamous order to his troops: "The main aim of the campaign against the Jewish-bolshevist system is the complete destruction of its forces and the extermination of the asiatic influence in the sphere of European culture. As a result, the troops have to take on tasks which go beyond the conventional purely military ones." He continued: "In the eastern sphere the soldier is not simply a fighter according to the rules of war, but the supporter of a ruthless racial ideology.... For this reason soldiers must show full understanding for the necessity for the severe but just atonement being required of the Jewish subhumans." Upon receiving a copy of Reichenau's order, the commander of Army Group South, Field Marshal Gerd von Rundstedt, decided to pass it along to the other armies under his command. A copy even reached Hitler, who "declared it to be outstanding, and ordered that it be sent to every unit on the eastern front." For his part, General Erich von Manstein echoed Reichenau's views in his order proclaiming: "The Jewish-Bolshevik system must be eradicated once and for all. Never again may it intrude upon our European living space."[97]

In a final example, the commander of the Seventeenth Army, General Hermann Hoth, authored his own order in support of Nazi racial objectives on November 17, 1941. Hoth asserted: "This battle can only end with the annihilation of one side or the other, there is no compromise.... Compassion and mildness with regard to the local population is completely out of place.... Resistance or any other type of intrigue by Jewish-Bolshevist rabble rousers is to be immediately and mercilessly exterminated."[98] The widespread dissemination of these types of orders combined with the criminal directives that preceded the attack into Russia clearly framed the conflict in the East as an apocalyptic battle between two antithetical ideologies. Seen in whole, these polices served to radicalize the conduct of the war and not just promoted but justified widespread acts of premeditated murder and cold-blooded atrocity across the eastern front. With respect to military and SS and police forces, the practice of murder found its most profound expression in the German prosecution of "antipartisan" war, or the war against "bandits" throughout the Soviet Union.

Comparing the American West and the Nazi East

The preceding discussion of U.S. Army strategy in the American West and German military strategy in the East reveal some points of similarity with respect to the use of rhetoric and in the conduct of operations at the tactical level. Army generals such as Sherman and Sheridan, like German generals in the East, made extensive use of annihilatory rhetoric, yet it is equally apparent that the implementation of such orders proved fundamentally different in terms of execution. Without doubt, Sheridan and Sherman, like many of their contemporaries, viewed and described Indians as "savages" and felt them capable of treachery and cruelty. In some cases individual generals, like John Pope, alternated between the rhetoric of extermination in 1862 and calls for a "defensive arrangement" against the tribes in 1865. Other military commanders such as Crook and Miles proved ready to use force to punish or coerce the Indians but still displayed a deep respect and admiration for their adversaries and their culture. In Crook's case his advocacy on behalf of the Apaches after their removal to Florida and Alabama is generally known, but he repeatedly sought to act in good faith and with "humanity" toward the tribes; for example, when, acting against Sheridan's orders, he chose not to disarm and dismount Sioux bands that had not engaged in battle with the army during the campaign in 1876. Similarly, Miles, despite the limits imposed by his own racial views, rejected calls for "destroying the whole race" of Indians and attempted "to act with justice and compassion toward his former enemies," including his unsuccessful attempt to intercede on behalf of Grey Beard in the wake of the Red River War and his contention that surrendering Sioux should be dealt with "fairly and justly" and prepared for "a pastoral life [that] would suit them well."[99]

The ultimate goal of military and political policy in the West involved the assimilation of the tribes under the guise of civilizing and Christianizing these "savage" and wayward children of a lesser God, even if this policy entailed the "cultural asphyxiation" of the Indians implied by confinement to the reservations.[100] In general, military force was used to enforce specific behaviors or to control the actions of the tribes. Likewise, the U.S. Army often found itself trapped between conflicting demands. On the one hand, its mission included the charter to prevent white encroachment upon the reservations and to protect Indian rights and property. On the other hand, it was responsible for "pursuing and punishing" tribes or bands of Indians who left the reservations or became involved in hostilities with white settlers. The Wehrmacht had no such obligation to the native peoples of the East. In fact, the racial and ideological imperatives that drove the war in Poland and the Soviet Union explicitly freed soldiers and SS and police forces from any legal responsibilities or restraints with respect to Slavs and Jews seen as "subhuman." Assimilation only applied to a select few who displayed supposed Aryan characteristics. The remaining Slavs, the vast majority of the population, were to be expelled, exploited through slave labor, starved, or exterminated when deemed appropriate. For the Jews, exploitation and annihilation were the only solutions, with the former often used as the means to achieve the latter.

One of the fundamental differences between the two national projects of conquest involved the role of political leaders in establishing the acceptable goals and limits related to military strategy. In the case of the American West, after the transfer of the Bureau of Indian Affairs to the Department of the Interior in 1849, military leaders felt that the bureau generally and congressionally appointed Indian agents specifically lacked "firmness" to deal with the Indians effectively. Nevertheless, the army found its scope of action significantly circumscribed by the bureau and its policies. Likewise, the authority of the president and Congress established guidance and limits for officers concerning military objectives and the parameters of acceptable action.[101] President Lincoln's personal intervention in the wake of the Santee Sioux uprising in 1862, in which he overturned 265 out of 303 death sentences handed down by a military commission despite the "vehement protests of Minnesota authorities," provides just one example of the role of the executive and the power of federal authority.[102] Likewise, Grant's Peace Policy provides further evidence of an initiative aimed at a nonviolent, if dictated, resolution to America's "Indian problem" through the creation of a system of reservations supervised by the army.

If U.S. political officials could and did choose on occasion to moderate military responses to the Indian tribes, such was clearly not the case for Hitler and his Nazi paladins in their dealings with Poland and the Soviet Union. Hitler's boasts of creating a new frontier in the East to rival that of America in the previous century not only demonstrated the Führer's limited understanding of the history of the American West but also exposed the genocidal impulse that underpinned his conception of conquest and exploitation in eastern Europe. The apocalyptic colonial fantasies expressed in General Plan East could only be realized by a combined force of military soldiers and the "political soldiers" of the SS willing to pursue the racial objectives of the regime through an unprecedented campaign of mass murder and atrocity. The first step in the creation of a German Garden of Eden did not involve the fashioning of a rib, but literally the creation of mountains of bones as the basis for a new race of "farmer-soldiers" and their progeny.

In short, the conceptualization and execution of military strategy in the two cases was fundamentally different based on the variant political and ideological goals that guided the implementation of these policies. Without doubt, acts of mass atrocity occurred in both historical cases; however, these actions must be compared using the standard of genocide. Against this standard, the issues of scale, scope, intent, and implementation are critical for reaching a judgment on the relative goals and objectives of each. This standard also does nothing to detract from the fact that acts of injustice and atrocity, both great and small, were associated with both national projects and the actions of specific military units. As the following chapter indicates, massacres and acts of atrocity became a signal feature in both the American West and the German East, offering an important point of comparison.

CHAPTER 4

MASSACRE AND ATROCITY

Atrocity and mass murder have been a part of warfare for millennia. In discussing the Peloponnesian War and the conflict between Athens and Sparta, Thucydides discussed the tragic fate of the Melians after their ill-fated attempt to form an alliance with the Spartans. After a protracted siege, the Melians chose to surrender to the Athenians in 416 B.C. Thucydides recorded their subsequent fate as the Athenians "put to death all the grown men whom they took, and sold the women and children for slaves, and subsequently sent out five hundred colonists and settled the place for themselves."[1] The very nature of armed conflict often creates an atmosphere in which one's adversary is vilified or dehumanized, establishing the explicit justification for his or her annihilation. Still, even if one accepts the premise that atrocity is a vestige of warfare, that does not necessarily imply that its scale, scope, and purpose are the same in all conflicts.

There is a clear distinction that can be made between "hot-blooded" and "cold-blooded" atrocity. The former most often occurs after a unit or group has experienced some trauma as a result of an armed engagement, treachery, or in a more contemporary case, the explosion of a roadside bomb. Under specific circumstances, soldiers bound by personal loyalty and angered by the death or wounding of their comrades have become involved in an orgy of blood lust that included the murder of civilians or the execution of captured prisoners.[2] Although indefensible and illegal, even the code of law makes a distinction between "crimes of passion" conducted in a moment of extreme emotional or mental duress and premeditation. Cold-blooded atrocity is a case of the latter, in which the actions cannot be rationalized as a primal response to the deaths of one's comrades or resulting from exposure to a situation of mortal danger and the activation of the "fight or flight reflex." It is distinguished by premeditation and the willingness to kill absent any threat to one's own safety. An atrocity conducted in this manner may serve a number of goals, including convenience, self-interest, apathy, or racial hatred.

Both the Nazi campaign in the East and the push for westward expansion provide numerous examples of hot-blooded and cold-blooded atrocity. But the scale and the scope of brutality and mass murder in the two cases offers an important point of comparison. The Nazi regime's direct murder of six million Jews during World War II is one example of the premeditated and cold-blooded murder of an entire group. In the case of the Final Solution, the cooperation of SS, police, and Wehrmacht forces in the execution of almost 34,000 Jews—men, women, and children—near the Ukrainian city of Kiev over the course of two days in September 1941 provides just one of many horrific examples of cold-blooded atrocity. Similarly, the "Hunger Policy" agreed to by German bureaucrats prior to the invasion of the Soviet Union assumed and embraced the death by starvation of *tens of millions* of Soviet citizens in order to feed the Wehrmacht from these conquered lands and to eliminate entire native populations. Likewise, the deaths of over three million Soviet POWs held by the Germans provides another example of mass murder and cold-blooded atrocity, even if the majority of prisoners perished by indirect methods such as disease, exhaustion, and starvation.[3]

Without a doubt, mass murder was one of the defining characteristics of Nazi Germany during the twelve-year history of the Third Reich, and one scholar estimated that Hitler's regime murdered between fifteen million and thirty-one million persons "by genocide, the murder of hostages, reprisal raids, forced labor, 'euthanasia,' starvation, exposure, medical experiments, terror bombing, and in the concentration and death camps."[4] The Nazi record of mass murder is made all the more extraordinary by the relatively brief time period in which the victims died and by the diversity of the groups and organizations involved in the slaughter.

In the case of westward expansion during the four decades between 1850 and 1890, there are also several cases of atrocity and mass murder. The infamous massacre at Sand Creek in 1864 and the slaughter of Sioux at Wounded Knee in 1890 remain dark chapters in U.S. history and indictments of the actions taken by federal, state, and military officials. In the former the carnage perpetrated by Colorado Volunteers was a premeditated act in which racial hatred played a key role, resulting in the deaths of 105 women and children and twenty-eight men. In the case of the latter, the attempt by members of the Seventh Cavalry to disarm a group of Indians encamped at Wounded Knee Creek escalated into an avoidable melee that resulted in the killing of at least 200 men, women, and children; the wounding of another 100 Sioux; and sixty-five U.S. Army casualties, in large part due to the poor judgment of an army commander.[5]

The conduct of massacre and atrocity in the West, however, was not limited to volunteers or members of the regular army but included the multifold acts of individuals and groups such as miners or ranchers. One historian estimated that these groups, including members of a volunteer militia acting on the "genocidal exhortations" of settlers and political leaders, were responsible for the decline of California's Indian population from 100,000 to 50,000 people between 1850 and 1870.[6] The involvement of civilians in mass murder found one of its most notorious examples in the so-called Camp Grant Massacre on April 30, 1871, when a group of Americans, Mexicans, and Tohono O'odham Indians attacked an Apache camp and murdered some 150 persons, mostly women and children, in an orgy of vigilante violence. Similarly, the historian Karl Jacoby argued that volunteers in Arizona "adopted a policy of killing whatever 'Apaches' they encountered on their patrols" as part of a "broad platform of extermination."[7]

From the examples above, it is evident that mass murder and atrocity occurred in the conquest of both the Nazi East and the American West, even if one admits to differences in their scale and the scope. The following discussion not only looks at specific cases of mass murder, but even more importantly it provides an overview of the political, military and racial factors that influenced the conduct of atrocity by framing the social and cultural environment in which these acts occurred as well as the variety of actors, both groups and individuals, involved and their motivations.

Violence and Atrocity in the "Wild West"

The term "wild, wild West" evolved not only as a function of the region's untamed nature, involving battle with the elements, the terrain, and wildlife, but also as a reflection of violence and conflict as facts of life. Popular culture did not give credit to the plow or the bible for taming the West, but rather to Sam Colt's revolver. In fact, gunslingers such as Wild Bill Hickock and Wyatt Earp emerged as iconic western figures famed for their ability to settle disputes or insults with a steady hand and a fast draw in single combat. Likewise, violence and vigilantism were frequent occurrences as small ranchers, farmers, and sheepherders fought against the efforts of the cattle kings to enclose the range and incorporate the lands under their control. In the case of Montana Territory, the "Hanging Tree" in Helena became a recognized symbol of the territory's reliance on vigilante justice. In 1865 alone "vigilance committees" there executed thirty-seven men, "the deadliest campaign of vigilante killing in American history."[8] The use of "frontier justice" among white settlers created its own precedent and dynamic for similar incidents involving Indians. But this dynamic of violence had long existed on the Great Plains, the site of warfare between the various tribes, even if the arrival of white settlers and fortune seekers dramatically raised the level of conflict and confrontation.

Much like the Italian city states of the Renaissance period, the Pueblo Indians of the Southwest, living in independent towns, "fought bitterly against each other" prior to the arrival of the Spanish. Likewise, they battled against Navajo, Apache, and Ute bands in the precolonial period.[9] In fact, the use of massacre as an intentional element of military strategy predated the arrival of Europeans to the New World. The anthropologist Lawrence Keeley discussed evidence of intertribal massacres, including one instance in South Dakota involving some five hundred men, women, and children "who had been slaughtered, scalped, and mutilated" in an attack dated to 1325. While mass atrocity constituted one facet of premodern warfare, the use of violence between tribes and settlers was a standard element in relations dating from the seventeenth century. In fact, Lance Blyth described the Chiricahua Apaches and the Hispanic population of Janos in Mexico as "communities of violence" during the two centuries between 1680 and 1880 in which violence and conflict provided the foundation for economic and social relations between the groups. He argued, "Violence was how these communities established, maintained, or changed their relationships." In another example, the westward migration and campaigns of conquest by the Sioux in the early nineteenth century allowed them to seize control of the northern plains. As Robert Utley stated, "the wave of white migration did not wash against a wall of Indian opposition but rather broke over a congeries of scattered groups that had been fighting one another for generations and would continue to fight one another to the day of their final conquest by the whites." With their arrival onto the Great Plains between 1820 and 1860, white settlers entered "probably the most viciously contested terrain of North America. The endemic intertribal conflict took at least as heavy a toll, and probably a much higher one, as later battles with the whites. . . . Raids and counter-raids chewed at populations, ripped apart families, and upset crazily the balance of men and women."[10]

Prior to the great influx of white settlers onto the plains, the major source of interaction between whites and the various tribes occurred in the form of trappers entering into the areas under Indian control. In many cases this contact resulted in trappers marrying Indian wives, an act that created "cultural and economic liaisons" between the two societies. Yet the competition for resources also spurred resentment and violence between the two groups. For example, sixteen-year-old Christopher "Kit" Carson left Missouri with a group of trappers in the summer of 1826 to seek his fortune in the West. His experiences were replete with both friendly and hostile meetings with various tribes. When encounters went bad, often quarter was neither given nor expected from either side. In one example, Carson and eleven of his companions, after losing sixty horses in a raid, trailed a group of Indians for a hundred miles and killed eight while taking three others prisoner.[11] In truth, those accused of horse stealing or cattle rustling, whether white or Indian, often suffered a similar fate. In Carson's case, his biographers argued: "Though he was an Indian fighter, he was not an Indian hater. No expression of hate or prejudice toward Indians is to be found in Carson's *Memoirs*."[12] Whatever the case, it is without a doubt that Kit Carson earned his fame by fighting and killing Indians in the American West.

The western experiences of a contemporary and later friend of Carson's, John Charles Frémont, during a series of surveys that resulted in his being named "the Pathfinder," offer another perspective for evaluating white and Indian interaction prior to the mass migration of white settlers into the West. Although Frémont displayed a fascination and admiration for the Indians and saw them as "misunderstood souls, often abused by whites," he supported their removal and the reservation policy. He also embraced a social, if not racial, hierarchy that placed Cherokees at the top and the Indians of the Great Basin at the bottom as "humanity . . . at its lowest form." Frémont encountered numerous bands over the course of his various travels, and the majority of these interactions proved peaceful, if not always friendly. During an 1846 survey of the Sacramento Valley, he was approached by white settlers seeking "protection" from Indian attacks. In this case Frémont allowed men from his party, including Kit Carson, to conduct an "expedition" against the Natives. Carson described this as an act of "chastisement" that resulted in "a perfect butchery." Two months later, while camped near Klamath Lake, a group of Indians surprised the party in a night raid and killed three members of the expedition, including one of Frémont's close friends. Throughout the next day and into the night, with the dead bodies of their comrades draped across their mules, Frémont's men circled Klamath Lake, indiscriminately killing any Indians they found as retribution for the attack of the previous night.[13]

Frémont's expeditions in the 1840s did much to map an uncharted land and certainly paved the way for future white settlement in the area. Likewise, his interaction with the Indians reflected the full spectrum of relations and the day-to-day reality of Indian-white relations by the mid-nineteenth century. Like Frémont, the majority of his U.S. Army peers believed that the fundamental maxim in dealing with the Indians was to "be fair but firm." But the concept and definition of "firmness" included a belief in the necessity and efficacy of punishment and the value of direct demonstrations of military power. Indeed, "chastisement" and operations to "pursue and punish" emerged as the standard response to real or alleged Indian depredations throughout the nineteenth century. Even officers such as Major General George Crook and Lieutenant Charles Gatewood, soldiers who showed real understanding and affection for Indians, still advocated the use of a strong hand. A successful leader of Apache scouts, Gatewood contended, "The Apache respects nothing, believes in nothing, & bows to nothing but force." Similarly, while on duty in the Pacific Northwest in 1858, Crook led a campaign to "punish" a group of Yakimas who had battled a unit of soldiers, killing six and wounding eleven. After capturing the Indians involved in the attack and obtaining a confession of their guilt, Crook authorized the summary execution of the five men, a task he found necessary but "exceedingly distasteful." Interestingly, at the outbreak of the Civil War and "fresh from Indian country," Crook condoned the summary execution of Confederate-sponsored "bushwhackers" during operations in West Virginia.[14] In this case it appears that his duty on the frontier had influenced his handling of guerrillas in the East.

The Sand Creek Massacre

Perhaps it should not be surprising that one of the most infamous examples of the atrocities committed against Indians occurred near the end of the Civil War. Indeed, the "War between the States" split families and the army's officer corps alike. William T. Sherman's pronouncement "War is cruelty, and you cannot refine it" was symbolized in his "march to the sea," a campaign that became emblematic of a style of "hard war" that spared neither soldier nor civilian. While some historians have noted Sherman's penchant for hyperbole and questioned the description of the Civil War as a "total war," the use of volunteers and militias throughout U.S. military history has been intertwined with the conduct of massacre and atrocity.[15] With the outbreak of the Civil War, the federal government had transferred regular-army units east to confront Confederate forces. As a result, many of the state and territorial governments raised militia and volunteer companies to oppose Confederate incursions and to maintain a constabulary force along the frontier. In Colorado Territory, Governor John Evans had appointed Colonel John M. Chivington to lead a unit of the Colorado Volunteers. In fact, Evans had requested approval from Washington to raise a regiment of 100-day volunteers specifically for action against the Indians and felt pressured to make use of the men or to accept the political embarrassment associated with raising the unit and never employing it in the field. The governor asserted, "They have been raised to kill Indians, and they must kill Indians."[16]

Many of these short-term volunteers included "rowdies and toughs recruited from the mining camps and Denver saloons," perfect choices to carry out orders to "burn villages and kill Cheyennes wherever and whenever found." Such men under Chivington's command prepared to fall upon the Indian encampment at Sand Creek in November 1864. For his part, Chivington was no stranger to acts of atrocity, as evidenced by his earlier decision to execute six Confederate prisoners despite being denied permission by higher authority to do so. In any event, he was eager for action as he had discussed "taking scalps" and "wading in gore." When one of the regular officers at Fort Lyon, Lieutenant James Connor, questioned the morality of the planned attack on Black Kettle's encampment and labeled the plan "murder in every sense of the word," Chivington responded in a rage: "I have come to kill Indians, and believe that it is right and honorable to use any means under God's heaven to kill Indians." Other officers at the fort were "stunned" by the treachery of Chivington's plan, but they received no support in their protests from the fort's commander, Major Scott Anthony, who supported the colonel's plan to "punish" the Cheyennes. In fact, subsequent testimony about Anthony stated that "he was in favor of killing all the Indians he came to."[17]

At daybreak on November 29, in a profound case of perfidy and bestiality, Chivington's volunteers, augmented by troops from Fort Lyon, prepared to attack the village. The Coloradoans initiated the attack on the camp, butchering 105 women and children and twenty-eight men. The massacre included sexual mutilations, scalpings, and the extensive taking of body parts as trophies. One historian described the scene: "For hours, the frenzied Coloradans, in an orgy of brutality and hate, went over the battlefield, murdering the wounded and scalping and mutilating the dead." Lieutenant Connor later testified on the "horrible manner" of the mutilations, "in which men had cut out the private parts of females and stretched them over the saddle-bows and wore them over their hats while riding in the ranks." Some soldiers refused to participate in the carnage. Captain Silas Soule refused to give the order to fire on the Indians, and he and his men simply watched as the massacre unfolded.[18]

Upon their return to Denver in the last week of December, Chivington and the "Blood Thirdsters" conducted a parade through the city's streets to the cheers of the assembled crowd and displayed their "trophies" of the Cheyenne body parts at a local theater. With the end of their enlistment, many of the volunteers found their way back to their "old haunts," where they openly admitted that "the big battle of Sand Creek was a cold-blooded massacre." In fact, the *Daily Mining Journal* interviewed some of the perpetrators of the slaughter and reported, "Many stories are told and incidents related by the actors in the bloody scene, which are too sickening to repeat." Sand Creek also sickened the famous Indian fighter Kit Carson, who described Chivington as a "dog" and his men as "dirty hounds." While admitting his own antipathy for "a hostile red skin [sic]," he remarked: "I've fought 'em, hard as any man. But I never yet drew a bead on a squaw or papoose, and I despise the man who would."[19]

A later congressional investigation by the Joint Committee on the Conduct of War found:

As to Colonel Chivington, your committee can hardly find fitting terms to describe his conduct. Wearing the uniform of the United States, which should be the emblem of justice and humanity; holding the important position of commander of a military district, and therefore having the honor of the government to that extent in his keeping, he deliberately planned and executed a foul and dastardly massacre which would have disgraced the verist [sic] savage among those who were the victims of his cruelty. Having full knowledge of their friendly character, having himself been instrumental to some extent in placing them in their position of fancied security, he took advantage of their in-apprehension [sic] and defenceless condition to gratify the worst passions that ever cursed the heart of man.[20]

For his part, Chivington escaped official punishment since he had resigned his commission in the army prior to the release of this report. Although he later ran for political office in Colorado and Ohio, his ambitions were crushed by the "ghosts of Sand Creek."[21]

In retrospect, the massacre at Sand Creek offers several insights into the nature of Indian and white relations in the West. First, the vacuum essentially created by the withdrawal of federal authority, specifically the regular-army presence in the West, put exactly those groups most closely associated with an exterminatory philosophy in control of Indian policy. In fact, one participant in the massacre discussed the unit's belief "that a war of extermination should be waged; that neither sex nor age should be spared." In contrast, the protests of the regular officers such as Connor in advance of the attack and Soule's refusal to participate provide a counterpoint to the actions and words of Chivington and his volunteers. A second insight involves the brutality and savagery of the massacre itself. The gratuitous violence and the sexual mutilations reflected the deep-seated antipathy of these "westerners" for their victims, just as the shock and revulsion shown by Congress and the friends of the Indians in the East highlighted the cultural and experiential chasm between the political power center of the nation and its frontier periphery. Finally, Sand Creek reflected an act of "cold-blooded atrocity," with clear premeditation and the successful dehumanization of the victim group. In this latter respect, a public speech made by Chivington in Denver prior to the massacre is revealing. In it he advocated the scalping of infants with the remark: "little and big, . . . [n]its make lice!"[22]

The "Fetterman Disaster"

The massacre at Sand Creek cast a long shadow across the Great Plains and sparked a bloody cycle of reprisal, retribution, and counterreprisal in 1864–65. In the summer of 1865, Brigadier General Patrick Connor led three columns of cavalry, mostly state volunteers, and almost two hundred Pawnee and Omaha scouts into the Powder River country on a punitive campaign. In preparation for the campaign, Connor told his men, "You will not receive overtures of peace or submission from Indians, but will attack and kill every male Indian over twelve years of age." On August 29, Connor and his force had the opportunity to put these words into action as his force fell upon an Arapaho encampment, resulting in a hand-to-hand melee that left between thirty-five to sixty-three Arapahos dead, including men, women, and children, against a loss of two soldiers and three scouts. According to one witness, the battle resulted in the capture of some thirty women and children, but "no Indian warrior was [left] alive." During a series of engagements in early September, the general lost twelve soldiers to hit-and-run attacks and eventually withdrew his forces in the face of the coming winter. Despite its stated goal, Connor's foray accomplished little except to "stir up a hornet's nest" and to demonstrate that the Indians of the northern plains were ready and capable of opposing incursions into their territory. It did display, however, the continuing use of a tactic that focused on the killing of warriors or military-age males, which had been employed in earlier campaigns in the Pacific Northwest and in the Desert Southwest. In the latter area, Colonel William Harney reacted to an alleged Indian raid in Texas by ordering his troops to find the offending tribe and "to exterminate if possible, every man in it, and make prisoners of the women and children."[23]

Connor's campaign also revealed that the most effective way for the federal government to protect the overland trails involved the establishment of a series of forts along the Bozeman Trail, a strategy that won increasing favor within the army by 1865. Yet forts to protect the movement of white settlers and fortune hunters through Indian country disturbed tribal hunting grounds and became a constant source of conflict. Finn Burnett, a frontiersman who traveled one overland trail, remembered the ubiquitous mounds along the road that marked the burial spots of those killed in attacks or who had perished as the result of accident or sickness.

Despite the success of the Indian Bureau in negotiating treaties with the northern Plains Indians to stop fighting and to withdraw from the existing overland routes, the establishment of Fort Reno and Fort Phil Kearny east of the Bighorn Mountains in present-day Wyoming proved a festering thorn in the side of the Sioux. With the end of the Civil War and the demobilization of state volunteers, General Sherman temporarily adopted a defensive strategy in the West focused on maintaining "comparative quiet . . . [until] we can have the new cavalry enlisted, equipped, and mounted, ready to go visit these Indians where they live."[24]

Sherman's hopes for a year of "comparative quiet" proved illusory on the northern plains despite the line of forts established along the Bozeman Trail. Since the erection of Fort Phil Kearny in July 1866, Sioux warriors had waged a series of hit-and-run attacks in its vicinity and along the entire route. During the first engagement on the seventeenth, a small group of warriors under Red Cloud stampeded the fort's mules and horses in an early morning raid. The subsequent chase led to the garrison's first casualties, with two soldiers killed and three wounded. En route back to the fort after an unsuccessful chase, soldiers came across a trader's wagon plundered of its contents of trinkets and illegal liquor. Among the wreckage were the mutilated bodies of the trader, French Pete Gazzous, and five of his traveling companions. Private John Ryan recalled, "The poor victims had been mutilated in the most horrible manner and it gave us all a most convincing lesson on what our fate would be should we fall into the hands of the Indians."[25] This initial engagement once again highlighted the often brutal nature of warfare in the West and demonstrated the use of violence and punishment as signals to one's adversary about the potential consequences associated with incursion into the area.

Throughout August and September, small groups of Sioux attacked and harassed traffic along the Bozeman Trail, including the ever-present woodcutting expeditions sent out in order to supply construction materials to finish Fort Phil Kearny before the snows came. The fort's commander, Colonel Henry Carrington, noted the "almost constant hostile demonstrations of some kind" that took place in September alone Even as Red Cloud's warriors made almost daily attacks near the post, Carrington continued to parlay with a band of Cheyennes under Black Horse, providing gifts of coffee, sugar, hardtack, and bacon. Shortly after the Cheyennes' arrival on

September 27, news came of an attack against a woodcutting party earlier that day in which a private, Patrick Smith, had been shot with arrows, scalped, and left for dead. A group of Smith's fellow troopers snuck out of the fort under the cover of darkness with the intent to inflict their revenge on the nearest Indians, in this case the Cheyennes camped nearby. Only the timely arrival of Carrington and a detachment of troops prevented the attack from taking place. An act of hot-blooded atrocity thus had been narrowly averted.[26]

After an Indian ambush of a work party on October 6 left another two soldiers dead and one wounded, Carrington recognized that the constant attacks frustrated and angered his men, making them "bitter against all Indians." By November, Red Cloud's own bitterness at the presence of this and other forts resulted in his search for additional Indian allies to aid in "destroying the whites." His plan was to use the coming winter as an ally to "starve them out . . . and kill them all." The arrival that same month of Captain William Fetterman, a Civil War veteran, increased the pressure on Carrington to take a more active policy against Red Cloud's warriors. Fetterman disdained the Indian's style of warfare and believed that offensive action was the tactic that would produce the best results. The captain's bravado included statements such as, "A single company of regulars could whip a thousand Indians," and, "With eighty men I could ride through the Sioux nation."[27]

On December 21, the eager and ambitious Fetterman got the chance that he had been seeking. After an attack on another woodcutting party, Carrington ordered the captain to take a mixed force of eighty cavalry troopers and infantrymen into the field. For whatever reason, Fetterman exceeded his orders by pursuing the retreating Sioux well beyond the bounds established by the colonel. Unfortunately for him and his men, the Sioux had developed a well-planned ambush involving as many as two thousand warriors. Overextended and beyond the support of the fort, Fetterman and his entire command fell victims to the Sioux trap. In a brief but ferocious engagement, all eighty men perished, the greatest army disaster in the Trans-Mississippi West until the Battle of Little Bighorn. In his official report of the action, Carrington described the gruesome scene that awaited the relief column: "Eyes torn out and laid on the rocks; ears cut off, entrails taken out and exposed, hands cut off, . . . punctures on every sensitive part of the body, even to the soles of the feet and palms of the hands." In contrast to the orgy of desecration inflicted by Chivington's men at Sand Creek, the mutilation of the soldiers' bodies were not simply gratuitous acts of violence but instead reflected the belief that disfiguring one's enemy "adversely affect[ed] the fate of the soul or spirit it once housed." Still, the practice of killing every man was not unique to the Sioux and not limited to combat with the army. For example, the Apaches and Comanches often killed all captured males and took only women and children prisoner. Likewise, Wolfkiller, a Navajo, recalled a raid by a band of Utes during which all the adult males were killed and the women and children taken captive.[28] In this respect, the nature of frontier warfare for both sides was often a "no quarter asked and no quarter given" affair, a practice equally applicable to intertribal combat.

After reporting on the loss of Fetterman and his men, Carrington was relieved of command and ordered to face a special commission. An army inquiry ended with little result, while a separate inquiry by the Department of the Interior found that the colonel had been placed in an untenable position and "furnished no more troops or supplies for this state of war than had been provided and furnished him for a state of profound peace."[29] In the end, lacking sufficient manpower and knowledge of his adversary, Carrington and his troops at Fort Phil Kearny proved unable to accomplish their mission on the northern plains, which was subsequently abandoned, at least temporarily. Ironically, one of the greatest disasters experienced by the U.S. Army during the Indian Wars led to the creation of a peace commission and the eventual abandonment of the Bozeman Trail forts.

The Baker Expedition: Anatomy of a Massacre

Despite the Laramie agreement and its implementation, the presence of white settlements in Montana Territory remained a point of friction. In the summer of 1869, reports of Indian raids on white settlers in the vicinity of Helena led to calls for a military response.[30] In a letter of August 3, 1869, Brigadier General Alfred Sully, the superintendent of Indian affairs for Montana, wrote to Commissioner Ely Parker of his concerns about the possibility of "serious difficulties between Indians and Whites" along with a request for additional military forces in the area. Sully argued that the current presence of some 400 troopers was entirely insufficient to deal with an Indian population he estimated at between 50,000 and 60,000 people. Sully warned that bands from the Powder River area, Canada, and other western territories frequently came into Montana to commit "depredations" against the white settlers, leading to reprisal killings against "*any* Indians they [white vigilantes] may chance to meet, sometimes in the most brutal and cowardly manner." He also identified a "rowdy and lawless" group of whites involved in the sale of whiskey as the culpable party for most of the bloodshed. Finally, the general provided the apparent rationale for his letter and his concerns for "open war" with his description of the "cowardly" murders of two Piegan Indians, an old man and a fourteen-year-old boy, who were gunned down in broad daylight on the street at Fort Benton. Although Sully informed the commissioner of his intent to arrest the murderers, he shared his doubts that he could gain a conviction in court for the killings. He concluded his letter by remarking that nothing could be done until the arrival of a military force strong enough to "clean out the roughs and whiskey sellers."[31]

After receiving the letter, Commissioner Parker wrote to the acting secretary of the interior on August 16 with an endorsement of Sully's request for additional military forces. Parker remarked that he had information from other sources that confirmed the fears of a possible "general war," information that he tied to the threat posed by Sioux bands operating in Montana Territory and the failure of Congress to appropriate promised funds to the Piegans, Bloods, and Blackfeet. On the following day the Department of the Interior forwarded copies of Sully's and Parker's letters to the secretary of war in hopes of "favorable consideration," an indication of the urgency and importance attached to the request. Due to the secretary's absence, the request was sent to Sherman, the commanding general of the army, on August 19. On the same day the acting secretary of the interior, William T. Otto, forwarded a telegram from Sully detailing alleged "outrages" committed by Blackfeet Indians in the territory, including an attack on a wagon train, raids to steal horses, and the shooting of two ranchers.[32]

Despite the apparent escalation of violence, the War Department proved slow to react to the request due in part to the annual mustering of new recruits into the army. This failure to act and along with continuing "depredations by Indians in Montana" led Otto to once again approach the secretary of war on October 12 with a call for "prompt actions." An accompanying letter from F. D. Pease, the Indian agent for the Blackfeet, dated August 31, 1869, demonstrates some of the problems associated with getting an accurate view of activities in the West. Pease emphatically noted that neither the Blackfeet nor the Bloods had been involved in the summer's incidents. Instead, he placed the blame for the depredations squarely on the Piegans and declared that the attacks, perpetrated by only a small number of Indians, had caused the main body of the tribe to move farther north in order to avoid retaliation. Another Indian agent, Alex Culbertson, added his support by describing the Blackfeet and Bloods as "perfectly friendly to the whites" and blaming the attacks on a "young rabble" of Piegans beyond the control of their chiefs. Culbertson observed that "a small amount of provisions" would go a long way in keeping the Indians "quiet," an existential necessity in light of the diminishing buffalo herds.[33]

The letters to and from the agencies provide several insights into Indian and white relations. First, the murder of the innocent Piegan man and boy and the absence of legal redress was responsible for inciting younger warriors to take reprisals. Second, the absence of appropriations and promised supplies was a clear source of dissatisfaction and tension in all the tribes. Third, these Indian agents were able to gain reliable information and to correct the false impression concerning the involvement of the Bloods and Blackfeet. Finally, the repeated requests for military action, or at least an increased military presence, came from the civilian leadership in the Department of the Interior and not the War Department.

In response to the Interior's latest appeal, Sherman ordered Phil Sheridan to take "such action as the case calls for" on October 12. Sheridan began to plan for a winter campaign to "strike" the Piegans and even suggested the date of January 15, 1870, as the time when "they will be very helpless, . . . [and] we might be able to give them a good hard blow." Two weeks later he received approval for this plan and the "punishment of these marauders." On January 16, the commander of the expedition, Major Eugene M. Baker, received his instructions from Colonel Phillipe Régis de Trobriand, commander of the Thirteenth Infantry. Colonel de Trobriand identified the location of the suspect Piegan encampment, led by Mountain Chief, on the Marias River and ordered Baker to avoid actions against the Bloods, Blackfeet, and two "friendly" Piegan bands. The colonel ended his instructions with the remark, "The details as to the best way to surprise the enemy and to carry on successfully the operations, is confidently left to your judgment and discretion according to circumstances, and to your experiences in such expeditions."[34]

On January 19, Baker's force moved north in the face of brutally cold conditions, estimated at thirty degrees below zero. In order to keep his approach a secret, the major only moved his column at night and counted on Joe Kipp and Joe Cobell, two local guides, to scout ahead during the day. As the troops approached the Marias River on January 23, they first came upon a small Piegan camp of five lodges under Gray Wolf. Under questioning, Gray Wolf admitted that at least two of the fugitives, Big Horn and Red Horn, were located in a Piegan camp farther downstream.

Later, Baker and his men approached the suspect Indians by using a ravine along the river to conceal their movements. Arriving early in the morning, they found a silent Piegan encampment composed of thirty-one lodges. Baker's two-hundred-man force moved to surround the camp and waited for a signal to attack. Kipp, having recognized the paintings on a lodge at the center of camp as identifying Heavy Runner, one of the known friendly chiefs, approached Baker with this news. Having endured a brutally cold three-day march and having successfully located a major Piegan village, the major was apparently in no mood to be denied his opportunity to punish the tribe. In response to Kipp's warning, he stated, "That makes no difference, one band or another of them; they are all Piegans and we will attack them."[35]

Fearing that Kipp might alert the sleeping camp, Baker placed the scout under arrest and ordered his men to shoot him if he cried out. At that moment, apparently alerted by the noise, Heavy Runner came out of his lodge, waving a good-conduct pass signed by Sully; before the Piegan chief made it to Baker's line, he was cut down by a solitary shot. The line of soldiers, tense and anticipating the order to attack, now unleashed a withering fusillade into the village. Taken by surprise, Piegan men, women, and children attempted to escape the village on foot, the troopers having captured the band's horses in the first minutes of the attack. Lieutenant Gustavus Doane, the commander of Company F, remarked, "Not an Indian got through [the encirclement] though several were followed high up on the slope of the opposite Bad Lands, and killed with revolvers." In reality, almost a hundred Piegans, including some warriors, successfully made it safely into the surrounding brush along the river.[36]

After almost an hour the firing subsided. Baker's men moved into the camp and began to search the individual lodges before pulling them down, in some cases on top of the dead, the dying, and the wounded; at this time the expedition experienced its one and only fatal casualty when Private Walter McKay was shot at point-blank range by a wounded warrior concealed beneath a buffalo robe. As Baker and his men moved through the camp, it quickly became evident that this was not Mountain Chief's band despite the identification of two "hostile chiefs" among the dead, Red Horn and Big Horn. An interrogation of some of the captured Indians by Kipp and Cobell revealed that Mountain Chief's camp was in fact located several miles farther downriver. At this, Baker proceeded with a force in search of his original target. Even now, despite clear evidence that he had attacked a friendly camp, the major ordered Doane to remain at the camp and to complete its destruction by burning the lodges and all their contents. Alerted either by the firing or by one of the Indians who had successfully slipped through army lines, Mountain Chief and his band hastily deserted their camp, and Baker's party had to settle for burning the remaining lodges before returning to the site of the massacre.[37]

Due to the "groans of the wounded [Piegans]" and the howling of the band's abandoned or ownerless dogs, according to Lieutenant Doane, the unit spent a "hideous" and restless night at the campsite. The next morning Baker met with chiefs from the Blackfeet tribes. After receiving promises of "good behavior," the major began his return trip to Fort Shaw, arriving there on January 29. On the same day Sheridan wrote Sherman to report the "complete success of the expedition." He then predicted, "I think this will end Indian trouble in Montana, and will do away with the necessity of sending additional troops there in the Spring as contemplated."[38]

Despite his initial statement, Sheridan would not receive a written copy of Baker's report until early March. In fact, the major waited almost two weeks after his return to Fort Ellis to write his account. He summarized the operation: "The result of the expedition is one hundred and seventy-three Indians killed, over one hundred prisoners, women and children, . . . forty-four lodges with all their supplies and stores destroyed, and three hundred horses captured." Baker's estimate of the killed and wounded is consistent with the historical average of eight Piegans per lodge, especially if one adds the destruction of the seven abandoned lodges at Mountain Chief's camp and those at Gray Wolf's camp in this total. Allowing for this, the total number of Piegans in Heavy Runner's camp at the time of the massacre was approximately three hundred. If his total estimate is reasonable, Baker's failure to identify the gender and ages of the 173 dead Piegans created immediate questions on the specific nature of the engagement. Since Sheridan's first report had made no mention of Indians taken captive, and based on the number of Piegan losses and the death of only one trooper, eastern newspapers immediately began to speculate on the operation and leveled claims of atrocity at Baker and his command. For example, newspapers in Boston; Albany, New York; and Jamestown, New York, all carried reports of the expedition under the headline "The Piegan Massacre." The subtitle to the story in the *Jamestown Journal* was "sickening details of Col. Baker's campaign," a clear indication of the editor's stance on the operation.[39] Sherman, for his part, recognized the adverse political consequences and the potential for public controversy. Already on January 29 he had instructed Sheridan to "[l]ook out for the cries of those who think the Indians are so harmless, and obtain all possible evidence concerning the murder charges on them."[40]

The number of women and children killed, combined with the absence of any male prisoners, immediately raised questions about the nature of the operation and Baker's actions. Likewise, the loss of only one trooper killed and one injured should have elicited concerns about the level of resistance offered by the Piegans.[41] Even a cursory comparison with the Seventh Cavalry's operation at Washita in November 1868 and army losses would have highlighted an important point of contrast. The questions surrounding Baker's actions led the Senate to request copies of all the orders associated with the expedition in preparation for its own investigation and increasing pressure for a more complete explanation of events.

At the end of February, however, Sheridan and Sherman were still waiting for a complete report of Baker's expedition against the Piegan village, more than a month after the massacre. This delay seems odd based on the fact that Sheridan's initial statement to Sherman had come only six days after the operation. On February 28, Sheridan assumed a defensive tone in a reply to Sherman by highlighting the loss of 800 men, women, and children to Indian attacks in the region since 1862, alleged sexual assaults against white women, and the mutilation of the victims of these attacks. He asked, "So far as the wild Indians are concerned the problem which the good peoples of the country must decide upon is, who shall be killed the whites or the Indians?" Sheridan then blamed the "Indian Ring" and those individuals who profited by plunder at the expense of the tribes for spreading false information and rumors of atrocity. Despite these protestations, the House of Representatives joined the Senate in demanding all information related to the expedition in a resolution of March 3.[42]

In a letter to Sherman on March 18, Sheridan once again voiced his growing frustration with the criticism of the campaign. "In taking the offensive," he stated, "I have to select that season when I can catch the fiends, and if a village is attacked, and women and children killed, the responsibility is not with the soldiers, but with the peoples whose armies necessitate the attack." He then reminded Sherman that during the Civil War and the sieges of Vicksburg and Atlanta, Union forces had not stopped shelling those cities due to the presence of women and children. Based on his long service on the frontier, he argued that he was convinced that the soldiers were the only "practical friends" of the Indians. In Sheridan's opinion the only solution to the problem was to "force the "wild Indians" onto the reservation."[43]

These letters reveal a great deal about Sheridan's thoughts concerning the tribes' and the army's role in westward expansion. First, the use of the term "fiends" provides a general insight into the way in which he had come to view the tribes in general and the Plains Indians in particular. He had developed this view during his time in Texas and the Pacific Northwest in the 1850s, when he had witnessed numerous acts of atrocity committed by both whites and Indians. In his memoir Sheridan routinely referenced acts of brutality and murder by both sides. Ironically, it was the brutal killing of an Indian mother, her two sons and three daughters, and an infant at the hands of white settlers in the Pacific Northwest that he described as "an unparalleled outrage which nothing can justify or extenuate." Still, Sheridan was a man who had little sympathy for the Indians and was a firm believer in the efficacy of punishment and military force as instruments to shape their behavior. In 1871, he expressed exactly this view in his annual report to the secretary of war: "As soon as active operations against Indians cease, our duties change from administering punishment to giving protection." Second, his reference to the Civil War is telling because the brutal nature of that war and the massive loss of life influenced his views with respect to human sacrifice, which would come to be shared by many Europeans, including Adolf Hitler, in the wake of the Great War. For a man who had been involved in battles that resulted in thousands and tens of thousands of casualties, war was by its nature a "ruthless" activity; victims numbering only in the hundreds seemed a small price to pay for keeping the peace on the frontier.[44] It was a philosophy Sheridan maintained during his entire time out west. Finally, his comment about soldiers as the only "practical friends" of the Indians reflected his belief that without the military posts to keep the Indians on the reservations and to keep whites off this land, a flood of white settlement would overwhelm the Native inhabitants.

In his response to Sheridan's letter of March 18, Sherman used the phrase "the Piegan massacre" but then paradoxically stated, "I prefer to believe that the majority of the killed at Mountain Chief's camp were warriors, that the firing ceased the moment resistance was at an end, and that quarter was given to all who asked." Despite what Sherman chose to believe, it strains credulity to think that no male Indians were wounded or captured from a number that reached 120 in Baker's own initial estimate, a fact that argues for the army's adoption of a plan to kill all military-age males. This practice had clear precedent from other previous army actions, including Connor's expedition into the Powder River against the Sioux and the Arapahos. Furthermore, the high number of women and children killed resulted in large part from the indiscriminate nature of surprise morning assaults against Indian camps and the army's reliance on this tactic.[45] But the most damning fact, and one avoided by Sheridan and Sherman except in the initial report, was that only one soldier was killed in the attack and another injured in a fall from his horse. If the Piegans had demonstrated the fanatical resistance that led to the killing of each and every able-bodied man, there undoubtedly would have been a greater loss of life among the major's troops and assuredly a larger number of wounded soldiers. In the end Baker's expedition was intended to "punish" the Piegans in order to create an example to the other tribal bands in Montana Territory.

For Sheridan and his epigones, the first rule of Indian warfare involved the belief that punishment was the only effective method for dealing with depredations. The general advocated: "The trouble heretofore with Indians has been caused by the absence of all punishment for crimes committed against the settlements. No people, especially those in a wild state, can be expected to behave themselves where there are no laws providing punishment for crime." As a consequence of this belief, the objective of U.S. Army strategy, especially during the reservation period, focused on operations to "pursue and punish" Indian bands that had abandoned the reservation. The purpose of these actions centered on the capture or killing of Indians accused of raiding or "depredations" and represented a continuation of the existing policy of punishment and coercion in contrast to complete annihilation. Although the army may have pursued a goal of the annihilation of the tribes' military power rather than their physical extermination, Baker's expedition demonstrates that such a distinction was certainly not evident to a group of Piegans camped on the Marias River in January 1870.[46]

Wounded Knee: Intentional Massacre or Avoidable Atrocity?

The slaughter of the Lakota on the banks of Wounded Knee Creek on December 29, 1890, resulting in almost 200 killed and another 100 wounded, was as unnecessary as it was tragic for the Sioux under Chief Big Foot.[47] By 1890, the "frontier" as an area of armed white-and-Indian conflict was fast becoming an anachronism as the reservation policy, the loss of the buffalo herds, the completion of the transcontinental railroads, the enormous influx of white settlement, and policies of isolation and assimilation were transforming the western landscape and severely weakening the tribes' ability to resist the onslaught of white settlement and culture. The decline in Native power and the diminished threat posed by the Plains Indians during this decade was dramatically demonstrated in the annual reports of the secretary of war.

Secretary of the War Robert T. Lincoln's report of November 10, 1881, highlighted the declining concern and focus of the army with respect to its role in Indian affairs. Lincoln observed, "no serious Indian or other war has occurred, but great progress has been made in collecting and locating Indians, hitherto hostile, on their proper reservations." He then noted that Sitting Bull and the remaining members of his band had returned from Canada and were being held as "prisoners of war." In fact, there was perhaps no greater indication of the decline in the power of the northern Plains Indians than that represented by the Sioux leader's humiliating return to Fort

Buford with 186 of his followers the previous July. Riding on a haggard pony, a weary, hungry, and sullen Sitting Bull and his bedraggled band returned to his home only to be imprisoned for actions from the Great Sioux War, a conflict that now seemed a distant memory of Indian power for whites and the Sioux alike. By 1885, the secretary's report focused not on Indian unrest, but rather on the army's role in keeping white settlers out of Indian Territory and evicting illegal homesteaders from this area, a largely successful effort that helped maintain the peace. On a more threatening note, it did mention "some trouble" with the Mescalero Apaches in New Mexico and the Utes in Colorado, a situation that was quickly remedied by the government's delivery of promised supplies and rations.[48] In one respect, the 1885 report provided cause for concern even if Secretary Lincoln failed to note it: fear, and even potential hysteria, at rumors of Indian unrest lurked beneath the apparently calm surface in many areas of the West.

At the end of 1890, the commanding general of the army, Lieutenant General John M. Schofield, confidently reported, "The past year, like the two or three preceding, has been marked by an almost total absence of hostilities with any of the Indians, or any indication on their part of a determination to again go upon the warpath." Despite this optimistic tone, the apparent surface calm on the northern plains was being disturbed from an unlikely source. A Paiute Shaman, Wovoka, residing in Nevada began to preach a message that combined elements of Christian theology and Native mysticism concerning the coming of an Indian messiah. Wovoka told those who came to hear him preach: "When you get home you must make a dance to continue five days. . . . When you get home I shall give you a good cloud [rainfall]. . . . In the fall there will be such a rain as I have never given you before. . . . Do not tell the white people about this." Although this Ghost Dance religion advocated nonviolence, it did contain an apocalyptic element with its reference to the biblical description of the great flood and the destruction of the white people. Wovoka also prophesied that in the spring of 1891 this new messiah "would wipe the whites from the face of the earth," resurrect all dead Indians, bring back the buffalo herds, and restore the power of tribes.[49]

The Sioux were one of many tribes that, after hearing Wovoka's prophesy, embraced the Ghost Dance and its promise for a literal rebirth of Native life and culture. Although the level of commitment varied, Elaine Goodale, a supervisor of education for the Lakotas, remarked, "Suddenly everyone seemed unable to talk of anything but the 'new religion.'" For some, the performance of the Ghost Dance became a ritual of hope and an act of rebellion, especially among conservative Sioux "who steadfastly resisted being acculturated into the white image." According to Luther Standing Bear: "The Indians were really serious about it. . . . They felt that this new religion was going to rid them of the hated pale-faces who had antagonized them so long." Whatever its purpose, the Ghost Dance created unease within white settlements. Initial reports of this feeling in November were followed by a growing sense of impatience and anger at the perceived delay in government action by the middle of December. Some newspapers, like the *Omaha Bee*, used the Ghost Dance to raise the fear of a general Indian uprising under story headings such as "Fanatical Ghost Dancers Threaten Anyone Who Interferes" and "A Squaw's Warning."[50]

As Lakota adherents of the Ghost Dance expanded their activities and moved from their villages to remote sections of the reservation, several inexperienced and incompetent Indian agents fell victim to a growing hysteria that this threatened government authority. As had happened prior to the Piegan Massacre, they sent warnings and requests for army troops to meet feared uprisings and to arrest the leaders of the movement. One alarmed Indian agent telegraphed the Indian Bureau: "Indians are dancing in the snow and are wild and crazy. . . . We need protection and we need it now. The leaders should be arrested and confined at some military post until the matter is quieted, and this should be done at once." The Indian agent at the Pine Ridge Agency in South Dakota also warned of the potential for violence since "every Indian on the reservation is armed with a Winchester rifle, and when they are requested to stop these dances they strip themselves and are ready to fight." In response, the army and Brigadier General Nelson Miles cautioned that "the ghost dances should not be disturbed nor anything be done to precipitate a conflict" until an adequate number of troops could be concentrated and "it can be judged of the measures that may be necessary and advisable."[51]

On November 13, President Benjamin Harrison ordered Secretary of War Redfield Proctor to take action, resulting in the transfer of units from across the United States into the area. The arrival of federal troops raised the level of tension across the reservations.

Chief Red Cloud blamed the Interior Department, not the army, for generating hysteria about the Ghost Dance, stating: "The Indian Department [sic] called for soldiers to shoot down the Indians whom it had starved into despair. . . . The army will, I hope, keep us safe and help us." As troops moved onto the reservations, the decision to arrest Sitting Bull as a "ringleader" of the movement led to a public outcry in the East after he was killed on December 15 in a gunfight between his supporters and the Indian policemen sent to take him into custody. An editorial in the *Omaha World Herald* joined the chorus of criticism against the government's handling of the situation by exclaiming: "There seems to be no end to the blunders, crimes and atrocities into which the government is led in the treatment of the Indians. It is time for a change."[52] Despite Sitting Bull's shooting, the Sioux remained peaceful, if justifiably wary, in the face of the overwhelming military force that confronted them.

The uneasy peace would be shattered on the banks of Wounded Knee Creek on December 29. A detachment of the Seventh Cavalry under Major Samuel Whitside searched for Big Foot's band with orders to "find his trail and follow, or find his hiding place and capture him," with additional instructions, "if he fights, destroy him." Whitside's troopers finally caught up with Big Foot's band of over 300 men, women, and children on the afternoon of December 28 and escorted them to the army's base camp on the creek. Since the Indians were hungry and many lacked adequate shelter for the evening, the major provided rations and several army tents for the overnight bivouac. Later that evening Colonel James W. Forsyth arrived and took command, with orders to disarm the Indians and to escort them to the railroad for shipment to a military prison in Nebraska. According to Turning Hawk, a Sioux at Pine Ridge, it was exactly the widespread and "oft-repeated" rumor that the army intended to disarm and dismount the tribes that had caused the greatest consternation among the Indians and most risked violent resistance.[53]

In preparation for disarming Big Foot's band, Forsyth surrounded the Indian encampment with 500 soldiers and placed four Hotchkiss cannons on a nearby hill. In his orders to local commanders, General Miles had repeatedly warned not to allow the soldiers "to become mixed up with the Indians friendly or otherwise." On the morning of December 29, the confrontation between Forsyth's command and the Sioux was about to reach its flash point with the order that the Indians relinquish their firearms, "their most cherished of all earthly possessions."⁵⁴ The soldiers, however, soon discovered that the Sioux were turning in obsolescent weapons, including two ancient "blunderbusses." During a subsequent search for concealed weapons, the situation turned volatile. As the soldiers rummaged through the Sioux tipis and tents, they found an assortment of tools and suspected weapons, including knives, axes, and even tent stakes. After the search of the camp, Forsyth then ordered a body search of the men. One warrior wearing a "Ghost shirt," believed to be impervious to bullets, became increasingly agitated and called for resistance to the order to surrender their arms. An Indian eyewitness, Spotted Horse, recalled hearing the first shot that "killed an [army] officer," which resulted in a volley of gunfire and a general melee between the soldiers and the warriors.⁵⁵

After waiting several minutes for a clear line of fire, the crews at the Hotchkiss guns loaded with canister and commenced shooting into the camp. When the firing stopped, some 200 Sioux lay dead or mortally wounded, including an estimated sixty-two women and children. In addition, twenty-five soldiers perished and thirty-five others were wounded during the exchange. The number of casualties on both sides resulted in part from the initial ferocity of the action and the resulting indiscriminate fire of both the artillery guns and individual soldiers. One newspaper correspondent at the scene wrote: "It was a war of extermination now with the troopers. . . . About the only tactic was to kill while it could be done whenever an Indian could be seen." From the events leading up to the shooting, it is apparent that the army had not intended to commit a massacre, but poor decision making by Forsyth and indiscriminate shooting, especially by the Hotchkiss crews, led to an act of avoidable atrocity that emerged alongside Sand Creek as a symbol of white repression. A later attempt by a military board of inquiry to censure Forsyth for his actions at Wounded Knee was overruled by General Schofield, who concluded that the colonel's command had displayed "excellent discipline" and "great forbearance." More telling, however, was Schofield's comment that ' the interests of the military service do not . . . demand any further proceedings in this case."⁵⁶

In any event, the ability of the U.S. Army to amass rapidly a major combat force in the area along with an offer to allow a Sioux delegation to travel to Washington, D.C., to present their "well founded grievances" helped prevent a major Indian war from erupting on the northern plains.⁵⁷ In his annual address to Congress in

1891, President Harrison reflected on the events at Wounded Knee, remarking, "these Indians had some just complaints, especially in the matter of the reduction of the appropriation for rations and in the delays attending the enactment of laws to enable the Department to perform the engagements entered into with them, is probably true." But he added, "the Sioux tribes are naturally warlike and turbulent, and their warriors were excited by their medicine men and chiefs, who preached the coming of an Indian messiah who was to give them power to destroy their enemies." In the end, the president proved equally willing to acknowledge the grounds for Sioux grievances as well as the army's response. In one of the most thoughtful evaluations of the events, Robert Utley described the actions at Wounded Knee as a "tragedy," but he conceded that "the vivid memory of shattered corpses and maimed survivors makes the Indians' preference for massacre wholly understandable. In a recent and detailed examination of the events at Wounded Knee, Jerome Greene used both terms, "tragedy" and "massacre," to describe the events that led to the confrontation and the aftershocks of the killings. From a Sioux perspective, "it was a slaughter, a massacre" in which innocent men, women, and children had been "shot down without even a chance to defend themselves."[58]

Whether seen as a "tragedy" or a "massacre," Wounded Knee effectively signaled the end of the Indian Wars. In his detailed study of the fighting, Greene determined, "It likely could have been avoided with improved communication and greater tolerance and patience all around, unfamiliar concepts at the time when the government sought to impress its control over tribal populations." Another historian perceptively concluded, "While it was the Indians who were doing the dancing it was really the whites who saw the ghosts." In this sense, Wounded Knee represents the essential element of Indian and white relations throughout the period of westward expansion, the inability or the unwillingness of either side to understand the culture or perspective of the other. Later in his life, Black Elk shared his visions of "butchered women and children lying heaped and scattered along the crooked gulch" and reflected on the ultimate consequence of the massacre: "And I can see that something else died there in the bloody mud. . . . A people's dream died there."[59]

The actions taken by the army at Sand Creek, Wounded Knee Creek, and on the Marias River clearly demonstrated a belief in the use of "punishment" or mass murder as a means to "chastise" or to "send a message" to the Indian tribes. Despite these cases of atrocity, it is important to note that such acts engendered controversy and protest in Congress and in the court of public opinion. Both the Indian Bureau and the War Department were forced to account for their actions, even if justice for the victims proved illusory. Likewise, it is the exceptional nature of such events that accounts for the iconic status of Sand Creek and Wounded Knee in American history.

If mass murder and atrocity proved the exception rather than the rule in army operations in the American West, this was clearly not the case for the actions of the Wehrmacht and SS and police forces on the eastern front.

Violence and Atrocity in the "Wild East"

From the discussion in the previous chapter, it is clear that acts of mass murder and atrocity were inextricably intertwined not only with conventional military operations in Poland and the Soviet Union but also in the actions of military and police forces in the everyday practice of subjugating the indigenous peoples of the East. But it was not only members of the Wehrmacht, SS, and police who participated in mass murder. The Nazi East, like the American West, had its own vigilantism as witnessed by the actions of ethnic Germans during the invasion of Poland. The organization and use of these residents in the conduct of mass murder represented a case of organized vigilantism that set a precedent for the later use of auxiliary units in the campaign against the Soviet Union. In Poland alone, approximately 100,000 men served as ethnic German auxiliaries, many as members of death squads that routinely participated in the torture of Polish gentiles and Jews and the summary execution of an estimated 10,000 persons.[60]

In discussing the conduct of massacres in the East, it is important to remember that deliberate atrocity formed a core element of Nazi thinking related to the subjugation and rule of the occupied territories. In fact, the issuing of the criminal orders that preceded the invasion into Russia demonstrates in part the method by which the road to annihilation was paved with the cooperation of military, SS, and police authorities, framing the campaign in apocalyptic terms of either victory and racial supremacy or defeat and racial extermination. Although the scope and scale of annihilatory practices in the East staggers the imagination, it should not be forgotten that the use of massacre and cold-blooded murder was not limited to Poland and the Soviet Union. The execution of American POWs by SS forces in December 1944 in the so-called Malmédy Massacre is widely acknowledged. Less well known, however, is the Wehrmacht's murder in 1940 of as many as 3,000 black African soldiers in French service and the hostage taking and brutal reprisal instituted in France during the military occupation.[61] Likewise, German generals ordered numerous massacres against the Third Reich's erstwhile Italian partners, actions described in a war-crimes investigation as constituting "a systematic policy of extermination, pillage, piracy, and terrorism." In a final example, the commander of German airborne forces, General Kurt Student, authorized large-scale reprisals against Cretan villages and the massacre of civilians on the island in the wake of the successful invasion in the spring of 1941.[62] If mass murder and reprisal manifested itself outside of the East based on the racial precepts of Nazi ideology, it should not be surprising that such actions formed a central element of occupation policies in Poland and the Soviet Union.

The following discussion provides a small sampling of the massacres committed by Wehrmacht soldiers, units of the SS and police, and indigenous auxiliaries. The examination of these cases is intended to offer specific detail on the circumstances, motives, and nature of mass murder in the East. The ability to look at these events in greater detail also provides additional evidence with which to compare and contrast the actions taken in the American West with those in the Nazi East.

Massacre at Ostrów

During the invasion of Poland and the establishment of Nazi rule, numerous acts of murder and atrocity were committed by SS and police forces as well as Wehrmacht soldiers (as detailed in the previous chapter). Yet the events that occurred in the Polish town of Ostrów Mazowieck on November 11, 1939, offer a glimpse into the methods by which racial hatred manifested itself in an act of mass murder and the first known case of the physical annihilation of an entire Jewish community in the East.[63] In this case it was "ordinary"

German policemen, not soldiers or members of the SS, who initiated the action that led to the cold-blooded murder of over 350 men, women, and children in less than two hours.

Located to the northeast of Warsaw in the General Government, Ostrów was a town with a small Jewish population. On November 9, the first anniversary of the *Kristallnacht*, or the "Night of Broken Glass," pogroms, the outbreak of a fire provided the pretext for a local Nazi *Kreisleiter* (district leader) to claim that the town's Jews were responsible for arson. To combat the blaze, the Nazi official ordered a group of Jews to work the reciprocating arms of a water pump, during which he along with several other men, including a soldier and a policeman, proceeded to deliver blows on the Jews in rhythm with the pumping action. The next day men from Reserve Police Battalion 11 gathered the town's Jews together, men, women, and children, and locked them into the basement of a local brewery, sending word of these arrests to the commander of Police Regiment Warsaw, Colonel of the Police Karl Brenner. Subsequently, Brenner ordered Captain of the Police Hans Hoffmann to assemble a group of men and to proceed to Ostrów to convene a police court in order to establish the facts and to punish the alleged arsonists.[64]

In reality, the fate of the Jews was sealed before the policemen left for Ostrów. The testimony of one of them confirms the decision to execute the Jews already had been made prior to the unit's departure from Warsaw. According to a senior enlisted member of the unit, Hoffman approached him on the night before the mission with orders to put together a group of men who were "especially brave" and "in possession of the necessary toughness" for a "very important affair" the following day.[65] In selecting Hoffmann to lead the action, Brenner had chosen well. The thirty-five-year-old Hoffman had joined the police in 1924 at the age of twenty and became an officer five years later. He was also an "old fighter," entering the Nazi Party in November 1932, and a member of the SS.[66]

Early on the morning of November 11, Hoffmann and a police contingent of some thirty-five men from Police Battalion 91 left Warsaw for Ostrów. When the policemen arrived in the town, they were informed that a group of Jews had been condemned to death for arson. Shortly thereafter, men from Police Battalion 11 began escorting the town's entire Jewish population from the basement of the brewery to the execution site. The fact that a mass grave was prepared *prior* to the arrival of the contingent from Warsaw is clear evidence of the premeditation involved. Armed with rifles and led by 1st Lieutenant of the Police Otto Franz (a pseudonym), a platoon leader and member of the SS, the policemen executed men, women, and children in groups of ten as the victims were led to the edge of the grave.

In his postwar testimony Franz remembered having to give the command to fire for the first group of victims. After this initial command, the policemen required no further prompting and fired on their own. The appearance of the children and infants did raise some concerns among the executioners. Franz claimed that when he saw children approaching the site, he requested to be replaced, a request refused by Hoffmann. Interestingly, it was not until the appearance of the children that Franz appeared to have second thoughts about the killings. Perhaps in reaction to these concerns, one participant remembered an officer justifying the murders by alleging Jewish complicity in a failed assassination attempt against Hitler in Munich a few days earlier.[67] The need for additional justification apparently was necessary when some of the policemen questioned the rationale for killing children and infants for the crime of arson, which they could not have committed. In the end, the men pulled their triggers and murdered 156 men and 208 women and children in groups of ten during the next ninety minutes.[68]

The massacre of the entire Jewish population of Ostrów by men from Police Battalion 91 was an important event based on its scale—an entire Jewish community—and the age of its victims, including children. Still, the murder of both Poles and Polish Jews began early in the occupation, and this event proved less an anomaly than a natural extension of previous actions. During a campaign designed to enflame racial hatred and an occupation built on the principle of exploitation, these murders provide but one example of the boundaries of the possible for the men serving in police units. The massacre also offers a clear example of a cold-blooded atrocity. These Jews had not fired upon German forces, nor had there been a loss of life in the fires they allegedly set. Additionally, the fact that a policeman who joined the battalion after the Polish campaign remembered being shown pictures of men and women kneeling before mass graves prior to their execution demonstrates that Ostrów was not seen as a dark chapter in the unit's history never to be opened again. Instead, showing pictures of executions to new members of the unit served two purposes. First, it demonstrated a sense of pride or accomplishment; second, it served to further socialize these new men by establishing the limits (or lack thereof) of accepted behavior and creating expectations for future actions. In the coming months and years, the men of both Police Battalion 11 and Police Battalion 91 became involved in mass murder on a scale that dwarfed the massacre at Ostrów, but it was in this small town that they first demonstrated their commitment to the regime and its racial objectives.[69]

Massacre at Babi Yar

Without doubt, the massacre of over 33,000 Jews in September 1941 at a site near the Ukrainian city of Kiev represents one of the most infamous examples of murder conducted one bullet at a time. As in the case of Ostrów two years earlier, the German administration took advantage of an incident to serve as the pretext for the murder of that city's entire Jewish population. After capturing Kiev on September 19, Wehrmacht forces, accompanied by a detachment from Einsatzgruppe C, entered and established their headquarters. The military administration then ordered the internment of the entire adult-male population of the city, a policy subsequently modified by infantry units focused on the internment of Jewish men and some Jewish women. A series of bomb explosions on September 24 destroyed German offices and military quarters and killed dozens of soldiers.[70] In the wake of the blasts, Wehrmacht, SS, police, and Nazi administrators met to discuss reprisal plans. This meeting led to the decision to eliminate Kiev's entire Jewish population despite the fact that there was no evidence connecting Jews to the bombings.[71]

In preparation for this, a military propaganda unit prepared thousands of leaflets and posted them throughout the city on September 28. The leaflets ordered all Jews to assemble at a street corner near the Jewish cemetery by 8:00 A.M. the following day, bringing with them "documents, money, valuables, as well as warm clothes" in preparation for their planned resettlement. The notices warned that any who failed to appear and were subsequently captured would be executed. On September 29 as directed, tens of thousands of Kiev's Jewish population assembled at the designated intersection. One Ukrainian woman watched the procession from her balcony and described the scene in her diary: "People are moving in an endless row, overflowing the entire street and sidewalks. Women and men are walking, young girls, children, old people, and entire families." She continued: "Many carry their belongings on wheelbarrows, but most of them are carrying things on their backs. . . . It went on like this for very long, the entire day and only in the evening did the crowd become smaller."[72] Over thirty thousand men, women, and children, with most of their worldly possessions, marched in the direction of the Jewish cemetery, where they were met by German officials who examined their papers and verified their ancestry.

Two police battalions, Ukrainian auxiliaries, and Wehrmacht soldiers established a cordon around the cemetery, which bordered a large ravine known locally as Babi Yar (Grandmother Ravine). After passing the initial checkpoint, the Germans confiscated the valuables and ordered the Jews to continue toward the ravine. Before reaching Babi Yar, they had to run a gauntlet no larger than five feet across lined by members of the cordoning force armed with truncheons and clubs. One female survivor recalled this horrifying part of the ordeal: "Blows rained down on the people as they passed through. . . . Brutal blows, immediately drawing blood. . . . The soldiers kept shouting: 'Schnell, schnell!' laughing happily, as if they were watching a circus act." The worst, however, was yet to come as Ukrainian militia ordered the battered and bloodied people to take off their clothes and enter the ravine, where members of Einsatzgruppe C waited with weapons in hand. A German eyewitness described what followed: "When they reached the bottom of the ravine they were seized by members of the police [sic] and made to lie down on top of Jews who had already been shot. . . . The corpses were literally in layers. A police marksman came along and shot each Jew in the neck with a submachine gun. . . . It went on this way uninterruptedly, with no distinction being made between men, women, and children."[73]

The executions continued throughout the day and, due to the large number of victims, were not concluded until the following day. The scale was in fact so great that the Wehrmacht had to supply the einsatzgruppe with additional ammunition. The continual firing could be heard clearly in the surrounding neighborhoods, and for non-Jewish Ukrainians the fate of their neighbors was apparent. After the two-day massacre, the einsatzgruppe reported the murder of a total of 33,771 Jews as military engineers detonated charges designed to collapse the walls of the ravine and cover the bodies. The following days were spent in sorting the banknotes, valuables, and clothing of the victims for shipment to the Third Reich, where the clothing was to be made available to ethnic Germans by the National Socialist Welfare Organization.[74]

The massacre at Babi Yar is perhaps the most notorious mass killing of World War II and in this tragic respect occupies the same iconic position as that of Sand Creek does for historians of the American West. It offers a number of insights into the conduct and objectives of the Nazi regime in the Soviet Union. First and foremost, the use of the einsatzgruppen as "purpose built" instruments of mass murder in support of Nazi annihilatory policy is plainly evident. The method of the killing and the number of victims is also stunning when one considers that the murders literally involved standing behind or climbing on top of the victims and firing from close range, a procedure that left the shooters with the blood and gore of their victims on their uniforms. Second, the murder of thousands of women and children, including infants, illustrates the ambition of Nazi racial planners and the determination displayed by those tasked with carrying out these policies. In this sense the massacre indicates that complete physical extermination, not punishment or coercion, formed the overarching objective toward the Jews. Third, the events at Babi Yar offers the ultimate example of cold-blooded atrocity, the distinguishing feature of German occupation policy in the East. Finally, the support provided by the police, the army, and local auxiliaries for the killings points to the broader complicity and cooperation of these groups in mass murder, a precedent established earlier during the Polish campaign. But subsequent massacres demonstrated that it was not only Himmler's SS and police forces who took a leading role in mass murder.

Baranivka

Babi Yar reveals the close relationship between SS, police, and the Wehrmacht during the campaign into Russia. In fact, Himmler valued good relations with his army counterparts and emphasized the same to his SS and police commanders. In a directive of August 2, 1941, he ordered these leaders to maintain the "greatest amity" with Wehrmacht headquarters and to "fulfill their wishes as far as possible." In one respect, the cooperation between army and SS and police forces not only reveals a convergence of goals but also reflects the practical considerations associated with securing a battlefront that stretched from Finland to the Caucasus. In short, the Wehrmacht required additional manpower to assist in the pacification and control of the areas behind the front as well as those areas placed under German civil administration. Although army commanders often facilitated and assisted in acts of mass murder and atrocity against the native populations of the East, they still recognized the leading role of Himmler's SS and police forces in the conduct of genocide. This relationship was emphasized in Wehrmacht directives, including an order of November 24, 1941, that discussed the fate of the Jews and the Sinti and Roma (Gypsies). Citing previous instructions, it stated, "the Jews must disappear from the countryside and the Gypsies also must be annihilated." In addition, "The conduct of *larger* Jewish actions is not the responsibility of units of the [army] division. These are to be conducted by civil and police authorities." Still, Wehrmacht forces did receive approval for actions against "larger or smaller groups of Jews" in cases that involved security concerns or in the conduct of reprisals.[75]

The existence of the November 24 directive and the emphasis on establishing lines of primary authority offers two important insights. First, it establishes the leading role of SS and police forces in large-scale killing operations. Second, and perhaps most interestingly, the order would not have been issued if army higher headquarters had not received information concerning Wehrmacht units taking their own initiative in the conduct of mass murder against the putative racial enemies of the Third Reich, the Jews and the "Gypsies." In fact, an incident that occurred in the Ukrainian village of Baranivka earlier that month provides an excellent example of the German army's involvement in massacre and acts of atrocity on the eastern front.

On the evening of November 4, 1941, a small group of military engineers, one officer and three enlisted soldiers, decided to stop at the village of Baranivka for the evening before continuing their journey to the headquarters of the Sixth Army. The officer, a Colonel Sinz, and his men took quarters with the village doctor and his family in the local clinic. Shortly thereafter, information on their presence reached a local partisan group, which made plans to attack. Sometime around midnight, the partisans surrounded the clinic and began their assault, killing Sinz and two soldiers while the remaining soldier escaped out of a window and into the nearby woods. The sole survivor, a Corporal Schneider, evaded the partisans and arrived days later at the German garrison to report the attack.[76]

The killing of a colonel attached to the headquarters staff of the Sixth Army, under the command of Field Marshal Walter von Reichenau, certainly received attention at the highest levels and raised the stakes for the German response. Reichenau earlier had instructed his troops in an order of October 10: "In the eastern sphere the soldier is not simply a fighter according to the rules of war, but the supporter of a ruthless racial ideology. . . . For this reason soldiers must show full understanding for the necessity for the severe but just atonement being required of the Jewish subhumans." His army responded with a number of punitive raids and antipartisan operations led by the 62nd Infantry Division. These series of actions over the following two months provide important insights into the army's use of "repressive violence," including hostage taking and reprisals.[77]

Reichenau's infamous order appears to have had a noticeable effect on his army even prior to the attack on Colonel Sinz. For example, a battalion of the 62nd Division assigned to Reichenau's command reported the summary execution of forty-five "partisans" and 168 Jews after entering the Ukrainian city of Myrhorod on October 28. The unit's commander justified the murder of the Jews based on their alleged "ties to the partisans." In fact, General Walter Keiner, the division's commander, had issued instructions to single out Jews for reprisal actions earlier that summer. Three days after the Myrhorod killings, the battalion executed twenty-one Ukrainians in another operation. This infantry battalion, composed mostly of German reservists who had been in intense combat over the previous four months, appeared to have little difficulty in adopting draconian reprisal actions against the local population. Such was the character of the unit given orders on November 9 to take the "harshest of reprisals" and "punitive measures against the guilty residents" involved in the attack on Sinz.[78]

That evening, soldiers from the battalion arrived at Baranivka, encircled the village, and assembled the villagers for interrogation. Residents at first refused to speak, but threats to execute hostages led one man to reveal the home of one of the alleged partisans. The husband was absent from the house, so the soldiers shot the wife and burned down the structure. After executing ten adult males from the village in plain sight of their spouses and children, the soldiers began a systematic effort to raze the village to the ground and to confiscate livestock and food stores. In truth, the limited number of executions made this a "very restrained reprisal" by German standards at that time. Only three days later, however, restraint was abandoned during an operation in the nearby village of Velyka Obukhivka when a company from the battalion came under fire upon approach. A brief but intense firefight resulted in eight German casualties and the deaths of numerous Soviet partisans, whose surviving comrades were forced to flee to a nearby swamp. After the fight, the Germans decided to take reprisal actions against the villagers for failing to warn them of the ambush. Soldiers deployed throughout Velyka and "began setting the houses on fire, working their way toward the center of the town and killing every man, woman, and child they could find. They shot people outside their homes as they attempted to flee from burning buildings or drove them into their houses and burned them alive." At the end of the day, the troops had destroyed the village and massacred between 200 and 300 men, women, and children.[79]

The actions of this infantry battalion offer several insights into the Wehrmacht's role in the conduct of atrocity in the East. First, the reprisal actions taken by these soldiers had been sanctioned at the highest levels of command prior to Baranivka. Additionally, the racial character of these orders, with the explicit identification of Jews as targets for mass murder and reprisal, was apparent, a practice also used by Wehrmacht units conducting reprisals in Serbia. In the Soviet Union, Wehrmacht units from the 707th Infantry Division murdered 10,000 Jews and 9,000 non-Jews in various operations, while units from the Eighteenth Army murdered 800 Jews in October 1941 and soldiers from the Sixteenth Army executed a total of 2,000 Jews from several villages. Likewise, battalion members who had proved willing to kill Jews in Myrhorod also executed twenty-three Jewish "refugees" on November 23 on racial grounds alone.[80] These racially motivated killings had the hallmark of cold-blooded atrocity. In contrast, an analysis of the incident at Velyka lends itself to the category of hot-blooded atrocity based on the losses suffered by the unit in the ambush, the short time between the combat and the reprisal action, and the fact that the victim group consisted of ethnic Ukrainians. In any event, both cases must be framed within the existing ideological and racial framework of the campaign in the East, one that not only promoted but also encouraged acts of mass killing. Finally, the use of hostage taking and reprisal killings emerged as a distinguishing feature of German military occupation policy in the East and provided ample precedent for mass murder by Wehrmacht forces throughout the war.

Cumulative Annihilation: Hostage Taking and Reprisal

The use of hostage taking and the conduct of reprisals by Wehrmacht forces occurred earlier during the campaign in Poland (as noted in chapter 3). This policy emerged from the very first days of the war as can be seen in the testimony of Władysława Bera concerning the killing of her husband and stepson by German soldiers on September 4, 1939. Bera recalled: "The men were surrounded and ordered to raise their hands. They were driven to a site near the fire station and stood up against a fence. I ran to them to save my husband. . . . I was eight months pregnant at the time, but a German kicked me, I fell and lost consciousness. When I awoke the execution was over. I saw the bodies of thirteen dead men." In another example, the wounding of a German soldier on September 9 near Bydgoszcz (Bromberg) resulted in an order from General Walter Braemer for the execution of 20 hostages in the city's market the following day, a number subsequently raised to 120. The conduct of such actions reflected a "veneration" of violence in the Third Reich. With respect to the Polish campaign, Alexander Rossino correctly observed that reprisal actions and the destruction of homes "brutalized the soldiers instructed to carry them out . . . [and] demonstrated . . . [a] willingness to kill civilians and destroy property."[81] Furthermore, this type of behavior reflected the essential belief in German racial superiority and a readiness to employ mass murder as a tool of occupation, which found expression in other areas under occupation as well.

The German occupation of Serbia in the spring of 1941 provides another example of an institutionalized Wehrmacht reprisal policy against the local population, typified by the "pitiless exercise of terror." General Franz Böhme, the commanding general in Serbia, issued instructions to the 342nd Infantry Division authorizing the execution of one hundred hostages for every German soldier killed and the execution of fifty hostages for every soldier wounded. Once again, the use of draconian reprisal policies in the Balkans campaigns mirrored the racial and ideological principles that provided the foundation for the later attack on the Soviet Union. Furthermore, the Wehrmacht in these areas, not the SS and police forces, took the initiative in establishing the standards for mass murder and organized atrocity, with predictable results. For example, an attack by Serbian partisans on the German garrison in Šabac on September 23 led to a ten-hour battle for control of the town before the partisans withdrew. In the wake of the attack, General Böhme ordered the roundup of the town's entire male population between the ages of fourteen and seventy and their incarceration in a concentration camp. On September 24, military forces (with some support from the police) took 4,459 males into custody and summarily executed an additional 75 men. During the first four weeks of their duty in Serbia, the 342nd Division executed 4,408 civilians and transferred an additional 25,735 to concentration camps. These actions were not exceptional as evidenced by the fact that Wehrmacht units executed over 20,000 civilians in the five-month period between September 1, 1941, and February 12, 1942, a murderous wave that, according to one historian, "allows for a comparison with the extermination of the Jews in the East."[82]

Although not a part of the campaign on the eastern front, the invasion of Crete and the occupation of Greece provide additional examples of the Wehrmacht's use of hostage taking and reprisal against populations. The airborne invasion of Crete encountered strong resistance from some of the island's residents and its British defenders. As a result of alleged atrocities against German soldiers, the commander of the Luftwaffe, Hermann Göring, ordered the conduct of reprisals against civilians independent of military-court review. As a result, German troops occupied villages and in several cases executed the entire male population, including in Alikianos, where the town's forty-two adult males were shot in front of the church before the eyes of their wives, mothers, and children. In May and June alone, Wehrmacht soldiers executed at least 400 persons, including men and women, and destroyed eighteen villages. Over two years later, on December 13, 1943, German soldiers once again demonstrated their willingness to engage in mass murder by executing more than 500 men and boys from the village of Kalavrita in the Peloponnese in reprisal for a partisan operation that resulted in the killing of eighty-one captured Germans on the seventh. The reprisal on Kalavrita included the destruction of the town by fire and the internment of the entire male population in the valley below. German troops then surrounded the men and the boys with machine guns and began to fire into the crowd. One young boy, fourteen-year-old Ntinos Dimopoulos, shouted "I'm still in school. I want to live!" before he was cut down by a bullet. As the smoke from the machine-gun fire cleared, individual soldiers moved among the group, firing single pistol shots as a coup de grace. From that day forward, Kalavrita became known as the "town of the widows."[83] By the end of the war, thousands of cities, towns, and villages could lay claim to the same title, or in many cases, "the town of the dead."

Comparing the Nazi East and the American West

The preceding discussion clearly demonstrates that atrocity and mass murder were common elements in both the American West and the Nazi campaigns of conquest, not only in the East but also throughout occupied Europe. Violence was a ubiquitous aspect of both national projects. In the West the threat or actuality of gunfights and physical conflict formed a pervasive aspect of everyday life, whether on the frontier, in mining settlements, or in the interaction between whites with Indians, whites with whites, and Indians with other tribes. According to Richard Brown, the cowboy's code was "frequently not a word and a blow but a word and a bullet." This culture of violence also found its expression in an "ideology of vigilantism," a willingness of individuals and groups to take the law into their own hands. In turn, vigilantism was usually a reflection of economic interests and an instrument of "the conservative, consolidating authority of capital" aimed at the "incorporation" of the West into the United States. In comparison, National Socialism as a political philosophy glorified violence and extolled struggle as part of the natural order of existence, but it was blood and race, not economic motives, that provided the fundamental impetus for conflict. In *Mein Kampf* Hitler framed this worldview with the statement, "He who wants to live should fight, therefore, and he who does not want to battle in this world of eternal struggle does not deserve to be alive." Nowhere more was this philosophy actualized than in the Nazi-occupied East, where in the words of one historian, "Violence was a constant presence in the war . . . , whether at the front, in the anti-partisan war or in the daily oppression and exploitation of the civilian population."[84]

As with the objectives of military strategy, the scale and the scope of massacre and atrocity in the East distinguishes it in a fundamental sense from the American West. Without doubt, the Sand Creek Massacre, the Piegan (or Marias River) Massacre, and the killings at Wounded Knee were reprehensible acts of slaughter aimed at "punishing" the Indians. Yet Sand Creek and Wounded Knee are also iconic events in western history in part because they represent the exceptional rather than the normal or routine. In contrast, the massacre of some 34,000 Jews at Babi Yar was only part of the larger mass murder of 1.5 million Jews in the killing fields of the East, literally one bullet at a time.[85] In fact, face-to-face killing was so widespread and sanguinary in the East that only the most horrific examples from among *thousands*, if not tens of thousands, of such actions are chosen to symbolize the whole. Likewise, the gas chambers and crematoria of Auschwitz remain the iconic symbols of Nazi atrocity. Despite the scale of Nazi mass murder, this does not lessen the crimes and murders perpetrated against the Native tribes, but it does demonstrate essential and important differences that distinguish these two national projects of conquest.

If the scope and scale of atrocity provide measures of comparison, then one also must consider the issues of intent and premeditation associated with the use of coercive force in each case. The Sand Creek and Piegan Massacres undoubtedly were premeditated acts. In the case of the former, the Colorado Volunteers acted on base racial prejudice while their commander, Colonel Chivington, combined racial prejudice with political ambition. In the case of the latter, Major Baker's planned attack against the Piegan encampment on the Marias River was intended to "punish" one specific band. This operation reflected a widespread belief that the selective use of deadly force against particular groups of Indians served the dual purpose of "chastising" the "guilty" and "signaling" other bands concerning the potential consequences of failing to abide by the rules and norms established by the Indian Bureau. Finally, both the Sand Creek and the Piegan Massacres were examples of cold-blooded atrocity. In comparison, Wounded Knee provides another example of atrocity, but it was incompetence and overreaction versus premeditation that led to an avoidable act of mass killing.

One factor that was not lacking on the eastern front was that of premeditation. In fact, the creation of militarized SS and police units with the explicit task of engaging in the systematic and routine murder of putative racial and political enemies is a critical point of distinction. The einsatzgruppen and the police battalions were purpose-built units established for the express purpose of mass killing and massacre. In a directive to his SS and police commanders, Himmler described this as a "holy duty," the obligation to "eliminate every source of resistance without consideration, to conduct the most severe measures involving the just execution of the enemies of the German people."[86] The campaign against the Soviet Union was framed by Hitler, the Nazi Party, and Wehrmacht leaders as a "war of annihilation," an apocalyptic contest that involved the necessity to discard "antiquated" concepts of chivalry and comradeship in favor of necessary harshness and brutality. The entire campaign, including the "hunger policy," was built upon the premise for cold-blooded, premeditated mass murder. The massacres at Ostrów and Babi Yar exemplified the objective of the extermination of the Jews, while the reprisals at Baranivka and Kalavrita provide examples of the use of mass killing as a reflection of perceived German racial and political dominance. For the conquered peoples under the heel of the Third Reich, mass murder and atrocity proved the rule and not the exception. In this regard, the conduct of antipartisan operations by SS and police forces and Wehrmacht soldiers provided the perfect pretext for annihilation.

CHAPTER 5

WAR IN THE SHADOWS

GUERRILLA WARFARE IN THE WEST AND THE EAST

The U.S. Army's operations against the Apaches in the Desert Southwest and the German prosecution of antipartisan operations in the East provide an apt point of comparison for evaluating the character and objectives of military strategy and the nature of policies designed to subjugate local populations. The choice of Apache warfare in the American Southwest results from the tribes' effective use of irregular, or guerrilla, tactics. Guerrilla warfare is often described as the "war of the weak" or the "war of the flea" because it is normally pursued by groups facing a disadvantage in terms of numbers of combatants or technology. In his writings on the subject, the Cuban revolutionary Che Guevara remarked: "The guerrilla band is not to be considered inferior to the army against which it fights simply because it is inferior in firepower. Guerrilla warfare is used by the side which is supported by a majority but which possesses a much smaller number of arms for use in defense against oppression." Although the guerrilla force is militarily weaker than its opponent, its major source of strength comes from the ability to gain popular support, which allows the fighter to gain intelligence, protection, and sustenance from the local population.[1]

Confronting the use of irregular tactics presents conventional armies with a number of difficulties, especially if the guerrillas have the advantage in popular support and a detailed knowledge of the terrain. Throughout history, armies faced with irregular tactics have been exasperated by their inability to achieve a decisive engagement. Brigadier General John Pope described the difficulty in "destroying or capturing" the Apaches: "When closely pursued the Indians scatter like partridges through the mountains, and the pursuit becomes the hunting down of individual Indians instead of open warfare." The superior knowledge of the terrain and the use of local intelligence has repeatedly allowed guerrillas to avoid the blows of a technologically superior force, leading to extreme frustration for the conventional force and often the adoption of indiscriminate reprisal and atrocity policies. For example, a British observer during the Boer War in South Africa observed, "If there is one certain education to be drawn from past experience it is that guerrilla tactics . . . [used] by a resourceful and persistent enemy, have invariably led to a protracted struggle, during which the invading armies against which they fought have suffered a series of minor disasters and regrettable incidents."[2] These "regrettable incidents" often involve the use of indiscriminate reprisals that serve the purpose of further reinforcing popular support for the guerrillas.

According to Mao Tse Tung, "the first law of [guerrilla] warfare is to preserve ourselves and destroy the enemy," a statement that perfectly echoed the Apaches' dictum "Kill your enemy and save yourself." In contrast, the defeat or isolation of guerrillas from their sources of support provides the formula for the conventional army to achieve victory. In *Counterinsurgency Warfare: Theory and Practice*, David Galula made the distinction between two general strategies for dealing with such partisan warfare: the direct and the indirect approach. The former focuses on a strategy of annihilation aimed at the destruction of the partisan and his means of support, while the latter attempts to separate the partisan from the population and his sources of local support. Using an analogy made famous by Mao, the indirect approach attempts to separate the "insurgent fish" from "the water of the population." In contrast, the direct approach attempts to "kill the fish by polluting the water."[3]

At the end of the nineteenth century, British colonel C. E. Callwell offered one of the clearest arguments for pursuing the direct approach in his book *Small Wars: Their Principles and Practice*. He defined small wars as "expeditions against savages and semi-civilised races . . . [and] campaigns undertaken to suppress rebellions and guerrilla warfare." Callwell also described the "great principle" of small wars as the "overawing of the enemy by bold initiative and by resolute action whether on the battlefield or as part of the general plan of campaign." Likewise, he advocated punishing insurgents and their supporters: "The most satisfactory way of bringing such foes to reason is by the rifle and sword, . . . their villages must be demolished and their crops and granaries destroyed." The U.S. Army's use of winter campaigns on the Great Plains offers one example of the use of the rifle and sword to strike at an adversary's means of subsistence. The echoes of the Indian Wars and the lessons learned in irregular warfare continued to reverberate into early years of the twentieth century during U.S. Army operations in the Philippines, when former "Indian fighters" used the knowledge gained on the plains in a fierce guerrilla war with Filipino nationalists.[4] Ultimately, it was in the Nazi East, however, that the definitive expression of Callwell's prescription to "overawe" one's adversary found its most brutal expression.

Irregular Warfare in the Desert Southwest

The traditional nature of Indian warfare reflected a number of the aspects of irregular warfare. From an early age, Native boys learned and practiced martial and hunting skills. The latter, based on knowledge of terrain, stealth, and precise aim, offered a primer on some of the key guerrilla principles. For example, Black Elk, a Sioux, discussed his own Spartan training that began at the age of five: "The little boys would gather together from the different bands of the tribe and fight each other with mud balls that they threw with willow sticks." He continued, "And the big boys played the game called 'Throwing-Them-Off-Their-Horses,' which is a battle all but the killing; and sometimes they got hurt." These games served a larger purpose, as Black Elk noted, "I was still too little to play war that summer, but I can remember watching the other boys, and I thought that when we all grew up and were big together, maybe we could kill all the *Wasichus* [whites] or drive them far away from our country." In a similar manner Geronimo, an Apache leader and one of the most skilled and famous of Indian warriors, recalled how his father "often told me of the brave deeds of our warriors, of the pleasures of the chase, and the glories of the warpath." As a young boy, Geronimo hunted and killed bears and mountain lions with a spear, and he remembered how he and the other boys would "spend hours in stealing upon grazing deer, . . . crawl[ing] long distances on the ground, keeping a weed or brush before us, so that our approach would not be noticed." Geronimo's success in this latter technique reflected the general mastery of the Apaches in the art of camouflage, a skill so highly developed that in the words of one contemporary observer, "any but the experienced would pass him by without detection at the distance of three or four yards."[5]

This type of childhood training not only resulted in the creation of warriors perfectly adapted to the conduct of irregular warfare but also reflected the central role of male martial prowess in establishing status within many Native societies. In fact, for many Native communities, warfare and martial prowess was an "essential" element of social and spiritual life and constituted a key rite of passage for young males.[6] In his examination of Indian warfare, the historian Robert Utley observed, "Warriors still practiced guerrilla tactics masterfully and made uncanny use of terrain, vegetation, and other natural conditions, all to the anguish of their military antagonists." A major source of "anguish" for white settlers and the U.S. Army involved the Apaches' use of raiding parties, a principal feature of their lifestyle that involved raids to capture horses, cattle, or slaves. In fact, this practice had existed since the start of colonial rule, when the Spanish, allied with the Pueblos and the Utes, fought a brutal "just war" against the hostile *bárbaros*, including the Apache and Comanche tribes. As early as 1779, a Spanish official, José de Galvez, described his frustration in battling the *indios bárbaros* and complained, "the kind of Indian who infests these regions cannot be exterminated or reduced with a decisive blow, or by that methodical series of wisely directed battles that make glorious campaigns in war between cultured nations." Indeed, the Apaches and the Comanches were a constant thorn in the side of the Spanish—and later the Mexicans and Americans—due to their skill at conducting raids using small groups of mounted warriors adept at surprising isolated settlers or wagon trains. Although raiding provided an opportunity for the warriors to display their martial skills and gain social status, it is important to note that it was not an optional activity but a necessity, since these operations often meant the difference between starvation and survival for individual clans.[7]

According to one account: "As a rule the Comanches relied upon surprise, upon the effect of a sudden and furious dash, accompanied by an unearthly, blood-curdling war whoop. They avoided a pitched battle when they were matched by an equal or greater number." Similarly, Lieutenant Charles Gatewood, an officer who worked closely with Apache scouts and became a recognized authority on Apache customs and warfare, offered the following description: "[Attacks occurred] generally at the break of day, a surprise—a rapid & furious attack, accompanied by the most demonical yells. The surprised party, paralyzed with fear [and] unable to make a concerted

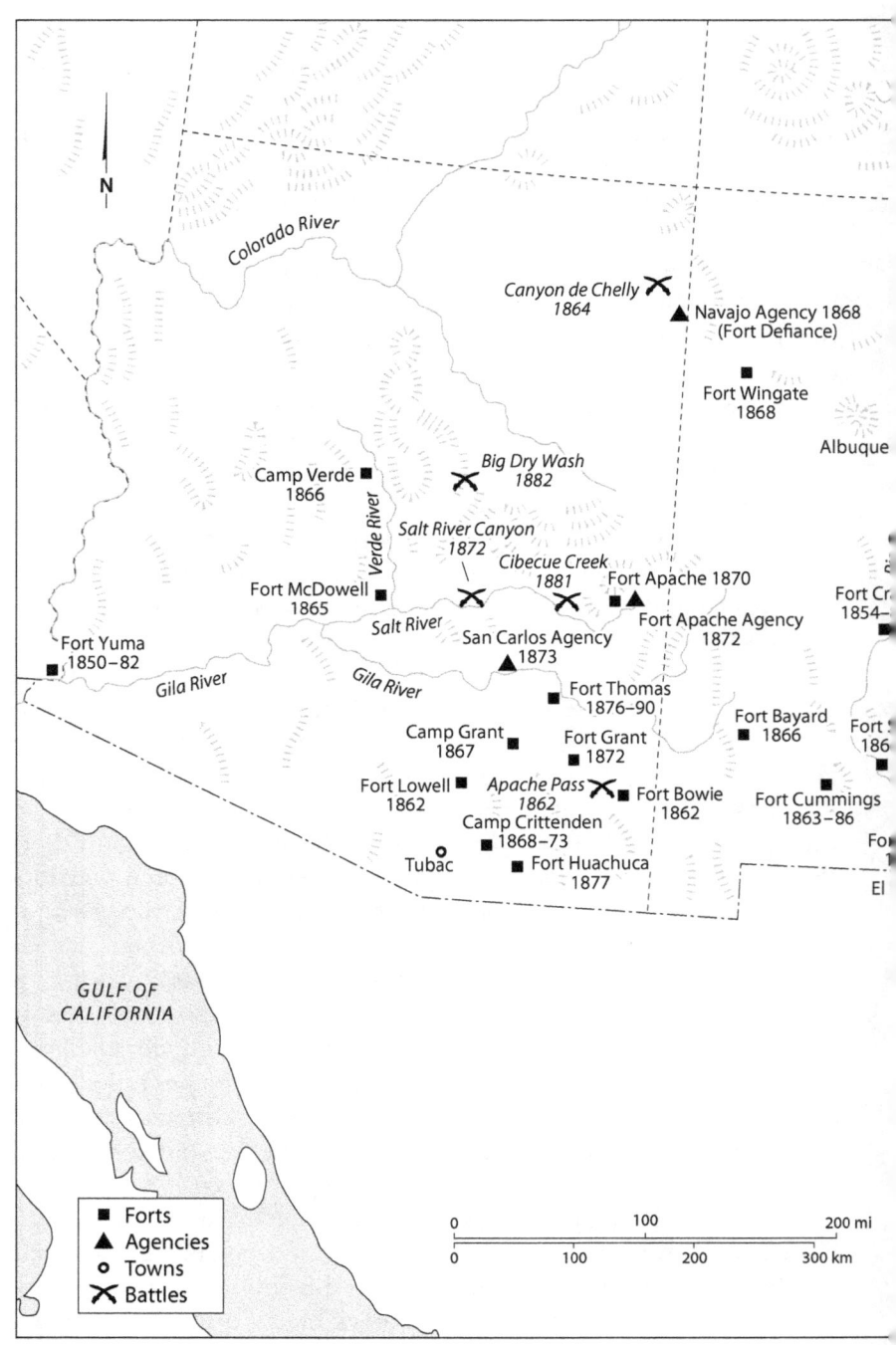

The Desert Southwest. Map by Bill Nelson. Copyright © 2016 by the University of Oklahoma Press.

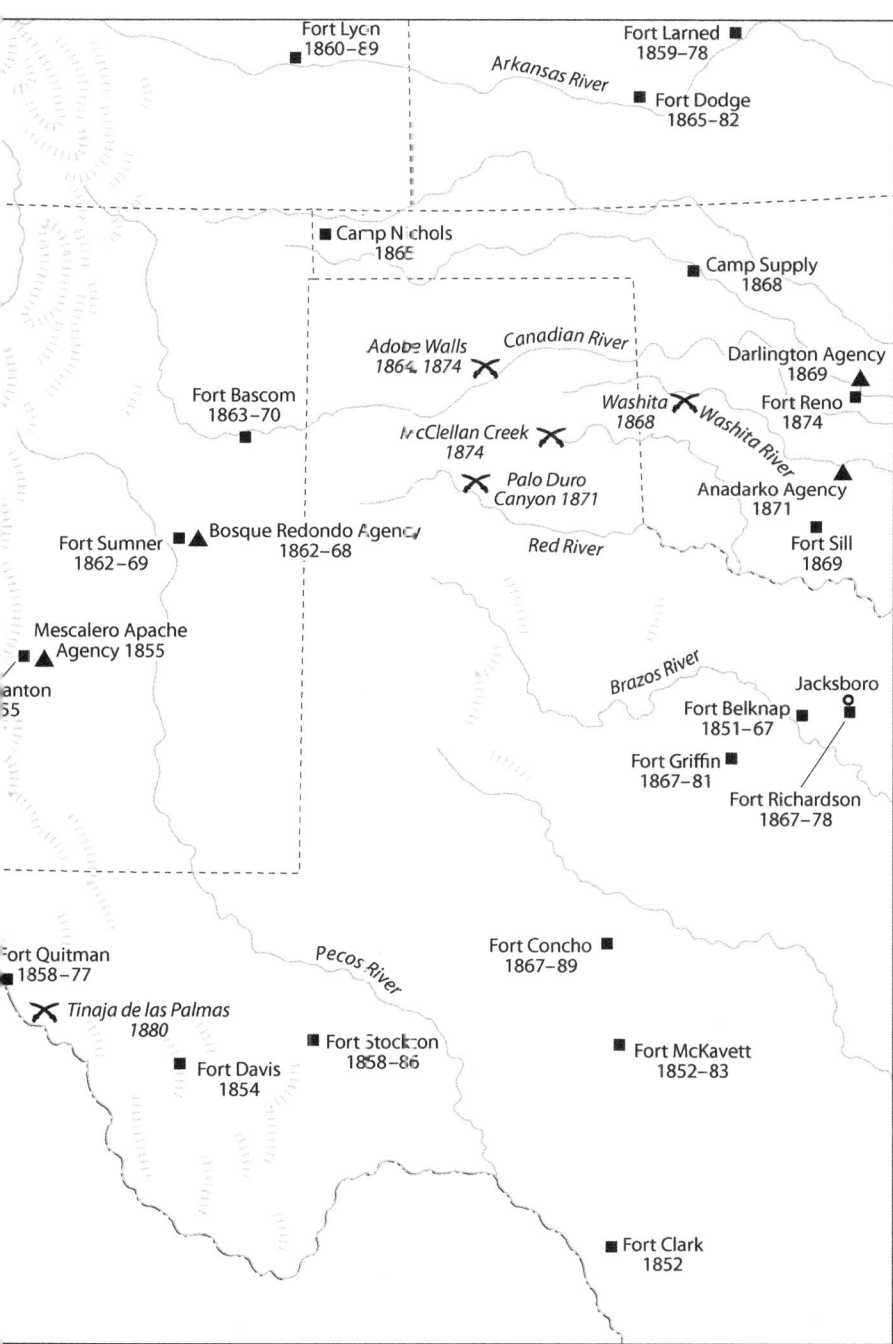

defense, massacred." In both accounts, surprise was the essential factor leading to Apache success. It was also a critical element in their use of the ambuscade or ambush, especially in the box canyons of New Mexico and Arizona. In this respect the Apaches' intimate knowledge of the terrain, and especially the areas with available water, made them masters of the ambush and a formidable foe for the U.S. Army units forced to chase this seemingly imperceptible foe across an arid and barren landscape.[8]

When being pursued by a larger group, the Apaches' favorite tactic involved the band scattering little by little until the pursuers were forced to follow individual Indian trails across the mountainous terrain of Arizona Territory. Utley described this challenge and the typical nature of army service as "characterized not by the stirring charge of blueclad horsemen—bugles blaring, banners snapping, sabers waving—but by the punishing, unheroic, usually fruitless reconnaissance over hostile terrain, pounded by rain, snow, or scorching sun, searching for an invisible enemy." Apaches often seemed to be an "invisible" foe even when soldiers succeeded in drawing them into combat. For example, the only evidence of the presence of Indians seen by one soldier over the course of an hour-long battle was the "smoke from the[ir] guns." The ability of the Natives, and especially of the Apaches and Comanches, to operate effectively in small groups was both a source of advantage and a critical weakness since these tactics inhibited the development of a unified organization, a flaw that precluded large-scale and coordinated operations.[9]

A key weakness in army operations against the tribes of the Southwest involved the lack of any official doctrine for dealing with an enemy employing irregular or unconventional tactics. One historian aptly remarked, "Soldiers trained only for the parade ground were no match for the western warriors in guerrilla warfare." Young lieutenants fresh from West Point had been schooled in Napoleonic tactics involving the movements of columns and divisions, not on the small-unit tactics employed by militias and frontiersmen during the French and Indian War (1756–63). Paradoxically, the "first American way of war" had reflected the use of "Indian warfare" by colonial militias and frontiersmen employing "the pillars of that tradition—extirpative war, ranging, and scalp hunting" as early as the seventeenth century. Likewise, Union forces battled Confederate guerrillas in a bloody and brutal campaign in the Upper South during the Civil War. This "uncivil war" also involved reprisals against civilians, such as the razing of homes, farms, and even entire towns by Union troops, and the executions of captured guerrillas and bushwhackers. As discussed earlier, George Crook had condoned the summary executions of Confederate-sponsored "bushwhackers" during operations in West Virginia.[10]

The Civil War experience of combating irregular forces also revealed the antipathy and revulsion among the leaders of conventional military forces for guerrillas as well as the frustration generated in trying to pin down an elusive enemy. For example, Major General William T. Sherman, at the time Union commander in Memphis, demanded that Confederate guerrillas be disbanded or reorganized into conventional units—if not, he threatened to release his troops to plunder the countryside. He warned Confederate leaders, "You know full well that it is to the interest of the people of the South that we should not disperse our troops as guerrillas; but at that game your guerrillas would meet their equals, and the world would be shocked by the acts of atrocity resulting from such warfare."[11] Sherman's warning illustrates that indiscipline, lawless behavior, and indiscriminate atrocity were inherent factors in the conduct of irregular warfare as understood at the time. These factors applied as much to white southerners during the Civil War as to the Indians of the Southwest.

Guerrilla Warfare in the Southwest

Based on the media attention devoted to them and the dramatic nature of events such as the Fetterman Disaster and the Battle of Little Bighorn, military operations waged against the Plains Indians in the post–Civil War period have overshadowed those conducted in the Desert Southwest. At the local level in settlements throughout Texas, Arizona, and New Mexico, the fear of Indian raids remained a basic fact of life, a situation that led to a great deal of settler-Indian hostility into the 1880s. Still, in 1871 in his annual report to Congress, Sherman, by then the commanding general of the army, viewed active operations in the southwest theater "to be at an end" with the exception of "a small number of Apaches."[12] Despite their small numbers, his optimism proved premature as clans and groups of Apaches continued their traditional practice of raiding and took advantage of the U.S.–Mexican border as an effective sanctuary.

One historian described the Southwest borderlands as a frontier dominated by "persistent ritual elements . . . of violence, gender, kinship, and masculine honor in long-term negotiations between colonists and Indians," an area of encounter where "confusion, revulsion, and massacre" came together. Similarly, Lance Blyth, in his study of the Chiricahua Apache, emphasized "the centrality of violence in the relationships and exchanges between and within borderland communities." Brian DeLay's trenchant analysis of the border between Texas, New Mexico, and Arizona and Mexico in the nineteenth century offers further support, revealing a frontier shaped by the forces of conflict, contestation, and cooperation between the various tribes and the Euro-American settlers on both sides of the international border. In but one example, Kickapoos operating from Mexico, and at times at the urging of agents of the Mexican government, generated fear and calls for reprisals from settlers in Texas. For its part, the Mexican government responded to cross-border Indian raids, mostly by Apache and Comanche bands, with demands for the United States to take action and prevent such attacks as stipulated in Article 11 of the Treaty of Guadalupe Hidalgo.[13]

One of the reasons that operations in the Southwest have received less attention in the history of the Indian Wars involves the smaller scale and scope of these actions. For example, Herman Lehmann, a boy taken captive and who spent nine years with the Apaches and Comanches, described his early experiences at raiding white settlements in order "to get more horses, and to kill as many of the palefaces as we could." The majority of these raids, conducted by small groups of warriors, focused on individual targets of opportunity, whether isolated homesteads, wagon trains, or individuals who crossed the Indians' path. Still, the stakes for both sides were high during these engagements since quarter often was neither given nor taken. During one raid in Texas, Lehmann recalled the capture of a white family of five. The Indians killed and scalped the father, the mother, and an infant and took the other two children, a young boy and his sister, captive. The band traveled with the children for four days before the children's refusal to eat and continual crying led the raiders to kill them by trampling them with their ponies. In this case as in others, the practice of killing adult male prisoners reflected a standard practice among the Apaches against both white and Native adversaries.[14]

In comparison, vigilante actions and acts of violence against the Indians could prove equally brutal. As early as May 1849, the Mexican state of Chihuahua passed a "scalp law," offering 200 pesos for every dead Indian warrior and additional bounties for captured men, women, and children. By 1851, states along the Mexican frontier were offering $200 for a scalp, $250 for a live warrior, and $150 for a captive Indian woman or child under the age of fourteen. A little over a decade later, during the Dakota War in Minnesota, Governor Alexander Ramsay offered a $25 bounty for male scalps, later raised to $200. As late as 1871, a group of Tohono O'odham (Papago) Indians collected ears from Apaches in Cochise's clan in order to claim a bounty from the Mexican government.[15] In the case of large-scale vigilante violence, the massacre of 150 Apaches, mostly women and children, by a group of whites, Mexicans, and Tohono O'odhams near Camp Grant, Arizona, on April 30, 1871, offers one of many horrific examples. Likewise, some army operations employed mass murder to "punish" or "chastise" tribes. For example, Lehmann noted that after a successful horse raid near Fort Griffin, his party joined another group of Apaches in order to disguise their trail before dispersing. Army soldiers in pursuit of the raiders came upon the camp of these innocent Indians and "murdered men, women, and children, and only a few squaws escaped to tell the tale." The main effect of these types of individual actions and acts of atrocity involved the creation of an escalatory spiral of reprisal, a dynamic that existed in every region of white and Indian interaction in the West. This cycle was further fueled by numerous examples of settler atrocities against fellow whites being falsely blamed on Indians.[16]

If the actions involving settlers and Indians illustrated the use of mass murder as an acceptable instrument by both sides, this practice also extended to formal military operations. During a raid into Mexico, Geronimo recalled preparing for an engagement with Mexican forces "to get possession of their horses, then surround the troops in the mountains, and destroy the whole company." In fact, he achieved this goal in an engagement with two companies of the Mexican army in 1873 by killing and scalping every soldier in these units.[17]

By the end of 1871, President Ulysses Grant's Peace Policy, although under siege, still provided the overarching goal of U.S. government policy. As a result, the government's response to the raiding of the Apaches under Cochise within Arizona involved a two-pronged approach aimed at ending the bloodshed. On the one hand, the threat of force provided the "stick" for federal policy. On the other hand, Vincent Colyer, sarcastically referred to as "Vincent the Good" and an "old philanthropic humbug" by local whites, offered the "carrot" of negotiations for a peaceful settlement to the growing unrest, an attempt derided by locals as an effort "to mesmerize the Apaches into peace."[18] Colyer's arrival resulted in the temporary suspension of military operations against the tribes in the territory as he worked to attain Apache agreement for relocation to the Tularosa Reservation.

Unlike the residents of Arizona, Brigadier General John Pope, commander of the Department of the Missouri and no stranger to exterminatory rhetoric, supported the mission and wrote, "I hope the [peace] experiment may be successful, and shall aid by all the means at my command." Between the efforts of Colyer and later Oliver Howard, a successful, albeit relatively brief agreement was achieved that led to the creation of multiple reservations and the government's promise to supply the tribes with rations and annuities. Unfortunately, a series of incidents between September 1871 and September 1872 led to the deaths of forty-four people, raising a public outcry within the territory, a call that convinced Commissioner of Indian Affairs Francis A. Walker that the time for a more forceful policy had arrived.[19]

Major General Oliver O. Howard held a council with Apache leaders at Camp Grant in April 1872, during which he warned the Indians that he had commanded 30,000 men in the Civil War and had the power to "exterminate them all" if he chose to. Thus, even Howard, a man who "combined military skill with an evangelical Christian zeal," was not above raising the specter of extermination in his interaction with the tribes. Still, President Grant's instructions to the "Christian soldier" Howard were to find "an equitable solution" for both the Apaches and the whites and to bring an end to the violence in Arizona.[20]

Lessons in Indian Warfare

Ultimately General Crook, the "old Indian fighter," was given the charge of dealing with the Apaches and bringing peace to the region. Lacking official army doctrine for Indian fighting, Crook, described by one historian as "the greatest of the U.S. Army's tactical leaders in the Indian Wars," developed a strategy for irregular warfare that would provide a template for defeating the tribes in the Desert Southwest. His formula for success involved several elements, including the employment of Indian scouts, the use of mules to pack supplies, and continual mobile operations designed to place constant pressure on the Indians. Crook described the Apache scouts as "invaluable," and their employment continued a practice that he had adopted in previous operations. During the Arizona campaign, the general was ably assisted by Lieutenant Walter S. Schuyler, an 1870 graduate of West Point, who proved capable of making the intellectual and practical adjustment from Napoleonic warfare to Indian fighting. Posted to the Fifth Cavalry in Arizona for his first assignment, Schuyler quickly realized that "[t]he campaigns in Arizona did not owe their ultimate success to any particular Waterloo-like victory, as much as they did to the covering of a great deal of ground by a comparatively small number of men, permitting the Indians no rest and rendering any and every hiding place insecure."[21]

The Apaches use of guerrilla warfare and their brutal tactics influenced the perceptions of many of the army officers who pursued them. In this sense the negative impression of Apaches held by white settlers in Arizona was mirrored by some army officers. Brigadier General B. J. D. Irwin characterized them as "one and all . . . alike; treacherous, bloodthirsty, and cowardly, and ever on alert to ambush small parties of incautious travelers." Irwin's description of Apaches as cowardly stemmed in part from the general belief among professional soldiers that guerrillas fought a lesser form of warfare and their refusal to engage in "proper" combat reflected their cowardice rather than the use of the only military advantage available. With respect to Irwin's use of the term "bloodthirsty," Apaches were feared for their use of torture and the mutilation of their victims. Lieutenant Gatewood observed, "stories of the most horrible torture and cruelties . . . on their captives are not exaggerations." Likewise, Sergeant Reuben Bernard recounted an incident during which eight Mexicans had been tied to their wagon wheels and burned to death, while two captured Americans "were held as prisoners for more refined tortures." After finding the remains of the incinerated Mexicans and the mutilated bodies of the Americans, a squad of soldiers called for hanging and burning their six Indian captives, members of Cochise's clan. The lieutenant in charge ordered the summary executions of the captured Apaches by hanging and left their bodies dangling for "months" as a warning to others. After returning to their fort, the squad released their surviving captives, an Indian woman and a young boy, and received a commendation for their action.[22]

These acts of torture and atrocity were not merely figments of hysterical settlers' imagination but were a reflection of general cultural practices, acts of revenge, and in some cases a form of psychological warfare. With respect to cultural mores, a standard punishment for Apache women convicted of adultery was to cut off their nose as an indelible "scarlet letter" for all to see.[23] Similarly, the ceremony of the Sun Dance by the Plains Indians involved acts of self-mortification, while one Apache punishment for serious offenses included suspending the individual above the ground by ropes tied to each wrist and each ankle until dead. It should be noted that the use of mutilation was not merely reserved for white settlers but extended to intertribal warfare as well. Finn Burnett, a frontiersman, described the Shoshone treatment of their Sioux rivals: "When the marauders were overtaken, their dead bodies were scalped and mutilated. The ears, hands, and other portions were cut off and borne to the Shoshone village in triumph, where the squaws would gloat and exclaim over the trophies." In fact, trophy taking, including scalping, was an integral part of the practices and rituals of many American Indian tribes and constituted "important ceremonial, social, and military functions."[24]

In some cases frontiersmen and even U.S. soldiers adopted these practices of trophy taking, including one account that refers to cutting the head off a dead Sioux warrior.[25] Similarly, physical and sexual assaults by white miners against Apache women often provoked fights and retaliation. These types of actions had the effect of escalating brutality on both sides and generating "tit for tat" reprisals to the point that brutality became a common occurrence. Geronimo commented on this cycle: "First a few Indians would be killed and then a few soldiers.... The number killed in these troubles did not amount to much, but this treachery on the part of the soldiers had angered the Indians."[26] This was the situation and the type of warfare that greeted Crook as he prepared for operations against the Apaches.

Although Crook believed that "the Apache is painted in darker colors than he really deserves," he still advocated "a sharp active campaign . . . [that] would save millions of dollars to the Treasury and the lives of many whites and Indians." The general received orders to strictly enforce the confinement of the Apaches to the reservations and to "attack all those who refused to come in and submit to the authority of the government." By the fall of 1872, attempts at a negotiated settlement had failed to end hostilities, and Crook intensified the campaign to find and confine the Apaches and Yavapais to their designated reservations. He therefore instituted the practice of a daily count of Indian males at the reservations and agencies in order to ascertain which warriors were missing at a given time. He also initiated a "grand offensive" to encircle the bands that had left the reservations with mobile cavalry columns supported by Indian scouts. Crook's orders were to induce surrender, but he noted that those choosing to fight "were to be hunted down until the last one in hostility had been killed or captured." He continued, "Every effort should be made to avoid the killing of women and children" and instructed that prisoners "should be guarded from ill-treatment of any kind."[27]

Crook continued this campaign into November 1872, with the intent of conducting a winter campaign designed to keep Apache and Yavapai bands on the move at a time when food and shelter were at a premium. The employment of Apache scouts proved to be a crucial factor in finding the encampments of their fellow Indians. Although these sites were usually abandoned in haste prior to the soldiers' arrival, Crook ordered that any food and belongings found to be destroyed, continuing a practice that had proved effective against the Plains Indians. Over the course of the winter, troops killed an estimated two hundred Indians during some twenty engagements. The major battle of the campaign occurred on December 28, when soldiers cornered approximately one hundred Yavapais in a cave at the Salt River Canyon and proceeded to lay down a withering fire that left seventy-six of them dead.[28]

These operations pressed on into the early months of 1873 in hopes of making the campaign against the Apaches "short, sharp, and decisive." In the meantime, Major General Oliver O. Howard made a separate agreement with Cochise's band, a group described by Crook as "the worst in the whole business." In the final major action of the campaign, a group of soldiers captured an Indian woman who revealed the position of an encampment at the top of a local mountain. The troops wrapped gunny sacks around their boots in order to silence their steps and began a nighttime climb to reach the peak. Arriving at the top just before daybreak, they opened fire on the camp at dawn on March 27, killing twenty-three Apaches. Although not present for the attack, Crook stated of this raid in his memoir, "All of the men were killed; most of the women and children were taken prisoners." He also noted that some of the prisoners had admitted that the band had been involved in the recent killing and torture of three white men, one of whom had been killed by sticking wood splinters into his flesh and setting them on fire. The Battle of Turret Mountain and Crook's description, however, raise some troubling questions. The deaths of "all the men" were explained by the surprise achieved in the assault and the fact that several of the warriors were so frightened and disoriented that they "jumped off the precipice and were mashed into a shapeless mass." In fact, it seems more likely that the surprise achieved by the unexpected assault in the early morning led to the capture of men, women, and children. It seems incredible that seasoned warriors with experience in the mountains would have been so frightened or disoriented that they would leap from the side of a cliff. Although a point of conjecture, the revelation of the band's involvement in the murder and torture of the white men may have provided sufficient grounds for pushing the remaining men off the side, an act of summary execution with existing precedent in earlier campaigns against the various tribes.[29]

The assault on Turret Mountain proved to be the final chapter in Cochise's War as the last of the Apaches surrendered on April 7, 1873. Upon seeing this group, Crook observed, "Had it not been for their barbarities, one would have been moved to pity by their appearance." He continued: "They were emaciated, clothes torn in tatters, some of their legs were not thicker than my arm. Some of them looked as if though they had dropped out of a comic almanac." In truth, there was little comical about the campaign, based on the tactics used by both sides. Crook's strategy of winter campaigning once again proved the effectiveness of striking at the tribes when they were at their most vulnerable, yet it also demonstrated the effects of such operations on the entire clan or tribe, not just the warriors charged with raiding. Although Crook's campaign ended depredations in Arizona, Apache warriors continued to raid into Sonora, with the Mexican government reporting over one hundred civilians killed in the first half of 1873. By the fall of 1873, the Indian Bureau counted over six thousand Apaches and Yavapais living on agencies and reservations in Arizona and New Mexico.[30] In sum, the campaign of 1872–73 foreshadowed the type of warfare that would characterize future operations in the Desert Southwest until the surrender of Geronimo in 1886.

Indian Scouts or Auxiliaries?

One of the major problems for the U.S. Army in fighting the Apaches (and most of the Indian tribes) involved the difficulty in locating them, surprising them, and bringing them to combat in classic military fashion. The keys to successful guerrilla warfare include accurate intelligence on the adversary's location, knowledge of the terrain, and mobility, advantages normally held by the Indians. The ability of groups of warriors to avoid cavalry, much less infantry, was a routine lament in official reporting, and it often reduced army horses "to hobbled, starved, and gasping nags."[31] Thomas Dunlay noted, "Commanders fresh from the Civil War battlefields found that they could march and countermarch along the trail from post to post without deterring the far more mobile raiders, and that offensive sweeps with cavalry through the hunting grounds generally failed to discover hostiles." The employment of Indian scouts thus proved to be one of the most effective measures for dealing with this shortcoming. General Crook, described by one historian as the "most devoted champion of the scouts," became an ardent believer in the effectiveness of Indian scouts, and a great deal of his success against the tribes was tied to their use. During operations in the Division of the Pacific in 1867, Crook established a precedent of raising scouts from bands "who were closely related to those he was fighting," a practice he would continue in his campaigns against the Apaches. For his part, Phil Sheridan experimented with the use of white scouts, but his success against the southern plains tribes in 1868 and 1869 came only after he "resorted to using formations of converging columns, hordes of allied Indian auxiliaries, and winter campaigns to force their submission." A report by the army's inspector general in the wake of an 1877 inspection of Indian-scout companies in Arizona stated, "I think they make good and efficient soldiers when they act with white troops—alone they are not reliable, and without them the white troopers are almost helpless in the pursuit of Indians." This comment is remarkable for a racial bias that on the one hand denigrates the ability of the scouts while on the other notes their importance to the success of army operations. In any event, the importance of Indian scouts and auxiliaries to the U.S. Army cannot be overestimated. In fact, one historian argued, "Indian allies greatly facilitated military conquest of the West, and in doing so may have prevented more truly genocidal wars than those that actually were fought." As the continuing campaigns in Arizona demonstrated, the use of Apache scouts was critical to the army's efforts "to achieve military dominance over the Apache" during the 1870s and 1880s.[32]

Victorio's War

The outbreak of a new round of hostilities with the Apaches resulted from a perennial source of tension between the tribes and the federal government, the boundaries of the reservation or forced movement to new areas. In his memoir Lieutenant Gatewood remarked, "The Indians were given their reservations, but . . . it is one thing to place them thereon & quite another to keep them there." The spark for renewed conflict arose when the Indian Bureau decided to move the Chiricahua Apache clans from their home on the Ojo Caliente (Warm Springs) Agency to the San Carlos Agency in 1876, a reservation designed to hold "nearly all of the most refractory Indians in the Territory." Victorio, an Apache chief, initially accepted the forced movement of his clan to a place that one of his people described as follows: "There was nothing but cactus, rattlesnakes, heat, rocks, and insects. No game; no edible plants. Many, many of our people died of starvation." In addition to these abysmal conditions, the management of San Carlos by the local Indian agent included all the worst excesses of profiteering and corruption intrinsic to the system of political appointments in the period. Colonel August V. Kautz notified the War Department: "I am in constant apprehension of an outbreak . . . on the San Carlos Reservation. . . . I charge this to the corrupt management." Faced with the choice between starvation or flight, Victorio led a force of approximately three hundred Mimbre and Chiricahua Apaches off the reservation in September 1877, initiating a three-year off-and-on pursuit of the skilled guerrilla leader, during which "the U.S. Army was unable to fulfil its political goal of defeating the hostile Apache."[33]

The resulting campaign against Victorio and his band followed closely the events of earlier operations against the Apaches as army troops chased on their heels but failed to capture the Indian leader or achieve a decisive battle. In contrast, Victorio used raids to supply his forces and conducted a series of hit-and-run attacks against his pursuers. In September 1879, he initiated a series of "fierce battles" with troopers from the Ninth Cavalry before crossing into Mexico. As a result of this attack and others that resulted in the deaths of thirty-one American and "New Mexican" citizens between September 1879 and February 1880, the army organized a force of four hundred cavalry, sixty infantry, and seventy-five Indian scouts to pursue the Apaches. Under the command of Colonel Edward Hatch, this force began operations in the spring of 1880 by moving onto the Mescalero Agency to disarm and dismount the Indians, an effort that resulted in the killing of fourteen Natives. General Pope described the resulting pursuit of Victorio as "simply a chase after the Indians from one range of mountains to another, with frequent skirmishes, but no decisive fight." As a result of this pressure and the practice of stationing troops at known watering holes, Victorio took his remaining band of two hundred warriors into the sanctuary of Mexico and began raiding on both sides of the border, the chief vowing "to die fighting."[34]

During the skirmishes in the first half of 1880, Hatch estimated that his forces had killed approximately one hundred Indians, but whatever their losses, Victorio's band continued their raids. Pope remarked that in order to "crush out these Indians," permission would be needed to pursue Victorio into Mexico. In fact, since 1875 the U.S. Army routinely crossed the border whether in "hot pursuit" or in deliberate operations, infuriating the Mexican government and threatening to escalate into open conflict between the two countries.[35] Pope placed the blame for the present hostilities squarely on the Department of the Interior and the Indian Bureau's decision to move Victorio's clan to the San Carlos Agency. From an army point of view, he asserted, "there is no doubt that it will be necessary to kill or capture the whole tribe before present military operations can be closed successfully." He continued, "The capture is not very probable, but the killing (cruel as it will be) can, I suppose be done in time."[36]

Pope's words exposed the crucial paradox faced by the military and the Indian Bureau in attempts to assimilate the tribes into white society. Commissioner of Indian Affairs Hiram Price remarked on exactly this issue in his annual report of 1881. Price argued: "[O]ne of two things must eventually take place, to wit, either civilization or extermination of the Indian. Savage and civilized life cannot live and prosper on the same ground. One of the two must die." For their part, Indians such as Victorio, Geronimo, Sitting Bull, and Crazy Horse recognized that assimilation was the equivalent to the end of their cultural existence and the extinction of their ethnic identity. Indeed, many warriors saw assimilation as a "threat to male honor."[37] Faced with such stark alternatives, the choice for many warriors from a culture that venerated martial deeds was to fight to the finish.

By October 1880, the final fight in Victorio's War was imminent. The Apaches' success on both sides of the border led to an agreement between the U.S. Army and the governor of Chihuahua, General Luis Terrazas, for a joint campaign against Victorio. The cooperation proved short lived, however, as Terrazas ordered army forces and Texas Rangers to return to the United States while he pursued the Apache leader. The Mexican army cornered Victorio and his band in the Tres Castillos Hills on October 14, 1880. In the resulting battle Terrazas's soldiers killed seventy-eight Apaches, including Victorio, and captured sixty-eight women and children. Even as the remnants of Victorio's band, including the septuagenarian Mimbre warrior Nana, fled back to the reservation, plans for a new round of hostilities were evolving that would lead to the emergence of one of the most famous leaders of the Indian Wars.

Geronimo's War

In his summary report for the secretary of war in 1881, General Pope reflected on the outbreak of hostilities in the Southwest: "The raids of the Apaches into Southern New Mexico for the last two years bear no resemblance to an Indian war or general outbreak. They rather resemble the operations of the cowboys and other bands of robbers on the frontier, or to the parties of train robbers in Missouri." He continued: "There is no great trouble in dealing with them when found. The difficulty is to find them."[38] Pope's comments are interesting in several respects and reflect a professional soldier's common misunderstanding of guerrilla warfare. First, Pope may have been attempting to insulate himself for any criticism on the failure of the army to capture Nana, or Victorio before him, by downplaying the activities of the previous two years, a sentiment certainly not shared by New Mexico Territory's civilian population. Second, the description of these raids as something other than "real warfare" demonstrated the existing prejudice of many professional officers against such operations, a bias that often prevented them from being able to conduct successful counteroperations. Third, the equation of the Indians with "bandits" and "criminals" is reflective of a wider trend to delegitimize guerrillas, a trend that had important implications for the treatment of partisans or suspected partisans in the Nazi East. Finally, Pope missed the key point about the essential nature of guerrilla warfare: bands purposefully operate in small groups in order to make it difficult for enemy forces to find them. Mobility and the use of small raiding parties was the tactic of choice and the best method for avoiding combat with a larger force.

The death of Victorio provided only a short respite in the war in the Southwest. According to an army report, Nana and his small band of warriors, after returning to the Mescalero Agency, began raiding again in the summer of 1881 "like a pack of hungry wolves, killing everybody they met and stealing all the horses they could lay their hands on." In response to these attacks, six companies of cavalry, including the famed Buffalo Soldiers of the Ninth Cavalry, chased the band into the mountains and pressed them so hard that Nana took his warriors back into Mexico. The proximity of Apache reservations to the Mexican border provided too great a temptation for tribes who had little regard for artificial boundaries and recognized the tactical advantage in using either country as a temporary sanctuary depending on the situation. In this respect the residents of the Mexican states of Chihuahua and Sonora suffered grievously from numerous raids and attacks between the 1831 and 1886. In fact, these areas had experienced the full brunt of Apache raiding, with one contemporary observer remarking on "the despairing terror which the bare mention of the Apaches conjures up to their [the Mexican inhabitants] diseased and horrified imaginations." For his part, Geronimo explained the practical and personal reasons behind his frequent forays that "followed the warpath" into "Old Mexico." In the case of the former, the lack of wild game in Arizona and the growth of white settlement pushed the Apaches farther south in the hunt for food. In the case of the latter, Geronimo's kinship with the

Nedni Apaches and his personal friendship with their chief, Whoa, were grounds for spending "much of our time in his territory." Additionally, the murder of his mother, wife, and three small children by Mexican troops provided additional motivation and led to his vow to seek vengeance upon all Mexican soldiers.[39]

The spark for the next round of Apache and white conflict stemmed from the killing of a medicine man and an Indian prophet, Nakaidoklini, in August 1881. Prefiguring the events of the Ghost Dance, the prophet had preached a special dance that promised to raise the Indian dead and rid the land of the white man. The Indian agent for the San Carlos Agency, J. C. Tiffany, requested the army's assistance in arresting or, if necessary, in killing Nakaidoklini. After an extended exchange between the army and the Indian Bureau, Colonel Eugene Carr, commander of the Sixth Cavalry, was ordered to arrest the holy man. Supported by eighty-five troops and a detachment of twenty-three Apache scouts, Carr took Nakaidoklini into custody on August 30. As this force returned with their captive, the shaman's supporters, including Carr's Apache scouts, attempted to free him. The resulting firefight left six troopers dead and two wounded. In addition, Nakaidoklini was shot and killed by the soldier guarding him.[40]

The killing of Nakaidoklini was another avoidable incident of Indian and white violence that catalyzed an uprising among the Apaches. A subsequent grand-jury investigation of Tiffany's management of the reservation found that he had committed "fraud against the government" and that "the constantly recurring outbreaks were due to the [agent's] criminal neglect or apathy." Whatever the causes, the consequences of this fight meant war. Initial newspaper accounts reported that Carr's entire command had been wiped out in the engagement, a report that raised hysteria and echoed fears of a southwestern Little Bighorn. As the actual facts of Carr's operation became known, General Sherman sent the following orders: "I want this annual Apache stampede to end right now and to effect that result will send every available man in the whole army if necessary." In his annual report Pope described his response as following the tactic of "close and persistent pursuit," but he also warned, "until the raiding Indians are killed or the Indian reservations removed, we may expect a renewal of these spasmodic raids at no very long intervals." He also noted that the governor of New Mexico Territory, Lionel Sheldon, had offered the services of "armed companies of volunteers" to assist the army by making further raids "so expensive in life to the Indians that they will probably not be often repeated." During his term, from 1881 to 1885, Sheldon, a Civil War veteran and militia commander, made repeated use of the territorial militia and citizens' posses against "disruptive" forces.[41] While Pope's comments once again reflected a "punishment strategy," his readiness to employ volunteers underscored his willingness to inflict significant casualties in the process.

With the flood of federal troops into the area and the activation of the territorial volunteers, it should have been no surprise that many Apaches began leaving the reservations and heading toward Mexico, understandably afraid of becoming victims in a punishment campaign based on the precedents of the past. Geronimo justified his decision to leave the reservation as that it was "more manly to die on the warpath than to be killed in prison." He led a band of warriors south toward the Sierra Madre, raiding and killing along the way while engaging and eluding his cavalry pursuers. Operating from this mountainous home base, Geronimo and other Apache bands conducted raids on both sides of the international border in the spring and summer of 1882, leading Mexican president Porfirio Díaz to agree to joint U.S.–Mexican military operations in order to stop the attacks, a major concession of national pride that demonstrated the severity of the situation in Sonora and Chihuahua.[42]

In response to renewed hostilities, Sherman appointed General Crook to assume command of the Department of Arizona on September 4, 1882, and to commence operations against the Apaches. For his part, Crook recognized the conditions that had led the Indians to war and argued that in the face of such abuses, they "had displayed remarkable forbearance in remaining at peace" for as long as they had. Based on his earlier experience with the Apaches, Crook instituted a rollcall of Indian males and issued each with an identity tag. This allowed the army to classify those who remained on the reservation as peaceful and those not present as hostile. The general also enlisted Apache scouts, acquired mules for pack trains, and prepared for continual mobile operations designed to put constant pressure on the marauding bands. Crook's actions brought relative calm to Arizona Territory, but bands under Geronimo and Chato initiated a series of attacks on both sides of the border in March 1883, a rampage during which they killed men and women, took children captive, and "created an uproar" throughout Arizona.

These attacks prompted the War Department to issue orders "to destroy hostile Apaches, to pursue them regardless of the department or national lines, and to proceed to such points as you [Crook] deem advisable."[43] In short, Crook received a free hand to "pursue and punish" the Apaches into Mexico, and he immediately began to coordinate with the Mexican army.

At the start of May, Crook pushed into Mexico with fifty troopers and 193 Indian scouts. But his top priority was negotiation, not punishment. The general remarked: "With all the interests at stake we cannot afford to fight them. We are too culpable, as a nation, for the existing condition of affairs." He continued, "It follows that we must satisfy them that hereafter they shall be treated with justice, and protected from the inroads of white men." In an engagement that lasted several hours on May 15, Crook's forces captured five Indian children and killed nine warriors. The subsequent capture of Geronimo's camp led to direct negotiations between the two leaders in which the majority of the Chiricahua bands, including Geronimo's, agreed to surrender. By the end of the month, 123 warriors and 251 women began the return journey to the reservation, arriving at San Carlos on June 24.[44] Geronimo and his warriors, as promised, arrived later in February 1884, driving a stolen herd of Mexican cattle with them.

This latest peace brokered by Crook held for over a year until Geronimo once again heard rumors of his pending imprisonment and execution; he decided to leave the reservation for Mexico in May 1885. The rumors of imprisonment may have been based in part on a recent prohibited *tizwin* (alcohol) party in which he and other warriors had participated in violation of reservation rules. Regardless, accompanied by thirty-four warriors, eight boys, and ninety-two women and children, Geronimo left and began raiding as he led his band southward. Upon hearing of the "breakout" and the raids, local newspapers fanned the flames of public hysteria.[45]

The news of the raids and public outrage once again led to the buildup of troops on both sides of the international border in preparation for operations against the fugitive bands. Facing insurmountable odds, Geronimo, described by one of his warriors as "the most intelligent and resourceful as well as the most vigorous and farsighted [military leader]," made plans for his own punishment campaign. The Apache leader recalled: "On our return through Old Mexico we attacked every Mexican found, even if for no other reason than to kill. We believed that they had asked the United States troops to come down to Mexico to fight us." He then aptly described his dilemma: "If we returned to the reservation we would be put in prison and killed; if we stayed in Mexico they would continue to send soldiers to fight us; so we gave no quarter to anyone and asked no favors." Intent on avoiding a return to the reservation and certain imprisonment, the Apaches engaged Crook's forces in a series of minor skirmishes throughout the summer and into the fall of 1885. In response to the "very considerable loss of life and the capture and destruction of much valuable property," Sheridan traveled to Arizona in November to meet with Crook and to discuss a strategy for dealing with the Apaches. His arrival coincided with a recent incursion into Arizona by the Apache band of Josanie, during which troops futilely chased the Indians for more than a thousand miles, a raid that took the lives of thirty-eight American settlers and one warrior.[46]

In reality, the small size of Geronimo's force by early 1886 made it impossible for him to seriously threaten either U.S. or Mexican interests beyond conducting raids at targets of opportunity, such as isolated ranches or supply trains. Still, the presence of the Apaches and the practice of giving no quarter created significant public pressure to capture or kill Geronimo and his followers. Furthermore, improved cooperation between the U.S. Army and the Mexican army deprived Geronimo of his sanctuary and put his people between a rock and a hard place. This constant military pressure, in many respects the result of Crook's decision to rely on Apache scouts, and the general exhaustion of his band finally led Geronimo to negotiate again with Crook. At their first meeting inside of the border of Mexico, the general told the Apache leaders that they had to decide "at once upon unconditional surrender or to fight it out." Crook warned that if they chose the latter option, "hostilities should be resumed at once and the last one of them killed if it took fifty years." He also noted that the leaders of the current uprising would be sent "east" for two years of imprisonment but allowed that wives and family could accompany them. After more discussion, the Apache leaders, including Geronimo, approved the terms of surrender and agreed to accompany the army back to Arizona. Later as the clans moved northward, an unscrupulous army trader sold the warriors mescal and told them of the horrific treatment that awaited them upon their return. With these visions in his head,

Geronimo and approximately thirty men, women, and children slipped out of camp and retraced their route back into Mexico. For his part, Geronimo justified his decision by stating that he "feared treachery and decided to remain in Mexico."[47]

Karl Marx asserted that "history repeats itself, first as tragedy, second as farce." The events following Geronimo's flight back to Mexico had more elements of tragedy than farce. The fact that the Apache leader and his band had been able to slip away from the army escort raised howls of derision and alarm from the citizens of Arizona and criticism from Sheridan of Crook's handling of the affair. As a result, the "old Indian fighter" offered his resignation, which Sheridan accepted and then made bitterer for Crook with the appointment of a personal rival, Brigadier General Nelson A. Miles, to assume the chase. The main element of tragedy in these events involved the fact that Miles would require another five-month campaign before forcing Geronimo's final surrender, a period during which Indians and citizens on both sides of the border would once again pay the ultimate price.

Miles and His Apache Campaign

Sheridan's appointment of Miles proved to be a good choice, especially based on the general's extensive experience in Indian warfare and his successful record on the southern and northern plains. Upon taking command, Miles assessed the major advantages enjoyed by his adversaries, including their intimate knowledge of the terrain and their ability to survive in the barren and arid desert conditions, where nature was an ally to the Indian and "fatal to the white man." Additionally, he recognized that the Apaches enjoyed a major advantage with regard to intelligence in the desert. Despite the presence of forty-three infantry companies and forty cavalry units, Geronimo and other Apache leaders continually displayed a knack for eluding their pursuers, if only by hours or even minutes. Miles's solution for improving army intelligence on the movement of the bands focused on two areas. First, he continued the use of Indian scouts, but based on his doubts concerning the loyalty of Apaches, he chose scouts from other tribes, a practice also employed by the Mexican army.[48] Second, the general took advantage of a relatively new signaling technology, the heliostat, to transmit information on the movement of the Indians. In fact, the dry climate of the Southwest proved perfect for this form of communication, which relied on mirrors and the use of visual Morse code to transmit messages. By establishing over fifty observation points across the mountain ranges of Arizona, troops used binoculars and telescopes to track movement on the plains and valleys below and the heliostat to transmit messages in relay (a more sophisticated form of Gondor's signal-fire system used in J. R. R. Tolkien's *Return of the King*).[49] Although a valuable signaling system, it was based on the premise that the Apache bands would be operating in Arizona and that they would not recognize its purpose.

On April 20, 1886, Miles issued his field orders, stating, "The chief object of the troops will be to capture or destroy any band of hostile Apache Indians found in this section of the country." He also mentioned the use of the mountain-top observation posts and the use of "reliable" Indians as scouts. Additionally, he instructed his troops to develop friendly relations with local citizens in order to gain valuable intelligence and demanded that "all the commanding officers will make themselves thoroughly familiar with the sections of country under their charge." The key element of Miles's strategy, however, mirrored Crook's earlier effort in one critical respect: the use of continual and overlapping pursuit operations by a combination of cavalry and, more importantly, infantry in order "to follow constantly . . . and to destroy or subdue them." As the general wrote in his memoir, "the argument in my mind was that no human being and no wild animal could endure being hunted persistently without eventually being subjugated."[50]

The strategy of constant pursuit placed exceptional demands upon the troops charged with executing it, as demonstrated by one operation during which the men pursued a group of Apaches for twenty-six hours straight despite running out of water eight hours into the chase. The intense heat not only dehydrated the soldiers but also made their weapons literally too hot to hold. Under these extreme conditions, some resorted to the questionable practice of cutting open their own veins "to moisten their burning lips with their own blood." The demands may have been high, but so were the potential rewards as the Apaches themselves suffered from the relentless pressure. Reflecting on Miles's campaign, Geronimo recalled the extreme thirst suffered by his people as well as the fact that the constant pursuit resulted in his camp being surprised on several occasions. Even the traditional tactic of scattering into smaller groups proved ineffective, for the army pursuers continued to follow groups as small as a single individual knowing that at some point they would rejoin with the band.[51] Despite this intense pressure, the Apaches managed to elude their pursuers and continued to subsist by raids on Sonoran communities.

By the end of August, Geronimo and his small band of twenty-four warriors were exhausted by the chase. The Apache leader negotiated a truce with the Mexican army by agreeing that his band would leave Mexico and return to the United States. Shortly thereafter, Lieutenant Gatewood arranged a meeting with Geronimo in his camp and offered him a last chance to surrender. If he did not, Gatewood warned, "they must all be killed eventually, or if surrendered or captured, the terms would not be so liberal." On September 3, Geronimo finally met Miles on the border to surrender, though first asking for assurances that his twenty-four warriors and fourteen women and children would not be killed. The general "simply told them to surrender and be sent to Florida to await the action of the president." Geronimo then ended the longest-running guerrilla war in U.S. history with the promise, "I will quit the warpath and live at peace hereafter."[52]

The Apache Wars ended with the transfer of Geronimo and over three hundred Chiricahua "prisoners of war" by train to their place of confinement in Florida. In the end, the contest was characterized by the ferocity and skill of the warriors and the ability of the federal government to mobilize thousands of troops against a force that never numbered over two hundred fighters. Although outnumbered, Geronimo and other Apache leaders provided a clinic in the art of guerrilla warfare, but the loss of their Mexican sanctuary eventually signaled the end of their uprising. For Miles, the final act in the Apache Wars came on November 8, 1887, with the presentation of a ceremonial sword by the citizens of Arizona in appreciation for his services "in ridding their country of the Apaches."[53] In one respect the presentation of a "very beautifully ornamented" sword provided an apt ending to a conflict that was concluded by negotiation, not annihilation.

On the eastern front in Europe, however, it would be cold steel and not words that would characterize German antipartisan operations in the occupied territories.

German Antipartisan Operations in the East

The war against the partisans provided a convenient cover for the murderous activities of SS and police units in the East, where Himmler's political soldiers partnered with the Wehrmacht in a campaign of annihilation aimed at the local Slavic population, the Sinti and Roma (Gypsies), Soviet POWs, and above all the Jews. The historian Isabell Hull identified the genesis of this genocidal violence within the "military culture" of the German Imperial Army during colonial campaigns in Southwest Africa. She concluded, this military culture "bequeathed practices, habits of action, and ways of behaving . . . [that] were easily harnessed for the ideological ends of even greater mass destruction and death" by the armies of the Third Reich, a case in which the military doctrines of the *Kaiserreich*, not Hitler's Reich, created the impetus for genocidal violence.[54]

Other historians have argued that the Wehrmacht's use of brutality and atrocity in antipartisan operations resulted from the army's obsessive fear of irregulars, a paranoia that emerged during the Franco-Prussian War (1870–71). The response of the Imperial Army to attacks by ununiformed franc-tireurs (free shooters) was to classify the guerrillas as criminals or terrorists. As a result, the army conducted reprisal acts against French civilians, both men and women, accused of sniping or other acts of resistance. In fact, the "Iron Chancellor," Otto von Bismarck, remarked, "We are hunting them down pitilessly. . . . They are not soldiers: we are treating them as murderers." In 1914, the specter of the franc-tireur arose once again to haunt imperial forces, contributing to German atrocities in the early stages of the Great War. These fears undoubtedly influenced the reaction of army leaders during World War II. But this paranoia did not drive German antipartisan policy, rather it served to further reinforce the racial philosophy that formed the essential foundation of this campaign in the occupied territories. As early as 1940, Himmler described the *Bandenkrieg* (guerrilla war) in Poland as "more unpleasant than an open battle," a type of warfare that required "soldiers and formations that were ideologically dependable." In this respect the use by Wehrmacht, SS, and police forces of terms such as "franc-tireur" and *Freischärler* (insurgents) acted as both euphemism and as the explicit justification for mass murder and reprisal.[55]

The widespread use of terror was an intrinsic element of occupation policy in the East and resulted in a situation in which "Soviet citizens could be killed at any time and for almost any reason." In fact, the Wehrmacht's senior leadership issued orders that advocated establishing security "not by legal prosecution of the guilty, but by the occupation forces spreading such terror as is alone appropriate to eradicate every inclination to resist." The historian Ben Shepherd identified two reasons for the brutality of the German antipartisan campaign. First, he argued that the ruthlessness of these actions resulted from the "racially and ideologically brutalized view of warfare which the Nazis espoused" combined with the army's own historical bias against guerrillas and the "brutalizing conditions of the war in the East as a whole." Second, he pointed to the adoption of terror as a "practical military necessity" to "compensate for the low levels of manpower" dedicated to rear-area security.[56] With regard to this second point, Wehrmacht leaders became increasingly complicit with SS and police forces as accomplices in mass murder and genocide under the guise of antipartisan operations during the campaigns in Poland, southeastern Europe, and the Soviet Union.

Raul Hilberg, one of the preeminent scholars of the Holocaust, has observed, "The generals had eased themselves into this pose of cooperation through the pretense that the Jewish population was a group of Bolshevist diehards who instigated, encouraged, and abetted the partisan war behind the German lines." He continued, "The army thus had to protect itself against the partisan menace by striking at its presumable source—the Jews." In postwar testimony one army general confirmed Hilberg's assessment by grudgingly admitting that "the ordering of the most severe measures for the prosecution of the war against the partisans by the highest authorities possibly had the final purpose to exploit the military war against the partisans by the army in order to make possible the ruthless liquidation of the Jews and other undesirable elements." After the war SS General Erich von dem Bach-Zelewski testified: "There is no question but that reprisals both by the Wehrmacht and SS and Police overshot the mark by a long way.... Moreover, the fight against partisans was gradually used as an excuse to carry out other measures, such as the extermination of Jews and gypsies [that is, Sinti and Roma]." In short, the conflation of Jews with partisans established the "cloak for the genocide of the Jews."[57]

During the initial months of the German invasion, policies and orders issued to the Wehrmacht and to SS and police forces demonstrated the level of officially sanctioned brutality for operations in the East. For example, the army's distribution of "Guidelines for the Combat of Partisans" offers evidence concerning the ultimate goals of antipartisan operations. Originally released by the Army High Command and then retransmitted to the police, with the remark to make them a "special object of training and discussion," the guidelines provided explicit directions on the handling of partisans: "The enemy must be *entirely wiped out*. The decision concerning the life or death of a captured partisan is difficult even for the toughest soldier. Action must be taken. He who completely disregards eventual sentiments of compassion and ruthlessly and mercilessly seizes the opportunity acts correctly."[58]

These types of orders translated not only into the Wehrmacht's willingness to kill former Soviet soldiers or those who took up arms against the Germans but also to a readiness to murder civilians suspected of supporting these groups. Army policies aimed primarily at civilians reflected earlier practices used in Serbia in "a campaign of hostage-taking and reprisals that was exceptional, even by Nazi standards, in the scale of indiscriminate butchery that if inflicted," a campaign that led to the deaths of some 1.75 million people, or 11 percent of the country's population. Another Wehrmacht directive issued to village leaders in Ukraine in November 1941 warned the region's farmers about the consequences of supporting partisans. The directive, which was to be posted throughout the countryside, stated that the villages of Baranowka and Obuchowka had been razed and their inhabitants executed for supporting the partisans and that "numerous partisan contacts" had been shot in several other villages. It declared that the battle in Ukraine was finished, and any person taking up arms would be considered a "bandit." Finally, military authorities offered a 10,000-ruble reward for information on suspected partisans and urged Ukrainians to join in the battle against the "Bolshevist regime."[59] Importantly, these instructions, initially intended for soldiers, came from the Wehrmacht and established extermination as the customary punishment for partisan activity, a standard embraced by SS and police forces throughout the East.

"Guidelines for the Combat of the Partisans" was not the first Wehrmacht directive on the subject passed on to police units. For example, the police battalions operating with the 221st Security Division received instructions in a division order on August 12, 1941, to consider "*all* [Soviet] soldiers encountered west of the

Beresina [River] as irregulars and to treat them accordingly." The next line of the order explained what was meant by this treatment as it called for daily reports on the numbers of irregulars executed. Five weeks later another published order distinguished between Soviet combat troops captured during battle and those who afterward "emerge[d] from their hiding places" to attack German lines of communication. In the case of the former, these men were to be taken prisoner, while the latter were to be handled as irregulars and treated accordingly. Additional instructions placed the responsibility for deciding to which group captured soldiers belonged in the hands of the senior commander based on the tactical situation, thus allowing each to act according to his own judgment.[60]

The nature and character of antipartisan warfare established in Poland in 1939 and 1940 found its most horrific expression during the invasion of the Soviet Union. Already in the first week of that operation, troops of the 35th Division had specifically identified Jews with the Soviet resistance movement and had initiated acts of mass killing, including the murder of approximately 100 Jewish men in the town of Lida. By the fall of 1941, the conflation of Jews and partisans had reached the small-unit level within the Wehrmacht. A former soldier with the 691st Infantry Regiment, Leopold Winter, testified about his unit's actions in a small village in Belorussia in October 1941. His company entered the town with orders to kill the entire Jewish population. Winter recalled, "it was said that the Jews of this town were to be liquidated, because they did things with the partisans." Based upon these instructions, the unit murdered at least 150 Jewish men, women, and children in cold blood. The 691st Regiment was not the only unit that got the message. In fact, army, SS, and police units used antipartisan operations as a cover to eliminate a plethora of "enemies" as evidenced by a monthly Wehrmacht report for October and November 1941, which detailed the army's cooperation with SS and police forces in the executions of 10,431 of 10,940 captured "partisans." Significantly, it noted the capture of a mere eighty-nine infantry weapons found among the entire number.[61] In other words, either these were surely the most ill-equipped partisans in history or units like the 691st simply killed unarmed men, women, and children as a matter of course in a campaign of racial annihilation.

Such use of mass killing found particular emphasis during an antipartisan conference held for the *Ostheer* (Eastern Army) and officers of the SS in September 1941. The conference emphasized the maxim "Where there's a Jew there's a partisan, and where there's a partisan there's a Jew." This belief mirrored the tortured logic espoused by Hitler and expressed in Nazi ideology in which "all Jews were Bolsheviks, all Bolsheviks were partisans (or at the very least supporters of partisans), and thus, all Jews were also partisans or partisan supporters." The conflation of Jews and partisans extended to female Jews in the East who "could be killed by German soldiers in what was to be counted as a form of "military action" without any judicial process."[62]

The acceptance of this formula by some Wehrmacht leaders can be seen in an order issued by General Erich von Manstein, commander of the Eleventh Army, on November 20, 1941. Manstein instructed his troops: "The Jewish-Bolshevist system must be annihilated once and for all. . . . The soldier must understand the necessity for the severe measures taken against the Jews, the spiritual carriers of Bolshevist terror." With such exhortations ringing in their ears, the men of the Eleventh Army on their own initiative executed Jewish men and women in operations in the Crimea and cooperated with SS and police forces in the annihilation of that region's Jewish population.[63] During the drive into Russia, Wehrmacht forces played a major role in the antipartisan campaign and became complicit in genocide. But Himmler's SS and police forces took the leading role in mass murder and atrocity.

The Command Staff RFSS

In addition to the einsatzgruppen, Himmler created the Command Staff RFSS (*Kommandostab Reichsführer SS*) to act as a headquarters and clearinghouse for gathering reports from SS and police formations to document their activities in the pacification of the Soviet Union. Composed of Waffen-SS and Order Police formations, these forces cut a bloody swath through the East in the first months of the invasion. At the end of July 1941, Himmler issued guidelines for the conduct of antipartisan operations to his SS mounted units operating with the Command Staff RFSS. In order to avoid casualties, he remarked on the need to use Luftwaffe aircraft to attack towns in which SS and police forces encountered particularly "stubborn resistance." To ensure the reliability of the local population, he ordered the recruitment of informers as well as the distribution of livestock and foodstuffs captured by German forces to those who provided information. In cases where the population displayed an anti-German attitude, Himmler's solution was more direct: "If the population in a national sense is adversarial, racially and physically inferior or even, as is often the case in swampy regions, composed of settled criminals, all those suspected of supporting the partisans are to be shot. Women and children are to be transported away, livestock and foodstuffs confiscated and secured. The villages are to be burned to the ground." Himmler then ended his instructions with the warning, "Either the villages and communities form a net of support bases whose inhabitants on their own accord exterminate every partisan or marauder and inform us of everything [that happens], or they cease to exist."[64]

A report by the 1st SS Brigade, covering the period between July 27 and July 30, provided an initial overview of the Command Staff's charter by stating its mission as "the capture or annihilation of (a) remnants of the 124th Soviet Infantry Division, (b) armed gangs, (c) irregulars, (d) persons who provided encouragement to the Bolshevist system." Operating with two police battalions from Police Regiment South, the brigade cited its success in the executions of 814 persons during the three-day period. The victims included nine Russian soldiers in civilian attire shot as irregulars, five Soviet functionaries (including one woman), and eight hundred Jewish females and males between the ages of sixteen and sixty executed for "aiding and abetting Bolshevism and as Bolshevist irregulars." One week later SS Infantry Regiment 10 reported on a "cleansing action" involving the executions of fourteen "agitators and Jews" and the capture of thirty prisoners, while a subsequent report noted the public hanging of two Jews in Zhitomir for providing "encouragement to gangs."[65]

In addition to providing support for the Waffen-SS, the police battalions demonstrated their own initiative in acts of mass murder in two separate reports dated August 19, 1941. The first report remarked on the participation of the units in the "combat of gangs" and noted the executions of twenty-five Jews and sixteen Ukrainians by Police Battalion 314. The second referred to the use of units from Police Regiment South in antipartisan operations that resulted in the killing of twenty-four suspected partisans and the capture of thirty-three prisoners. After interrogating the prisoners, the police shot them. In addition, Police Battalion 45 executed 322 Jews in the town of Slavuta. The second report also indicated the disproportional forces involved in these operations, with the loss of only one man and the wounding of four policemen.[66]

On the following day the regiment's staff company, composed of members of both the SS and the police, reported the executions of 514 Jews and 2 armed partisans, while units from Police Regiment South recorded 212 partisans killed and 19 captured at a cost of two casualties. Additionally, a report of August 21 boasted of the executions of 367 Jews by Police Battalion 314 in a "cleansing action" to secure German supply lines. Finally, a report on August 22 recorded the executions of five prisoners (including three partisan women), nineteen "bandits," and 537 Jews by Police Battalion 45, while Police Battalion 314 executed twenty-eight Ukrainians on charges of "arson."[67]

These early reports of the activities of the Command Staff RFSS are important in a number of respects. First, they highlight the close cooperation between Waffen-SS and police forces in the conduct of antipartisan operations. Second, the clear emphasis in the report on highlighting the executions of Jews and the size of these massacres clearly shows that the police were not afraid to take the lead in the conduct of racial policy. Third, the high number of enemy killed and the low number of prisoners taken, combined with the relatively light losses experienced by the police forces, argues that many of those killed as partisans were unarmed and clearly not even members of a guerrilla group. Fourth, they offer examples of the use of euphemism to characterize both the victims and to justify their executions. Finally, the reports seemed to indicate a rising trend of murder and atrocity as these units became accustomed to their duties.

The last week of August proved to be an especially bloody period for the Command Staff. Status reports on August 24 detailed the capture of 19 prisoners by SS Infantry Regiment 8 and the capture of 85 prisoners by SS Infantry Regiment 10 as well as the executions of 283 "Bolshevist Jews." During this time, the police battalions proved equally adept at killing, including the executions of 294 Jews by Police Battalion 314, 61 Jews by Police Battalion 45, and 113 Jews by the police mounted formation. On August 25, the 1st SS Brigade reported the executions of the 85 prisoners taken the previous day, and Police Regiment South announced the executions of 1,342 Jews, while Police Battalion 304 captured and executed eight Soviet paratroopers. Again on August 27, the SS and police forces recorded their

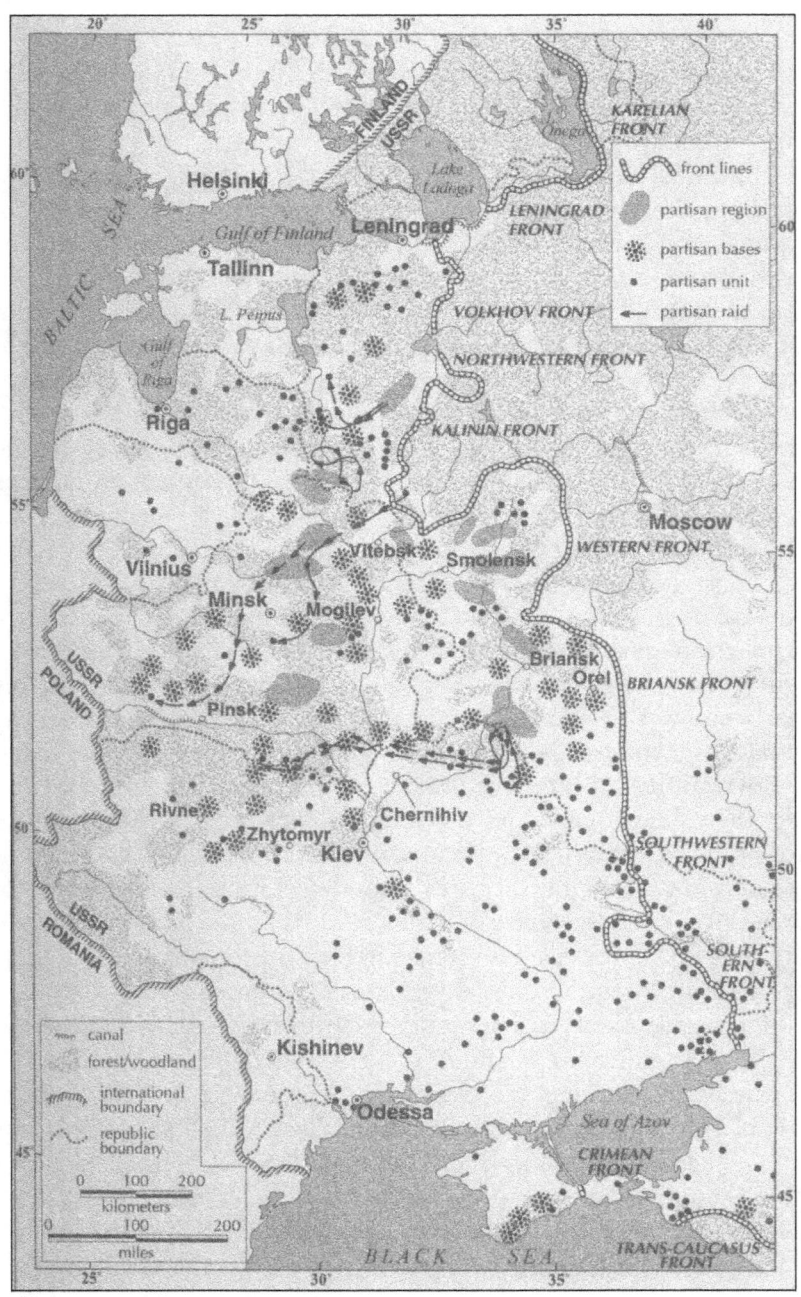

Partisan Operations and Bases on the Eastern Front, Winter 1941–1942. From Kenneth Slepyan, *Stalin's Guerrillas: Soviet Partisans in World War II* (2006), courtesy of the University Press of Kansas. Map by Dick Gilbreath.

success by noting the capture of 145 prisoners and the executions of 98 Jews by Waffen-SS forces, but it was once again the police that led the way, including the capture of 23 prisoners and the executions of 2,078 Jews.[68]

The totals of victims provided in this incomplete sampling of the month between July 27 and August 27 begins to numb the mind of the reader as numbers follow numbers in a litany that effaces the identities and human faces of those killed. Based on these reports alone, Waffen-SS formations murdered 1,294 persons, including 1,195 Jews; the police battalions killed 4,905 people, including 4,593 Jews; and the regiment's staff company executed 1,062 persons, of whom 1,060 were Jews. In other words, *an astounding 94 percent* of the victims were Jews. Furthermore, the SS mounted formations reported the executions of "approximately 3,000 Jews and irregulars" in the week between July 27 and August 3 alone. It is important to remember that this orgy of murder proceeded independently of the einsatzgruppen activities as these formations cut their own deadly paths eastward. The routine participation by numerous police battalions, both regular and reserves, in these activities in the rear areas of Army Group South alone during the second month of the invasion aptly highlights the emergence of these battalions as the "foot soldiers of annihilation."[69]

One of the critical aspects involving the use of antipartisan operations, especially in 1941, involves the fact that Soviet forces did not pose a credible guerrilla threat. In fact, it was not until the summer of 1942 that one can speak of an organized and centrally directed partisan effort.[70] In other words, the specter of partisan warfare was primarily created as a cover for Nazi genocidal policy on the part of SS and police forces and as a method for achieving the Wehrmacht's participation and complicity in these operations; this process expanded by the middle of 1942 with the emergence of a credible Soviet guerrilla threat.

The Soviet Partisan Movement

As reports of rapid Wehrmacht penetrations into the Soviet Union reached an incredulous Stalin, he issued an address to the Soviet people on July 3 that called on them "to foment guerrilla warfare everywhere." He also demanded that German forces "must be hounded and annihilated at every step and their measures frustrated." Despite Stalin's appeal, military and political realities prevented the organization of a viable partisan force in the first months of the German invasion. The Soviet regime's own brutality against its citizens and the indications of a rapid German victory resulted in the willingness of only party members and members of the secret police to risk their lives by joining partisan forces. Likewise, with the exception of the secret police, most early partisans lacked military training and the necessary weapons and supplies for guerrilla operations, severely limiting their effectiveness. In fact, Soviet partisan forces were nearly wiped out and almost "collapsed" by the end of the invasion's first winter.[71]

After teetering on the brink of destruction, the Soviet General Staff recognized the growing potential of partisans, forces that had grown to some 72,000 combatants by the spring of 1942. In order to further strengthen them, Soviet commandos parachuted into German-occupied territories to organize partisan groups, and the Soviet Air Force delivered supplies and munitions. By that summer, the guerrillas were "solidly established" and numbered 125,000 women and men. The brutal nature of German occupation policies and the practice of executing former Soviet soldiers after capture provide the primary explanation for the large growth in partisan forces between the spring and summer. Individuals and groups of former soldiers, including escaped POWs, banded together and hid out in forests and swampy areas to form guerrilla bands. Although lacking communication equipment, supplies, and weapons, they had military experience and the desire and ability to fight. Operating primarily in small groups, the partisans concentrated on interdicting German supply lines or attacking isolated garrisons. One German soldier recounted their tactics: "Trains were derailed, supply columns attacked and munitions depots blown up. . . . [W]eak staging posts were attacked with all Germans killed." He continued, "The embitterment was great on both sides and not infrequently it came to barbarity."[72]

The use of "barbarity" in dealing with real or perceived partisan threats by military and police forces was not a practice limited to the Soviet Union. Former German soldier Josef Lücking recalled his participation in antipartisan operations in Serbia: "The partisans used treacherous methods of fighting. . . . [W]e carried out reprisals on a 1:10 ratio: ten hostages killed for every German. The whole thing got so out of hand that in the end it was all just a matter of killing as many as possible. It was a relentless and merciless way of fighting." The mention of Serbia was appropriate since Wehrmacht actions in southeastern Europe in many respects set the stage for later actions in Russia. In Kiev, for example, the military commander, General Kurt Eberhard, authorized the executions of hundreds of the city's residents in October and November as reprisals for acts of "arson and sabotage." In another case, an attack on the German communication system resulted in the murder of four hundred male hostages.[73]

Whether operating in the city or the countryside, German forces routinely used reprisal killings as a means to coerce the local population into submission. Yet the massive use of reprisals backfired and led to increased resistance on the part of the residents. A historian of the Soviet partisan movement argued, "The more vicious German reprisals became, the more the peasantry turned to the partisans as their only viable alternative." The guerrilla war in the East also experienced its own escalatory spiral of violence as Soviet partisans not only conducted actions against the German occupiers but also targeted killings and the destruction of villages that refused to support the resistance or allegedly provided support to the invaders. The use of violence against their fellow citizens highlights the fact that the partisan movement in the East incorporated two separate but related centers of power, one political and the other military.[74] On the one hand, Soviet forces sought to defeat the Germans militarily, but on the other, the political objective of establishing Communist control over the partisan movement was equally, if not more, important in this effort.

The Killing Year, 1942

By the summer of 1942, mass murder had not only become standard operating procedure but also had been institutionalized and promoted at the highest levels. Not coincidentally, approximately 3,000,000 Jews were murdered during the calendar year 1942, approximately 50 percent of all Jews killed in the Holocaust. In a secret report of July 31, 1942, titled "Combat of Partisans and Jewish Action in the White Russian District," Wilhelm Kube, the commissioner general for Belorussia, identified the Jews as the "primary bearers" of the partisan movement and laid out plans for their complete elimination. Kube noted that in the previous ten weeks alone, 55,000 Jews had been "liquidated." He also mentioned plans for the pending executions of some 20,000 Jews, which he believed would end "the danger" of partisans receiving support from the Jews in his region.[75] In this case, the growing partisan movement was used by the Nazi leadership not only to brutally suppress armed opposition to German rule but once again as a rationale for killing Jews, a logical extension of the Final Solution authorized at the Wannsee Conference in January 1942.

After the reverses suffered by the Wehrmacht in fall of 1941, Hitler and his army leaders were betting on a "year of decision" in which a well-timed blow would collapse an exhausted and overextended Russian colossus. The army's subsequent success in achieving conventional "battles of annihilation" at Kharkov and at Kerch in May and June 1942 resulted in the capture of almost 500,000 Soviet soldiers and the destruction of thousands of tanks and artillery pieces, offering hope to planners for a rapid, if belated, conclusion to the campaign in the East. Despite these initial successes, the resistance offered by Soviet conventional forces and the increasing effectiveness of partisan activities dampened German euphoria by the end of the summer. In an order of August 18, 1942, Hitler decried the "unbearable scope" of partisan activity and authorized the "extermination" of these forces through the combined use of the Wehrmacht, the SS, and the police.[76] His order became in many respects a blank check, promoting atrocity and offering institutional approval for these acts.

In the fall of 1942, Himmler reported to Hitler that the war against the "partisans" in Ukraine had resulted in the executions of 387,370 "gang helpers" and "suspected gangs," of whom 363,211 were Jews, almost 94 percent of the total killed. Similarly, a telegram of September 2, 1942, from Einsatzgruppe A concerning operations in the Baltic states provided further evidence of mass murder, especially of Jews. The death squad recorded the killing of 136,421 Jews, 1,064 Communists, 653 mentally ill persons, and a mere 56 partisans; of this total, 55,556 were women and 34,464 were children. In this case, the einsatzgruppen had no need to resort to semantic camouflage or euphemism since their explicit mission involved the murder of Jews, who by definition constituted a partisan threat. In the case of Himmler's report on the killings in Ukraine, the intentional use of the term "gangs" could not conceal its function as the pretext for the genocide of the region's Jewish population. As in the American West, there was an effort to criminalize partisan behavior by labeling those who opposed German occupation policies as bandits.[77]

Himmler Takes Charge of the Antipartisan Effort

During a private audience with Benito Mussolini in October 1942, Hermann Göring described the "ideal" antipartisan soldier. The Reich marshal discussed the conduct of antipartisan operations in the East and explained the German practice of confiscating all livestock and foodstuffs in partisan areas as well as interning men, women, and children from these areas in work camps and burning down their villages. He then discussed the practice of lining up all the men and informing the women of a village that they all will be shot unless they identify persons who do not belong to the community. Interestingly, Göring revealed: "Members of the Party carry out this task much more harshly and better. That's why armies that are ideologically committed, like the Germans (or the Russians) fight much harder than the others. The SS, the guard of the old fighters who have a personal connection to the Führer and constitute an elite, confirm this principle."[78]

Göring's comments to Mussolini referred in part to a recent change in the overall command of the antipartisan efforts. His suggestion that members of the Nazi Party and the SS were best suited for this difficult duty had found its expression in July 1942 with Hitler's appointment of Himmler to head antipartisan efforts in areas behind the frontlines. This decision identified fighting partisans as "primarily the task of the police" and called for the "energetic combat" of the threat and its elimination by the start of the coming winter.[79] Although the Wehrmacht retained responsibility for operations against partisans in the combat zones, Hitler's selection of Himmler clearly constituted a bureaucratic victory for the leader of the SS and demonstrated the increasing reliance on SS and police forces in the East.[80]

After his appointment, Himmler discussed the "so-called partisans" and informed his SS and police forces, "I am personally taking over the direction of the combat against gangs, franc-tireurs, and criminals." He also transferred regional responsibility for the antipartisan campaign to his higher SS and police leaders (HSSPFs).[81] Himmler's comment on the threat and the use of terms such as "gangs," "guerrillas," and "criminals" found its expression in one of his first actions prohibiting the use of the term "partisan" and replacing it with either "gangs" or "gangs of robbers," thus setting the tone for his stewardship of this effort.[82] The linguistic "criminalization" of these groups provided the ostensible pretext for the actions taken to reestablish law and order and legitimized the wholesale massacre of persons so designated.

One indication of the nature of his campaign can be found in a personal letter from Himmler's chief of staff, Gottlob Berger, on June 17, 1942. In it Berger argued that experience in the General Government with "attacks by gangs" seemed to argue for a policy of "better to shoot one Pole too many than one Pole too few."[83] To be sure, this appeared to be the motto of German forces within the occupied territories. In any event, Himmler quickly translated his new authority into action by organizing a vast antipartisan effort throughout the East in early August. In his instructions to the HSSPFs, he remarked on the cooperation of the Wehrmacht in the planned campaign in providing blocking and security duties. He also emphasized the combined efforts of the Order Police with forces from the Security Police and SD to ensure the "annihilation of the gangs." Furthermore, he reminded his SS and police leaders of the necessity for secrecy in preparation and for "tough and ruthless" measures in the execution of these operations.[84]

The selection of Himmler and his SS and police forces to lead the antipartisan effort guaranteed that murder and atrocity would emerge as institutional norms. With Himmler's political soldiers in charge, men tasked with upholding the racial and ideological precepts of the order and experienced in the mass murder of Jews and others, the escalating radicalization of the antipartisan effort was assured. One example of this involved Hitler's order to take the "toughest measures" against all those who joined or supported these irregular forces. The police responded by providing several guidelines for dealing with the partisans. On September 15, 1942, German rural police forces in Ukraine received the following orders: "If it is conclusively established, that members of a family are active with the bandits, then the entire family is to be made responsible and exterminated with agreement of the SD." In these cases the order also allowed for the immediate expropriation of the family's property and the burning down of their homes or farms without special permission.[85]

For those living in the countryside, open support or collaboration with either the partisans or the Germans could prove deadly. While German forces did not hesitate to kill alleged collaborators and to destroy entire villages, partisan groups also took action against individuals and villages supporting the Germans. In one case a group of ten fighters from the famous Bielski partisans was forced to seek refuge at the home of a Belorussian farmer, a friend of two of the men, in March 1943. The farmer, however, sent his son to the police with information on the group's presence. The police subsequently killed nine partisans while the farmer's son murdered the other with an axe when he emerged from a hiding place after the police had departed. Upon hearing this news, Tuvia Bielski sent scouts to investigate. They questioned a female witness about the events, and after a "good beating" she confessed to the farmer's treachery. Afterward, Tuvia and a group of partisans visited the farmer and executed him and his entire family before freeing the animals and setting the farm on fire. In another example, Leo Kahn, a Jewish partisan fighter, recalled the executions of villagers, who had participated in the murder of "hundreds of Jews," shortly before the arrival of Soviet forces in 1944. The partisans first read them a list of their crimes, then ordered them to kneel as they shot the collaborators in the village square.[86] As these examples demonstrate, residents were caught between a hammer and an anvil, but active or suspected collaboration with either side was a risky, if sometimes unavoidable, fact of life.

The Face of Annihilation

By the fall of 1942, SS and police forces certainly constituted the cutting edge of the process of annihilation, but they were by no means alone in their efforts. For example, Gendarmerie Battalion 1 (motorized), in cooperation with a police company, led an effort aimed at "herds of bandits" in the vicinity of Miedzyrzec within the General Government. The one-day operation involved the encirclement of several small villages, which were then thoroughly searched. The after-action report described the results: "Bandits were not found in the towns. From the group of wanted suspects, several were apprehended. Non-local Jews were staying in several villages and nearby forests. They were shot. During the operation, it became especially apparent that younger men and women attempted to run away and escape into the forests as the police approached. Some of these persons were arrested or shot while running away." The mission resulted in the executions of two bandits, thirteen persons who "attempted to run away," and twenty-five Jews as well as the razing of the farm of an alleged partisan helper. In addition, the police arrested one Pole and rounded up fifty-eight men and women for forced-labor duties.[87]

The commander of the gendarmerie battalion later reflected on several aspects of this action. First, he observed that since the attitude of the local population had shown a fear of the police, they obviously had a "bad conscience." He also remarked that the attempts of the young men and women to run away demonstrated that they were not willing to contribute in the Reich's "construction efforts," and "therefore no reservations existed regarding the shooting of these elements as they fled." He then suggested that unemployed young women be included in future operations to roundup forced laborers as they were inclined to become friends with the bandits and provide them support. He also provided a personal opinion: "They [the young women] are under certain circumstances more dangerous than the men."[88]

The experience of the police in this operation offers several important insights into the prosecution of the antipartisan campaign. First, there were no Security Police or SD men available to participate, but this did not prevent these uniformed policemen from acting on their own initiative. Second, the course of the action indicates the wide latitude and authority enjoyed by local police commanders in the prosecution of the antipartisan campaign. Third, the use of the term "herds of bandits" is reminiscent of the army's use of the phrase "herds of partisans." This equation of the partisans with herds of animals was deliberate and provided another method by which the police and soldiers dehumanized their victims in the East. Such a mindset reinforced the tendency for increasing brutality and for showing no mercy. For example, a former police-platoon leader recalled that he could not remember a single instance in which prisoners were taken during battles with partisans in the vicinity of Chotimsk in the summer of 1942.[89]

Helping Hands: Auxiliaries and the Antipartisan War

In operations against the partisans, local auxiliaries under German command played a key role in assisting the police. One of the first initiatives pursued by SS and police leaders in the eastern territories involved the creation of local units to support the German occupation, a move supported by Hitler. Already in July 1941, Himmler authorized the immediate formation of auxiliaries from the conquered territories. Chief of the Order Police Kurt Daluege admitted that based on the chronic manpower shortage faced by German forces, "auxiliary forces from the occupied territories had to be included and organized, trained, and equipped for the fulfillment of police tasks." Designated as *Schutzmannschaften*, these units primarily consisted of volunteers and members of the former police and armed forces of their respective areas, in some cases even released POWs.[90] By the end of 1941, the auxiliaries serving in the occupied Soviet territories numbered approximately 45,000 men.[91] One year later these numbers exploded to some 300,000 auxiliaries, including 100,000 Ukrainians alone, an increase that coincided with a massive wave of killing aimed at the Jews and the growing number of partisans.[92]

Despite the unreliability of some members, the auxiliaries proved an effective instrument for supporting German efforts. A six-week-long operation in early 1943, Operation Winter Magic, involved SS and police forces, Luftwaffe aircraft, a Wehrmacht antiaircraft section, and Latvian auxiliaries under German police command, with the objective of creating a "dead zone" within a small area in the Latvian countryside. In the course of this action, a senior Order Police officer named Colonel Knecht reminded his subordinates that executions were to be the primary responsibility of the SD. But he allowed: "In the event that executions [are] necessary by the [auxiliary] troops, because the SD is not in the vicinity, executions are to take place in houses. The bodies are to be covered with hay and straw and the houses set on fire." The after-action report concerning the performance of the Order Police and the Latvian auxiliaries detailed the killing of 77 "bandits" in combat, the capture of 9 others, the "special handling" of 875 bandits and bandit helpers, and the turnover of an additional 1,389 persons to the SD between February 16 and March 31.[93] Additionally, a Security Police report noted 132 enemy casualties, 2,588 executed "bandit helpers," twenty-two arrests, and the forced deportation of almost 4,000 persons.[94]

In the fight against the partisans and the extermination of the Jews, the auxiliary battalions, like their German police counterparts, proved to be an effective and deadly instrument.[95] One former policeman recalled two antipartisan operations involving Auxiliary Battalion 57. In the first action the battalion entered a small village and determined that the entire population of some twenty men, women, and children belonged to the partisans. On the orders of a police lieutenant, the auxiliaries executed every inhabitant and burned down their houses and barns. Similarly, during a second action, another, much larger village experienced the same fate as the battalion murdered the entire population and burnt their homes to the ground. One policeman highlighted the unit's conflation of Jews and partisans and stated that it followed the motto "Whoever was regarded as a Jew or suspected partisan was bumped off."[96]

It was not only the auxiliary police battalions that murdered, however. In the case of Belorussia, auxiliary policemen from a regional station routinely cooperated with German policemen in the murder of the local Jewish population, mostly scattered throughout the countryside in small towns and villages. In these cases "Belorussian policemen and German gendarmes used to come to a village or small town, collect all the Jewish inhabitants, and then murder them. Each killing operation resulted in ten to forty victims, depending on how many Jews resided in a specific place." Oswald Rufeisen, a Jew using a false identity, personally witnessed in the town of Kryniczno one such combined action under the command of a German gendarme, Karl Schultz, a man he described as being of "low intelligence, a pathological murderer, and a sadist." A baker before the war, Schultz kept a personal log of the names of his victims, except for those under the age of sixteen, who he simply noted as "pieces" (*Stücke*). Rufeisen remembered the killings, especially the actions of one Belorussian policeman who had taken a particular interest in two beautiful Jewish girls: "To my horror I saw him bend down. Next I realized that he was busy taking off the dead girl's handmade sweater.... The others too continued to examine the rest of the bodies impassively, methodically. When they discovered any signs of life they shot again."[97]

Comparing the Nazi East and the American West

The use of guerrilla warfare by the Apaches in the Desert Southwest and the partisan war in the occupied East shared certain similarities at the tactical level, including the employment of small mobile groups conducting operations against vulnerable targets of opportunity, the use of raids to secure provisions, and the practice of using knowledge of the local terrain to escape pursuit or avoid detection. Likewise, there is some parallel in the character of warfare in both areas in which local civilians became the objects of violence or coercive measures. Once again, however, the issue of the scale and scope as well as the role played by military and government-sanctioned forces against the guerrillas offer a major contrast between the American West and the Nazi East.

In the American West, U.S. Army forces employed constant pursuit to wear down and "punish" the Apaches, and while killing was an element of this strategy, so too was negotiation. The threat of complete physical extermination, although often cited, remained a rhetorical device for coercing the bands to peace. In the East, anti-partisan operations served a two-fold purpose. On the one hand, these actions provided a pretext for a larger effort, in line with Nazi racial ideology, that encompassed the physical extermination of the region's Jewish population and the wholesale killing of other suspect groups, including Communists, Sinti and Roma, and the mentally ill. On the other hand, the emergence of a genuine partisan movement was met by ruthless and brutal policies designed to exterminate this threat. Even here, however, the widespread characterization of partisans as Bolsheviks and Bolsheviks as Jews reflected the regime's racial precepts and justified mass murder as not just a necessary, but in fact a desired response. Likewise, the use of imagery describing Jews as pestilent or plague ridden and partisans as "dirty" created an explicit rationale for *Säuberungsaktionen* (cleansing actions) designed to completely eradicate putative sources of infection. In short, the Wehrmacht, like SS and police forces, "favored a terroristic doctrine of counterinsurgency warfare" that embraced officially sanctioned atrocity such as the widespread destruction of villages, the use of summary executions, a policy of not taking prisoners, and the mass murder of Jews and other politically and racially suspect groups.[98]

The fact that Hitler and his generals embraced this philosophy is seen in the plethora of orders, directives, and policies conveyed to the Wehrmacht, SS and police forces, and German auxiliaries promoting mass murder. With regard to the latter, the German auxiliaries were in fact 'purpose built' instruments of annihilation and critical to the prosecution of genocide in the East. In contrast, as Thomas Dunlay argues, Indian scouts and auxiliaries at times may have acted brutally against their tribal adversaries, but these forces often served to circumscribe the level of violence and killing associated with army operations in the West.[99]

With respect to rhetoric, the orders and instructions of some U.S. Army commanders employed exterminatory language as did many stories in the frontier press and among white settlers. Certainly, military officers such as Crook, Miles, and Gatewood made it plain to Apache leaders during negotiations that a refusal to surrender threatened the members of their bands with annihilation, but the fact that there were negotiations at all reflected a desire or a willingness by the government to end these conflicts without resort to extermination. In this respect Geronimo's ability to surrender to Miles for the "fourth time" after a series of on-again, off-again raiding forays over a period of years provides one key point of difference between policy in the American West and the Nazi East. Likewise, another distinction can be found in the actual course and conduct of army operations against the tribes. Miles's orders to his troops at the start of the campaign stating that the primary object was "to capture or destroy any band of hostile Apache Indians" differs fundamentally from those issued by Wehrmacht generals, including Manstein, during the invasion of the Soviet Union that argued: "The Jewish-Bolshevist system must be annihilated once and for all. . . . The soldier must understand the necessity for the severe measures taken against the Jews, the spiritual carriers of Bolshevist terror." The differing practical manifestations of such instructions can be seen in the German policy of taking no prisoners and the routine use of summary executions and large-scale reprisals. In comparison, the case of the Battle of Turret Mountain raises suspicions concerning summary execution in reprisal for the torture and murder of the white settlers, but even in this case Indian women and children were spared and taken prisoner.

Despite individual acts of atrocity, including the vigilante action at Camp Grant, the U.S. Army never adopted a sanctioned policy of mass annihilation during its battles against the Apaches. The limitations on the character and scale of these operations occurred in part because of the role played by the president and Congress in directing and overseeing the political objectives associated with the displacement of the Apaches and other tribes in the Southwest. This political guidance did not establish annihilation as its aim, but rather attempted to isolate the tribes on the reservations with the goal of assimilation or at the very least submission to white society, even if this assumed the loss of tribal identity. Starting with Grant's Peace Policy in 1869, subsequent presidents into the 1880s also focused on efforts designed to place the tribes on reservations and to promote assimilation. In his 1880 address to Congress, President Rutherford B. Hayes remarked on the end of Victorio's War and his hopes for an end to the Indian Wars. Furthermore, he promoted the concept of severalty for Indian lands and asserted that the Natives were increasingly "building houses and engaging in the occupations of civilized life." Three years later President Chester A. Arthur informed Congress about Crook's campaign against Geronimo and expressed his confidence that serious outbreaks were at an end and his expectation that the tribes "will hereafter remain in peaceable submission."[100]

These statements can be compared to a series of orders and directives from Hitler that not only promoted but actually endorsed genocide, including his orders to the Wehrmacht in December 1942: "The army is justified and duty bound in this battle [against the partisans] to employ every means without restriction, also against women and children, when it leads to success."[101] Furthermore, he prohibited disciplinary or legal action against soldiers who committed acts of murder or atrocity during these operations. In sum, the scope and scale of the campaigns in the Southwest differed significantly from the operations in the occupied East as did the fundamental objectives of the U.S. government when compared to those pursued by Hitler and the Nazi bureaucracy.

Finally, there was an essential difference between the Apaches and "Stalin's guerrillas" based on their respective level of organization and their political goals. By the beginning of 1944, Soviet partisans numbered over 180,000 and were a potent military force equipped with modern weaponry and supplied by the government. Organized into military formations up to brigade size, these units provided a "major contribution" to Soviet military operations, including the disruption of German resupply efforts by targeting rail lines.[102] In contrast, the guerrilla bands under Victorio and

Geronimo were small and reliant on raiding forays for their sustenance. They never constituted an existential threat to U.S. political control in the Southwest or a major military threat for the army. The primary effect of their presence was psychological and resulted from the fear and hysteria created by the media and among civilians on both sides of the border. Likewise, the Soviet partisan force was guided by a clear political objective involving the reestablishment of Communist control over the occupied territories. In contrast, the Apache Wars constituted a form of resistance and protest against the federal government's reservation policy and the corrupt administration of these areas. In this respect, once off the reservation, the Apaches could not count on the support of the local population since this was exactly the group that benefited most from their confinement to those areas. White settlers may have derided the army or scoffed at the soldiers' efforts, but their allegiance always remained with them and against the Indians.

Conclusion

As Geronimo and his small band of warriors along with their families traveled east toward incarceration in Florida in October 1886, they rode in passenger cars guarded by some twenty soldiers with orders to "kill anyone who attempted to escape." The image of Apaches locked into railcars and guarded by federal troops undoubtedly evokes similar images of European Jews packed into cattle cars as trains of the Reichsbahn carried them to the infamous killing centers in Poland. The fate of Geronimo and the Chiricahuas, however, was not foreordained as was that of the millions of European Jews heading to their annihilation. Despite the promise made to keep families together, Geronimo and his warriors were separated from theirs before the trip. In his memoir the Apache leader bitterly recalled this breach of faith and described his incarceration at Fort Pickens, near Pensacola, as a period of hard labor that included "sawing up large logs, . . . work every day." It was not until May of the following year that the Apache warriors were reunited with their families as promised. In the meantime, the sultry climate combined with hard labor led to the deaths of about a hundred of Geronimo's clan as a result of disease, most likely a combination of malaria and tuberculosis. Similarly, the forced removal of many of the children to the Indian School at Carlisle, Pennsylvania, provided an additional punishment to the proud and fiercely clannish Apaches, especially since some of these children subsequently perished from disease after their abduction.[1]

In response to this bleak situation, groups of Indian reformers in the East, including Major General George Crook, mounted a campaign to relocate the Apaches to a more suitable climate. Their return to Arizona remained barred as the territory's population refused to consider the return of a man who had assumed near mythic status as a symbol of settlers' fears. In the wake of Geronimo's capture, press coverage in the East and the West focused on the issue of punishment, with one report echoing a common refrain, "it seems probable that Geronimo will be executed, either by the civil or military authorities." In fact, Conrad M. Zulick, governor of the Arizona

Territory, traveled to Washington, D.C., to speak with President Grover Cleveland, reportedly demanding "the head of the cruel chief on a charger or at the end of a rope."[2]

Commissioner of Indian Affairs John D. Atkins confirmed Geronimo's status as a prisoner of war and stated that the final decision on his prosecution rested with the president. Atkins, however, offered his personal opinion that Geronimo "ought to be hanged" as a deterrent to "other young men in the tribe." In the end President Cleveland opted for imprisonment instead of execution. He even addressed the issue in his annual message to Congress on December 6, 1886, asserting: "[I]t was considered best to imprison them [the Apaches] in such manner as to prevent their ever engaging in such outrages again, instead of trying them for murder. Fort Pickens having been selected as a safe place of confinement, all the adult males were sent thither and will be closely guarded as prisoners." In his message Cleveland also referenced the treatment of the other Chiricahua Apaches: "In the meantime the residue of the band, who, though still remaining upon the reservation, were regarded as unsafe and suspected of furnishing aid to those on the war path, had been removed to Fort Marion. The women and larger children of the hostiles were also taken there, and arrangements have been made for putting the children of proper age in Indian schools." In April 1887, the Chiricahuas imprisoned at Fort Marion were transferred to Mount Vernon, Alabama, and in May 1888 were joined by Geronimo and his remaining warriors. They remained in Alabama for six years until their final relocation to Fort Sill, Oklahoma, in 1894, a transfer that owed much to the efforts of Crook and Major General Oliver O. Howard.[3]

The incarceration and treatment of Geronimo and the Chiricahuas was in many respects emblematic of the federal government's treatment of all Indian tribes in the last half of the nineteenth century. Those Natives who resisted their incarceration on the reservations, as in the cases of Geronimo and the Apaches and Big Foot and the Minneconjou Sioux during the Ghost Dance, faced two stark choices: submission or armed opposition. The former guaranteed them a place on a reservation but meant a bare existence supplemented with oft-broken promises of food and provisions, the slow decay of pride and Native traditions, and ultimately the loss of cultural identity. By the end of the nineteenth century, armed resistance meant facing overwhelming federal power, which might be successfully resisted for a time, but whose vast numerical and material advantages ultimately presaged death or surrender.

The Holocaust historian Christopher Browning has argued for "preserving the distinctions between policies of population decimation, genocide, and [the] Final Solution."[4] In the end the subjugation of the Indian tribes in the West between 1850 and 1890 was not a policy of intentional genocide like that pursued by the Nazis, even if it did embrace the use of military force. In the conquest of the American West, military force served as a coercive mechanism for achieving federal control, while the Nazi East witnessed force as an intrinsic and unrestrained instrument for mass murder and genocide. Although the U.S. military did not pursue an intentional policy of annihilation, it did embrace, however, an intentional policy of subjugation that entailed specific acts of atrocity and massacre. Federal policy undoubtedly sought to achieve a fundamental transformation of tribal and cultural identity for those Indians willing to assimilate. For those unwilling, the reservations and agencies became sites of isolation and marginalization, but not annihilation. One historian of the West described the intent of reservation policy as an "alternative to extinction" in which "American Indian cultures would probably die out but Indian bloodlines would survive."[5] In contrast, the Nazi use of force was intended from the start to serve as an instrument for mass extermination of the "Jewish bloodline" rather than as a coercive mechanism for achieving the submission or acquiescence of conquered populations.

Annihilation may not have been the goal of federal policy, but governmental plans and actions progressively marginalized the tribes and increasingly limited their rights and prerogatives. In an address to graduating cadets at West Point in 1884, Crook commented on the dilemma facing the tribes: "[T]here is no longer a frontier, and war with the Indian tribes can never again assume formidable dimensions. The savage is hemmed in by civilization, and he sees the inevitable must be faced. He is more ready to abandon his old habits and accept civilization, than civilization is to accept him." Likewise Lieutenant General Phil Sheridan, clearly no friend of the tribes, reflected more deeply and more precisely on this process when remarking: "[A]long came the nineteenth-century progress, or whatever it may be called, to disturb their happy condition. . . . In other words, we took away their country and their means of support, broke up their mode of living, their habits of life, introduced disease and decay among them, and it was for this and against this that they made war. Could anyone expect less?"⁶

Conflict, violence, acts of atrocity, and episodes of mass killing undoubtedly accompanied the battle for control of the West between the U.S. Army and the Native tribes. Likewise, the identity and intent of those involved in these actions is a critical point of consideration. According to the historian Samuel Watson, prior to 1850, "massacres were almost entirely the province of citizen soldiers . . . , militias and volunteers, and of individuals who killed natives out of hatred, greed or revenge." In the second half of the nineteenth century, the growth of federal power resulted in a corresponding increase in the role of the army in operations against the Indians. As such, individual commanders on the ground had great latitude in the ways they chose to interpret orders to "punish" or "chastise" specific tribes. The nature of warfare in the West, highlighted by the inability of the army to bring the Indians to battle on its terms and thus the need for achieving surprise, resulted in morning attacks aimed at entire villages that "often guaranteed a heavy [casualty] toll of women and children." Similarly, racism at Sand Creek and command ineptitude at Wounded Knee led to incontrovertible massacres, events that have become iconic symbols not because of their ubiquity, but rather because they largely provide the exception rather than the rule for federal military operations from 1850 to 1890. In his examination of the demographic collapse of the Indian tribes, Russell Thornton noted: "During the nineteenth century the total North American Indian population was not reduced nearly as much from warfare and genocide as from disease and other causes, though individual tribes in some regions were reduced virtually to extinction by them."⁷

Over the course of the Indian Wars, a War Department report estimated 930 engagements occurred between the various tribes and the U.S. Army between 1866 and 1891. The vast majority of these actions were fought by units at the company level or below, and 140 of these engagements, 15 percent of the total for the entire period, occurred in 1868 alone. Over this twenty-five-year period, the U.S. Army lost 932 men killed in action and counted an additional 1,061 as wounded. Settler losses during the same time included 461 civilians killed and another 116 wounded. With respect to the tribes, the army report estimated 5,519 Indians as killed or wounded, a number certainly lower than the actual losses due to the practice of warriors risking their own lives to recover the bodies of wounded or fallen comrades from the battlefield. This reckoning also does not include those who perished from disease or the secondary effects of military campaigns.[8]

While these losses are significant, they in no way approach the number of victims in Hitler's crusade in the East. This campaign literally involved the mass murder of millions in death camps and at the hands of specially prepared death squads, such as the notorious einsatzgruppen and Himmler's black and green legions of SS and police forces. In fact, the einsatzgruppen alone murdered almost 1.5 million Jewish men, women, and children, the majority, like the victims at Babi Yar, perishing at the hands of SS and police executioners with a bullet to the back of the head.[9] Beyond the death squads, though, police battalions, mounted SS units, indigenous auxiliaries, and Wehrmacht forces contributed to the murder of millions more, including Slavs, prisoners of war, Sinti and Roma, and Jews. While U.S. presidents and Congress debated policies aimed at the "civilization" and "Christianization" of the tribes, the supreme leader of Nazi Germany spoke of Slavs as "subhumans" and described Jews as a "plague" and a "sickness-causing bacteria."[10] In this respect Hitler viewed complete extermination, not assimilation, as the final solution to the danger posed by the indigenous peoples of the East.

The metaphor of disease offers another appropriate point of comparison between the two national projects. While Hitler and his Nazi cohort characterized Jews and Slavs in terms of a plague and bacteria, his solution was to eradicate the sources of such contagion. But no such metaphor was applied to the Indian tribes of the West by the U.S. government. Hitler and his Nazi administrators in the East employed a dual strategy that sought to "immunize" the German population by the annihilation of these "carriers of disease," on the one hand, while literally denying these populations "vaccinations" with which to resist disease, on the other. In comparison, true diseases, such as smallpox and measles, certainly devastated American Indian populations, especially in the sixteenth and seventeenth centuries, when "whole societies fell apart, values crumbled, and old ways of life lost all shred of meaning." Even in the nineteenth century, smallpox still posed a threat to some North American tribes, as seen in the Piegan experience in the winter of 1870, but federal efforts to promote vaccination among the tribes assisted in bringing this scourge under control. In fact, a federal inoculation program proved critical in protecting a number of Sioux bands during a smallpox outbreak in 1832, and these efforts resulted in the vaccination of more than 17,000 Indians nationwide by February 1833. Similarly, Thornton acknowledges, "Although there was a comparatively large number of smallpox epidemics between 1870 and the end of the nineteenth century, the story for the most part is one of localizing the outbreaks by active precautionary measures, and reducing mortality by active efforts at vaccination."[11] In this case the western tribes were neither identified as pathogens nor denied the vaccinations with which to resist them.

A comparison of American westward expansion with the Nazi quest for living space in the East demonstrates the inherent difficulty in comparing historical events that shared similar objectives—conquest and exploitation—but also fundamentally differed in both the rationale and the scope and scale of the actions taken to achieve these objectives. In the East, the goal involved the murder of every Jew within the grasp of the Nazi empire, regardless of age or gender. In the American West, it was an economic imperative and not a racial imperative that drove the dynamic of dispossession and isolation. This is not to argue that the project of westward expansion was free from atrocity, injustice, and racial bias. Indeed, the federal government, the U.S. Army, and the hordes of settlers who streamed into the West created a system that favored whites and led to the dispossession of the Native tribes, with the essential premise "that Indian ways of life were inferior." At the heart of this process, however, economic considerations dominated the government's policies toward the Indians, combined with a patronizing sense of paternalism. The ultimate objective with respect to the tribes involved remaking them in the image of "civilized" white Christians and eventually assimilating them into American society. In contrast, for Nazi racial planners, the very possibility of Jewish assimilation constituted an existential threat to "the foundation of Germandom: its racial substance."[12]

Recent scholarship on the Nazi conquest and exploitation of occupied eastern Europe has focused on the issue of agency and the corresponding roles played by decision makers at the "center" in Berlin and at the periphery in the occupied areas themselves. This discussion seeks to define the relative importance of the role of policymakers such as Hitler and Himmler in directing the Final Solution versus the actions and decisions made by lower-level Nazi

Party officials and bureaucrats in the occupied territories themselves. In addressing this issue, Peter Longerich argued, "it becomes irrefutably clear that the German power holders on the 'periphery' were always acting in the context of an overall policy guided by the 'centre,' meaning Hitler and the SS leadership." He continues, "However, the centre was only able to guide this process and set it in motion because it knew that impulses issuing from the centre were picked up with great independent initiative by the authorities in the 'periphery.'" In other words, the murder of the Jews in the Nazi East was a process initiated and shaped by Hitler and the SS but implemented by lower-level regional functionaries who demonstrated their own initiative in the process of annihilation. These men may have made local policy, but in their own minds they were simply "working towards the Führer" and his vision of new Germanic world empire.[13]

In contrast to the Nazi East, the overwhelming demands for annihilation of the Indians existed at the periphery, among those living in the West in closest proximity to the tribes. Calls for radical solutions to the "Indian Problem" such as extermination emerged not from the federal power center in Washington, D.C., but rather from the periphery itself in the words of settlers, speculators, frontier newspaper editors, and territorial officials. On the frontier it was the state and territorial volunteers and militias who demanded the right to "operate with genocidal freedom against fragments of Native American societies." In contrast, "[U.S.] policymakers still nourished some humane obligation" toward the tribes and recognized that "without federal protection, . . . American Indians faced extermination." As such it was federal officials, the U.S. Army, Indian reformers, and religious organizations at the center who were seen by those on the periphery as the primary obstacle to a "final solution of the Indian question." An opinion piece in the *Tombstone Daily Epitaph* framed this perspective by contending: "The trouble with the East, in relation to this Indian question is, that Arizona is thought to be too much out of the world. . . . [T]he New England humanitarians believe—or profess to believe—that the whites are the aggressors. . . . If it were only possible for Geronimo to go on one of these murderous raids in the Eastern States, the Indian question would soon be solved." Another editorial writer not only criticized those in the East for misplaced compassion but also went so far as to argue that the struggle on the frontier was an existential one between white settlers and the Native tribes: "People who live far from the scenes of Indian vengeance, the bloody work of his tomahawk and scalping knife, are not the safest or most intelligent counselors." He continued, "If their line of policy were observed, settlers upon the borders of western civilization would become the indiscriminate subjects of savage cruelty—if not total extermination."[14]

Despite the level of settler antipathy to the tribes, successful dispossession of Native lands could lead to a change in attitude. The anthropologist Lawrence Keeley described this attitudinal volte face: "Most Westerners still in direct contact with 'wild' Indians . . . regarded them as dangerous vermin, turbulent brigands, or useless beggars to be expelled or exterminated at any opportunity." He then noted, "Once the natives were safely reduced to living on reservations, however, Westerners were just as inclined to become sentimental about them and their traditional ways of life as Easterners were." In this case the rhetoric of extermination could be exchanged for that of nostalgia once the process of isolation and economic dispossession had taken place. For Nazi administrators in the East, however, extermination was not simply a rhetorical device to be discarded after successful conquest but "a crucial precondition for accomplishing the historical task of reasserting the nation's collective identity and purging it of everything that polluted and undermined it."[15]

In both the East and the West, one finds the use of language as a means to create cultural and racial separation between the objects of conquest and those seeking to supplant them. In the American West, the description of Indians as "savages" served itself as an explicit rationale for a multitude of aims, including dispossession, "civilization," assimilation, and extermination. In the case of colonial America, the historian Wayne Lee argued that the description of the Iroquois and other tribes as "barbarians" provided a potential rationale for atrocity and mass killing that "profoundly shaped" the nature of the conflict between colonists and the Indians. Even in this case, however, Lee cautioned that despite racism and prejudice, early Americans were "prepared to absorb them if they [the Indians] changed their ways." In short, white and Indian relations in the West were predicated on the belief that the tribes could in fact join in the "American project" if they were willing to submit, to abandon their cultural and religious heritage, and to become farmers. In contrast, the Nazi description of Jews and Slavs as "subhumans" created a dynamic in which these groups were specifically excluded from assimilation and incorporation into the socially constructed Aryan *Volk*. In fact, the Nazi linguistic assault against Jews not only began with the publication of Hitler's *Mein Kampf* in 1925 but also continued in the pages of German mass media in the 1930s, involving the "racialization of the category 'Jew' and its separation from [the concept of] Germanness."[16]

The process of "othering" or dehumanizing putative enemies has been, and remains, a hallmark of warfare and conflict to the present. This process, however, in both the American West and the Nazi East resulted in the use of apocalyptic imagery and language in dealing with policymakers' multiple pronouncements on both the "solution of the Indian problem" and "the final solution of the Jewish question."[17] In the case of the former, the use of exterminatory rhetoric repeatedly appeared in the writings and utterances of politicians, soldiers, frontiersmen, and in the editorial columns of major newspapers. Still, such rhetoric was often invoked not as a desired end state, but rather as a situation that had to (or could) be prevented. Four years before President Grant's inauguration and the proclamation of his so-called Peace Policy, a *New York Times* editorial in September 1865 proclaimed: "Many of the western settlers are very anxious for a war of extermination against the Indians, and assert that outrages and atrocities will never cease until this is adopted and ended. But this in itself would be an atrocity of the most gigantic and inexcusable character."[18] In addition to the moral arguments against such a policy, the editorial noted the cost and bloodshed associated with such an undertaking, arguments made all the more powerful in the wake of the death and destruction of the American Civil War.

If costs in blood and treasure were cited as arguments against extermination in the West, such was not the case with the Nazi East. Indeed, the exterminatory rhetoric and the language of annihilation was transformed into concrete actions, whether in the form of the Commissar Order, the "hunger policy," or most significantly in the discussions of Nazi bureaucrats at Wannsee concerning Hitler's decision on the "evacuation" of the Jews to the East. In this case "evacuation" was simply a euphemism for genocide, as Adolf Eichmann, the "Jewish expert" in the SS, later conceded with his admission, "In the end, final solution meant extermination."[19]

If the SS was the principal agency charged with exterminating the Jews, it is also equally clear from the secretly recorded conversations of German POWs that "practically all German soldiers knew or suspected that Jews were being murdered en masse." In fact, this knowledge was in part gained through the Wehrmacht's own support to SS units and participation in both a war of annihilation and a "partisan war" that became its own justification for the mass murder of millions. In the end, as Mark Roseman correctly argued, "Whatever Hitler's precise intentions, his rhetoric thus provided the justification for others' actions, assuring the perpetrators that murder was appropriate."[20]

If Hitler repeatedly prophesied the annihilation of the Jews and emerged as the architect of the Final Solution, Indian policy and the so-called Indian question in the American West were driven by a diverse range of individuals of varying social, religious, and political outlooks. Without a doubt, political rhetoric and governmental policy played a major role in determining the treatment of the Indians. President Andrew Jackson's policy of removal from 1829 to 1837 offers one extreme, while the "peace offensive" of the Grant administration in 1869 provides a significant contrast.[21] Additionally, congressional oversight often played a key role in shaping policy and its execution, especially with respect to appropriations and treaty and agreement ratification throughout the period of westward expansion. In this respect the chronological breadth of U.S.–American Indian relations poses its own challenges when compared with the much more focused and consistent Nazi racial policies aimed at the conquered populations of the East.

Even if one accepts that the results of the two efforts shared a common goal, the victims of Hitler's campaign in the East could not attempt to challenge Nazi policies in the Reichstag, in the courts, or in the realm of public opinion. In contrast, religious and social-reform groups were created in cities throughout the eastern United States and became strong advocates for the Native tribes, with the ability to influence the formulation and implementation of Indian policy. Humanitarians throughout this period may have been a minority, but they were "close to President Grant's ear" and forcefully argued for the federal government to keep its treaty obligations to the tribes. Likewise, Quaker Indian agents remained ardent supporters of the concept of assimilation even as they gradually were forced out of or resigned their positions during reforms initiated by Secretary of the Interior Carl Schurz between 1877 and 1882. The Jews and eastern European Slavs enjoyed no such support from within the Third

Reich. Additionally, the National Socialist Party and Nazi administrators "worked towards the Führer" and established the fundamental principles of governance for the occupied East. In this respect the party and the state created plans for the settlement and expansion of empire from Berlin with inputs from the periphery. In contrast, the settlement of the American West was influenced by the dynamic of pioneers, fortune seekers, and frontiersmen who, on their own initiative and for personal gain, continually pushed against every temporary and "permanent" Indian frontier established by the government since the first days of European settlement. This led one frustrated army officer to complain, "All our *Indian wars*, with very few exceptions, are brought on either by our *frontier settlers* . . . or the traders in the Indian country, who as a class, are an unmitigated set of *scoundrels*."[22]

The comparison between the Nazi East and the American West reveals key points of congruence but equally important points of dissimilarity. In both cases the dynamic of conquest and subjugation entailed ominous consequences for the defeated, and both national projects shared similar processes involving isolation, expropriation, and mass killing. To admit the singular nature of the genocidal impulse that drove Nazi visions of a racial utopia "cleansed" of Jews and other racial undesirables does not detract from the elements of violence, brutality, and atrocity that accompanied U.S. expansion into the West. Likewise, it should not be surprising that for the Native tribes and individual Indians, the loss of life and land would evoke comparisons to the Shoah. From this perspective, Wilma Mankiller's description of the Trail of Tears as "our holocaust" is completely understandable. Still, the injustice and atrocity symbolized by the massacres at Sand Creek and Wounded Knee did not create a historical trajectory to Babi Yar and the killing fields of Himmler's SS and police empire in the East, even if Hitler made this comparison explicit in his remark that the conquest of the American West had been attained "after the white man had shot down the millions of redskins to a few hundred thousand."[23]

In this sense the importance of Hitler's declaration is not related to the accuracy or inaccuracy of his assessment, but rather to *his own belief* in the historical truth of this statement. Indeed, if Hitler envisioned the conquest of the American West as a process that included the murder of millions, then he also could imagine the subjugation of German lebensraum in the East through a process of mass annihilation. Hitler's boasts on creating a new frontier in the East to rival that of the American West in the previous century not only demonstrated his limited understanding of U.S. history but, more importantly, exposed the genocidal fantasy that framed his conception of conquest and exploitation in eastern Europe.

Notes

Abbreviations

BA-MA	Bundesarchiv-Militärarchiv, Freiburg, Germany
BArch	Bundesarchiv, Berlin, Germany
LOC	Library of Congress, Washington, D.C.
NARA	National Archives and Records Administration, College Park, Md./Washington, D.C.
USMMA	U.S. Holocaust Memorial Museum Archives, Washington, D.C.
ZStl	Zentrale Stelle der Landesjustizverwaltungen, Ludwigsburg, Germany

Introduction

1. Kershaw, *Hitler: 1936–1945 Nemesis*, 434. Hitler's comment is intended to indicate that Nazi Germany's colonial empire would begin in Europe.
2. Stahel, *Operation Typhoon*, 230; Kershaw, *Fateful Choices*, 387; Baranowski, *Nazi Empire*, 140–41. According to Baranowski, "Hitler's visions drank deeply from the popularity of [German] fiction on the American frontier."
3. Limerick, *Legacy of Conquest*, 26, 27–28; Kocka, "Asymmetrical Historical Comparison," 49.
4. Hinton, "Critical Genocide Studies," 45–46; Huttenbach, "From the Editor," 319; Huttenbach, "Vita Felix, Via Dolorossa," 57 (quote, emphasis added).
5. Churchill, *Struggle for the Land*, 203; Churchill, *Little Matter of Genocide*; Stannard, *American Holocaust*, 254–55; Thornton, *American Indian Holocaust*, xv–xvi. See also Stannard, "Uniqueness as Denial."
6. Gwynne, *Empire of the Summer Moon*, 2; G. Anderson, *Conquest of Texas*, 259, 359–60. The term "ethnic cleansing" came out of the conflicts in Yugoslavia in the 1990s and was defined by a UN commission as "rendering an area ethnically homogenous by using force or intimidation to remove persons of given groups from the area." Ethnic cleansing may involve acts of "murder, torture, arbitrary arrest and detention, extra-judicial executions, rape, and sexual assaults." The terms "genocide" and "ethnic cleansing," however, are not synonymous. For an extended discussion of this issue, see Lieberman, "'Ethnic Cleansing' versus Genocide?"

7. Kakel, *American West and the Nazi East*, 3; Fischer, review of *The American West and the Nazi East*, 502.
8. Ostler, "Question of Genocide in U.S. History," 118, 120; G. Anderson, *Ethnic Cleansing and the Indian*, 6; Alvarez, *Native America and the Question of Genocide*, 166; Stone, *Historiography of the Holocaust*, 4.
9. For a discussion of this neo-Marxian perspective, see Carmichael, *Genocide before the Holocaust*, 58–59. Examples of scholars who use the concept of postcolonial theory include Zimmerer, "Colonialism and the Holocaust"; Zimmerer, "Birth of the *Ostland*"; Wolfe, "Settler Colonialism and the Elimination of the Native"; and Moses, "Genocide and Settler Society in Australian History." For a dissenting view on the role of the settling of the American West in shaping Nazi policy, see Guettel, "U.S. Frontier as Rationale for the Nazi East?"
10. Hixson, *American Settler Colonialism*, 140 (quote, emphasis added). Hixson concluded, "in the final analysis the United States pursued a continuous 'foreign policy' of colonial genocide targeting indigenous North Americans as well as Hawaiians." Ibid., 197.
11. McDonnell and Moses, "Raphael Lemkin as Historian of Genocide in the Americas," 501; Convention on the Prevention and Punishment of Genocide, accessed Apr. 4, 2012.
12. Lemkin, *Axis Rule in Occupied Europe*, 79. For a discussion of this issue, see Moses, "Raphael Lemkin, Culture, and the Concept of Genocide."
13. Weiss-Wendt, "Problems in Comparative Genocide Scholarship," 44, 65. In fact, Weiss-Wendt contended that this definitional quagmire has left the field itself stuck in a state of "crisis."
14. Hinton, "Critical Genocide Studies," 51; Rosenberg and Silina, "Genocide by Attrition," 111.
15. Katz, *Holocaust and Mass Death*, 128.
16. Shaw and Bartov, "Question of Genocide in Palestine," 246, 253.
17. For examples, see Wippermann, *Europäischer Faschismus im Vergleich*; and Arendt, *Origins of Totalitarianism*.
18. Glover, *Humanity*, 306.
19. Casas, *Short Account of the Destruction of the Indies*, 3; Taylor, *American Colonies*, 51; Weber, *Spanish Frontier in North America*, 339. For a detailed critique of the effects of the "black legend," see Powell, *Tree of Hate*.
20. West, *Last Indian War*, xx. For the ramifications of disease, see McNeill, *Plagues and Peoples*; and Ramenofsky, *Vectors of Death*. For the influence of warfare in early American history, see I. Steele, *Warpaths*; and Grenier, *First Way of War*.
21. Coffman, *Old Army*, 3–4, 215; Utley, *Indian Frontier*, 4.
22. Weinberg, *Visions of Victory*, 18. See also Mallmann and Cüppers, *Halbmond und Hakenkreuz*; and Weinberg, *Visions of Victory*, 8–18.
23. Greene, *Yellowstone Command*, 4. Greene used the term "cultural asphyxiation" to refer to the fate of Sioux and Northern Cheyenne confined to the reservations.

24. West, *Contested Plains*, xxii. See also DeLay, *War of a Thousand Deserts*, xiv, xxi.
25. Lower, *Nazi Empire-Building*, 20–24; Hermand, *Old Dreams of a New Reich*, 240; Bogue, "Agricultural Empire," 289 (Jefferson); White, *"It's Your Misfortune,"* 72; Turner, *Significance of the Frontier in American History*, 3.
26. Lower, *Nazi Empire-Building*, 23; H. Smith, *Virgin Land*, 123–32; West, *Contested Plains*, 98; Bogue, "Agricultural Empire," 285; Prucha, *Great Father*, 44.
27. Longerich, *Holocaust*, 428. See also Lower, *Nazi Empire-Building*, 71–78. Samuel Watson also discussed this concept in respect to the U.S. Army being caught between demands and policies emanating from Washington, D.C., on the one hand and from the frontier on the other. See Watson, *Peacekeepers and Conquerors*, 3.

Chapter 1

1. West, *Contested Plains*, xxiii; W. Smith, *Ideological Origins of Nazi Imperialism*, 242; Kershaw, *Hitler: 1889–1936 Hubris*, 252; Weinberg, *World at Arms*, 44.
2. For detailed discussions of Comanche social, political, and military organization, see Hämäläinen, *Comanche Empire*; and DeLay, *War of a Thousand Deserts*.
3. Cecil, *Myth of the Master Race*, 8–9; Longerich, *Heinrich Himmler*, 273 (quote); Liulevicius, *War Land on the Eastern Front*, 278.
4. Hietala, *Manifest Design*, 176; Horsman, *Race and Manifest Destiny*, 87 (quote, emphasis in original); O'Sullivan, "Annexation," 5; Merk, *Manifest Destiny and Mission*, 261.
5. Grund, *Americans in Their Moral, Social, and Political Relations*, 8.
6. Hietala, *Manifest Design*, 214; Coffman, *Old Army*, 70, 73.
7. West, *Contested Plains*, 12; Bowes, *Exiles and Pioneers*, 4, 220–21. Bowes examined the removal and relocation of some of the Great Lakes tribes to Kansas and discussed the difficulty of the federal government in exercising control in these areas. He noted, "Although the absence of federal authority allowed for the persistence of native autonomy, it also provided traders, settlers, speculators, and local officials countless opportunities to promote their agendas at the expense of both federal policies and Indian interests." Ibid., 4.
8. Wallace and Hoebel, *Comanches*, 32.
9. Quoted in H. Smith, *Virgin Land*, 37.
10. Greenberg, *Wicked War*, 173; Merk, *Manifest Destiny and Mission*, 28; Morgan, *William McKinley and His America*, 225.
11. For a discussion of the various manifestations of this idea between 1840 and 1898, see Merk, *Manifest Destiny and Mission*, 24–266.
12. Greenberg, *Wicked War*, 55 (Polk), 76; Pratt, *Expansionists of 1898*, 2–5; Sherman, *Memoirs*, chap. 26, ebook 4361.
13. White, *"It's Your Misfortune,"* 246; Angevine, "Individuals, Organizations, and Engineering." See also Ostler, *Plains Sioux and U.S. Colonialism*, 59; and Utley, *Cavalier in Buckskin*, 124–25.

14. *Annual Report of the Secretary of War* (1880), accessed Aug. 20, 2012.
15. Turner, *Frontier in American History*, 2–3. For a discussion of the responses to Turner's thesis, see Aron, "Lessons in Conquest."
16. West, *Last Indian War*, 282; Greene, *American Carnage*, 215–46, 288.
17. McPherson and Hogue, *Ordeal by Fire*, 19; Daly, *Covering America*, 57–58, 85 (Bennett), 96–98; West, *Contested Plains*, 180; S. Vaughn, *Encyclopedia of American Journalism* (New York: Routledge, 2008), s.v. "Yellow Journalism," by Emily Erickson.
18. Greenberg, *Wicked War*, 96–97; Knight, *Following the Indian Wars*, 4–5, 28–29, 31, 66; Daly, *Covering America*, 122–23; *Annual Report of the Secretary of War* (1883), accessed Nov. 20, 2014.
19. McLaurin, *Celia*, 82; Mueller, *Shooting Arrows and Slinging Mud*, 148; West, *Contested Plains*, 123.
20. S. Smith, *View from Officers' Row*, 105; C. Robinson, *General Crook*, 114; Jacoby, *Shadows at Dawn*, 226; O. Howard, *Autobiography*, 447; Gatewood, *Apache Wars Memoir*, 113.
21. C. Robinson, *General Crook*, 235. See also Crook, *Autobiography*, 233–34.
22. Quoted in Prucha, *Great Father*, 184.
23. McPherson, *Battle Cry of Freedom*; Mardock, *Reformers and the American Indian*, 199; Quinton, "Woman's National Indian Association," 71–73. *The Indian's Friend* was first published in 1888.
24. *New York Herald*, 17 May 1856; G. D. R. Boyd, "The Indian War in Oregon," *New York Herald*, July 18, 1856, 6; "Indian Hostilities—The Probable Extermination of that Race in Our Territories," *New York Herald*, July 31, 1865, 4; "Virginia City and the Silver Mines," *Boston Daily Advertiser*, Aug. 28, 1865, 2.
25. Jas. S. Reynolds, "Caleb Once More," *Idaho Tri-Weekly Statesman* (Boise), June 14, 1866, 2.
26. Daly, *Covering America*, 79–80, 109. Daly describes the emergence of the Associated Press and its influence on news reporting in the United States.
27. "Our Indian Troubles," *New York Herald*, July 29, 1867, 4.
28. *National Republican* (Washington, D.C.), June 21, 1876; "The Indians," *Memphis Daily Appeal*, Aug. 26, 1876; *Morning Star and Catholic Messenger* (New Orleans), Nov. 26, 1876.
29. "The Indian Question," *Iola (Kans.) Register*, Sept. 9, 1876, 1; Sweeney, *From Cochise to Geronimo*, 558 (Lawton).
30. Nye, *Unembarrassed Muse*, 200; Bold, *Selling the West*, xiii, 4; Johannsen, *House of Beadle and Adams*, accessed Sept. 7, 2012; Mueller, *Shooting Arrows and Slinging Mud*, 3–4.
31. Nye, *Unembarrassed Muse*, 201–202.
32. Bold, *Selling the West*, xii, 1, 6, 11–12; Johannsen, *House of Beadle and Adams*, accessed Sept. 7, 2012.
33. Nye, *Unembarrassed Muse*, 203, 205; Bold, *Selling the West*, 14.
34. For a critical discussion of James Fenimore Cooper's writing, see Folsom, *American Western Novel*, 36–59.

35. S. Smith, *View from Officers' Row*, 19; Faragher, *Women and Men on the Overland Trail*, 31–32.
36. Bold, *Selling the West*, 11–13.
37. As quoted in Nye, *Unembarrassed Muse*, 207.
38. Ibid., 201, 287.
39. Rickey, *Forty Miles a Day on Beans and Hay*, 23; Nye, *Unembarrassed Muse*, 284; Bold, *Selling the West*, xii.
40. McNenly, *Native Performers in Wild West Shows*, 5; Russell, *Buffalo Bill*, 193–96 (reviews).
41. Nye, *Unembarrassed Muse*, 192, 193; Wilson, *Buffalo Bill's Wild West*, 29–189, 56 (Twain); Russell, *Buffalo Bill*, 316–17.
42. Penny, *Kindred by Choice*, 60–62; Usbeck, *Fellow Tribesmen*, 24–25; May, *Mein Leben und Streben*, chap. 7, accessed Sept. 7, 2012. In his autobiography, devoted primarily to his legal and financial troubles, May mentions the accusation that he has taken his western figures from Buffalo Bill, among others.
43. Kershaw, *Hitler: 1889–1936 Hubris*, 15, 387. See also Penny, *Kindred by Choice*, 152–55.
44. Hitler, *Mein Kampf* (1939), 419. One manifestation of this influence can be found in Hitler's contention that the "American continent was opened" by "Aryans," who eventually conquered the land "when their increasing number and better instruments permitted them to clear the wild soil for tillage and to resist the aborigines [i.e., Indians]."
45. W. Smith, *Ideological Origins of Nazi Imperialism*, 240; Picker, *Tischgespräche*, 69; Whittlesey, "Haushofer," 399–400, 407, 408, 410–11.
46. Hitler, *Mein Kampf* (1939), 180, 935, 936, 940. Significantly, Hitler compared the size and strength of the European states with the "American Union" (i.e., the United States).
47. Ibid., 947; , 948–49.
48. Ibid., 950–51; Baranowski, *Nazi Empire*, 142; Hitler, *Mein Kampf* (1939), 951–52.
49. Weinberg, *Hitler's Second Book*, 18, 49, 51, 53.
50. Ibid., 149, 158.
51. Weinberg, *Visions of Victory*, 8; W. Smith, *Ideological Origins of Nazi Imperialism*, 255; Kühne, "Colonialism and the Holocaust," 349. For a discussion of the concept of "serial genocide," see Gellately, "Third Reich, the Holocaust, and Visions of Serial Genocide."
52. Weinberg, *Germany, Hitler, and World War II*, 155. For a more detailed discussion of Hitler's global ambitions of conquest, see Goda, *Tomorrow the World*.
53. Hitler, *Mein Kampf* (1939), 949; Picker, *Tischgespräche*, 215, 247, 440–41; Gruner, *Jewish Forced Labor under the Nazis*, 196–213; Lower, *Nazi Empire-Building*, 143–50.
54. Weinberg, *Foreign Policy of Hitler's Germany*, 538.
55. Hitler, *Mein Kampf* (1939), 227–28, 232, 234; Kershaw, *Hitler: 1889–1936 Hubris*, 301.

56. Quoted in Reuth, *Goebbels*, 167; and Noakes, *German Home Front*, 465.
57. Noakes, *German Home Front*, 466.
58. Reuth, *Goebbels*, 176, 177; Kershaw, *Hitler: 1889–1936 Hubris*, 453–54.
59. Quoted in Kershaw, *Hitler: 1936–1945 Nemesis*, 201; and Noakes, *German Home Front*, 470.
60. Kershaw, *Hitler: 1936–1945 Nemesis*, 241; Reuth, *Goebbels*, 256.
61. Combs, *Voice of the SS*, 20; Matthäus et al., *Ausbildungsziel Judenmord?*, 38; "Der Reichsführer SS und Chef der Deutschen Polizei im Reichsministerium des Innern, O-Kdo P I (1a) Nr.168 III/39, Betrifft: Aushängekästen für 'Das Schwarze Korps.' [Oct. 28, 1939]," T175, Records of the Reichsführer SS and Chief of the German Police, reel 227, frame 2766127, NARA.
62. Combs, *Voice of the SS*, 31, 41–42, 70, 107, 304.
63. Ibid., 129–38, 376–77.
64. Donson, "Why Did German Youth become Fascists?," 344; Oberkommando der Wehrmacht, *Kampf um Norwegen*, 7; Mielke, *Heldenkampf um Narvik*; Bathe, *Feldzug der 18 Tage*, vi, xvii, 168.
65. Koschorke, *Polizeireiter in Polen*, 5–6, 12, 23, 49.
66. Ibid., 44–47.
67. Koschorke, *Polizei greift ein!*, 13, 16, 21, 49.
68. Quoted in H. Hoffmann, *Triumph of Propaganda*, vi. For a description of heroic military film portrayals, see Giesen, *Nazi Propaganda Films*, 51–92.
69. Giesen, *Nazi Propaganda Films*, 122–28.
70. Tegel, *Jew Süss*, 185; Manz, *Mind in Prison*, 78; Giesen, *Nazi Propaganda Films*, 132–33; Westermann, *Hitler's Police Battalions*, 118; Burleigh, *Moral Combat*, 396.
71. H. Hoffmann, *Triumph of Propaganda*, 173; Giesen, *Nazi Propaganda Films*, 137–38.
72. Kershaw, *Hitler: 1936–1945 Nemesis*, 582–83 (quote); Matthäus et al, *Ausbildungsziel Judenmord?*, 60.
73. H. Hoffmann, *Triumph of Propaganda*, 176.
74. Weinberg, *World at Arms*, 190; Rürup, *Krieg gegen die Sowjetunion*, 42; Hermand, *Old Dreams of a New Reich*, 272; Noakes, *German Home Front*, 475 (quotes).
75. Reuth, *Goebbels*, 293, 301; H. Hoffmann, *Triumph of Propaganda*, 171.
76. Snyder, *Bloodlands*, 287; H. Hoffmann, *Triumph of Propaganda*, 172.
77. Steinweis, "Eastern Europe and the Notion of the 'Frontier,'" 60–61.
78. Merk, *Manifest Destiny and Mission*, 57; Greenberg, *Wicked War*, 193–99; Gorn et al., *Constructing the American Past*, 86–87 (quote).

Chapter 2

1. Weinberg, *World at Arms*, 190.
2. Greenberg, *Wicked War*, 131–33, 213; Williams, *Savage Anxieties*, 210–17. Williams examines the concept of the "savage" from the perspective of the founders of the American Republic.

3. Banner, *How the Indians Lost Their Land*, 4.
4. Cohen, *Handbook of Federal Indian Law*, 69; draft of first inaugural address, n.d., Ulysses S. Grant Papers, reel 4, LOC. The inaugural address was delivered on March 4, 1869.
5. Cohen, *Handbook of Federal Indian Law*, 69. For a discussion of the Indian Reform Movement, see Mardock, *Reformers and the American Indian*.
6. B. Steele, *Jefferson and American Nationhood*, 174; Jefferson, "Third Annual Message to Congress," accessed June 11, 2015; Jefferson, "Fourth Annual Message to Congress," accessed June 11, 2015; Banner, *How the Indians Lost Their Land*, 193–94.
7. Banner, *How the Indians Lost Their Land*, 199–201.
8. *Cherokee Nation v. Georgia* (1831); Banner, *How the Indians Lost Their Land*, 220.
9. *Worcester v. Georgia* (1832); Jackson, "Second Annual Message to Congress," accessed Oct. 12, 2012.
10. Banner, *How the Indians Lost Their Land*, 217–18, 224–25; Hietala, *Manifest Design*, 203.
11. Watson, *Peacekeepers and Conquerors*, 176. For an in-depth discussion of the army's role in removal, see ibid., 141–77.
12. White, *"It's Your Misfortune,"* 87.
13. Utley, *Indian Frontier*, 37. For a detailed discussion of this process, see Prucha, *American Indian Treaties*, 156–82.
14. Jackson, "Fifth Annual Message to Congress," accessed Oct. 12, 2012; White, *"It's Your Misfortune,"* 103. In contrast to White, Reginald Horsman argued that as early as 1850 "a clear pattern" of racialized thinking and Anglo-Saxon superiority was emerging in the United States. See *Race and Manifest Destiny*, 5. Horsman also discussed the political and social contestation of this idea with respect to the Indians and noted the debates on their ability or inability to be assimilated into white society.
15. Adams and DeLuzio, *On the Borders of Love and Power*, 3, 5.
16. Cohen, *Handbook of Federal Indian Law*, 73.
17. Ball, *Army Regulars*, xii.
18. C. Robinson, *General Crook*, 102–103; S. Smith, *View from Officers' Row*, 93–94.
19. Banner, *How the Indians Lost Their Land*, 228; White, *"It's Your Misfortune,"* 92. For examples of this failure to meet treaty obligations and to provide provisions, see S. Robinson, *Apache Voices*, 70; Wooster, *Nelson A. Miles*, 72; and Greene, *American Carnage*, 88–89. See also G. Anderson, *Conquest of Texas*, 259–76.
20. Prucha, *Great Father*, 54, 57.
21. Quoted in ibid., 100.
22. Quoted in ibid., 102.
23. *Annual Report of the Commissioner of Indian Affairs* (1875), accessed Sept. 21, 2012; Todd, "Education of Indian Girls in the West," 39–40.
24. Quoted in Adams, *Education for Extinction*, 27.

25. Ibid., 97–135; Prucha, *Great Father*, 239 (quote).
26. Child, *Boarding School Seasons*, 13; Greene, *American Carnage*, 61 (unidentified Sioux); Stahl, "U.S. and Native American Education." The emphasis on boarding school education changed in 1928 as a result of the "Meriam Report" which advocated the use of reservation schools. Subsequent legislation led to the opening of public schools for Native American children.
27. Child, *Boarding School Seasons*, 13.
28. Ball, *Army Regulars*, xx.
29. Prucha, *Great Father*, 47.
30. *Annual Report of the Commissioner of Indian Affairs* (1851), accessed Oct. 18, 2012.
31. White, *Railroaded*, xxii.
32. Neihardt, *Black Elk Speaks*, 8–9; Utley, *Frontier Regulars*, 115; *Annual Report of the Commissioner of Indian Affairs* (1868), accessed Oct. 18, 2012; Weigley, *American Way of War*, 158.
33. Reilly, *Bound to Have Blood*, 32, 33 (first quote) 34 (second quote).
34. Utley, *Frontier Regulars*, 122–23, 125; *Annual Report of the Secretary of War* (1867), M997, reel 15, NARA.
35. Kavanagh, *Comanches*, 411. Kavanagh placed the blame for this conflict on "various 'designing persons,'" including the governor of Kansas, Samuel J. Crawford.
36. Prucha, *Great Father*, 155–56; *Annual Report of the Commissioner of Indian Affairs* (1868), accessed Nov. 18, 2014; Utley, *Frontier Regulars*, 137 (Sherman).
37. *Annual Report of the Commissioner of Indian Affairs* (1868), accessed Nov. 18, 2014; Sherman, *Memoirs*, chap. 26, ebook 4361; Prucha, *American Indian Treaties*, 280–81.
38. Prucha, *Great Father*, 156; "Ratified Treaty No. 371," accessed Oct. 18, 2012; White, *"It's Your Misfortune,"* 97; Sherman, *Memoirs*, chap. 26, ebook 4361.
39. Ostler, *Plains Sioux and U.S. Colonialism*, 36; Mardock, *Reformers and the American Indian*, 50.
40. Milner, *With Good Intentions*, 1, 2–3; draft of first inaugural address, n.d., Grant Papers, reel 4, LOC.
41. Draft of first inaugural address, n.d., Grant Papers, reel 4, LOC. Significantly, Grant followed his comments on the Indians with a plea for the ratification of the pending Fifteenth Amendment.
42. Bogue, "Agricultural Empire," 289.
43. Draft of first annual address to Congress, n.d., Grant Papers, reel 4, LOC; Sherman, *Memoirs*, chap. 26, ebook 4361.
44. Draft of first annual address to Congress, n.d., Grant Papers, reel 4, LOC.
45. Mardock, *Reformers and the American Indian*, 2; Milner, *With Good Intentions*, 4.
46. Mardock, *Reformers and the American Indian*, 55; Utley, *Frontier Regulars*, 133, 198; Prucha, *Great Father*, 161.

47. Quoted in Prucha, *Great Father*, 159, 160.
48. Banner, *How the Indians Lost Their Land*, 252; Prucha, *Great Father*, 164; White, "It's Your Misfortune," 116–17.
49. Draft of fourth annual address to Congress, Dec. 2, 1872, Grant Papers, reel 5, LOC.
50. Prucha, *Great Father*, 167 (quote); "The Indians," *Dallas Weekly Herald*, Dec. 30, 1871, 1.
51. Haviland to Sheridan, July 30, 1874, Philip H. Sheridan Papers, reel 6, LOC.
52. Ibid.
53. Mardock, *Reformers and the American Indian*, 117–18; Prucha, *Great Father*, 170 (quote). Grant later commuted two of the death sentences into life imprisonment at Alcatraz Island in San Francisco Bay.
54. Mardock, *Reformers and the American Indian*, 119–20.
55. U.S. Senate Select Committee, *Testimony in Regard to the Sioux Indians, Dakota*, 81.
56. Adams, *Education for Extinction*, 16–17; C. Robinson, *General Crook*, 294; Prucha, *Great Father*, 226; Milner, *With Good Intentions*, 193 (quote); Adams and DeLuzio, *On the Borders of Love and Power*, 5; Mardock, *Reformers and the American Indian*, 217.
57. Prucha, *Great Father*, 227; Milner, *With Good Intentions*, 197.
58. Adams, *Education for Extinction*, 8, 15.
59. Weinberg, *Germany, Hitler, and World War II*, 32, 35; Hitler, *Mein Kampf* (1962), 231.
60. Quoted in Noakes and Pridham, *Foreign Policy, War, and Racial Extermination*, 737.
61. Ibid., 739, 741, 743 (quotes); Rossino, *Hitler Strikes Poland*, 9–10.
62. Quoted in Rutherford, *Prelude to the Final Solution*, 4.
63. Kershaw, *Hitler: 1936–1945 Nemesis*, 244–245.
64. Noakes and Pridham, *Foreign Policy, War, and Racial Extermination*, 930; Epstein, *Model Nazi*, 130 (quote).
65. Epstein, *Model Nazi*, 172–90
66. Yahil, *Holocaust*, 164; Hilberg, *Destruction of the European Jews*, student ed., 74. For a differing perspective on the creation of ghettos, employing a cultural, semantic, and linguistic approach, see Michman, *Jewish Ghettos during the Holocaust*.
67. Hilberg, *Destruction of the European Jews*, student ed., 81–84, 94–95.
68. Kaplan, *Warsaw Diary*, 277; Hilberg, *Destruction of the European Jews*, student ed., 95–96; Yahil, *Holocaust*, 165 (second quote).
69. Noakes and Pridham, *Foreign Policy, War, and Racial Extermination*, 958; Yahil, *Holocaust*, 152–53; Breitman, *Architect of Genocide*, 242; Kershaw, *Hitler: 1936–1945 Nemesis*, 240–41.
70. Noakes and Pridham, *Foreign Policy, War, and Racial Extermination*, 959–60; Yahil, *Holocaust*, 160 (quote).
71. Quoted in Noakes and Pridham, *Foreign Policy, War, and Racial Extermination*, 962 (quote, emphasis added).
72. Ibid., 965 (Frank); "III.,'Polizei-Regiment-Mitte, Bericht vom 16.2. bis 28.2.1942 [Mar. 1, 1942]," RG 48.004M, Records of the Military

Historical Institute, Prague, reel 2, frame 201479, USHMMA; Lissance, *Halder Diaries*, 565.
73. Sandkühler, *Endlösung in Galizien*, 30.
74. Quoted in Noakes and Pridham, *Foreign Policy, War, and Racial Extermination*, 988.
75. Ibid., 932; Yahil, *Holocaust*, 254; Breitman, *Architect of Genocide*, 122; Westermann, *Hitler's Police Battalions*, 81–82.
76. Hitler, *Mein Kampf* (1962), 950; Snyder, *Bloodlands*, 159; Weinberg, *Hitler's Second Book*, 158; Kershaw, *Hitler: 1936–1945 Nemesis*, 336.
77. Kershaw, *Hitler: 1936–1945 Nemesis*, 343; Förster, "Operation Barbarossa," 482.
78. Krausnick, *Hitlers Einsatzgruppen*, 100–101; Rürup, *Krieg gegen die Sowjetunion*, 42.
79. Förster, "Operation Barbarossa," 496–507.
80. Klein, *Einsatzgruppen in der besetzten Sowjetunion*, 367–68.
81. "Oberkommando des Heeres, Betr.: Unterweisung über den vorgesehen Einsatz [May 6, 1941]," NS 19, folder 2818, fiche 1, frame 1, BArch.
82. Kay, "Germany's Staatssekretäre," 685; Snyder, *Bloodlands*, 162–63 (quote).
83. Rutherford, *Prelude to the Final Solution*, 218; Tooze, *Wages of Destruction*, 468, 472; Snyder, *Bloodlands*, 160; Kershaw, *Hitler: 1936–1945 Nemesis*, 434.
84. Müller, *Hitlers Ostkrieg*, 25–26, 34–39, 86; Dallin, *German Rule in Russia*, 323.
85. Lower, *Nazi Empire-Building*, 163; Tooze, *Wages of Destruction*, 473; Yahil, *Holocaust*, 159.
86. Zimmerer, "Birth of the Ostland," 202 (quote); Picker, *Tischgespräche*, 214, 454; Berkhoff, *Harvest of Despair*, 191.
87. Berkhoff, *Harvest of Despair*, 195–96; Weinberg, *Visions of Victory*, 22; Lower, *Nazi Empire-Building*, 117–18.
88. Picker, *Tischgespräche*, 453; Lower, *Nazi Empire-Building*, 111–12.
89. Krausnick, *Hitlers Einsatzgruppen*, 121–78.
90. Earl, *Nuremberg SS-Einsatzgruppen Trial*, 55–56; Longerich, *Holocaust*, 254; Headland, *Messages of Murder*, 105–106; Kershaw, *Hitler: 1936–1945 Nemesis*, 434–35.
91. Kershaw, *Hitler, the Germans, and the Final Solution*, 89–116.
92. Quoted in Noakes and Pridham, *Foreign Policy, War, and Racial Extermination*, 1095; and Lang, *Eichmann Interrogated*, 122.
93. Rhodes, *Masters of Death*, 154; Kogon et al., *Nazi Mass Murder*, 14–15, 37. The total number of killings of the handicapped during the war by the Nazis throughout Europe is estimated at 275,000. See Bergen, *War and Genocide*, 132.
94. Kogon et al, *Nazi Mass Murder*, 37–40, 52–64.
95. Yahil, *Holocaust*, 310–11, 312.
96. Quoted in Noakes and Pridham, *Foreign Policy, War, and Racial Extermination*, 1131.
97. Quoted in Kershaw, *Hitler: 1936–1945 Nemesis*, 494.

98. Quoted in Noakes and Pridham, *Foreign Policy, War, and Racial Extermination,* 1098.
99. Quoted in Kershaw, *Hitler: 1936–1945 Nemesis,* 495.
100. Zimmerer, "Kolonialer Genozid?," 123; Lower, *Nazi Empire-Building,* 143–50.
101. Ball, *Army Regulars,* 18; Watson, *Peacekeepers and Conquerors,* 7; Utley, *Geronimo,* 230.
102. White, *"It's Your Misfortune,"* 32–33. See also Weber, "Spanish-Mexican Rim," 63–70. For a discussion of the exploitation of Chinese labor in the building of the U.S. railroads, see White, *Railroaded,* 29–30.
103. Roseman, *Wannsee Conference,* 25.
104. Ball, *Army Regulars,* 15. In contrast to the hopes for being sites of assimilation, by the 1930s, one Sioux observer described the reservation as a "government prison" and a place of "spiritual deterioration" for the tribes. See Standing Bear, *Land of the Spotted Eagle,* 266.
105. Quoted in Noakes and Pridham, *Foreign Policy, War, and Racial Extermination,* 933.
106. Ball, *Army Regulars,* 17.

Chapter 3

1. Clausewitz, *On War,* 87.
2. Stahel, *Kiev,* 61, 66; Citino, *German Way of War,* xiii.
3. Wooster, *Military and United States Indian Policy,* 207; Beck, *Columns of Vengeance,* 44.
4. Weigley, *American Way of War,* 153; Linn, "American Way of War Revisited," 505. See also Wooster, *Military and United States Indian Policy,* 214.
5. Sherman, *Memoirs,* chap. 22, ebook 4361.
6. Grenier, *First Way of War,* 5; Lee, *Barbarians and Brothers,* 222. Sullivan and his regular forces set out looking for a set-piece battle in order to destroy Iroquois military power. But as in the American West, the Indians refused to engage in direct combat and chose simply to harass the Continentals before melting away in the forests.
7. For an excellent discussion of the ritual role of violence during the Seminole Wars, see Strang, "Violence, Ethnicity, and Human Remains during the Second Seminole War." I would like to thank Don Fixico for bringing this article to my attention.
8. Beck, *Columns of Vengeance,* 67. This practice was reciprocated by many of the tribes. For example, the Comanche "generally killed adult males on the spot." See Rivaya-Martínez, "Becoming Comanches," 49.
9. Heidler and Heidler, *Old Hickory's War,* 226.
10. Millett and Maslowski, *For the Common Defense,* 237; Watson, *Peacekeepers and Conquerors,* 3; Grenier, *First Way of War,* 11. See also Watson, *Peacekeepers and Conquerors,* 6–8.
11. White, *"It's Your Misfortune,"* 90–91.
12. Annual Report of the Secretary of War (1857), M997, reel 11, NARA.

13. Ibid. This comment referred explicitly to the seemingly interminable campaign against the Seminoles in Florida but reflected a general frustration in bringing Indians to battle.
14. Utley, *Frontier Regulars*, 47.
15. Ball, *Army Regulars*, 39–44; West, *Contested Plains*, 12–13.
16. Watson, *Peacekeepers and Conquerors*, 6.
17. S. Smith, *View from Officers' Row*, 92.
18. Weigley, *American Way of War*, 153, 159; draft of first annual address to Congress, n.d., Ulysses S. Grant Papers, reel 4, LOC. Wording denotes changes made by Grant to the original draft of the text.
19. Hutton, *Sheridan and His Army*, 180, 222 (quote); Mulroy, *Freedom on the Border*, 119. Mackenzie's force included thirty-four Seminole Maroons as scouts.
20. Watt, "Apaches without and Enemies Within," 176; Dunlay, *Wolves for the Blue Soldiers*, 73; DeLay, *War of a Thousand Deserts*, 43, 131–33. For a Navajo perspective on this type of warfare, see Wetherill and Leake, *Wolfkiller*, 98–99.
21. Rickey, *Forty Miles a Day on Beans and Hay*, 283. For a detailed examination of the effects of attrition on the Comanche, see Riva-ya-Martínez, "Different Look at Native American Depopulation."
22. S. Smith, *View from Officers' Row*, 99–100. For a discussion of Sheridan's view on punishment of the tribes, see Hutton, *Sheridan and His Army*, 183–84.
23. Sheridan to the Secretary of War, Sept. 25, 1874, Philip H. Sheridan Papers, reel 6, LOC; Ostler, *Plains Sioux and U.S. Colonialism*, 59; Utley, *Cavalier in Buckskin*, 133; Larson, *Gall*, 93–96. Both Ostler and Utley noted that the expedition had a clear if unstated goal of determining the availability of gold in the Black Hills.
24. Hämäläinen, *Comanche Empire*, 336–37. In this chapter I use the more commonly known term "buffalo" versus the technically correct "bison."
25. Utley, *Indian Frontier*, 174–75; Sheridan to R. Williams, Oct, 5, 1874, Sheridan Papers, reel 6, LOC.
26. Hämäläinen, *Comanche Empire*, 339.
27. Utley, *Indian Frontier*, 176; Sheridan to Brig. Gen. Christopher C. Augur, Nov. 20, 1874, Sheridan Papers, reel 6, LOC; Hämäläinen, *Comanche Empire*, 341.
28. Hutton, *Sheridan and His Army*, 51–56; Wooster, *Military and United States Indian Policy*, 132–33.
29. West, *Contested Plains*, 90; Wallace and Hoebel, *Comanches*, 70.
30. Wallace and Hoebel, *Comanches*, 64; West, *Contested Plains*, 90, 92; White, *"It's Your Misfortune,"* 216. See also Andrew C. Isenberg, *The Destruction of the Bison: An Environmental History, 1750–1920* (Cambridge: Cambridge University Press, 2000). For a discussion of the multicausal factors in the disappearance of the buffalo herds, see Flores, "Bison Ecology and Bison Diplomacy"; Dobak, "Killing the Canadian Buffalo"; and Smits, "Frontier Army and the Destruction of the Buffalo."

31. White, *"It's Your Misfortune,"* 219; Davis, *Ten Days on the Plains*, 14, 16.
32. C. Robinson, *General Crook*, 59–71; Ball, *Army Regulars*, 46–48. Ball provides an overview of the Sioux Expedition of 1855 and its effects.
33. Smits, "Frontier Army and the Destruction of the Buffalo," 338.
34. Yenne, *Indian Wars*, 277; *Annual Report of the Commissioner of Indian Affairs* (1875), accessed Sept. 29, 2012.
35. Annual Report of the Secretary of War (1875), M997, reel 24, NARA.
36. Sheridan to U.S. Army Headquarters, Nov. 23, 1874, Sheridan Papers, reel 6, LOC.
37. Annual Report of the Secretary of War (1876), M997, reel 26, NARA; Utley, *Cavalier in Buckskin*, 147; Ostler, *Plains Sioux and U.S. Colonialism*, 60.
38. Wooster, *Military and United States Indian Policy*, 165; C. Robinson, *General Crook*, 170; Greene, *Lakota and Cheyenne*, 3–8 (quote); S. Smith, *Sagebrush Soldier*, 55 (quote); Annual Report of the Secretary of War (1876), M997, reel 26, NARA.
39. S. Smith, *Sagebrush Soldier*, 23 (quote); J. Vaughn, *With Crook at Rosebud*, 4.
40. Annual Report of the Secretary of War (1876), M997, reel 26, NARA. See also J. Vaughn, *With Crook at Rosebud*, 15.
41. Crook, *Autobiography*, 213. See also J. Vaughn, *With Crook at Rosebud*, 22–24.
42. Quoted in C. Robinson, *General Crook*, 183. See also J. Vaughn, *With Crook at Rosebud*, 46.
43. J. Vaughn, *With Crook at Rosebud*, 50, 97; Neihardt, *Black Elk Speaks*, 103.
44. Annual Report of the Secretary of War (1876), M997, reel 26, NARA; C. Robinson, *General Crook*, 185. For a detailed analysis of Indian losses in the battle, see Hardorff, *Hokahey!*
45. Utley, *Cavalier in Buckskin*, 177, 179; Whittaker, *Complete Life of General George A. Custer*, 575 (quoting an order by Capt. E. W. Smith, acting assistant adjutant general to Custer).
46. Quoted in Greene, *Lakota and Cheyenne*, 37, 48.
47. Larson, *Gall*, 132. The desecration of the dead reflected the cultural belief that any enemy crippled or disfigured would be unable to exact revenge in the afterlife.
48. Strang, "Violence, Ethnicity, and Human Remains," 979; Rivaya-Martínez, "Captivity of Macario Leal," 387; Keeley, *War before Civilization*, 83–84. Although Strang's observation relates to the Second Seminole War, it has application to the conflict in the trans-Mississippi West as well.
49. Utley, *Indian Frontier*, 184; Annual Report of the Secretary of War (1876), M997, reel 26, NARA; Greene, *Lakota and Cheyenne*, 40, 46 (quote); Greene, *Yellowstone Command*, 33, 40.
50. Reilly, *Bound to Have Blood*, 40; Knight, *Following the Indian Wars*, 195. For an alternative view, see Mueller, *Shooting Arrows and Slinging*

Mud. Mueller argued that press coverage of the Great Sioux War and Custer's death was relatively brief and that the major focus of the media was on the presidential election of 1876.
51. Hays, *Race at Bay*, 143 (quote); Reilly, *Bound to Have Blood*, 54, 55; Beck, *Columns of Vengeance*, 66–67.
52. Ostler, *Plains Sioux and U.S. Colonialism*, 63; S. Smith, *Sagebrush Soldier*, 130.
53. Russell, *Buffalo Bill*, 222; Greene, *Yellowstone Command*, 16, 64; Greene, *Lakota and Cheyenne*, 82 (quote). Beaver Heart contended that Yellow Hair, acting as a forward scout for the band, died as a result of a volley in the initial contact with the soldiers.
54. Sheridan to the Secretary of War, Oct. 13, 1876, Sheridan Papers, reel 8, LOC.
55. Annual Report of the Secretary of War (1876), M997, reel 26, NARA.
56. Ibid.; Greene, *Yellowstone Command*, 44, 51–52.
57. Greene, *Yellowstone Command*, 63 (Gibbon); Crook, *Autobiography*, 208; C. Robinson, *General Crook*, 196; Greene, *Lakota and Cheyenne*, 86 (Red Horse).
58. Crook, *Autobiography*, 211.
59. Ibid., 212; Sheridan to the Secretary of War, Nov. 6, 1876, Sheridan Papers, reel 8, LOC; Annual Report of the Secretary of War (1876), M997, reel 26, NARA.
60. S. Smith, *Sagebrush Soldier*, 66, 78–81.
61. Ibid., 82, 87, 96, 130; Utley, *Indian Frontier*, 184; Greene, *Lakota and Cheyenne*, 114 (Iron Teeth).
62. Greene, *Yellowstone Command*, 89, 96. The lack of sufficient ammunition proved a perennial handicap to many of the tribes as they attempted to oppose federal authority in the West. See also Watt, "Apaches without and Enemies Within," 152; and Wetherill and Leake, *Wolfkiller*, 102.
63. Greene, *Yellowstone Command*, 71 (Miles).
64. Ibid., 96–105.
65. Annual Report of the Secretary of War (1876), M997, reel 26, NARA; Greene, *Yellowstone Command*, 115 (Sherman); Utley, *Frontier Regulars*, 283.
66. Annual Report of the Secretary of War (1877), M997, reel 28, NARA; Utley, *Indian Frontier*, 186; Ostler, *Plains Sioux and U.S. Colonialism*, 85.
67. Ostler, *Plains Sioux and U.S. Colonialism*, 63.
68. West, *Last Indian War*, xvi.
69. Weigley, *American Way of War*, 163.
70. Weinberg, *Germany, Hitler, and World War II*, 130, 157; Megargee, *Hitler's High Command*, 68.
71. Citino, *German Way of War*, 254; Noakes and Pridham, *Foreign Policy, War, and Racial Extermination*, 735–36; Megargee, *Hitler's High Command*, 68.
72. Citino, *German Way of War*, 256–64; Burleigh, *Moral Combat*, 120.

73. Rossino, *Hitler Strikes Poland*, xiii.
74. See Westermann, *Hitler's Police Battalions*, 89–90; Westermann, "Partners in Genocide," 773.
75. Rossino, *Hitler Strikes Poland*, 129.
76. Rossino, *Hitler Strikes Poland*, 62. For examples of the German depiction of Polish actions in Bromberg, see Bathe, *Feldzug der 18 Tage*, 29–44; and Koschorke, *Polizeireiter in Polen*, 40–50.
77. Rossino, *Hitler Strikes Poland*, 64; Mallmann, "'Mißgeburten,'" 74.
78. Rossino, *Hitler Strikes Poland*, 125; Böhler, "'Tragische Verstrickung,'" 40; Burleigh, *Moral Combat*, 126.
79. Mallmann, "'Mißgeburten,'" 73; Burleigh, *Moral Combat*, 121; Böhler, "'Tragische Verstrickung,'" 49–50.
80. Krausnick and Wilhelm, *Truppen des Weltanschauungskrieges*, 29; Borodziej, *Terror und Politik*, 26; Böhler, *Auftakt zum Vernichtungskrieg*, 241; Rossino, *Hitler Strikes Poland*, 1, 14, 234.
81. Hilberg, *Destruction of the European Jews*, student ed., 339; Rutherford, *Prelude to the Final Solution*, 219; Böhler, "'Tragische Verstrickung,'" 50; Hartmann, *Wehrmacht im Ostkrieg*, 637, 638 (Fried); Neitzel and Welzer, *Soldaten*, 141. One explanation for the greater participation of lower ranks might be explained by the effectiveness of Nazi propaganda and the socialization of these younger men under National Socialism.
82. Fritz, *Ostkrieg*, 72 (quote); Kershaw, *Hitler: 1936–1945 Nemesis*, 395; DiNardo, *Mechanized Juggernaut or Military Anachronism*.
83. Citino, *German Way of War*, 292 (quote); Megargee, *War of Annihilation*, 25.
84. Kershaw, *Hitler: 1936–1945 Nemesis*, 391 (quote); Citino, *German Way of War*, 293–94.
85. Kershaw, *Hitler: 1936–1945 Nemesis*, 391 (quote); Citino, *German Way of War*, 295–96; Megargee, *War of Annihilation*, 26–28; Stahel, *Operation Typhoon*, 92.
86. Megargee, *War of Annihilation*, 83; Fritz, *Ostkrieg*, 385; Megargee, *War of Annihilation*, 99–115 (quote, 99).
87. Kay, "Transition to Genocide," 414; Longerich, *Holocaust*, 247, 248; Streit, *Keine Kameraden*, 104.
88. Longerich, *Holocaust*, 248; Neitzel and Welzer, *Soldaten*, 92; Snyder, *Bloodlands*, 184; Streit, *Keine Kameraden*, 245–46; Jarausch and Arnold, "Das stille Sterben," 307.
89. Ropp, *War in the Modern World*, 228, 252; Holmes, *Oxford Companion to Military History*, 852.
90. Pohl, *Herrschaft der Wehrmacht*, 337.
91. Stahel, *Kiev*, 66; Reese, *Stranger to Myself*, 98.
92. Pohl, *Herrschaft der Wehrmacht*, 96, 264, 340.
93. Stahel, *Kiev*, 248, 278. Following Hitler's orders, the German army pursued just such a premeditated starvation strategy against the besieged city of Leningrad, with an estimated population of 2.5 million.
94. Liddell Hart, *German Generals Talk*.

95. Quoted in Megargee, *War of Annihilation*, 33.
96. Quoted in ibid., 38.
97. Quoted in Noakes and Pridham, *Foreign Policy, War, and Racial Extermination*, 1096; and Megargee, *War of Annihilation*, 125. Not surprisingly, Manstein did not mention this order or his role in a racial war of annihilation in his autobiographical critique of Hitler, *Lost Victories*.
98. Rürup, *Krieg gegen die Sowjetunion*, 63.
99. Larson, *Gall*, 58; Beck, *Columns of Vengeance*, 43; C. Robinson, *General Crook*, 201, 306; Wooster, *Nelson A. Miles*, 72, 74, 85, 161–62.
100. Greene, *Yellowstone Command*, 4.
101. Watson, *Peacekeepers and Conquerors*, 438–39.
102. See Berg, *38 Nooses*; and Utley, *Indian Frontier*, 81.

Chapter 4

1. Strassler, *Landmark Thucydides*, 357.
2. Westermann, *Hitler's Police Battalions*, 18–19; Turse, *Kill Anything That Moves*, 25–26.
3. Westermann, *Hitler's Police Battalions*, 171; Kay, "Germany's Staatssekretäre," 685–700; Streit, *Keine Kameraden*.
4. Rummel, *Democide*, 11.
5. For accounts of the events at Wounded Knee Creek, see Greene, *American Carnage*, 215–46; Cox-Richardson, *Wounded Knee*, 247–83; and Ostler, *Plains Sioux and U.S. Colonialism*, 338–60.
6. Cave, "Genocide in the Americas," 288; Sousa, "'Hunted Down like Wild Beasts and Destroyed!,'" 206. With respect to this population decline, Sousa noted, "the majority of the population decline was not directly the result of murder at the hands of white Californians." See also Madley, "Patterns of Frontier Genocide."
7. Jacoby, *Shadows at Dawn*; Jacoby, "Broad Platform of Extermination," 249, 253.
8. R. Brown, "Violence," 398, 401–402; Allen, *Decent Orderly Lynching*, 328.
9. White, *"It's Your Misfortune,"* 10. The antipathy between the Utes and the Navajos continued well into the second half of the nineteenth century as Ute raids involved the murder of Navajo men and, in some cases, women and children. For one account, see Wolfkiller's testimony in Wetherill and Leake, *Wolfkiller*, 99–105.
10. Keeley, *War before Civilization*, 68–69; Blyth, *Chiricahua and Janos*, 211; Utley, *Indian Frontier*, 11; West, *Contested Plains*, 78. For an extended discussion of this process, see Hyde, "Hard Choices."
11. West, *Contested Plains*, 183; Guild and Carter, *Kit Carson*, 42. Carson's biographers noted parenthetically that the subsequent fate of the three hostages was not given.
12. Guild and Carter, *Kit Carson*, x.
13. Chafin, *Pathfinder*, 33, 290–91, 309–11.
14. S. Smith, *View from Officers' Row*, 97; Gatewood, *Apache Wars Memoir*, 50; Crook, *Autobiography*, 64, 87.

15. Weigley, *American Way of War*, 152. For a critique of the concept of the Civil War as total war, see Neely, "Was the Civil War a Total War?" For a discussion of volunteers conducting acts of atrocity, see Grenier, *First Way of War*, 5; Watson, *Peacekeepers and Conquerors*, 7; and Greenberg, *Wicked War*, 131–34.
16. Millett and Maslowski, *For the Common Defense*, 236; U.S. Senate, *Sand Creek Massacre*; Bridger, *Buffalo Bill and Sitting Bull*, 109 (quote).
17. Utley and Washburn, *Indian Wars*, 206; Reilly, *Bound to Have Blood*, 18, 20; Crowe, *War Crimes, Genocide, and Justice*, 48 (quote); U.S. Senate, *Sand Creek Massacre*.
18. Ostler, *Plains Sioux and U.S. Colonialism*, 45; Reilly, *Bound to Have Blood*, 21; Connell, *Son of the Morning Star*, 177; Alvarez, *Native America and the Question of Genocide*, 95. For a detailed examination of the massacre, see Hoig, *Sand Creek Massacre*. For a discussion of the memory and historical legacy of the event, see Kelman, *Misplaced Massacre*.
19. Hoig, *Sand Creek Massacre*, 160; Kelman, *Misplaced Massacre*, 39–40; Reilly, *Bound to Have Blood*, 23; Alvarez, *Native America and the Question of Genocide*, 96 (quote).
20. *Report of the Joint Committee on the Conduct of War*, accessed July 14, 2012.
21. Reilly, *Bound to Have Blood*, 29.
22. Quoted in Alvarez, *Native America and the Question of Genocide*, 99–100; and Waller, *Becoming Evil*, 27.
23. Utley, *Indian Frontier*, 95, 99; D. Brown, *Fort Phil Kearny*, 14; Yenne, *Indian Wars*, 116; David, *Finn Burnett*, 89; Beck, *Columns of Vengeance*, 67; C. Robinson, *General Crook*, 22–24; G. Anderson, *Conquest of Texas*, 254. The subsequent raid on a Lipan Apache village resulted in the killing of "several" Indians and the capture of eighteen women and children as prisoners.
24. Larson, *Gall*, 59; David, *Finn Burnett*, 58; Ostler, *Plains Sioux and U.S. Colonialism*, 45; Utley, *Frontier Regulars*, 97.
25. D. Brown, *Fort Phil Kearny*, 77, 78. Gazzous's Indian wife and their five children were spared in the attack.
26. Ibid., 107, 125–27.
27. Ibid., 130–31, 147, 149, 150.
28. Utley, *Indian Frontier*, 103–105; Wooster, *Military and United States Indian Policy*, 68; David, *Finn Burnett*, 134–35 (quote); Keeley, *War before Civilization*, 100; DeLay, *War of a Thousand Deserts*, 90; Cremony, *Life among the Apache*, 74; Wetherill and Leake, *Wolfkiller*, 98–99.
29. Utley, *Frontier Regulars*, 111.
30. Secondary-source descriptions of the massacre can be found in Hutton, *Sheridan and His Army*, 196–200; and Graybill, *Red and the White*, 121–30. Hutton focuses on the military aspects of the operation and Sheridan's response to later criticism, while Graybill focuses his account on the impact of the kinship bonds that led to the massacre and the aftereffects of the massacre on the participants and their families.

31. Brig. Gen. Alfred Sully to Commissioner Ely S. Parker, Aug. 3, 1869, Philip H. Sheridan Papers, reel 88, LOC (quote, emphasis in original).
32. Commissioner Ely S. Parker to Acting Secretary of the Interior William T. Otto, Aug. 16, 1869, ibid.; telegram, General Sully to Commissioner Parker, Aug. 18, 1869, ibid.
33. General Sheridan to General Sherman, Oct. 21, 1869, ibid.; Secretary of the Interior to the Secretary of War, Oct. 12, 1869, ibid.; Major Pease, acting Indian agent, to Alfred Sully, Aug. 31, 1869, ibid.; Brig. Gen. Alfred Sully to Commissioner Ely S. Parker, Sept. 2, 1869, ibid.
34. General Sheridan to General Sherman, Oct. 21, 1869, ibid.; Adjutant General to General Sheridan, Nov. 4, 1869, ibid.; Colonel de Trobriand to Major Baker, Jan. 16, 1870, ibid.
35. Robert Ege, *Strike Them Hard*, 43; Wischmann, *Frontier Diplomats*, 330.
36. Ege, *Strike Them Hard*, 43, 45; Bonney and Bonney, *Battle Drums and Geysers*, 24.
37. Ege, *Strike Them Hard*, 44; Wischmann, *Frontier Diplomats*, 331. See also U.S. House, *Expedition against Piegan Indians*.
38. Bonney and Bonney, *Battle Drums and Geysers*, 25; U.S. House, *Expedition against Piegan Indians*; General Sheridan to General Sherman, Jan. 29, 1870, Sheridan Papers, reel 88, LOC.
39. U.S. House, *Expedition against Piegan Indians*; *Annual Report of the Commissioner of Indian Affairs* (1858), accessed Aug. 21, 2013; *Boston Daily Advertiser*, Mar. 11, 1870; *Jamestown (N.Y.) Journal*, Mar. 11, 1870; *Albany (N.Y.) Evening Journal*, Mar. 11, 1870. The article in this case used Baker's brevet rank instead of his permanent grade.
40. General Sherman to General Sheridan, Jan. 29, 1870, Sheridan Papers, reel 88, LOC.
41. General Sheridan to General Sherman, Jan. 29, 1870, ibid. The one soldier was injured in a fall from his horse.
42. Adjutant General to General Sheridan, Feb. 26, 1870, ibid.; General Sheridan to General Sherman, Feb. 28, 1870, ibid.; U.S. House, *Expedition against Piegan Indians*.
43. General Sheridan to General Sherman, Mar. 18, 1870, ibid.
44. Sheridan, *Memoirs*, chap. 6, ebook 4362; *Annual Report of the Secretary of War* (1871), M997, reel 24, NARA; Hutton, *Sheridan and His Army*, 17.
45. General Sherman to General Sheridan, Mar. 24, 1870, Sheridan Papers, reel 88, LOC; Dunlay, *Wolves for the Blue Soldiers*, 73.
46. S. Smith, *View from Officers' Row*, 99–100; Hämäläinen, *Comanche Empire*.
47. This account is primarily based on Greene, *American Carnage*. Other accounts include Heather Cox-Richardson's argument that Wounded Knee was an act of massacre involving wanton cruelty and brutality that serves as a "condemnation of extreme American [Republican] party politics" and reflects the political corruption of the Gilded Age. *Wounded Knee*, 313. Similarly, Jeffrey Ostler contends that the

massacre was the fault of the U.S. Army and involved acts of cold-blooded murder against women and children and represents but one event in "a long and ongoing history of injustice." *Plains Sioux and U.S. Colonialism,* 368.

48. *Annual Report of the Secretary of War* (1881), M997, reel 38, NARA; Utley, *Lance and the Shield,* 231–32; *Annual Report of the Secretary of War* (1885), M997, reel 50, NARA.
49. *Annual Report of the Secretary of War* (1890), M997, reel 64, NARA; Demaille, "Lakota Ghost Dance," 185–88; Standing Bear, *My People the Sioux,* 218; Greene, *American Carnage,* 69–70. Standing Bear details a conversation between Indian Agent J. George Wright and Short Bull.
50. Greene, *American Carnage,* 71, 72; Standing Bear, *My People the Sioux,* 219; Pine Ridge Agency Situation Report, Nov. 24, 1890, ARC ID 285038, RG 75, Records of the Bureau of Indian Affairs, NARA; telegram from Pine Ridge Agency, Dec. 20, 1890 ARC ID 285042; Reilly, *Bound to Have Blood,* 114–16.
51. Thornton, *American Indian Holocaust,* 148 (quote); Gorn et al., *Constructing the American Past,* 40 (quote); military correspondence signed R. Williams, assistant adjutant general, Division of the Missouri, Nov. 24, 1890, RG 75, Records of the Bureau of Indian Affairs, NARA.
52. Greene, *American Carnage,* 132; Standing Bear, *My People the Sioux,* 221; Rickey, *Encyclopedia of South Dakota Indians,* 226 (quote); Larson, *Gall,* 216–17; Reilly, *Bound to Have Blood,* 119 (quote).
53. Greene, *American Carnage,* 209, 214; Gorn et al., *Constructing the American Past,* 51 (quote).
54. Wooster, *Nelson A. Miles,* 180; Greene, *American Carnage,* 223, 229. Greene provides a facsimile of a map showing troop dispositions on December 29, 1890.
55. Greene, *American Carnage,* 225–27; Gorn et al., *Constructing the American Past,* 51 (quote).
56. U.S. House, *Report of the Secretary of War;* Greene, *American Carnage,* 234–36 (quote, 236), 322 (quote).
57. U.S. House, *Report of the Secretary of War.* In his account Luther Standing Bear attributes this to the efforts of his father, Chief Standing Bear, and other Sioux chiefs who negotiated the peace with their fellow tribesmen. See *My People the Sioux,* 227–30.
58. Harrison, "Third Annual Message," accessed Oct. 12, 2012; Utley, *Frontier Regulars,* 418; Greene, *American Carnage,* 3, 378–80; Standing Bear, *My People the Sioux,* 224.
59. Greene, *American Carnage,* 380 (quote); Neihardt, *Black Elk Speaks,* 270.
60. See Jansen and Weckbecker, "*Volksdeutsche Selbstschutz" in Polen.*
61. See Scheck, *Hitler's African Victims,* 165; and Neumaier, "Escalation of German Reprisal Policy."
62. Pezzino, "German Military Occupation of Italy," 177; Weinberg, *World at Arms,* 229.

63. Mallmann, "'Mißgeburten,'" 79.
64. "Der Oberbefehlshaber Ost, Ic/Ac, B.Nr.991/39 geh., Betr.: Vorgänge in Ostrow Maz. am 9.11.39 [Dec. 7, 1939]," Verschiedenes 301 Bt., folder 153, pp. 26–27, ZStl; testimony of Polizeiobermeister Josef K., Feb. 16, 1960, 211 AR-Z 350/59, folder 1, p. 124, ibid. See also Mallmann, "'Mißgeburten,'" 78–79.
65. Testimony of Polizeihauptkommissar Otto F., Feb. 22, 1960, 211 AR-Z 350/59, folder 1, p. 141; testimony of Polizeiobermeister Josef K., Feb. 16, 1960, ibid., 124–26. Josef K. stated that Hoffmann did not share the nature of the mission with him, a very unlikely story based on his position within the company staff.
66. Ibid., 26, 115. This information comes from background material accumulated by the federal prosecutor's office.
67. Testimony of Otto F., Feb. 22, 1960 ibid., 170–72; testimony of Otto F., Feb. 22, 1960, ibid., 143. For details on the failed assassination attempt against Hitler on the night of November 8, 1939, see P. Hoffmann, *Hitler's Personal Security*, 105–11.
68. Mallmann, "'Mißgeburten,'" 79; testimony of Ernst T., Feb. 5, 1960, 211 AR-Z 350/59, folder 1, p. 101, ZStl. Mallmann provides an account of one policeman who tore an infant from his mother's arm and shot the child while holding it in front of him.
69. Testimony of Wilhelm M., n.d., 211 AR-Z 350/59, folder 1, p. 40, ZStl; Klemp, "Nicht Ermittelt," 106–13, 206–14.
70. Pohl, *Herrschaft der Wehrmacht*, 259; Snyder, *Bloodlands*, 201. Retreating Soviet forces had left the bombs, armed with time-delayed fuses, in key governmental buildings.
71. Pohl, *Herrschaft der Wehrmacht*, 260.
72. Rhodes, *Masters of Death*, 172; Snyder, *Bloodlands*, 201–202; Berkhoff, *Harvest of Despair*, 65.
73. Snyder, *Bloodlands*, 202; Rhodes, *Masters of Death*, 174–76 (quotes).
74. Pohl, *Herrschaft der Wehrmacht*, 260; Rhodes, *Masters of Death*, 178.
75. "Der Reichsführer SS und Chef der Deutschen Polizei," Aug. 2, 1941, folder 333, p. 5, R 19, Chef der Ordnungspolizei, Hauptamt Ordnungspolizei, BArch; "Der Kommandant in Weissruthenien des Wehrmachtbefehlshaber Ostland," Nov. 24, 1941, RG 53.002M, Selected Records of the Belarus Central State Archive, Minsk, folder 698, USHMMA (quote, emphasis in original).
76. T. Anderson, "Incident at Baranivka," 585–86.
77. Noakes and Pridham, *Foreign Policy, War, and Racial Extermination*, 1096 (quote); T. Anderson, "Incident at Baranivka," 587, 589.
78. T. Anderson, "Incident at Baranivka," 601, 603, 605.
79. Ibid., 608–609, 612, 613.
80. Shepherd, *Terror in the Balkans*, 245; Hartmann, *Wehrmacht im Ostkrieg*, 657; Pohl, *Herrschaft der Wehrmacht*, 262; T. Anderson, "Incident at Baranivka," 616. In the case of the 707th Infantry Division, one German historian described the unit's actions as the "terrible apex, not the norm, for military pacification policy." See Hartmann, *Wehrmacht*

im Ostkrieg, 657n156.
81. Kennedy, *Shock of War*, 84–85 (quote); Röhr, *Faschistische Okkupationspolitik in Polen*, 114; Rossino, *Hitler Strikes Poland*, 138.
82. Shepherd, *Terror in the Balkans*, 245; Manoschek, "Kriegsverbrechen und Judenvernichtung in Serbien," 127–31; Pohl, *Herrschaft der Wehrmacht*, 77.
83. Pohl, *Herrschaft der Wehrmacht*, 78; Eberhard Rondholz, "Die Erde über den Gräbern bewegte sich noch," *Zeit-Punkte* 3 (1995): 27; Roland Kirchbach, "Ich gehe noch zur Schule. Ich will leben!," *Zeit-Punkte* 3 (1995): 31–32.
84. R. Brown, "Violence," 395, 396; Hitler, *Mein Kampf* (1962), 397; Pohl, *Herrschaft der Wehrmacht*, 115.
85. Desbois, *Holocaust by Bullets*.
86. Hartmann, *Wehrmacht im Ostkrieg*, 653; "Polizei-Einsatzstab Südost, Veldes, Tagesbefehl Nr. 5 [Jan. 9, 1942]," 503 AR-Z 9/1965, folder 1, p. 280, ZStl.

Chapter 5

1. Guevara, *Guerrilla Warfare*, 52; Mao, *On Guerrilla Warfare*, 48–49.
2. Annual Report of the Secretary of War (1880), accessed Aug. 20, 2012; Guevara, *Guerilla Warfare*, 4 (quote).
3. Mao, *On Guerrilla Warfare*, 47; Russell, *One Hundred and Three Fights*, 16; Galula, *Counterinsurgency Warfare*, 44–46; Kitson, *Low Intensity Operations* 49.
4. Callwell, *Small Wars*, 21, 24, 41. For a discussion of this campaign and references to the Indian Wars, see Miller, *Benevolent Assimilation*; and Linn, *Philippine War*.
5. Neihardt, *Black Elk Speaks*, 15; Geronimo, *Geronimo*, 12, 19–20; Cremony, *Life among the Apaches*, 189.
6. Kavanagh, *Comanche Ethnography*, 57–59; Kavanagh, *Comanches*, 28; Standing Bear, *My People the Sioux*, 3–4; Strang, "Violence, Ethnicity, and Human Remains," 975. Strang noted that young men without martial experience were referred to as "old women" or "*Este dogo*, you are nobody," among the Seminoles and the Creeks.
7. Utley, *Indian Frontier*, 169; White, "*It's Your Misfortune*," 13; Weber, *Bárbaros*, 157; Newcomb, *Indians of Texas*, 358.
8. Wallace and Hoebel, *Comanches*, 257; Gatewood, *Apache Wars Memoir*, 16; Cremony, *Life among the Apaches*, 174–75.
9. Russell, *One Hundred and Three Fights*, 78; Utley, *Indian Frontier*, 161; Sweeney, *From Cochise to Geronimo*, 426; DeLay, "Wider World of the Handsome Man," 112; Newcomb, *Indians of Texas*, 336. For their part, the Comanche often were successful in organizing large-scale raids into Texas and Mexico, but as DeLay has noted, "By the late 1850s Comanches and Kiowas were more commonly sending small parties into Texas and into northernmost Mexico in search of horses and slow-moving cattle."
10. Rickey, *Forty Miles a Day on Beans and Hay*, 280; Watson, *Peacekeepers*

and Conquerors, 181; Grenier, First Way of War, 19; Mackey, Uncivil War, 14–15, 32, 36; Crook, Autobiography, 87.
11. Mackey, Uncivil War, 35.
12. Annual Report of the Secretary of War (1871), M997, reel 18, NARA.
13. Brooks, Captives and Cousins, 4, 26; Blyth, Chiricahua and Janos, 5; DeLay, War of a Thousand Deserts, xiii–xxi, 297–310; Hutton, Sheridan and His Army, 222; Mulroy, Freedom on the Border, 117–18.
14. Lehmann, Nine Years among the Indians, 38, 40–41; Cremony, Life among the Apaches, 74; S. Robinson, Apache Voices, 133–34; Riva-ya-Martínez, "Captivity of Macario Leal," 387.
15. Chamberlain, Victorio, 71; G. Anderson, Conquest of Texas, 232; Mulroy, Freedom on the Border, 68; Beck, Columns of Vengeance, 45; Sweeney, From Cochise to Geronimo, 223. Mexican state governments continued to offer a scalp bounty into the 1870s. See also C. Robinson, General Crook, 112.
16. Jacoby, Shadows at Dawn, 1–2; Lehmann, Nine Years among the Indians, 77; Russell, One Hundred and Three Fights, 155; Geronimo, Geronimo, 70; G. Anderson, Conquest of Texas, 254. Anderson noted that this practice extended to both "renegade Mexicans and Americans."
17. Geronimo, Geronimo, 44, 60.
18. Utley, Frontier Regulars, 200; Sweeney, From Cochise to Geronimo, 321.
19. Annual Report of the Secretary of War (1871), M997, reel 18, NARA; C. Robinson, General Crook, 115; Utley, Frontier Regulars, 201–202. In addition to the forty-four deaths, sixteen people were wounded in these incidents.
20. Crook, Autobiography, 171; Chamberlain, Victorio, 128; C. Robinson, General Crook, 119.
21. Yenne, Indian Wars, 304; Crook, Autobiography, 175–77; C. Robinson, General Crook, 111; Utley, Indian Frontier, 157 (quote).
22. Russell, One Hundred and Three Fights, 17 (quote), 22, 27; Gatewood, Apache Wars Memoir, 17.
23. Lehmann, Nine Years among the Indians, 38. This practice also was used by the Shoshonis. See David, Finn Burnett, 281.
24. Gatewood, Apache Wars Memoir, 57; O. Howard, Autobiography, 493; David, Finn Burnett, 282; Keeley, War before Civilization, 101; Strang, "Violence, Ethnicity, and Human Remains," 973–94.
25. David, Finn Burnett, 191. See also Beck, Columns of Vengeance, 109.
26. Chamberlain, Victorio, 86; Geronimo, Geronimo, 71.
27. C. Robinson, General Crook, 116 (quote), 127.
28. Crook, Autobiography, 175–76; Utley, Frontier Regulars, 203.
29. Crook, Autobiography, 176–77, 178; Utley, Frontier Regulars, 203–204; Beck, Columns of Vengeance, 36.
30. Crook, Autobiography, 179; Sweeney, From Cochise to Geronimo, 380–85; Utley, Frontier Regulars, 204.
31. Dunlay, Wolves for the Blue Soldiers, 74; Ball, Army Regulars, 21; Wooster, Nelson A. Miles, 60. The smaller Indian ponies proved more durable and better adapted to survival on the Great Plains and in the

desert than their larger, fodder-dependent counterparts. For a detailed discussion of the intentional Apache tactic of "ruining" U.S. Army mounts, see Watt, "Apaches without and Enemies Within," 153–57.
32. Dunlay, *Wolves for the Blue Soldiers*, 3, 33, 65, 76; C. Robinson, *General Crook*, 89; Hutton, *Sheridan and His Army*, 49; Wooster, *Nelson A. Miles*, 60; Jacoby, "Broad Platform of Extermination," 262.
33. Gatewood, *Apache Wars Memoir*, 33; Annual Report of the Secretary of War (1877), M997, reel 28, NARA; Utley, *Indian Frontier*, 196 (quote); Clendenen, *Blood on the Border*, 95 (quote); Watt, "Apaches without and Enemies Within," 148.
34. Watt, "Apaches without and Enemies Within," 151; Annual Report of the Secretary of War (1880), accessed Aug. 20, 2012; S. Robinson, *Apache Voices*, 148 (quote).
35. Annual Report of the Secretary of War (1880), accessed Aug. 20, 2012; Watt, "Apaches without and Enemies Within," 166–68. Watt noted that the Mexican government was willing to "cooperate" in joint operations against the Apaches as long as U.S. troops did not cross the border without permission.
36. Annual Report of the Secretary of Wart (1880), accessed Aug. 20, 2012.
37. *Annual Report of the Commissioner of Indian Affairs* (1881), accessed Aug. 21, 2012; Beck, *Columns of Vengeance*, 22.
38. Annual Report of the Secretary of War (1881), M997, reel 38, NARA.
39. Ibid.; Utley, *Geronimo*, 9, 18, 19, 24; Cremony, *Life among the Apaches*, 195; Geronimo, *Geronimo*, 29–30, 60.
40. Utley, *Frontier Regulars*, 381–82.
41. Leonard, *Men of Color*, 112; Crook, *Autobiography*, 243 (quote); Utley, *Frontier Regulars*, 383 (quote); Annual Report of the Secretary of War (1881), M997, reel 38, NARA; New Mexico Office of the State Historian, "Biography of Lionel Sheldon," accessed Aug. 21, 2012.
42. Geronimo, *Geronimo*, 79; Wooster, *Military and United States Indian Policy*, 95–96. Diaz initially demanded a reciprocal agreement that would allow Mexican forces to conduct operations across the international border in pursuit of hostile Indians. See Watt, "Apaches without and Enemies Within," 167.
43. Crook, *Autobiography*, 244, 246 (quote); C. Robinson, *General Crook*, 257–60.
44. Annual Report of the Secretary of War (1883), M997, NARA; Utley, *Frontier Regulars*, 389; Crook, *Autobiography*, 248. Crook put the numbers at fifty-three warriors and 273 women and children.
45. C. Robinson, *General Crook*, 273; Utley, *Frontier Regulars*, 393.
46. Utley, *Frontier Regulars*, 375 (quote); Geronimo, *Geronimo*, 83; Annual Report of the Secretary of War (1885), M997, reel 50, NARA; C. Robinson, *General Crook*, 276.
47. Gatewood, *Apache Wars Memoir*, 116 (quote), 118; Geronimo, *Geronimo*, 82.
48. Utley, *Indian Frontier*, 186–93; Miles, *Personal Recollections*, 447. Sheridan had been especially critical of Crook's use of Apache scouts in the campaign against Geronimo. Miles initially replaced them with

Yumas, but he later also enlisted Apaches. See Utley, *Geronimo*, 193, 200; and Wooster, *Nelson A. Miles*, 147.
49. Miles, *Personal Recollections*, 481–84, 495.
50. Ibid., 485–86 (quote); Wooster, *Nelson A. Miles*, 148.
51. Miles, *Personal Recollections*, 491, 493; Geronimo, *Geronimo*, 83.
52. Utley, *Geronimo*, 202, 217; Geronimo, *Geronimo*, 83, 85; Gatewood, *Apache Wars Memoir*, 139.
53. Sweeney, *From Cochise to Geronimo*, 577; Miles, *Personal Recollections*, 532.
54. Hull, *Absolute Destruction*, 333.
55. M. Howard, *Franco-Prussian War*, 251; Horne and Kramer, "German 'Atrocities' and Franco-German Opinion," 17; International Military Tribunal, *Trials of the Major War Criminals*, 29:103; De Zayas, *Wehrmacht War Crimes Bureau*, 140–41; Streit, *Keine Kameraden*, 106–108.
56. Stahel, *Battle for Moscow*, 28; International Military Tribunal, *Trials of the Major War Criminals*, 15:479; Shepherd and Pattinson, "Partisan and Anti-Partisan Warfare in German-Occupied Europe," 688.
57. Hilberg, *Destruction of the European Jews*, rev. ed., 301; International Military Tribunal, *Trials of the Major War Criminals*, 32:478 (Document 3713-PS); Stahel, *Battle for Moscow*, 31; Hartmann, *Wehrmacht im Ostkrieg*, 658.
58. "Der Chef der Ordnungspolizei, Kdo. I-Ia (1) 5 Nr. 5/41 [Nov. 17, 1941]," T175, Records of the Reichsführer SS and Chief of the German Police, reel 3, frame 2503434, NARA (quote, emphasis in the original).
59. Shepherd, *Terror in the Balkans*, 1; Meyer, *Wehrmachtsverbrechen*, 88–89.
60. "Sich-Division 221, AbtIa, Divisionsbefehl [Aug. 12, 1941]," RH 26-221, Oberkommando des Heeres/Sicherungs-Division 221, folder 13b, BA-MA (quote, emphasis in the original); "Der Befehlshaber des rückw. Heeres-Gebietes Mitte, Ia, Korpsbefehl Nr. 54 [Sept. 19, 1941]," ibid., folder 13a. These instructions followed upon the heels of guidelines issued by the Army High Command on September 13, 1941.
61. Wildermuth, "Widening the Circle," 312–13; Beorn, "Calculus of Complicity," 308; Streit, *Keine Kameraden*, 107–108.
62. Shepherd, *War in the Wild East*, 89; Beorn, "Calculus of Complicity," 314; Kipp, "Holocaust in the Letters of German Soldiers," 607.
63. Oldenburg, *Ideologie und militärisches Kalkül*, 160–62.
64. "Kommandostab RFSS, Abt. Ia, Tgb.-Nr. Ia 18/0/41 geh., Betrifft: Richtlinien für die Durchkämmung und Durchstreifung von Sumpfgebieten durch Reitereinheiten [July 28, 1941]," CSSR (Russland), folder 147, pp. 59a–59d, ZStl.
65. "1. SS-Brigade, Tätigkeitsbericht für die Zeit vom 27.7.41/12.00 Uhr-30.7.41/12.00 Uhr [July 30, 1941]," ibid., 1–2; "1. SS-Brigade, Tätigkeitsbericht für die Zeit vom 6.8.41/12.00 Uhr-10.8.41/12.00 Uhr [Aug. 1941]," ibid., 3; "Funkspruch, 1.SS-Brig [Aug. 9, 1941]," ibid., 4.
66. "Fernschreiben, von Pol.Praes.Berlin [Aug. 19, 1941]," ibid., folder 147, p. 7; "Fernschreiben [Aug. 19, 1941]," ibid., 8.

67. "Fernschreiben [Aug. 20, 1941]," ibid., 10; "Fernschreiben [Aug. 21, 1941]," ibid., 14; "Fernschreiben [Aug. 22, 1941]," ibid., 13.
68. "Fernschreiben [Aug. 24, 1941]," ibid., 17; "Funkspruch [Aug. 24, 1941]," ibid., 19; "Fernschreiben [Aug. 25, 1941]," ibid., 22; "Funkspruch [Aug. 27, 1941]," ibid., 25; "Fernschreiben [Aug. 27, 1941]," ibid., 24.
69. "Kommandostab RF-SS, Abt Ia, Betrifft: Bericht des Kdo.Stabes RF-SS über die Tätigkeit für die Zeit vom 28.7. bis 3.8.1941 einschl. [Aug. 6, 1941]," ibid., 77; Mallmann, "Vom Fußvolk der 'Endlösung,'" 355.
70. Pohl, *Herrschaft der Wehrmacht*, 285.
71. Slepyan, *Stalin's Guerrillas*, 15, 26–34.
72. Grenkevich, *Soviet Partisan Movement*, 205, 207–208; Slepyan, *Stalin's Guerrillas*, 36; Stahel, *Operation Typhoon*, 123 (quote).
73. Steinhoff, Pechel, and Showalter, *Voices from the Third Reich*, 269–70; Pohl, *Herrschaft der Wehrmacht*, 78; Berkhoff, *Harvest of Despair*, 147; Meyer, *Wehrmachtsverbrechen*, 89.
74. Slepyan, *Stalin's Guerrillas*, 39; Tec, *Defiance*, 96–97.
75. Bergen, *War and Genocide*, 167–68; International Military Tribunal, *Trials of the Major War Criminals*, 32:279–82.
76. Citino, *Death of the Wehrmacht*, 87, 108–14; "Der Führer, OKW/WFst/ Op. Nr. 002 81/42g.K. [Aug. 18, 1942]," RW 4, Oberkommando der Wehrmacht/Wehrmachtführungsstab, folder 554, BA-MA.
77. Mallmann, "Vom Fußvolk der 'Endlösung,'" 373; Rürup, *Krieg gegen die Sowjetunion*, 105; "Befehlshaber der Ordnungspolizei Alpenland, Tagesbefehl Nr. 27 [July 31, 1942]," RG 48.004M, Records of the Military Historical Institute, Prague, reel 2, frame 201616, USHMMA. See also "Tagesbefehl Nr. 12, Partisanenbekämpfung [Aug. 8, 1942], RG 53.002M Selected Records of the Belarus Central State Archive, Minsk, reel 3, fond 389, folder 1, ibid.
78. International Military Tribunal, *Trials of the Major War Criminals*, 35:408 (Document 729-D).
79. "Oberkommando der Wehrmacht, Nr. 0025 2/42 g.K./WFST/Qu(II), Betr.: Partisanenbekaempfung [July 23, 1942]," NS 19, Persönlicher Stab Reichsführer-SS, reel 1671, frames 81–82, BArch. See also "Der Reichsminister für die besetzten Ostgebiete, II 1 d 963/42 GRs, Betr.: Verstärkte Bekämpfung des Bandenunwesens in den besetzten Ostgebieten [Aug. 25, 1942]," ibid., reel 1671, frame 110.
80. Von dem Bach to Himmler, [Sept. 5, 1942], ibid., reel 1671, frames 118–19.
81. "Kommandostab RF-SS, Abt. Ia, TgbNr. Ia 567/42 geh., Betr.: Führung in der Bandenbekämpfung [July 28, 1942]," ibid., frame 77. A HSSPF was equivalent to an SS general officer and had control over all SS and police organizations in a given area. He was ostensibly under the control of the local Nazi Party governor, but Himmler exercised a separate and powerful line of authority over these men.
82. "Befehlshaber der Ordnungspolizei, Alpenland, Befehlsstelle Veldes, Tagesbefehl Nr. 27 [July 31, 1942]," RG 48.004M, Records of the Military Historical Institute, Prague, reel 2, frames 201615–16, USHMMA.

83. "Der Reichsführer SS, Chef des SS-Hauptamtes, VS-Nr. 2140/42, Entwurf [June 17, 1942]," Former BDC, Daluege Collection. In this letter Berger asked for permission to comb German prisons for convicted poachers in order to create a special detachment for antipartisan activities based on the notorious *Sonderkommando Dirlewanger*.
84. "Der Reichsführer-SS, Kommandostab, Abt. Ia, Tgb.Nr. Ia 490/42 g.Kdos, Betr.: Unterdrückung der Bandentätigkeit in Weißruthenien [Aug. 7, 1942]," NS 19, Persönlicher Stab Reichsführer-SS, reel 1671, frames 87–88, BArch. See also "Der Reichsführer-SS, Kommandostab, Abt. Ia, Tgb.Nr. Ia 491/42 g.Kdos, Betr.:Unterdrückung der Bandentätigkeit in Bialystock [sic] [Aug. 7, 1942]," ibid., frames 90–91.
85. "Der Reichminister für die besetzten Ostgebiete, II 1 d 963/42 GRs, Betr.:Verstärkte Bekämpfung des Bandenunwesens in den besetzten Ostgebieten [Aug. 25, 1942]," ibid., frame 110; "Der Kdeur.d.Gend.Shitomir, Gend.Hauptmschft.Mosyr, Hauptmannschaftsbefehl Nr. 3 [Sept. 15, 1942]," RG 53.002M, Selected Records of the Belarus Central State Archive, Minsk, reel 5, fond 658, folder 3, USHMMA.
86. Tec, *Defiance*, 102–103; Kahn, *No Time to Mourn*, 119.
87. "1. Gend.-Btl. (mot.), Einsatzbericht über den Einsatz des 1.Gend.-Batl. (mot.) am 19.9.1942 im Raume Drelow, 10 km südostwärts Miedzyrzec [Sept. 20, 1942]," RG 15.011M, Der Kommandeur der Gendarmerie im Distrikt Lublin, reel 21, file 276, USHMMA.
88. Ibid.
89. Testimony of Erwin L., 208 AR-Z 30/62, folder 1, p. 108, ZStl.
90. "Der Reichminister für die besetzten Ostgebiete, II 1 d 963/42 GRs, Betr.:Verstärkte Bekämpfung des Bandenunwesens in den besetzten Ostgebieten [Aug. 25, 1942]," NS 19, Persönlicher Stab Reichsführer-SS, reel 1671, frame 111, BArch; Browning and Matthäus, *Origins of the Final Solution*, 274; "Der Chef der Ordnungspolizei, Vortrag über den Kräfte- und Kriegseinsatz der Ordnungspolizei im Jahre 1941, [Feb. 1942]," T580, Captured German Documents Microfilmed at the Berlin Document Center, reel 96, NARA. See also Pohl, "Ukrainische Hilfskräfte beim Mord an den Juden," 210.
91. "Der Chef der Ordnungspolizei, Vortrag über den Kräfte- und Kriegseinsatz der Ordnungspolizei im Jahre 1941, [Feb. 1942]," T580, Captured German Documents Microfilmed at the Berlin Document Center, reel 96, NARA. At the end of 1941, Daluege estimated that there were a total of 31,652 auxiliaries in the Reichkommissariat Ostland and 14,452 in the *Reichkommissariat Ukraine*.
92. Browning and Matthäus, *Origins of the Final Solution*, 274–75. See also Pohl, "Ukrainische Hilfskräfte beim Mord an den Juden," 211.
93. Birn, "'Zaunkönig' an 'Uhrmacher,'" 104–105, 111; "Der Höhere SS- und Polizeiführer für das Ostland und Rußland Nord, Führungsstab, IA, Befehl über Abschluß des Unternehmens 'Winterzauber' [Mar. 30, 1943]," UdSSR 245 Af, pp. 161–64, 191, ZStl. The high number of transferred persons is a direct reflection of the initial orders given to the policemen prior to the start of the operation.

94. Birn, "'Zaunkönig' an 'Uhrmacher,'" 115. Birn also listed another report showing 137 enemy combatant deaths, 51 arrests, and the execution of 1,807 "suspects." While acknowledging the role of the German police leadership, Birn emphasized the role of the auxiliaries in the executions conducted by the police forces.
95. For an in-depth analysis of the activities of the auxiliaries, see Black, "Foot Soldiers of the Final Solution."
96. Testimony of Erwin Z., 2C2 AR 165/61, folder 1, pp. 62–63, ZStl; testimony of Johann H., ibid., 80.
97. Tec, *In the Lion's Den*, 89, 94–95.
98. Kipp, "Holocaust in the Letters of German Soldiers," 609; Shepherd, *Terror in the Balkans*, 256.
99. Dunlay, *Wolves for the Blue Soldiers*, 3.
100. Hayes, "Fourth Annual Message to Congress," accessed Aug. 26, 2012; Arthur, "Third Annual Message to Congress," accessed Aug. 26, 2012.
101. Gorzka and Stang, *Vernichtungskrieg im Osten*, 46–47.
102. Slepyan, *Stalin's Guerrillas*, 188; Grenkevich, *Soviet Partisan Movement*, 241–42, 255.

Conclusion

1. S. Robinson, *Apache Voices*, 90; Gatewood, *Apache Wars Memoir*, 154; Geronimo, *Geronimo*, 91, 101; Roberts, *Like the Wind*, 302; Child, *Boarding School Seasons*, 6.
2. *Macon (Ga.) Telegraph*, Oct. 1, 1886.
3. "Geronimo Ought to be Hung," *Boston Morning Journal*, Sept. 11, 1886; Cleveland, "Second Annual Message to Congress," accessed 20 Dec. 2012; C. Robinson, *General Crook*, 301–309.
4. Browning, *Nazi Policy, Jewish Workers, German Killers*, 30. I am indebted to Thomas Kühne for his observation on the difference between "intent-focused" and "results-focused" processes.
5. Ball, *Army Regulars*, 15.
6. Crook, "Address to the Graduates of the United States Military Academy"; Knight, *Following the Indian Wars*, 6 (quote).
7. Watson, *Peacekeepers and Conquerors*, 8; Ball, *Army Regulars*, 54; Thornton, *American Indian Holocaust*, 104. For an argument about a specific case of alleged genocide, see Madley, "California's Yuki Indians," 330.
8. Knight, *Following the Indian Wars*, 9–12.
9. See Westermann, *Hitler's Police Battalions*; and Desbois, *Holocaust by Bullets*.
10. Weinberg, *Hitler's Second Book*, 114.
11. Picker, *Tischgespräche*, 453; McNeill, *Plagues and Peoples*, 215; Ostler, *Plains Sioux and U.S. Colonialism*, 31; Fenn, *Encounters at the Heart of the World*, 324; Thornton, *American Indian Holocaust*, 101 (quote). Despite the 1832 vaccination effort, Fenn has argued that federal authorities "intentionally" excluded some northern tribes from the program.

12. Ostler, *Plains Sioux and U.S. Colonialism*, 15; Ingrao, *Believe and Destroy*, 106.
13. Longerich, *Holocaust*, 428; Kershaw, "'Working towards the Führer,'" 103–18.
14. Ostler, *Plains Sioux and U.S. Colonialism*, 15; Watson, *Peacekeepers and Conquerors*, 7; Ball, *Army Regulars*, 15, 18; *Tombstone (Ariz.) Daily Epitaph*, 2 May 1886; Mueller, *Shooting Arrows and Slinging Mud*, 149 (quote).
15. Keeley, *War before Civilization*, 167; Bartov, *Mirrors of Destruction*, 143.
16. Lee, *Barbarians and Brothers*, 241; Pegelow, "'German Jews,' 'National Jews,' 'Jewish Volk,' or 'Racial Jews'?," 197.
17. Prucha, *Great Father*, 225. Carl Schurz, along with a host of newspaper writers, routinely employed this term or a variation thereof when discussing Indian policy.
18. Quoted in Hays, *Race at Bay*, 1.
19. Lang, *Eichmann Interrogated*, 130.
20. Neitzel and Welzer, *Soldaten*, 101; Roseman, *Wannsee Conference*, 50.
21. Prucha, *Great Father*, 68–77, 152–66.
22. White, *"It's Your Misfortune,"* 102–17; Ostler, *Plains Sioux and U.S. Colonialism*, 60–61; Milner, *With Good Intentions*, 188; Kershaw, *Hitler: 1936–1945 Nemesis*, 249; Ball, *Army Regulars*, 19 (quote, emphasis in original).
23. Mankiller, "Reflections on Removal," 186; Kershaw, *Fateful Choices*, 387 (quote).

Bibliography

Archives and Research Centers

Bundesarchiv, Berlin, Germany
    NS 19. Persönlicher Stab Reichsführer-SS.
    R 19. Chef der Ordnungspolizei, Hauptamt Ordnungspolizei.
Bundesarchiv-Militärarchiv, Freiburg, Germany
    RH 26-221. Oberkommando des Heeres/Sicherungs—Division 221.
    RW 4. Oberkommando der Wehrmacht/Wehrmachtführungsstab.
Library of Congress, Washington, D.C.
    Philip H. Sheridan Papers.
    Ulysses S. Grant Papers.
National Archives and Records Administration, College Park, Md.
    T175. Records of the Reichsführer SS and Chief of the German Police.
    T580. Captured German Documents Microfilmed at the Berlin Document Center.
National Archives and Records Administration, Washington, D.C.
    M997. Annual Reports of the Secretary of War (1857, 1867, 1871, 1875, 1876, 1877, 1881, 1885, 1890).
    RG75. Records of the Bureau of Indian Affairs.
U.S. Holocaust Memorial Museum Archives, Washington, D.C.
    RG 15.011M. Der Kommandeur der Gendarmerie im Distrikt Lublin.
    RG 48.004M. Records of the Military Historical Institute, Prague.
    RG 53.002M. Selected Records of the Belarus Central State Archive, Minsk.
U.S. Military Academy, West Point, N.Y.
    Crook, George. "Address to the Graduates of the United States Military Academy, West Point, New York, of the Class of 1884."
Zentrale Stelle der Landesjustizverwaltungen, Ludwigsburg, Germany
    Case Investigations
        202 AR 165/61
        208 AR-Z 30/62
        211 AR-Z 350/59
        503 AR-Z 9/1965
    Document Collections
        CSSR (Russland)
        Verschiedenes 301 Bt.
        UdSSR 245 Af.

Newspapers and Magazines

Albany (N.Y.) Evening Journal
Boston Daily Advertiser

Boston Morning Journal
Dallas Weekly Herald
Idaho Tri-Weekly Statesman (Boise)
Iola (Kans.) Register
Jamestown (N.Y.) Journal
Macon (Ga.) Telegraph
Memphis Daily Appeal
Morning Star and Catholic Messenger (New Orleans)
National Republican (Washington, D.C.)
New York Herald
Tombstone (Ariz.) Daily Epitaph
Zeit-Punkte (Hamburg, Ger.)

Internet/Electronic Sources

Annual Report of the Commissioner of Indian Affairs (1851). http://digital.library.wisc.edu/1711.dl/History.AnnRep51.

Annual Report of the Commissioner of Indian Affairs (1858). http://digital.library.wisc.edu/1711.dl/History.AnnRep58.

Annual Report of the Commissioner of Indian Affairs (1868). http://digital.library.wisc.edu/1711.dl/History.AnnRep68.

Annual Report of the Commissioner of Indian Affairs (1875). http://digital.library.wisc.edu/1711.dl/History.AnnRep75.

Annual Report of the Commissioner of Indian Affairs (1881). http://digital.library.wisc.edu/1711.dl/History.AnnRep81.

Annual Report of the Secretary of War (1880). https://books.google.com/books?id=LLMsAAAAIAAJ&printsec=frontcover&source=gbs_ge_summary_r&cad=0#v=onepage&q&f=false.

Annual Report of the Secretary of War (1883). http://babel.hathitrust.org/cgi/pt?id=uc1.b2979942;view=1up;seq=8.

Arthur, Chester A. "Third Annual Message to Congress." December 4, 1883. American Presidency Project. http://www.presidency.ucsb.edu/ws/index.php?pid=29524.

Cleveland, Grover. "Second Annual Message to Congress." December 6, 1886. American Presidency Project. http://www.presidency.ucsb.edu/ws/index.php?pid=29527.

"Convention on the Prevention and Punishment of Genocide." Modern History Sourcebook: UN Resolution 260, 1948—On Genocide. Fordham University. http://www.fordham.edu/halsall/mod/UN-GENO.asp.

Harrison, Benjamin. "Third Annual Message to Congress." December 9, 1891. American Presidency Project. http://www.presidency.ucsb.edu/ws/index.php?pid=29532.

Hayes, Rutherford B. "Fourth Annual Message to Congress." December 6, 1880. American Presidency Project. http://www.presidency.ucsb.edu/ws/index.php?pid=29521.

Johannsen, Albert. *The House of Beadle and Adams and Its Dime and Nickel Novels: The Story of a Vanished Literature*. House of Beadle

& Adams Online. Northern Illinois University Libraries. http://www.ulib.niu.edu/badndp/contents2.html.
Jackson, Andrew. "Fifth Annual Message to Congress." December 3, 1833. American Presidency Project. http://www.presidency.ucsb.edu/ws/index.php?pid=29475.
———. "Second Annual Message to Congress." December 6, 1830. American Presidency Project. http://www.presidency.ucsb.edu/ws/index.php?pid=29472.
Jefferson, Thomas. "Fourth Annual Message to Congress." November 8, 1804. American Presidency Project. http://www.presidency.ucsb.edu/ws/index.php?pid=29446.
———. "Third Annual Message to Congress." October 17, 1803. American Presidency Project. http://www.presidency.ucsb.edu/ws/index.php?pid=29445.
May, Karl. *Mein Leben und Streben*. Freiburg im Breisgau: F. E. Fehsenfeld, 1910. Project Gutenberg, etext #2779. http://eremita.di.uminho.pt/gutenberg/2/7/7/2779/2779-h/2779-h.htm.
New Mexico Office of the State Historian. "Biography of Lionel Sheldon." New Mexico History. http://www.newmexicohistory.org/people/biography-of-lionel-sheldon.
"Ratified Treaty No. 371: Documents Relating to the Negotiation of the Treaty of May 10, 1868, with the Northern Cheyenne and Northern Arapaho Indians." http://digital.library.wisc.edu/1711.dl/History.IT1868no371.
Report of the Joint Committee on the Conduct of War at the Second Session of the Thirty-eighth Congress. http://quod.lib.umich.edu/m/moa/ABY3709.0003.001.
Sheridan, Philip H. *The Memoirs of General P. H. Sheridan*. Project Gutenberg, ebook #4362. http://www.gutenberg.org/files/4362/4362-h/4362-h.htm.
Sherman, William T. *The Memoirs of General W. T. Sherman*. Project Gutenberg, ebook #4361. http://www.gutenberg.org/files/4361/4361-h/4361-h.htm.

Government Documents

Cherokee Nation v. Georgia 30 U.S. 1 (1831).
International Military Tribunal. *Trials of the Major War Criminals before the International Military Tribunal*. Vols. 15, 29, 32, 35. Nuremberg, Ger.: Secretariat of the Military Tribunal, 1948.
U.S. House of Representatives. *Expedition against Piegan Indians*. 41st Cong., 2nd sess., 1870. H. Ex. Doc. 197.
———. *Report of the Secretary of War*. 52nd Cong., 1st sess., 1892. H. Ex. Doc. 1, pt. 2.
U.S. Senate. *Sand Creek Massacre*. 39th Cong., 2nd sess., 1867. S. Ex. Doc. 26.
———. Select Committee to Examine into the Condition of the Sioux and Crow Indians. *Testimony in Regard to the Sioux Indians, Dakota*. 48th Cong., 1st sess., 1883. S. Rep. 283.
Worcester v. Georgia 31 U.S. 515 (1832).

Books and Articles

Adams, David Wallace. *Education for Extinction: American Indians and the Boarding School Experience, 1875–1928*. Lawrence: University Press of Kansas, 1995.

Adams, David Wallace, and Crista DeLuzio, eds. *On the Borders of Love and Power: Families and Kinship in the Intercultural American Southwest*. Berkeley: University of California Press, 2012.

Allen, Frederick. *A Decent Orderly Lynching: The Montana Vigilantes*. Norman: University of Oklahoma Press, 2004.

Alvarez, Alex. *Native America and the Question of Genocide*. Lanham, Md.: Rowman and Littlefield, 2014.

Anderson, Gary. *The Conquest of Texas: Ethnic Cleansing in the Promised Land, 1820–1875*. Norman: University of Oklahoma Press, 2005.

———. *Ethnic Cleansing and the Indian: The Crime That Should Haunt America*. Norman: University of Oklahoma Press, 2014.

Anderson, Truman. "Incident at Baranivka: German Reprisals and the Soviet Partisan Movement in Ukraine, October–December 1941." *Journal of Modern History* 71 (September 1999): 585–621.

Angevine, Robert. "Individuals, Organizations, and Engineering: U.S. Army Officers and the American Railroads, 1827–1838." *Technology and Culture* 42 (April 2001): 292–320.

Arendt, Hannah. *The Origins of Totalitarianism*. New York: Harcourt, Brace, and World, 1966.

Aron, Stephen. "Lessons in Conquest: Towards a Greater Western History." *Pacific Historical Review* 61 (February 1992): 125–47.

Ball, Durwood. *Army Regulars on the Western Frontier, 1848–1861*. Norman: University of Oklahoma Press, 2001.

Banner, Stuart. *How the Indians Lost Their Land: Law and Power on the Frontier*. Cambridge, Mass.: Harvard Belknap, 2005.

Baranowski, Shelley. *Nazi Empire: German Colonialism and Imperialism from Bismarck to Hitler*. Cambridge: Cambridge University Press, 2011.

Bartov, Omer. *Mirrors of Destruction: War, Genocide, and Modern Identity*. Oxford: Oxford University Press, 2000.

Bathe, Rolf. *Der Feldzug der 18 Tage: Chronik des polnischen Dramas*. Oldenbourg I.O.: Gerhard Stalling Verlagsbuchhandlung, 1939.

Beck, Paul. *Columns of Vengeance: Soldiers, Sioux, and the Punitive Expeditions, 1863–1864*. Norman: University of Oklahoma Press, 2013.

Beorn, Waitman W. "A Calculus of Complicity: The Wehrmacht, the Anti-Partisan War, and the Final Solution in White Russia, 1941–42." *Central European History* 44 (June 2011): 308–37.

Berg, Scott. *38 Nooses: Lincoln, Little Crow, and the Beginning of the Frontier's End*. New York: Vintage Books, 2012.

Bergen, Doris. *War and Genocide: A Concise History of the Holocaust*. 2nd ed. Lanham, Md.: Rowman and Littlefield, 2003.

Berkhoff, Karel. *Harvest of Despair: Life and Death in Ukraine, 1941–1944*. Cambridge, Mass.: Harvard University Press, 2004.

Birn, Ruth Bettina. "'Zaunkönig' an 'Uhrmacher.' Große Partisanenaktionen 1942/43 am Beispiel des 'Unternehmens Winterzauber.'" *Militärgeschichtliche Zeitschrift* 60 (2001): 99–118.
Black, Peter. "Foot Soldiers of the Final Solution: The Trawniki Training Camp and Operation Reinhard." *Holocaust and Genocide Studies* 25 (Spring 2011): 1–99.
Blyth, Lance. *Chiricahua and Janos: Communities of Violence in the Southwestern Borderlands, 1680–1880*. Lincoln: University of Nebraska Press, 2012.
Bogue, Allan G. "An Agricultural Empire." In *The Oxford History of the American West*, edited by Clyde Milner II, Carol O'Connor, and Martha Sandweiss, 275–313. New York: Oxford University Press, 1994.
Böhler, Jochen. *Auftakt zum Vernichtungskrieg: Die Wehrmacht in Polen 1939*. Frankfurt/Main: Fischer, 2006.
———. "'Tragische Verstrickung' oder Auftakt zum Vernichtungskrieg?: Die Wehrmacht in Polen 1939." In *Genesis des Genozids: Polen, 1939–1941*, edited by Klaus-Michael Mallmann and Bogdan Musial, 36–56. Darmstadt: Wissenschaftliche Buchgesellschaft, 2004.
Bold, Christine. *Selling the West: Popular Western Fiction, 1860–1960*. Bloomington: Indiana University Press, 1987.
Bonney, Orrin, and Lorraine Bonney. *Battle Drums and Geysers: The Life and Journals of Lt. Gustavus Cheyney Doane*. Chicago: Swallow, 1970.
Borodziej, Włodzimierz. *Terror und Politik: Die Deutsche Polizei und die Polnische Widerstandsbewegung im Generalgouvernement, 1939–1944*. Mainz: Verlag Philipp von Zabern, 1999.
Bowes, John P. *Exiles and Pioneers: Eastern Indians in the Trans-Mississippi West*. Cambridge: Cambridge University Press, 2007.
Breitman, Richard. *The Architect of Genocide: Himmler and the Final Solution*. New York: Alfred A. Knopf, 1991.
Bridger, Bobby. *Buffalo Bill and Sitting Bull: Inventing the Wild West*. Austin: University of Texas Press, 2002.
Brooks, James F. *Captives and Cousins: Slavery, Kinship, and Community in the Southwest Borderlands*. Chapel Hill: University of North Carolina Press, 2002.
Brown, Dee. *Fort Phil Kearny: An American Saga*. Lincoln: University of Nebraska Press, 1962.
Brown, Richard Maxwell. "Violence." In *The Oxford History of the American West*, edited by Clyde Milner II, Carol O'Connor, and Martha Sandweiss, 393–425. New York: Oxford University Press, 1994.
Browning, Christopher. *Nazi Policy, Jewish Workers, German Killers*. Cambridge: Cambridge University Press, 2000.
———. *Ordinary Men: Reserve Police Battalion 101 and the Final Solution in Poland*. New York: Harper Collins, 1992.
Browning, Christopher, and Jürgen Matthäus. *The Origins of the Final Solution: The Evolution of Nazi Jewish Policy, September 1939–March 1942*. Lincoln: University of Nebraska Press, 2004.

Burleigh, Michael. *Moral Combat: Good and Evil in World War II*. New York: Harper Collins, 2011.
Callwell, C. E. *Small Wars: Their Principles and Practice*. 3rd ed. Lincoln: University of Nebraska Press, 1996.
Carmichael, Cathie. *Genocide before the Holocaust*. New Haven, Conn.: Yale University Press, 2009.
Casas, Bartolomé de las. *A Short Account of the Destruction of the Indies*. Translated by Nigel Griffin. New York: Penguin, 1992.
Cave, Alfred A. "Genocide in the Americas." In *The Historiography of Genocide*, edited by Dan Stone, 273–95. New York: Palgrave Macmillan, 2008.
Cecil, Robert. *The Myth of the Master Race: Alfred Rosenberg and Nazi Ideology*. New York: Dodd, Mead, 1972.
Chafin, Tom. *Pathfinder: John Charles Frémont and the Course of American Empire*. New York: Hill and Wang, 2002.
Chamberlain, Kathleen. *Victorio: Apache Warrior and Chief*. Norman: University of Oklahoma Press, 2007.
Child, Brenda J. *Boarding School Seasons: American Indian Families, 1900–1940*. Lincoln: University of Nebraska Press, 2000.
Churchill, Ward. *A Little Matter of Genocide: Holocaust and Denial in the Americas 1492 to the Present*. San Francisco: City Lights Books, 1998.
———. *Struggle for the Land: Indigenous Resistance to Genocide, Ecocide, and Expropriation in Contemporary North America*. Monroe, Maine: Common Courage, 1993.
Citino, Robert. *The Death of the Wehrmacht: The German Campaigns of 1942*. Lawrence: University Press of Kansas, 2007.
———. *The German Way of War: From the Thirty Years' War to the Third Reich*. Lawrence: University Press of Kansas, 2005.
Clausewitz, Carl von. *On War*. Edited and translated by Michael Howard and Peter Paret. Princeton, N.J.: Princeton University Press, 1976.
Clendenen, Clarence C. *Blood on the Border: The United States Army and the Mexican Irregulars*. New York: Macmillan, 1969.
Coffman, Edward M. *The Old Army: A Portrait of the American Army in Peacetime*. New York: Oxford University Press, 1986.
Cohen, Felix S. *Handbook of Federal Indian Law*. Washington, D.C.: Government Printing Office, 1941.
Combs, William L. *The Voice of the SS: A History of the SS Journal 'Das Schwarze Korps.'* New York: Peter Lang, 1986.
Connell, Evan. *Son of the Morning Star: Custer and the Little Bighorn*. New York: Farrar, Straus, and Giroux, 1984.
Cox-Richardson, Heather. *Wounded Knee: Party Politics and the Road to an American Massacre*. New York: Basic Books, 2010.
Cremony, John C. *Life among the Apache*. San Francisco: A. Roman, 1868.
Crook, George. *His Autobiography*. Edited by Martin Schmitt. Norman: University of Oklahoma Press, 1946.
Crowe, David. *War Crimes, Genocide, and Justice: A Global History*. New York: Palgrave Macmillan, 2014.

Dallin, Alexander. *German Rule in Russia, 1941–1945: A Study of Occupation Policies.* New York: St. Martin's, 1957.
Daly, Christopher B. *Covering America: A Narrative of a Nation's Journalism.* Amherst: University of Massachusetts Press, 2012.
David, Robert Beebe. *Finn Burnett, Frontiersman.* Glendale, Calif.: Arthur H. Clark, 1937. Reprint, Mechanicsburg, Penn.: Stackpole, 2003.
Davis, Henry E. *Ten Days on the Plains.* Edited by Paul Andrew Hutton. Dallas: Southern Methodist University Press, 1985.
DeLay, Brian. *War of a Thousand Deserts: Indian Raids and the U.S.–Mexican War.* New Haven, Conn.: Yale University Press, 2008.
———. "The Wider World of the Handsome Man: Southern Plains Indians Invade Mexico, 1830–1848." *Journal of the Early Republic* 27 (Spring 2007): 83–113.
Demaille, Raymond J., Jr. "The Lakota Ghost Dance: An Ethnohistorical Account." In *The American Indian: Past and Present,* edited by Roger L. Nichols, 179–91. New York: MacGraw-Hill, 1999.
Desbois, Patrick. *The Holocaust by Bullets: A Priest's Journey to Uncover the Truth behind the Murder of 1.5 Million Jews.* New York: Palgrave Macmillan, 2008.
De Zayas, Alfred M. *The Wehrmacht War Crimes Bureau, 1939–1945.* Lincoln: University of Nebraska Press, 1989.
DiNardo, Richard. *Mechanized Juggernaut or Military Anachronism: Horses and the German Army of World War II.* New York: Greenwood, 1991.
Dobak, William. "Killing the Canadian Buffalo, 1821–1881." *Western Historical Quarterly* 27 (Spring 1996): 33–52.
Donson, Andrew. "Why Did German Youth become Fascists? Nationalist Males Born 1900 to 1908 in War and Revolution." *Social History* 31 (August 2006): 337–58.
Dunlay, Thomas W. *Wolves for the Blue Soldiers: Indian Scouts and Auxiliaries with the United States Army, 1860–90.* Lincoln: University of Nebraska Press, 1982.
Earl, Hilary. *The Nuremberg SS-Einsatzgruppen Trial: Atrocity, Law, and History.* Cambridge: Cambridge University Press, 2009.
Ege, Robert. *Tell Baker to Strike Them Hard: Incident on the Marias, 23 January 1870.* Bellevue, Neb.: Old Army, 1970.
Epstein, Catherine. *Model Nazi: Arthur Greiser and the Occupation of Western Poland.* Oxford: Oxford University Press, 2010.
Faragher, John Mack. *Women and Men on the Overland Trail.* 2nd ed. New Haven, Conn.: Yale University Press, 1979.
Fenn, Elizabeth A. *Encounters at the Heart of the World: A History of the Mandan People.* New York: Hill and Wang, 2014.
Fischer, Klaus P. Review of *The American West and the Nazi East: A Comparative and Interpretive Perspective,* by Carrol P. Kakel III. In *Holocaust and Genocide Studies* 26 (Winter 2012): 499–502.
Flores, Dan. "Bison Ecology and Bison Diplomacy: The Southern Plains from 1800 to 1850." *Journal of American History* 78 (September 1991): 465–85.

Folsom, James K. *The American Western Novel*. New Haven, Conn.: College and University Press, 1966.
Förster, Jürgen. "Operation Barbarossa as a War of Conquest and Annihilation." In *The Attack on the Soviet Union*, edited by Research Institute for Military History and translated by Dean S. McMurry, Ewald Osers, and Louise Wilmot. Oxford: Clarendon, 1998.
Fritz, Stephen. *Ostkrieg: Hitler's War of Extermination in the East*. Lexington: University Press of Kentucky, 2011.
Galula, David. *Counterinsurgency Warfare: Theory and Practice*. New York: Praeger, 1964. Reprint, Westport, Conn.: Praeger Security International, 2006.
Gatewood, Charles B. *Lt. Charles Gatewood and His Apache Wars Memoir*. Edited by Louis Kraft. Lincoln: University of Nebraska Press, 2005.
Gellately, Robert. "The Third Reich, the Holocaust, and Visions of Serial Genocide." In *The Specter of Genocide: Mass Murder in Historical Perspective*, edited by Robert Gellately and Ben Kiernan, 241–64. Cambridge: Cambridge University Press, 2003.
Geronimo. *Geronimo: The True Story of America's Most Ferocious Warrior*. Edited by S. M. Barrett. New York: Skyhorse, 2011.
Giesen, Rolf. *Nazi Propaganda Films: A History and Filmography*. Jefferson, N.C.: McFarland, 2003.
Glover, Jonathan. *Humanity: A Moral History of the 20th Century*. New Haven, Conn.: Yale University Press, 2000.
Goda, Norman. *Tomorrow the World: Hitler, Northwest Africa, and the Path toward America*. College Station: Texas A&M University Press, 1998.
Gorn, Elliot, Randy Roberts, and Terry D. Bilhartz. *Constructing the American Past: A Sourcebook of a People's History*. Vol. 2. 5th ed. New York: Pearson Longman, 2005.
Gorzka, Gabriele, and Knut Stang, eds. *Der Vernichtungskrieg im Osten: Verbrechen der Wehrmacht in der Sowjetunion aus Sicht russischer Historiker*. Kassel: Kassel Universitätsverlag, 1999.
Graybill, Andrew. *The Red and the White: A Family Saga of the American West*. New York: Liveright, 2013.
Greenberg, Amy. *A Wicked War: Polk, Clay, Lincoln, and the 1846 Invasion of Mexico*. New York: Vintage Books, 2012.
Greene, Jerome. *American Carnage: Wounded Knee, 1890*. Norman: University of Oklahoma Press, 2014.
———. *Yellowstone Command: Colonel Nelson A. Miles and the Great Sioux War, 1876–1877*. Lincoln: University of Nebraska Press, 1991.
———, ed. *Lakota and Cheyenne: Indian Views of the Great Sioux War, 1876–1877*. Norman: University of Oklahoma Press, 1994.
Grenier, John. *The First Way of War: American War Making on the Frontier*. New York: Cambridge University Press, 2005.
Grenkevich, Leonid D. *The Soviet Partisan Movement, 1941–1944*. London: Frank Cass, 1999.

Grund, Francis Joseph. *The Americans in Their Moral, Social, and Political Relations*. Vol. 2. London: Longman, Orme Rees, 1837.
Gruner, Wolf. *Jewish Forced Labor under the Nazis: Economic Needs and Racial Aims, 1938–1944*. Translated by Kathleen M. Dell'Orto. Cambridge: Cambridge University Press, 2006.
Guettel, Jens-Uwe. "The U.S. Frontier as Rationale for the Nazi East? Settler Colonialism and Genocide in Nazi-Occupied Eastern Europe and the American West." *Journal of Genocide Research* 15 (2013): 401–19.
Guevara, Che. *Guerrilla Warfare*. 3rd ed. Lincoln: University of Nebraska Press, 1985. Reprint, Lanham, Md.: SR Books, 1997.
Guild, Thelma, and Harvey Carter. *Kit Carson: A Pattern for Heroes*. Lincoln: University of Nebraska Press, 1984.
Gwynne, S. C. *Empire of the Summer Moon*. New York: Scribner, 2010.
Hämäläinen, Pekka. *The Comanche Empire*. New Haven, Conn.: Yale University Press, 2008.
Hardorff, Richard G. *Hokahey! A Good Day to Die: The Indian Casualties of the Custer Fight*. Lincoln: University of Nebraska Press, 1999.
Hartmann, Christian. *Wehrmacht im Ostkrieg: Front und militärisches Hinterland, 1941/42*. Munich: R. Oldenbourg, 2009.
Hays, Robert G. *A Race at Bay*. New York Times *Editorials on "the Indian Problem," 1860–1900*. Carbondale: Southern Illinois University, 1997.
Headland, Ronald. *Messages of Murder: A Study of the Reports of the Einsatzgruppen of the Security Police and the Security Service, 1941–1943*. Rutherford, N.J.: Fairleigh Dickinson University Press, 1992.
Heidler, David, and Jeanne T. Heidler. *Old Hickory's War: Andrew Jackson and the Quest for Empire*. Mechanicsburg, Pa.: Stackpole, 1996.
Hermand, Jost. *Old Dreams of a New Reich: Volkish Utopias and National Socialism*. Bloomington: Indiana University Press, 1992.
Hietala, Thomas R. *Manifest Design: American Exceptionalism and Empire*. Rev. ed. Ithaca, N.Y.: Cornell University Press, 1985.
Hilberg, Raul. *The Destruction of the European Jews*. Student ed. New York: Holmes and Meier, 1985.
———. *The Destruction of the European Jews*. Vol. 3. Rev. ed. New York: Holmes and Meier, 1985.
Hinton, Alexander L. "Critical Genocide Studies." In *Genocide Matters: Ongoing Issues and Emerging Perspectives*, edited by Joyce Apsel and Ernesto Verdeja, 42–58. New York: Routledge, 2013.
Hitler, Adolf. *Mein Kampf*. Translated by Alvin Johnson. New York: Reynal and Hitchcock, 1939.
———. *Mein Kampf*. Translated by Ralph Manheim. Boston: Houghton Mifflin, 1962.
Hixson, Walter. *American Settler Colonialism: A History*. New York: Palgrave Macmillan, 2013.
Hoffmann, Hilmar. *The Triumph of Propaganda: Film and National Socialism, 1933–1945*. Translated by John A. Broadwin and V. R. Berghahn. Providence, R.I.: Berghahn Books, 1996.

Hoffmann, Peter. *Hitler's Personal Security: Protecting the Führer, 1921–1945*. Boston, Mass.: Da Capo, 2000.
Hoig, Stan. *The Sand Creek Massacre*. Norman: University of Oklahoma Press, 1961.
Holmes, Richard, ed. *The Oxford Companion to Military History*. Oxford: Oxford University Press, 2001.
Horne, John, and Alan Kramer. "German 'Atrocities' and Franco-German Opinion, 1914: The Evidence of German Soldiers' Diaries." *Journal of Modern History* 66 (March 1994): 1–33.
Horsman, Reginald. *Race and Manifest Destiny: The Origins of American Racial Anglo-Saxonism*. Cambridge, Mass.: Harvard University Press, 1981.
Howard, Michael. *The Franco-Prussian War: The German Invasion of France, 1870–1871*. New York: Dorset, 1961.
Howard, Oliver O. *Autobiography of Oliver Otis Howard*. New York: Baker and Taylor, 1907.
Hull, Isabell. *Absolute Destruction: Military Culture and the Practices of War in Imperial Germany*. Ithaca, N.Y.: Cornell University Press, 2005.
Huttenbach, Henry. "From the Editor: No Comparing, No Thinking—the Unavoidable Future of Studying Genocide." *Journal of Genocide Research* 2 (2000): 319–20.
———. "Vita Felix, Via Dolorossa: An Academic Journey towards Genocide." In *Pioneers of Genocide Studies*, edited by Samuel Totten and Steven Leonard Jacobs, 47–58. New Brunswick, N.J.: Transaction, 2002.
Hutton, Paul Andrew. *Phil Sheridan and His Army*. Norman: University of Oklahoma Press, 1999.
Hyde, Anne F. "Hard Choices: Mixed Race Families and Strategies of Acculturation in the U.S. West after 1848." In Adams and DeLuzio, *On the Borders of Love and Power*, 93–115.
Ingrao, Christian. *Believe and Destroy: Intellectuals in the SS War Machine*. Translated by Andrew Brown. Malden, Mass.: Polity, 2013.
Jacoby, Karl. "'The Broad Platform of Extermination': Nature and Violence in the Nineteenth Century North American Borderlands." *Journal of Genocide Research* 10 (June 2008): 249–67.
———. *Shadows at Dawn: A Borderlands Massacre and the Violence of History*. New York: Penguin, 2008.
Jansen, Christian, and Arno Weckbecker. *Der "Volksdeutsche Selbstschutz" in Polen, 1939/40*. Munich: Oldenbourg, 1992.
Jarausch, Konrad, and Klaus Jochen Arnold, eds. *"Das stille Sterben": Feldpostbriefe von Konrad Jarausch aus Polen und Russland, 1939–1942*. Paderborn: Ferdinand Schöningh, 2008.
Kahn, Leo. *No Time to Mourn: The True Story of a Jewish Partisan Fighter*. Vancouver, Canada: Ronsdale, 2004.
Kakel, Carroll P., III. *The American West and the Nazi East: A Comparative and Interpretive Perspective*. New York: Palgrave Macmillan, 2011.

Kaplan, Chaim. *The Warsaw Diary of Chaim A. Kaplan.* Translated and edited by Abraham Katsh. New York: Collier, 1973.
Katz, Stephen. *The Holocaust and Mass Death before the Modern Age.* Vol. 1 of *The Holocaust in Historical Context.* New York: Oxford University Press, 1994.
Kavanagh, Thomas. *The Comanches: A History, 1706–1875.* Lincoln: University of Nebraska Press, 1996.
Kavanagh, Thomas, ed. *Comanche Ethnography: Field Notes of E. Adamson Hoebel, Waldo R. Wedel, Gustav G. Carlson, and Robert H. Lowie.* Lincoln: University of Nebraska Press, 2008.
Kay, Alex J. "Germany's Staatssekretäre, Mass Starvation and the Meeting of 2 May 1941." *Journal of Contemporary History* 41 (October 2006): 685–700.
———. "Transition to Genocide, July 1941: Einsatzkommando 9 and the Annihilation of Soviet Jewry." *Holocaust and Genocide Studies* 27 (Winter 2013): 411–42.
Keeley, Lawrence H. *War before Civilization.* Oxford: Oxford University Press, 1996.
Kelman, Ari. *A Misplaced Massacre: Struggling over the Memory of Sand Creek.* Cambridge, Mass.: Harvard University Press, 2013.
Kennedy, Sean. *The Shock of War: Civilian Experiences, 1937–1945.* Toronto: Toronto Press, 2011.
Kershaw, Ian. *Fateful Choices: Ten Decisions That Changed the World, 1940–1941.* New York: Penguin, 2007.
———. *Hitler: 1889–1936 Hubris.* New York: W. W. Norton, 1998.
———. *Hitler: 1936–1945 Nemesis.* New York: W. W. Norton, 2000.
———. *Hitler, the Germans, and the Final Solution.* New Haven, Conn.: Yale University Press, 2008.
———. "'Working towards the Führer': Reflections on the Nature of the Hitler Dictatorship." *Central European History* 2 (July 1993): 103–18.
Kipp, Michaela. "The Holocaust in the Letters of German Soldiers on the Eastern Front (1939–1944)." *Journal of Genocide Research* (December 2007): 601–15.
Kitson, Frank. *Low Intensity Operations: Subversion, Insurgency, Peacekeeping.* Hamden, Conn.: Archon, 1974.
Klein, Peter, ed. *Die Einsatzgruppen in der besetzten Sowjetunion, 1941/42.* Berlin: Druckhaus Hentrich, 1997.
Klemp, Stefan. *"Nicht Ermittelt": Polizeibataillone und die Nachkriegsjustiz-Ein Handbuch.* Essen: Klartext Verlag, 2005.
Kocka, Jürgen. "Asymmetrical Historical Comparison: The Case of the German *Sonderweg.*" *Forum on Comparative Historiography* (1999): 40–50.
Kogon, Eugen, Hermann Langbein, and Adalbert Rückerl, eds. *Nazi Mass Murder: A Documentary History of the Use of Poison Gas.* New Haven, Conn.: Yale University Press, 1993.
Koschorke, Helmuth. *Polizei greift ein!: Kriegsberichte aus Ost, West und Nord.* Berlin: Franz Schneider Verlag, 1941.

———. *Polizeireiter in Polen*. Berlin: Franz Schneider Verlag, 1940.
Knight, Oliver. *Following the Indian Wars: The Story of the Newspaper Correspondents among the Indian Campaigners*. Norman: University of Oklahoma Press, 1960.
Krausnick, Helmut. *Hitlers Einsatzgruppen: Die Truppen des Weltanschauungskrieges, 1939–1942*. Frankfurt/Main: Fischer Taschenbuch, 1981.
Krausnick, Helmut, and Hans-Heinrich Wilhelm. *Die Truppen des Weltanschauungskrieges: Die Einsatzgruppen der Sicherheitspolizei und des SD, 1938–1942*. Stuttgart: Deutsche Verlags-Anstalt, 1981.
Kühne, Thomas. "Colonialism and the Holocaust: Continuities, Causations, and Complexities." *Journal of Genocide Research* 15 (September 2013): 339–62.
Lang, Jochen von, ed. *Eichmann Interrogated*. Translated by Ralph Mannheim. New York: Farrar, Straus, and Giroux, 1983.
Larson, Robert W. *Gall: Lakota War Chief*. Norman: University Press of Oklahoma, 2007.
Lasch-Quinn, Elisabeth. "Democracy in the Ivory Tower?" In *Reconstructing History: The Emergence of a New Historical Society*, edited by Elizabeth Fox-Genovese and Elisabeth Lasch-Quinn, 23–34. New York: Routledge, 1999.
Lee, Wayne. *Barbarians and Brothers: Anglo-American Warfare, 1500–1865*. Oxford: Oxford University Press, 2011.
Lehmann, Herman. *Nine Years among the Indians, 1870–1879*. Edited by J. Marvin Hunter. Albuquerque: University of New Mexico Press, 1993.
Lemkin, Raphael. *Axis Rule in Occupied Europe*. Washington, D.C.: Carnegie Council, 1944.
Leonard, Elizabeth D. *Men of Color to Arms!: Black Soldiers, Indian Wars, and the Quest for Equality*. New York: W.W. Norton, 2010.
Liddell Hart, B. H. *The German Generals Talk*. New York: W. Morrow, 1948. Reprint, New York: Quill, 1971.
Lieberman, Benjamin. "'Ethnic Cleansing' versus Genocide?" In *The Oxford Handbook of Genocide Studies*, edited by Donald Bloxham and A. Dirk Moses, 42–60. Oxford: Oxford University Press, 2010.
Limerick, Patricia Nelson. *The Legacy of Conquest: The Unbroken Past of the American West*. New York: W. W. Norton, 1987.
Linn, Brian M. "The American Way of War Revisited." *Journal of Military History* 66 (April 2002): 501–33.
———. *The Philippine War, 1899–1902*. Lawrence: University Press of Kansas, 2000.
Lissance, Arnold, ed. *The Halder Diaries*. Vol. 1. Boulder, Colo.: Westview, 1976.
Liulevicius, Vejas Gabriel. *War Land on the Eastern Front: Culture, National Identity, and German Occupation in World War I*. Cambridge: Cambridge University Press, 2000.
Longerich, Peter. *Heinrich Himmler*. Oxford: Oxford University Press, 2012.

———. *Holocaust: The Nazi Persecution and Murder of the Jews*. Oxford: Oxford University Press, 2010.
Lower, Wendy. *Nazi Empire-Building and the Holocaust in Ukraine*. Chapel Hill: University of North Carolina Press, 2005.
Mackey, Robert R. *The Uncivil War: Irregular Warfare in the Upper South, 1861–1865*. Norman: University of Oklahoma Press, 2004.
Madley, Benjamin. "California's Yuki Indians: Defining Genocide in Native American History." *Western Historical Quarterly* 39 (Autumn 2008): 303–32.
———. "Patterns of Frontier Genocide, 1803–1910: The Aboriginal Tasmanians, the Yuki of California, and the Herero of Namibia." *Journal of Genocide Research* 6 (June 2004): 167–92.
Mallmann, Klaus-Michael. "'Mißgeburten, die nicht auf diese Welt gehören': Die deutsche Ordnungspolizei in Polen, 1939–1941.'" In *Genesis des Genozids: Polen, 1939–1941*, edited by Klaus-Michael Mallmann and Bogdan Musial, 71–89. Darmstadt: Wissenschaftliche Buchgesellschaft, 2004.
———. "Vom Fußvolk der 'Endlösung': Ordnungspolizei, Ostkrieg und Judenmord." *Tel Aviver Jahrbuch für deutsche Geschichte* 26 (1997): 355–91.
Mallmann, Klaus-Michael, and Martin Cüppers. *Halbmond und Hakenkreuz: Das "Dritte Reich," die Araber und Palästina*. Darmstadt: Wissenschaftliche Buchgesellschaft, 2006.
Mankiller, Wilma. "Reflections on Removal." In *The Cherokee Removal: A Brief History with Documents*, edited by Theda Perdue and Michael D. Green, 186–87. Boston: Bedford/St. Martin's, 2005.
Manoschek, Walter. "Kriegsverbrechen und Judenvernichtung in Serbien, 1941–1942." In *Kriegsverbrechen im 20. Jahrhundert*, edited by Wolfram Wette and Gerd Ueberschär, 123–36. Darmstadt: Primus Verlag, 2001.
Manz, Bruno. *A Mind in Prison: The Memoir of a Son and Soldier of the Third Reich*. Washington, D.C.: Brassey's, 2000.
Mao Tse-Tung. *On Guerrilla Warfare*. New York: Frederick Praeger, 1961. Reprint, Norwalk, Conn.: Easton, 1996.
Mardock, Robert Winston. *The Reformers and the American Indian*. Columbia: University of Missouri Press, 1971.
Matthäus, Jürgen, Konrad Kwiet, Jürgen Förster, and Richard Breitman. *Ausbildungsziel Judenmord? Zum Stellenwert der "weltanschaulichen Erziehung" von SS und Polizei im Rahmen der "Endlösung."* Frankfurt/Main: Fischer Taschenbuch, 2003.
McDonnell, Michael, and A. Dirk Moses. "Raphael Lemkin as Historian of Genocide in the Americas." *Journal of Genocide Research* 7 (December 2005): 501–29.
McLaurin, Melton. *Celia: A Slave*. New York: Harper Collins, 1991.
McNeill, William H. *Plagues and Peoples*. New York: Doubleday, 1976.
McNenly, Linda. *Native Performers in Wild West Shows: From Buffalo Bill to Euro Disney*. Norman: University of Oklahoma Press, 2012.

McPherson, James. *Battle Cry of Freedom: The Civil War Era.* New York: Ballantine, 1989.
McPherson, James, and James Hogue. *Ordeal by Fire: The Civil War and Reconstruction.* 4th ed. New York: McGraw Hill, 2009.
Megargee, Geoffrey. *Inside Hitler's High Command.* Lawrence: University Press of Kansas, 2000.
———. *War of Annihilation: Combat and Genocide on the Eastern Front, 1941.* Lanham, Md.: Rowman and Littlefield, 2006.
Merk, Frederick. *Manifest Destiny and Mission in American History: A Reinterpretation.* New York: Alfred A. Knopf, 1970.
Meyer, Gert, ed. *Wehrmachtsverbrechen: Dokumente aus sowjetischen Archiven.* Cologne: PapyRossa Verlag, 1997.
Michman, Dan. *The Emergence of Jewish Ghettos during the Holocaust.* Cambridge: Cambridge University Press, 2011.
Mielke, Otto. *Der Heldenkampf um Narvik.* Berlin: Steiniger-Verlag, 1940.
Miles, Nelson A. *Personal Recollections and Observations of General Nelson A. Miles.* Chicago: Werner, 1897.
Millett, Allan, and Peter Maslowski. *For the Common Defense: A Military History of the United States of America.* New York: Free Press, 1984.
Miller, Stuart Creighton. *Benevolent Assimilation: The American Conquest of the Philippines.* New Haven, Conn.: Yale University Press, 1982.
Milner, Clyde A., II. *With Good Intentions: Quaker Work among the Pawnees, Otos, and Omahas in the 1870s.* Lincoln: University of Nebraska Press, 1982.
Morgan, H. Wayne. *William McKinley and His America.* Rev. ed. Kent, Ohio: Kent State University Press, 2003.
Moses, A. Dirk. "Genocide and Settler Society in Australian History." In *Genocide and Settler Society: Frontier Violence and Stolen Indigenous Children in Australian History,* edited by A. Dirk Moses, 3–48. New York: Berghahn Books, 2004.
———. "Raphael Lemkin, Culture, and the Concept of Genocide." In *The Oxford Handbook of Genocide Studies,* edited by Donald Bloxham and A. Dirk Moses, 19–41. Oxford: Oxford University Press, 2010.
Mueller, James E. *Shooting Arrows and Slinging Mud: Custer, the Press, and the Little Bighorn.* Norman: University of Oklahoma Press, 2013.
Müller, Rolf-Dieter. *Hitlers Ostkrieg und die deutsche Siedlungspolitik.* Frankfurt/Main: Fischer Taschenbuch, 1991.
Mulroy, Kevin. *Freedom on the Border: The Seminole Maroons in Florida, the Indian Territory, Coahuila, and Texas.* Lubbock: Texas Tech University Press, 1993.
Neely, Mark, Jr. "Was the Civil War a Total War?" *Civil War History* 37 (March 1991): 5–28.
Neihardt, John, ed. *Black Elk Speaks: Being the Life Story of a Holy Man of the Oglala Sioux.* New York: William Morrow, 1932. Reprint, Lincoln: University of Nebraska Press, 1979.
Neitzel, Sönke, and Harald Welzer. *Soldaten: On Fighting, Killing, and Dying.* New York: Alfred A. Knopf, 2012.

Neumaier, Christopher. "The Escalation of German Reprisal Policy in Occupied France, 1941–1942." *Journal of Contemporary History* 41 (January 2006): 113–31.
Newcomb, W. W., Jr. *The Indians of Texas: From Prehistoric to Modern Times*. Austin: University of Texas Press, 1961.
Noakes, Jeremy, ed. *The German Home Front in World War II: A Documentary Reader*. Vol. 4 of *Nazism, 1919–1945*. Exeter: University of Exeter Press, 1998.
Noakes, Jeremy, and Geoffrey Pridham, eds. *Foreign Policy, War, and Racial Extermination: A Documentary Reader*. Vol. 3 of *Nazism, 1919–1945*. Exeter: University of Exeter Press, 1988.
Nye, Russel. *The Unembarrassed Muse: The Popular Arts in America*. New York: Dial, 1970.
Oberkommando der Wehrmacht, ed. *Kampf um Norwegen: Berichte und Bilder vom Kriege gegen England*. Berlin: Zeitgeschichte-Verlag, 1940.
Oldenburg, Manfred. *Ideologie und militärisches Kalkül: Die Besatzungspolitik der Wehrmacht in der Sowjetunion, 1942*. Cologne: Böhlau, 2004.
Ostler, Jeffrey. *The Plains Sioux and U.S. Colonialism from Lewis and Clark to Wounded Knee*. Cambridge: Cambridge University Press, 2004.
———. "The Question of Genocide in U.S. History." In *Genocide in History*, edited by Adam Jones, 2:115–26. Los Angeles: Sage, 2008.
O'Sullivan, John L. "Annexation." *The United States Democratic Review* 17 (July–August 1845): 5–10.
Pegelow, Thomas. "'German Jews,' 'National Jews,' 'Jewish Volk,' or 'Racial Jews'?: The Constitution and the Contestation of 'Jewishness' in Newspapers of Nazi Germany, 1933–1938." *Central European History* 35 (June 2002): 195–221.
Penny, H. Glenn. *Kindred by Choice: Germans and American Indians since 1800*. Chapel Hill: University of North Carolina Press, 2013.
Pezzino, Paolo. "The German Military Occupation of Italy and the War against Civilians." *Modern Italy* 12 (June 2007): 173–88.
Picker, Henry. *Hitlers Tischgespräche im Führerhauptquartier*. Frankfurt/Main: Ullstein, 1993.
Pohl, Dieter. *Die Herrschaft der Wehrmacht: Deutsche Militärbesatzung und einheimische Bevölkerung in der Sowjetunion, 1941–1944*. Frankfurt/Main: Fischer Taschenbuch Verlag, 2011.
———. "Ukrainische Hilfskräfte beim Mord an den Juden." In *Die Täter der Shoah: Fanatische Nationalsozialisten oder ganz normale Deutsche?*, edited by Gerhard Paul, 205–34. Göttingen: Wallstein, 2002.
Powell, Philip Wayne. *Tree of Hate: Propaganda and Prejudices Affecting United States Relations with the Hispanic World*. New York: Basic Books, 1971.
Pratt, Julius W. *Expansionists of 1898: The Acquisition of Hawaii and the Spanish Islands*. Chicago: Quadrangle Books, 1936.

Prucha, Francis Paul. *American Indian Treaties: The History of a Political Anomaly*. Berkeley: University of California Press, 1994.
———. *The Great Father: The United States Government and the American Indians*. Abridged ed. Lincoln: University of Nebraska Press, 1984.
Quinton, Amelia S. "The Woman's National Indian Association." In *The Congress of Women: Held in the Woman's Building, World's Colombian Exposition, Chicago, U.S.A., 1893*, edited by Mary Kavanaugh Oldham, 71–71. Chicago: Monarch, 1894.
Ramenofsky, Ann F. *Vectors of Death: The Archaeology of European Contact*. Albuquerque: University of New Mexico Press, 1987.
Reese, Willy Peter. *A Stranger to Myself: The Inhumanity of War*. Translated by Michael Hofmann. New York: Farrar, Straus and Giroux, 2005.
Reilly, Hugh J. *Bound to Have Blood: Frontier Newspapers and the Plains Indian Wars*. Lincoln: University of Nebraska Press, 2010.
Reuth, Ralf Georg. *Goebbels*. Translated by Krishna Winston. New York: Harcourt Brace, 1993.
Rhodes, Richard. *Masters of Death: The SS Einsatzgruppen and the Invention of the Holocaust*. New York: Alfred A. Knopf, 2002.
Rickey, Jr. Donald. *Encyclopedia of South Dakota Indians*. St. Clair Shores, Mich.: Somerset Publishers, 2000.
———. *Forty Miles a Day on Beans and Hay*. Norman: University of Oklahoma Press, 1963.
Riley Sousa, Ashley. "'They Will Be Hunted Down like Wild Beasts and Destroyed!': A Comparative Study of Genocide in California and Tasmania." *Journal of Genocide Research* 6 (June 2004): 193–209.
Rivaya-Martínez, Joaquín. "Becoming Comanches: Patterns of Captive Incorporation into Comanche Kinship Networks, 1820–1875." In Adams and DeLuzio, *On the Borders of Love and Power*, 47–70.
———. "The Captivity of Macario Leal: A Tejano among the Comanches, 1847–1854." *Southwestern Historical Quarterly* 117 (April 2014): 373–402.
———. "A Different Look at Native American Depopulation: Comanche Raiding, Captive Taking, and Population Decline." *Ethnohistory* 61 (Summer 2014): 393–418.
Robinson, Charles M., III. *General Crook and the Western Frontier*. Norman: University of Oklahoma Press, 2001.
Robinson, Sherry. *Apache Voices: Their Stories as Told to Eve Ball*. Albuquerque: University of New Mexico Press, 2000.
Röhr, Werner, ed. *Die faschistische Okkupationspolitik in Polen, 1939–1945*. Cologne: Pahl-Rugenstein Verlag, 1989.
Ropp, Theodore. *War in the Modern World*. Durham, N.C.: Duke University Press, 1959.
Roseman, Mark. *The Wannsee Conference and the Final Solution: A Reconsideration*. London: Folio Society, 2012.
Rosenberg, Sheri, and Everita Silina. "Genocide by Attrition: Silent and Efficient." In *Genocide Matters: Ongoing Issues and Emerging*

Perspectives, edited by Joyce Apsel and Ernesto Verdeja, 106–26. New York: Routledge, 2013.
Rossino, Alexander. *Hitler Strikes Poland: Blitzkrieg, Ideology, and Atrocity*. Lawrence: University Press of Kansas, 2003.
Rummel, R. J. *Democide: Nazi Genocide and Mass Murder*. New Brunswick, N.J.: Transaction, 1992.
Rürup, Reinhard. *Der Krieg gegen die Sowjetunion, 1941–1945*. Berlin: Argon-Verlag, 1991.
Russell, Don. *The Lives and Legends of Buffalo Bill*. Norman: University of Oklahoma Press, 1979.
———. *One Hundred and Three Fights and Scrimmages: The Story of General Reuben F. Bernard*. Mechanicsburg, Pa.: Stackpole Books, 2003.
Rutherford, Phillip T. *Prelude to the Final Solution: The Nazi Program for Deporting Ethnic Poles, 1939–1941*. Lawrence: University Press of Kansas, 2007.
Sandkühler, Thomas. *Endlösung in Galizien: Der Judenmord in Ostpolen und die Rettungsinitiativen von Berthold Beitz, 1941–1944*. Bonn: Verlag JHW Dietz, 1996
Scheck, Raffael. *Hitler's African Victims: The German Army Massacres of Black French Soldiers in 1940*. Cambridge: Cambridge University Press, 2006.
Shaw, Martin, and Omer Bartov. "The Question of Genocide in Palestine, 1948: An Exchange between Martin Shaw and Omer Bartov." *Journal of Genocide Research* 12 (December 2010): 243–59.
Shepherd, Ben. *Terror in the Balkans: German Armies and Partisan War*. Cambridge, Mass.: Harvard University Press, 2012.
———. *War in the Wild East: The German Army and Soviet Partisans*. Cambridge, Mass.: Harvard University Press, 2004.
Shepherd, Ben, and Juliette Pattinson. "Partisan and Anti-Partisan Warfare in German-Occupied Europe, 1939–1945: Views from Above and Lessons from the Past." *Journal of Strategic Studies* 31 (October 2008): 675–93.
Slepyan, Kenneth. *Stalin's Guerrillas: Soviet Partisans in World War II*. Lawrence: University Press of Kansas, 2006.
Smith, Henry Nash. *Virgin Land: The American West as Symbol and Myth*. Cambridge: Harvard University Press, 1950.
Smith, Sherry L. *Sagebrush Soldier: Private William Earl Smith's View of the Sioux War of 1876*. Norman: University of Oklahoma Press, 1989.
———. *The View from Officers' Row: Army Perceptions of Western Indians*. Tucson: University of Arizona Press, 1990.
Smith, Woodruff D. *The Ideological Origins of Nazi Imperialism*. New York: Oxford University Press, 1986.
Smits, David. "The Frontier Army and the Destruction of the Buffalo, 1865–1883." *Western Historical Quarterly* 25 (Autumn 1995): 312–38.
Snyder, Timothy. *Bloodlands: Europe between Hitler and Stalin*. New York: Basic Books, 2010.

Stahel, David. *The Battle for Moscow*. Cambridge: Cambridge University Press, 2015.
———. *Kiev 1941: Hitler's Battle for Supremacy in the East*. Cambridge: Cambridge University Press, 2012.
———. *Operation Typhoon: Hitler's March on Moscow, October 1941*. Cambridge: Cambridge University Press, 2013.
Stahl, Wayne K. "The U.S. and Native American Education: A Survey of Federal Legislation." *Journal of American Indian Education* 18 (May 1979): 28–32.
Standing Bear, Luther. *Land of the Spotted Eagle*. Rev. ed. Lincoln: University of Nebraska Press, 1978.
———. *My People the Sioux*. Rev. ed. Lincoln: University of Nebraska Press, 1975.
Stannard, David. *The American Holocaust: Columbus and the Conquest of the New World*. New York: Oxford University Press, 1992.
———. "Uniqueness as Denial: The Politics of Genocide Scholarship." In *Is the Holocaust Unique?: Perspectives on Comparative Genocide*, edited by Alan Rosenbaum, 163–208. Boulder, Colo.: Westview, 1996.
Steele, Brian. *Thomas Jefferson and American Nationhood*. Cambridge: Cambridge University Press, 2012.
Steele, Ian. *Warpaths: Invasions of North America*. New York: Oxford University Press, 1994.
Steinhoff, Johannes, Peter Pechel, and Dennis Showalter. *Voices from the Third Reich: An Oral History*. Washington, D.C.: Regnery Gateway, 1989.
Steinweis, Alan E. "Eastern Europe and the Notion of the 'Frontier' in Germany to 1945." In *Germany and Eastern Europe: Cultural Identities and Cultural Differences*, edited by Keith Bullivant and Geoffrey Giles, 56–69. Amsterdam: Rodopi, 1999.
Stone, Dan, ed. *The Historiography of the Holocaust*. New York: Palgrave Macmillan, 2010.
Strang, Cameron B. "Violence, Ethnicity, and Human Remains during the Second Seminole War." *Journal of American History* 100 (March 2014): 973–94.
Strassler, Robert, ed. *The Landmark Thucydides: A Comprehensive Guide to the Peloponnesian War*. New York: Free Press, 1996.
Streit, Christian. *Keine Kameraden: Die Wehrmacht und die sowjetischen Kriegsgefangen, 1941–1945*. Bonn: JHW Dietz, 1991.
Sweeney, Edwin R. *From Cochise to Geronimo: The Chiricahua Apaches, 1874–1886*. Norman: University of Oklahoma Press, 2010.
Taylor, Alan. *American Colonies: The Settling of North America*. New York: Penguin Books, 2001.
Tec, Nechama. *Defiance: The Bielski Partisans*. New York: Oxford University Press, 1993.
———. *In the Lion's Den: The Life of Oswald Rufeisen*. Oxford: Oxford University Press, 1990.
Tegel, Susan. *Jew Süss: Life, Legend, Fiction, Film*. London: Continuum, 2011.

Thornton, Russell. *American Indian Holocaust and Survival: A Population History since 1492*. Norman: University of Oklahoma Press, 1987.
Todd, Mary. "Education of Indian Girls in the West." In *The Congress of Women Held in the Woman's Building, World's Columbian Exposition, Chicago, USA 1893*, edited by Mary Kavanaugh Oldham, 39–40. Chicago: Monarch, 1894.
Tooze, Adam. *The Wages of Destruction: The Making and Breaking of the Nazi Economy*. New York: Viking, 2006.
Turner, Frederick Jackson. *The Frontier in American History*. New York: Henry Holt, 1921. Reprint, New York: Barnes and Noble, 2009.
——. *The Significance of the Frontier in American History*. Madison: State Historical Society of Wisconsin, 1894.
Turse, Nick. *Kill Anything That Moves: The Real American War in Vietnam*. New York: Metropolitan Books, 2013.
Usbeck, Frank. *Fellow Tribesmen: The Image of Native Americans, National Identity, and Nazi Ideology in Germany*. New York: Berghahn, 2015.
Utley, Robert. *Cavalier in Buckskin: George Armstrong Custer and the Western Military Frontier* Norman: University of Oklahoma Press, 1988.
——. *Frontier Regulars: The United States Army and the Indian, 1866–1890*. New York: Macmillan, 1973.
——. *Geronimo*. New Haven, Conn.: Yale University Press, 2012.
——. *The Indian Frontier of the American West, 1846–1890*. Albuquerque: University of New Mexico Press, 1984.
——. *The Lance and the Shield: The Life and Times of Sitting Bull*. New York: Henry Holt, 1993.
Utley, Robert, and Wilcomb Washburn. *Indian Wars*. Boston: Mariner Books, 2002.
Vaughn, J. W. *With Crook at Rosebud*. Lincoln: University of Nebraska Press, 1956.
Vaughn, Stephen, ed. *Encyclopedia of American Journalism*. New York: Routledge, 2008.
Wallace, Ernest, and E. Adamson Hoebel. *The Comanches: Lords of the South Plains*. Norman: University of Oklahoma Press, 1952.
Waller, James. *Becoming Evil: How Ordinary People Commit Genocide and Mass Killing*. Oxford: Oxford University Press, 2002.
Watson, Samuel J. *Peacekeepers and Conquerors: The Army Officer Corps on the American Frontier. 1821–1846*. Lawrence: University Press of Kansas, 2013.
Watt, Robert. "Apaches without and Enemies within: The US Army in New Mexico, 1871–1881.' *War in History* 18 (April 2011): 148–83.
Weber, David J. *Bárbaros: Spaniards and their Savages in the Age of Enlightenment*. New Haven, Conn.: Yale University Press, 2005.
——. *The Spanish Frontier in North America*. New Haven, Conn.: Yale University Press, 1992.

———. "The Spanish-Mexican Rim." In *The Oxford History of the American West*, edited by Clyde Milner II, Carol O'Connor, and Martha Sandweiss, 45–77. Oxford: Oxford University Press, 1994.

Weigley, Russell. *The American Way of War: A History of United States Military Strategy and Policy*. Bloomington: Indiana University Press, 1973.

Weinberg, Gerhard L. *The Foreign Policy of Hitler's Germany: Starting World War II*. Chicago: University of Chicago Press, 1980; reprint Atlantic Highlands, N.J.: Humanities Press, 1994.

———. *Germany, Hitler, and World War II: Essays in Modern German and World History*. Cambridge: Cambridge University Press, 1995.

———. *Visions of Victory: The Hopes of Eight World War II Leaders*. Cambridge: Cambridge University Press, 2005.

———. *A World at Arms: A Global History of World War II*. New York: Cambridge University Press, 1994.

———, ed. *Hitler's Second Book*. New York: Enigma Books, 2003.

Weiss-Wendt, Anton. "Problems in Comparative Genocide Scholarship." In *The Historiography of the Holocaust*, edited by Dan Stone, 42–70. New York: Palgrave Macmillan, 2010.

West, Elliot. *The Contested Plains: Indians, Goldseekers, and the Rush to Colorado*. Lawrence: University Press of Kansas, 1998.

———. *The Last Indian War: The Nez Perce Story*. New York: Oxford University Press, 2009.

Westermann, Edward B. *Hitler's Police Battalions: Enforcing Racial War in the East*. Lawrence: University Press of Kansas, 2005.

———. "Partners in Genocide: The German Police and the Wehrmacht in the Soviet Union." *Journal of Strategic Studies* 31 (October 2008): 771–96.

Wetherill, Louisa Wade, and Harvey Leake, eds. *Wolfkiller: Wisdom from a Nineteenth-Century Navajo Shepherd*. Layton, Utah: Gibbs Smith, 2007.

White, Richard. *"It's Your Misfortune and None of My Own": A New History of the American West*. Norman: University of Oklahoma Press, 1991.

———. *Railroaded: The Transcontinentals and the Making of Modern America*. New York: W. W. Norton, 2011.

Whittaker, Frederick. *A Complete Life of General George A. Custer: From Appomattox to the Little Big Horn*. Vol. 2. New York: Sheldon, 1876. Reprint, Lincoln: University of Nebraska Press, 1993.

Whittlesey, Derwent. "Haushofer: The Geopoliticians." In *Makers of Modern Strategy: Military Thought from Machiavelli to Hitler*, edited by Edward Mead Earle, 388–411. Princeton, N.J.: Princeton University Press, 1943.

Wildermuth, David. "Widening the Circle: General Weikersthal and the War of Annihilation, 1941–42." *Central European History* 45 (June 2012): 306–24.

Williams, Robert A., Jr. *Savage Anxieties: The Invention of Western Civilization*. New York: Palgrave Macmillan, 2012.

Wilson, R. L., with Greg Martin. *Buffalo Bill's Wild West: An American Legend*. New York: Random House, 1998.
Wippermann, Wolfgang. *Europäischer Faschismus im Vergleich*. Frankfurt/Main: Suhrkamp, 1983.
Wischmann, Lesley. *Frontier Diplomats: The Life and Times of Alexander Culbertson and Natoyist-Siksina*. Spokane, Wash.: Arthur H. Clark, 2000.
Wolfe, Patrick. "Settler Colonialism and the Elimination of the Native." *Journal of Genocide Research* 8 (December 2006): 387–409.
Wooster, Robert. *The Military and United States Indian Policy, 1865–1903*. New Haven, Conn.: Yale University Press, 1988.
———. *Nelson A. Miles and the Twilight of the Frontier Army*. Lincoln: University of Nebraska Press, 1993.
Yahil, Leni. *The Holocaust: The Fate of European Jewry*. Translated by Ina Friedman and Haya Galai. Oxford: Oxford University Press, 1990.
Yenne, Bill. *Indian Wars: The Campaign for the American West*. Yardley, Pa.: Westholme, 2006.
Zimmerer, Jürgen. "The Birth of the *Ostland* out of the Spirit of Colonialism: A Postcolonial Perspective on the Nazi Policy of Conquest and Extermination." *Patterns of Prejudice* 39 (2005): 197–219.
———. "Colonialism and the Holocaust: Towards an Archeology of Genocide." In *Genocide and Settler Society: Frontier Violence and Stolen Indigenous Children in Australian History*, edited by A. Dirk Moses, 49–76. New York: Berghahn Books, 2004.
———. "Kolonialer Genozid?: Vom Nutzen und Nachteil einer historischen Kategorie für eine Globalgeschichte des Völkermords." In *Enteignet, Vertrieben, Ermordet: Beiträge zur Genozidforschung*, edited by Dominik Schaller, Rupert Boyadjian, and Vivianne Berg, 109–28. Zurich: Chronos, 2004.

Index

Adams, John Quincy, 19
Africa, 6, 53, 85–86, 186, 201, 227
Alikianos, Greece, 196
Alvarez, Alex, 6
American Indian Aid Association, 77
Anderson, Gary, 5
Anthony, Scott, 166
antipartisan warfare, 6, 10, 115, 200–202, 286n83; and auxiliaries, use of, 243–44; as cover for mass murder of Jews, 228–31, 235–38, 244–46, 258; in Serbia, 195–96; in Soviet Union, 108, 115, 152–53, 191–95, 227–44; strategies of, 201; Wehrmacht policies on, 229
Apache, 6, 18, 27, 99, 116–17, 121, 130, 247, 250; as army scouts, 31, 105, 164, 211, 213–16, 220–21, 223, 283n48; Chiricahua, 106, 162, 208, 216, 226, 249–50; and intertribal warfare, 162; and male prisoners, 171, 208, 211; Mescalero, 180; Mimbre, 216, 218; Nedni, 220; and punishment for adultery, 212; and raids into Mexico, 207; size of, 214; style of warfare, 200–226, 245; and treaty negotiations, 69
Apache Wars, 31, 116–17, 141, 200–226
Arapaho, 69, 117, 124, 168, 178
Arizona, 26–27, 31, 107, 161, 206–226, 249, 255
Arizona Miner, 27
Arizona Star, 27
Armenia, 9
Arthur, Chester A., 247
Ash Creek, 140
Atkins, John D., 250
Auschwitz, 94, 112, 198
Australia, 6, 53

Babi Yar Massacre, 189–91, 198–99, 253, 259
Bach-Zelewski, Erich von dem, 228
Baker, Eugene, 73, 198; and Piegan Massacre, 173–79
Baldwin, Frank, 140
Balkans, 115, 195
Baltics, 18
Banner, Stuart, 55
Baranivka, Ukraine, 191–95, 199
Baranowka, Ukraine, 229
Baranowski, Shelley, 261n2
Bartov, Omer, 8
Bathe, Rolf, 44
Battle of Cedar Creek, 140
Battle of Little Bighorn, 30, 36, 66, 129, 139, 141, 170, 207, 220; details of, 133–38; and media response, 135
Battle of Palo Duro Canyon, 123
Battle of Rosebud Creek, 131–33
Battle of the Somme, 152
Battle of Turret Mountain, 213–14, 246
Beadle Publishing, 32
Beaver Heart, 274n53
Belknap, William, 129–31
Bełżec, 94
Bennett, James, 25
Bera, Władysława, 195
Berger, Gottlob, 240, 286n83
Bernard, Reuben, 211
Bielski, Tuvia, 241
Big Foot, 179, 182, 250
Big Horn, 174–75
Bird, Robert, 34
Bismarck, Otto von, 227
bison. *See* buffalo
Black Corps, 42–43
Black Elk, 184, 202
Blackfeet (Indian tribe), 172–75
Black Hills, 101, 122, 129–30, 135, 139, 272n23

Black Horse, 169
Black Kettle, 165
Black Legend, 10
Blimp, Colonel, 152
Blitzkrieg, 10, 115, 143, 149
Blood (Indian tribe), 172–73
Blut und Boden (Blood and Soil), 12
Blyth, Lance, 162, 208
Board of Indian Commissioners, 26–27, 73–74, 77
Bock, Fedor von, 145
Boer War, 201
Böhme, Franz, 195–96
Bonner, Mary, 28
Boston Daily Advertiser, 29, 70
Boston Indian Citizenship Committee, 27
Bourke, John G., 132
Bowes, John P., 263n7
Bozeman Trail, 18, 66, 70, 168
Braemer, Walter, 195
Brauchitsch, Walther von, 154
Brave Wolf, 133
Brenner, Karl, 187
"Bromberg's Bloody Sunday," 144–45
Brown, Orlando, 63
Brown, Richard, 197
Browning, Christopher, 251
buffalo, 102, 272n24; decimation of, 122, 124–28, 272n30; and Ghost Dance prophecy, 180
Buffalo Bill. *See* Cody, William F. "Buffalo Bill"
Buntline, Ned, 33, 35
Bureau of Indian Affairs, 15, 30, 66, 169, 198; and Apache Wars, 214–15; annuities and provisions, 103, 173; criticism of, 130, 157, 217; Indian agents and superintendents, 72–73, 99, 125, 172–73, 181, 220; organization of, 61; response to Battle of Little Bighorn, 135; response to Fetterman massacre, 67; response to Ghost Dance, 181; transfer of, 61
Burnett, Finn, 168, 212
Bydgoszcz (Bromberg), Poland, 144–45, 195

California, 19, 22, 29, 76, 78, 120, 161, 164, 276n6
Callwell, C. E., 201–202
Cambodia, 9
Cameron, James D., 136
Camp Grant Massacre, 27, 161, 209–10, 246
Camp Supply, Indian Territory, 103
Canada, 97, 137, 141, 172, 179
Canby, Edward S., 76
Carleton, James, 117
Carlisle School, 64, 249
Carr, Eugene, 220
Carrington, Henry, 67, 169–71
Carson, Christopher "Kit," 163–64, 166
Casas, Bartolomé de las, 10
Chato, 221
Chełmno, 82, 94
Cherokee Nation v. Georgia, 57
Cherokees, 57–59
Cheyennes, 18, 69, 77, 129; conflict with army, 118–19; and destruction of buffalo, 125; in Fetterman disaster, 169–71; and Great Sioux War, 131–39; and Red River War, 123–24; and Sand Creek Massacre, 165–67; and treaty negotiations, 117; at War Bonnet Creek, 136
Chickasaws, 59
Chief Joseph, 24, 141
Chihuahua, Mexico, 209, 218, 221
Chivington, John, 68, 165–67, 171, 198
Choctaws, 59
Chotimsk, 242
Christianity, 11
Churchill, Ward, 4
Citino, Robert, 114
Civil War, 10, 32, 55, 71, 115, 119, 128, 134, 215, 221; and guerrilla operations, 206–207; as "hard war," 165; and media, 25–26; influence on operations in the West, 177–78, 257
Clausewitz, Carl von, 114
Clemens, Samuel (Mark Twain), 35
Cleveland, Grover, 250

Cobell, Joe, 174–75
Cochise, 209–11, 213–14
Cody, William F. "Buffalo Bill," 33, 265n42; and Great Sioux War, 136; and "Wild West" Show, 34–36
Colorado, 21, 68, 160, 165–67, 180, 198
Colyer, Vincent, 26, 210
Comanches, 5, 17, 21, 77, 121, 125, 129, 206; Kwahada, 123–24; and male captives, 134, 171, 208, 271n8; raids, use of, 203, 208, 281n9; and Red River War, 123–24; and treaty negotiations, 69
Commissar Order (*Kommissarbefehl*), 88, 257
Connor, James, 165–67
Connor, Patrick, 168, 178
Cooper, James Fenimore, 33
Cooper, Peter, 77
Crawford, Samuel J., 268n35
Crawford, T. Hartley, 63
Crazy Horse, 132–38, 141, 218
Creeks, 59
Crete, 196
Crook, George, 128, 130, 214, 225, 247, 251; advocacy on behalf of Apaches, 156, 222, 249–50; on Apache scouts, 212, 215; in Apache Wars, 210–24; exterminatory rhetoric, 223, 246; in Great Sioux War, 131–38; on role of the media, 25–26; use of summary execution, 164, 207
Crow Indians, 132
Culbertson, Alex, 173
Cultural Asphyxiation, 12
Custer, George A., 30–31, 68, 128, 140; at Battle of Little Bighorn, 133–38; and Black Hills expedition, 122; in popular culture, 36
Czechs, 90

Daily Mining Journal, 166
Dakota Territory, 70, 122, 130, 137
Dallas Morning News, 31
Dallas Weekly Herald, 75

Daluege, Kurt, 88, 243, 286n91
Daly, Christopher, 264n26
Darwin, Charles, 22
Dawes Act, 78, 247
Delano, Columbus, 76
Delaware Indians, 119
Delay, Brian, 208
Denver, 166–67
Díaz, Porfirio, 221, 283n42
Dimopoulos, Ntinos, 197
Directive 21, 86–88
disease, 6, 10, 84, 98, 249, 253; denial of vaccinations to Slavs, 92, 252–53; in ghettos, 82–83
Doane, Gustavus, 174–75
Douglas, Stephen, 22
Drang nach Osten (Drive to the East), 16, 18
Dull Knife Fight, 138–39
Dundy, Elmer S., 27
Dunlay, Thomas, 215, 246

Earp, Wyatt, 161
Eastern Reform Groups (U.S.), 12, 117; advocacy for Indians, 27, 258; advocacy of severalty, 78; goals of, 12, 28, 97; response to Piegan Massacre, 73; response to Sand Creek Massacre, 167; role in education, 64; views of Native Americans, 12, 97; views on reservations, 65, 77–78
Eberhard, Kurt, 237
education, 62–65, 107, 250
Eichmann, Adolf, 94, 257
einsatzgruppen (special-mission units), 16, 92–94, 199, 235, 253; and Babi Yar Massacre, 189–91; operations in Poland, 146; operations in the Soviet Union, 238, 253; and Soviet POWs, 151–52; and Wehrmacht, cooperation with, 151–53
England. *See* Great Britain
Eternal Jew (film), 46–48
Ethnic Cleansing, 5–6, 261n6
Ethnic Germans, 44, 81–82, 144, 185, 191
Evans, John, 165

Fetterman, William, 66, 170–71
Fetterman disaster, 70, 134, 207; description of, 168–71
Fifth U.S. Cavalry, 136, 211
Fifth U.S. Infantry, 139–40
"Final Solution," 4–5, 43, 93–97, 160, 238, 251–58
First U.S. Cavalry, 118
Five Civilized Tribes, 58
Fixico, Donald, 271n7
Floyd, John B., 118
forced labor. *See* slave labor
Forsyth, James W., 182–83
Fort Abraham Lincoln, 131–32
Fort Benton, 172
Fort Buford, 180
Fort Ellis, 132, 175
Fort Fetterman, 130, 132
Fort Griffin, 209
Fort Laramie Treaty (1851), 117
Fort Laramie Treaty (1868), 67, 69, 171
Fort Lyon, 165–66
Fort Marion, 250
Fort Phil Kearny, 66, 132, 169–71
Fort Pickens, 106, 249–50
Fort Reno, 132, 169
Fort Shaw, 175
Fort Sill, 124, 250
France, 82, 85, 115, 142, 144
Franco-Prussian War (1870–71), 227
Frank, Hans, 80–81; on mass murder in Poland, 83–85; on purpose of ghettos, 98
Franz, Otto, 188
Frémont, John Charles, 163–64
French and Indian War (1756–63), 206
Fried, Lieutenant, 147–48

Galula, David, 201
Galvez, José de, 203
Gates, Merrill, 64
Gatewood, Charles, 31, 246; on Apache warfare, 203, 206, 211; on reservations, 216; and surrender of Geronimo, 226; views on Apaches, 164
Gazzous, French Pete, 169
Gem of the West, 75–76

General Allotment Act (1887). *See* Dawes Act
General Government (Poland), 13; as reservation, 80, 84–85; as site of mass murder, 83–85, 187, 240–42
Generalplan Ost (General Plan East), 15, 19, 89–91, 157–58
genocide, 5, 12, 53; definitions of, 6, 8, 12; in Poland, 146–48; question of intent, 7–9l; in the Soviet Union, 152
genocide studies, 4
Georgia, 57–58
German police, 16, 187–90, 199; and antipartisan operations, 115, 239–42, 287n94; cooperation with Wehrmacht, 45, 87–88, 143, 146, 153, 227–30, 240; and massacre at Ostrów Mazowieck, 186–89, 280n68; and mass murder, 84–85, 111, 113, 145–46, 153, 157–58, 232–35, 241–42, 253; police auxiliaries, 16, 113, 115, 190–91, 243–44, 246, 286n91, 287n94; use of propaganda literature, 44–45
Geronimo, 31, 212, 218, 224–25, 248–50, 255; on incarceration, 249; on male honor, 221; as military leader, 222; martial training of, 202; raids in Mexico, 209, 219–23; and role of press, 27; surrender of, 226, 246; transfer to Florida, 106, 226, 249
Gettysburg, 68
ghettos, 81–83, 96, 98, 110
Ghost Dance, 24, 180–82, 220, 250
Gibbon, John, 132–33
Gilpin, William, 21
Goebbels, Joseph, 81; on annihilation of the Jews, 96; anti-Semitism, 42; on propaganda, 40–41; use of film, 46–49
Goodale, Elaine, 181
Goose Creek, 133
Göring, Hermann, 87–88, 148, 196, 239
Grant, Ulysses S., 27, 73, 122; and death sentences, 269n53; exterminatory rhetoric, 120; on

Indian policy, goals of, 72–75, 120, 268n41; peace policy of, 55, 70–73, 77, 120, 124, 130, 157, 209, 247, 257–58; on railroads 72; on reservations, 72, 74–75; on settlers and Indian relations, 20, 72
Gray Wolf, 174, 176
Great Britain, 11, 54, 95
Greater Reconstruction, 10
Great Sioux War (1876–77), 18, 30, 122, 128–39, 141, 180
Greely, Horace, 25
Greene, Jerome, 184, 262n23
Greiser, Arthur, 80–82
Grey Beard, 156
Grierson, Benjamin, 26
Grund, Francis Joseph, 20
guerrilla warfare. *See* antipartisan warfare
Guettel, Jens-Uwe, 262n9
Guevara, Che, 200
Gwynne, S. C., 5
Gypsies. *See* Sinti and Roma

Halder, Franz, 80, 85, 87, 149
Hancock, Winfield S., 68
Hanseatic League, 18
Hardorff, Richard, 273n44
Harney, William, 168
Harrison, Benjamin, 181, 184
Hartmann, Christian, 146
Hatch, Edward, 217
Haushofer, Karl, 36–37, 50
Haviland, C. Augustus, 75–76
"Hay Action," 91–92
Hayes, Rutherford B., 141, 247
Hearst, William Randolph, 25, 51
Heavy Runner (Piegan chief), 174, 176
heliostat, 224–25
Heydrich, Reinhard, 87–88, 95
Hickock, James B. "Wild Bill," 33, 161
Hilberg, Raul, 228
Himmler, Heinrich, 3, 16, 43, 46, 81, 143–44, 199, 253, 285n81; and annihilation of Jews, 33–84, 254; and antipartisan effort, 239–40; on auxiliaries, 243; and Command Staff RFSS, 231–35; control of einsatzgruppen, 92–93; on cooperation with army, 191; and creation of the death camps, 94–95; on education in occupied East, 99; on guerrilla warfare, 227, 231–32, 238–40; and Madagascar Plan, 85–86; as Reich Commissioner, 81, 89; on settlements in the East, 90; on slave labor, 91; on Teutonic Knights, 18
Hinton, Alexander, 8
Hippler, Fritz, 46–47
Hitler, Adolf, 4, 83, 178, 197, 199, 231, 239; and anti-Semitism, 37–39, 47–48, 79, 155, 253, 258; and auxiliaries, 243; on creation of reservation in Poland, 84–85; depiction of Native Americans, 3, 259, 265n44; depiction of U.S. West, 14, 16, 93, 157, 259–60; on invasion of Poland, 79–80, 142; on invasion of Soviet Union, 54, 86–87, 148–49; on *Lebensraum*, 3, 9–13, 17–18, 36–39, 50–51, 79–80, 86–87; orders for mass murder, 85, 87, 93, 96, 254; and partisans, 238, 240, 245–47; on propaganda, 40; radio broadcast to Wehrmacht, 150; reading of Karl May, 36; on Slavic peoples, 37–39, 48, 91, 153, 253; and "T4" program, 94; and Teutonic Knights, 37; threat to annihilate Jews, 95, 258; writings of, 37–38, 257, 265n46
Hixson, Walter, 6, 262n10
Hoepner, Erich, 154
Hoffmann, Hans, 187–88
Hoffmann, Hilmar, 45, 48
Holocaust, 4–8, 38, 93, 228, 237, 251, 259
Homestead Act (1862), 71
Horsman, Reginald, 267n14
Horthy, Nikolaus, 48
Höss, Rudolf, 94
Hoth, Hermann, 155
Howard, Oliver O., 210, 213, 250
Hull, Isabel, 227
"Hunger Policy," 88, 160, 199, 257, 275n93

316 INDEX

Idaho Tri-Weekly Statesman, 29
In the Katyn Forest (film), 49
Indian question, 31, 128, 255, 258
Indian Ring, 61, 77, 99, 177, 216
Indian Territory, 27, 61, 63, 69, 75–76, 103, 118–20, 180
Indian Trade and Intercourse Act (1834), 60
Indian's Friend, 28
Iola Register, 31
Ireland, 11, 95
Iron Hawk, 132
Iron Teeth, 139
Iroquois, 116, 256, 271n6
Irwin, B. J. D., 211
Isatai, 123
Italy, 9

Jackson, Andrew, 19, 58–59, 258
Jacoby, Karl, 161
Jamestown Journal, 176
Janos, Mexico, 162
Jefferson, Thomas, 12, 56–57, 78
Jew Süß (film), 46–48
Jews, 4, 5, 9, 17, 227; as contagion, 98; deportation of, 85–86; economic exploitation versus annihilation, 83–84, 95–96; in film, 46–47; ghettoization of, 82–83, 110; mass murder of, 92–96, 112, 146, 152–53, 157–58, 186–95, 228–35; Nazi policy toward, 11, 229–30, 254–56, 259; as partisans, 228–31, 237–38, 244; as prisoners of war, 146; for slave labor, 39, 91, 95, 109
Josanie (Apache band), 223

Kahn, Leo, 241
Kakel, Carroll P. III, 5
Kalavrita, Greece, 196–97, 199
Kansas, 31–32, 68–69, 120, 124, 263n7
Kaplan, Chaim, 82
Kate Bighead (Cheyenne), 131
Katyn, Poland, 49
Katz, Steven, 8
Kautz, August V., 216
Keeley, Lawrence, 162, 256
Keiner, Walter, 193
Keitel, Wilhelm, 87

Kerch, 238
Kesselschlacht (cauldron battle), 114, 149
Kharkov, 238
Kickapoos, 121, 208
Kiev, Ukraine, 92, 150, 160, 189–91, 237
Kiowa, 69, 77, 123–24, 129
Kipling, Rudyard, 52
Kipp, Joe, 174–75
Knecht, Colonel, 243
Kocka, Jürgen, 4
Koschorke, Helmuth, 44–45
Kristallnacht (Night of Broken Glass), 187
Kryniczno, 244
Kube, Wilhelm, 237
Kühne, Thomas, 287n4
Kwahada. *See* Comanches

Lamar, Lucius Q., 79
Lawton, Henry, 31
Lea, Luke, 66
lebensraum (living space), 3–6, 9–14, 17–18, 36–39, 44, 50–51, 259–60
Lee, Wayne, 256
Lehmann, Herman, 208–9
Lemkin, Raphael, 7–8
Leningrad, 149–50, 275n93
Lida, Belarus, 230
Liddell Hart, B. H., 154
Limerick, Patricia Nelson, 3–4
Lincoln, Abraham, 157
Lincoln, Robert T., 179–80
Lipan Apaches, 277n23
Little Bighorn, Battle of. *See* Battle of Little Big Horn
Lo (Indian tribe), 29
Łódź, 82–83
Logan, John A., 30, 77
Longerich, Peter, 255
Looking Glass (Nez Perce), 104
Louisiana, 60
Louisiana Purchase, 56
Lower, Wendy, 13
Lublin Reservation, 13, 84
Lücking, Josef, 236
Luther Standing Bear, 181, 271n104, 279n49, 279n57
Lyon, Caleb, 29

Mackenzie, Ranald, 121, 138–39
Madagascar Plan, 85–86
Malmédy Massacre, 186
Manifest Destiny, 3, 6, 14; discourse on, 17, 19–22; philosophy of, 50–52; propaganda and, 24–36
Mankiller, Wilma, 259
Manstein, Erich von, 155, 231, 246, 276n97
Manz, Bruno, 46
Mao Tse Tung, 201
Marian, Ferdinand, 46
Marias River, 173–74, 179, 184, 198
Marshall, John, 57
Marx, Karl, 224
Mauthausen, 109
May, Karl, 36, 265n42
McCook, Alexander, 119–20
McKay, Walter, 175
McKenney, Thomas L., 62–63
McKinley, William, 22
Mein Kampf, 37, 39, 86, 197, 257
Memphis Daily Appeal, 30
"Meriam Report," 268n26
Mescalero Agency, 217, 219
Mexican-American War (1846–48), 18–22, 25, 60; and atrocity, 54; Whig Party opposition to, 51
Mexican Army, 121, 218, 220–24
Mexico, 11, 19–22, 54, 97, 121, 207, 225–226; as Apache sanctuary, 217, 219, 223–224; and scalp bounties, 209, 282n15; and Treaty of Guadalupe Hidalgo, 208
Michman, Dan, 269n66
Miedzyrzec, Poland, 241
Miles, Nelson A., 31, 106, 246; and Apache Wars, 224–26; on campaign against Nez Perce, 141; depiction of Indians, 156; and Great Sioux War, 137–41; use of Indian scouts, 224–25, 283–284n48; and Wounded Knee Massacre, 181–82
Minnesota, 60, 157, 209
Missionaries, 12, 30, 73–74, 78
Modocs, 76–77
Molotov, Vyacheslav, 86, 142
Montana, 24, 73, 132, 162, 171–79

Morgan, Thomas Jefferson, 64
Morning Star (Dull Knife), 138
Morning Star and Catholic Messenger, 30
Moscow, 149–50, 154
Mountain Chief, 173–74, 178
Mount Vernon, Alabama, 250
Mussolini, Benito, 9, 239
Myrhorod, Ukraine, 193–94

Nakaidoklini, 220
Nana (Mimbre warrior), 218–19
National Republican, 30
National Socialism, 9; and film, 45–49; and Jews, 9, 11, 15, 37–39, 42, 79, 253, 256; and propaganda, 40–49, 275n81; and radio, 41; and Slavs, 11–12, 15, 37–39, 41–42, 79, 256; and violence, glorification of, 197
National Socialist German Worker's Party, 5, 15, 18, 40, 80, 95–96
National Socialist Welfare Organization, 191
Native Americans, 3–5; agency of, 12; and attrition, effects of, 121, 272n21; casualties in Indian wars, 252–53; dime novel depictions of, 32–34; and disease, 6, 10, 249, 252–53; goals for assimilation of, 21, 28; and the horse, role of, 282–283n31; intertribal warfare, 162–63, 171, 276n9; and loss of buffalo, effects of, 125–26; and male honor, 212, 218, 221, 281n6; martial prowess of, 202–203; organization of, 11; population size, 10, 21; proposal for incarceration, 75–77; scalping and mutilation in warfare, 134, 139, 162, 170–71, 208, 212, 273n47; sexual assault of, 212; style of warfare, 115, 118, 132, 162, 171, 203, 208, 274n62; as wards of the state, 74
Navajo, 162, 171, 272n20, 276n9
Nebraska, 69, 71, 129, 136, 182
Neurath, Konstantin von, 142
New Mexico, 105, 180, 206–208, 215, 218–20

newspapers, 11, 249; attacks on federal officials, 26–27; criticism of federal policy, 75, 182; exterminatory rhetoric, 28–30, 255–56; and Great Sioux War, 274n50; reporting of Piegan Massacre, 176; reporting of Wounded Knee Massacre, 183; role in westward expansion, 25–31; sectional divide between East and West, 28–30, 76, 257; sensational accounts, 66–67, 181, 220, 222
New York Herald, 25, 28, 30–31
New York Times, 135, 257
New York Tribune, 25
Nez Perce, 24, 104, 141
Ninth U.S. Cavalry, 217, 219
North Dakota, 24, 132
Northwest Ordinance (1787), 56

Obuchowka, Ukraine, 229
Ojo Caliente Agency, 216
Oklahoma, 250
Omaha Bee, 135, 181
Omaha Indians, 168
Omaha Weekly Herald, 27, 67, 135
Omaha World Herald, 182
Operation Barbarossa, 89, 148
Operation Tannenberg, 146
Operation Winter Magic, 243
Oregon Territory, 22, 28
Ostheer (Eastern Army), 230
Ostkrieg (War in the East), 7
Ostler, Jeffrey, 5, 135
Ostrów Mazowieck, Poland, 186, 199
O'Sullivan, John, 19–20
Otto, William T., 172

Palo Duro Canyon, Battle of, 123
Parker, Ely S., 71, 73–74, 171–72
Pawnee Fork, 68
Pawnees, 168
Peace Policy. *See* Grant, Ulysses S.
Philippines, 202
Phoenix Indian School, 107
Piegan Indians, 171–79, 253
Piegan Massacre, 77, 171–79, 181, 198, 277n30, 278n41

Pine Ridge Agency, 181–82
Pohl, Dieter, 152–53
Pol Pot, 9
Poland, 4, 10, 18, 86–87, 98; dismemberment of, 80–84, 90; and gas vans, use of, 94; Germanization of, 81; invasion of, 39, 42, 79–82, 115, 142–48; liquidation of ghettos, 96; massacre at Ostrów Mazowieck, 186–89; and mass murder, 82, 85, 89, 94, 112, 144–48, 185; propaganda against, 41–45, 48–49; and slave labor, 82
Polk, James K., 21–22, 51
Poncas, 27
Pope, John, 156, 210, 219; on Apache warfare, 200, 217–21; and criticism of Indian Bureau, 217
Powder River, 131, 138, 168, 172, 178
Pratt, Julius, 22
prisoners of war (POWs), 94, 123–24, 242, 253; and Chiricahua Apaches, 226; as German auxiliaries, 243–44; massacre of U.S. POWs, 186; as partisans, 236; in Polish campaign, 143, 145–46; and Sitting Bull, 179; in Soviet Union, 149–52, 159, 227, 231–32, 238
Proctor, Redfield, 181
Pueblo Indians, 162, 203

Quakers. *See* Society of Friends
Quinton, Amelia, 28

railroads, 19–20, 23, 39, 66, 68–70, 72, 98, 179, 182; and Chinese labor, 271n102
Ramsay, Alexander, 209
Ratzel, Friedrich, 50
Red Army, 88–89, 149
Red Cloud, 66–67, 70, 138; criticism of Interior Department, 182; opposition to forts along Bozeman Trail, 169–70
Red Cloud Agency, 130, 136, 138, 141
Red Horn, 174–75
Red Horse, 134, 137

INDEX   319

Red Leaf, 138
Red River War, 77, 122–24, 156
Reichenau, Walter von, 154–55, 193
Removal Act (1830), 58
Reno, Marcus, 133–34
reservations, 13, 21, 27, 30, 99, 128, 137, 179, 213, 248; establishment of, 69, 72; purpose of, 61–62, 247; as sites of isolation and marginalization, 98, 247, 250–51, 271n104; U.S. Army's policing of, 65–66, 120, 123, 156, 178, 214–16
Reynolds, James S., 29
Reynolds, Joseph, 131
Rosebud Creek, Battle of, 131–33
Rosebud Reservation, 62
Roseman, Mark, 258
Rosenberg, Alfred, 18, 91
Rossino, Alexander, 143, 195
Rufeisen, Oswald, 244
Rundstedt, Gerd von, 155
Russia, 19, 54. *See* Soviet Union
Ryan, John, 169

Šabac, Serbia, 196
Sachsenhausen, 47
San Carlos Reservation, 62, 99, 215–17, 220, 222
Sand Creek Massacre, 68, 159–60, 183–84, 191, 198, 252, 259; description of, 165–67; effects of, 168
Sandkühler, Thomas, 85
Santa Fe Trail, 117
scalping, 134, 139, 208–209, 212; at Fetterman disaster, 170–71; at Sand Creek, 166–67; settler fear of, 256
Schneider, Corporal, 193
Schofield, John M., 180, 183
schools. *See* education
Schultz, Karl, 244
Schurz, Carl, 258, 288n17
Schutzmannschaften (auxiliaries), 243
Schuyler, Walter, 137, 211
Seminoles, 59, 116, 272n13, 272n19, 281n6; as scouts, 272n19

Serbia, 194–96, 229, 236–37
settler colonialism, 6, 262n9
settlers, 6, 11, 13, 207, 209, 252, 256
Seventh U.S. Cavalry, 128, 137, 140, 176; at Battle of Little Bighorn, 133–38; at Wounded Knee, 160, 182–84
severalty. *See* Dawes Act
Seyß-Inquart, Arthur, 84
Sheldon, Lionel, 220–21
Shepherd, Ben, 228
Sheridan, Philip, 75–76, 116; and Apache Wars, 223–24; army scouts, views on, 215, 283n48; on decimation of the buffalo, 125–26; on disarming and dismounting Indians, 138; exterminatory rhetoric, 120–21; Indian Bureau, criticism of, 130, 177; and Indians, attitudes toward, 122, 129–30, 156, 176–79, 251–52, 272n22; and labor riots, 141; and Piegan Massacre, 173, 175–79; on railroads, 23; strategy for Great Sioux War, 131–32, 136, 140; strategy for Red River War, 123–24
Sherman, William T., 73, 117, 131, 140, 156, 207; and Apaches, 220; exterminatory rhetoric, 67, 120; influence of Civil War on, 116; on nature of war, 165; and Piegan Massacre, 172–73; and reprisals, threat to use, 207; on role of peace commission, 68–69; on role of the railroads, 22–23, 70; and strategy, 169
Sherman Institute, 64
She Walks with Her Shawl, 134
Shoah. *See* Holocaust
Short Bull, 279n49
Shoshoni, 132, 212
Sioux, 18, 24, 27, 30, 66–67, 70, 77, 121, 130, 156, 172, 178, 212; along Bozeman Trail, 169–71; and Ghost Dance, 180–81, 250; and Great Sioux War, 128–39, 180; martial prowess of, 202–203; as prisoners of war, 179–80; reaction to Black Hills expedition, 122;

Sioux (continued)
reaction to boarding schools, 64; and Santee Sioux uprising, 157; and treaty negotiations, 117; and vaccinations, 253–54; and Wounded Knee, 160–61
Sioux Expedition (1855), 128, 273n32
Sinti and Roma (Gypsies), 82, 152, 192, 227–28, 245, 253
Sinz, Colonel, 192–93
Sitting Bull, 36, 77, 218; and Great Sioux War, 129–30, 134–41; and killing of, 182; as prisoner of war, 179–80
Sixth U.S. Cavalry, 220
slave labor, 39, 81–82, 85, 91–92, 97–98, 109, 112, 146, 152, 157, 160, 242
Slavs, 3, 11, 12, 80, 99, 115, 154, 253, 256; forced sterilization of, 92; plans for killing of, 90, 97; use in slave labor, 91–92, 157
Smith, Edward, 129
Smith, Patrick, 179
Snyder, Timothy, 88
Sobibor, 94
Social Darwinism, 37, 51, 79–80
Society of Friends, 71, 258
Söderbaum, Kristina, 46
Sonderkommando Dirlewanger, 286n83
Sonora, Mexico, 214, 219, 221
Soule, Silas, 166–67
South Dakota, 162, 181
Soviet General Staff, 236
Soviet Paradise (film), 49
Soviet Union, 3, 10, 12, 17, 37, 39, 41, 43, 53, 85, 93, 157, 196, 199, 246; and ethnic Germans, 81; and gas vans, use of, 94; invasion of, 3, 86–89, 114, 148–49; military casualties, 149; Nazi depiction of, 48–49; partisan movement of, 115, 155, 230–31, 235–37, 247–48; policy of terror against, 85, 90, 93, 111, 142, 145, 151, 160, 185–86, 191, 194, 227–28
Spain, 10, 18, 22, 51, 54, 95
Spotted Horse, 183

SS (Schutzstaffel), 3, 16, 285n81; in antipartisan campaign, 240–44; and Command Staff RFSS, 231–35; cooperation with police, 16, 45, 87–88, 92–93, 146, 153, 185, 240–44; and death camps, 94, 112; and deportation planning, 86; massacre of U.S. prisoners of war, 186; and mass murder, 84, 87, 92–96, 111, 151–53, 157–58, 189–91, 231–35, 253, 257; and settlements in the East, 90–91; and Waffen-SS, 231–35
Stalin, Josef, 142, 235–36, 247
Standing Bear v. Crook, 27
Stannard, David, 4–5
state militias (U.S.), 16, 117, 135, 220–21; and atrocity, 161, 165–67, 252, 255, 277n15; demobilization of, 169
Stone, Dan, 6
Strang, Cameron, 134, 273n48
Street and Smith Publishers, 32
Student, Kurt, 186
Sullivan, Thomas, 116, 271n6
Sully, Alfred, 171–72, 174
Sumner, Edwin, 118–19
Sumner, William Graham, 51
Sun Dance, 123, 212
Switzerland, 95

"T4" Program ("Euthanasia Program"), 94, 270n93
Taylor, Nathaniel, 68–69
telegraph, 20
Terrazas, Luis, 218
Terry, Alfred, 131–33, 135–37
Teutonic Knights, 18, 37, 48
Texas, 5, 19, 22, 60, 121–25, 168, 177, 207–208
Texas Rangers, 117, 218
Thirteenth U.S. Infantry, 173
Thornton, Russell, 4–5, 252, 254
Thucydides, 159
Tibbles, Thomas H., 27
Tiffany, J. C., 220
Todd, Mary, 63–64
Tohono O'odham, 161, 209
Tombstone Daily Epitaph, 255

Tonawanda Seneca, 71
Torzeniec, Poland, 145
Trail of Tears, 58, 259
Treaty of Guadalupe Hidalgo (1848), 60, 208
Treaty of Medicine Lodge Creek (1867), 69
Treblinka, 94
Tres Castillos Hills, 218
Trobriand, Phillipe Régis de, 173
Turner, Frederick Jackson, 12–13, 15, 23–24, 34, 50
Turning Hawk, 182
Twain, Mark. See Clemens, Samuel (Mark Twain)
Twenty-Second U.S. Infantry, 141

Ukrainians, 86, 90, 92, 189–94, 229, 232–33, 243
United Nations Resolution, 260, 4, 6–8
Untermenschen (subhumans), 15, 115
U.S. Army, 5–6, 15–16, 19, 68, 78, 101, 118–19, 120–21, 128, 168; and Apache Wars, 202–226; and Bozeman trail forts, 70, 171; conduct of Great Sioux War, 128–39; conduct of Red River War, 122–24; conflict with settlers, 20, 117, 259; and frontier forts, 60–61, 118; as Indian Agents, 72–73; and Indian scouts, reliance on, 105, 119, 132, 138, 168, 211, 213, 215–16, 220–21, 224–25; lawsuits against, 217; and Mexican Army, cooperation with, 218, 221–23, 283n35, 283n42; and Mexico, operations into, 217; policing reservations, 65, 99–100, 120, 156, 178; and reprisal, use of, 211–12; role in removal, 58; role at Sand Creek Massacre, 166; role at Wounded Knee Massacre, 179–85; size of, 10; strategy of, 115–42, 155, 179, 201–226, 245–46, 252; targeting warriors, 121, 168, 178, 214, 277n23; and trophy taking, 212; unconventional warfare doctrine, lack of, 206, 219

U.S. Congress, 22, 52, 59, 66, 72, 77–78, 120, 129, 136; and Bureau of Indian Affairs, 61; and Dawes Act, 78; and end of treaty making, 74; failure to appropriate annuities, 59–62, 67, 98, 122, 173, 180, 184, 250, 267n19; and federal Indian policy, 59–60; and Indian policy, 55–56, 58, 61, 64, 68, 70, 129, 157, 247, 258; and Piegan Massacre, 176; and Sand Creek Massacre, 166–67; and Wounded Knee Massacre, 185
U.S. Department of the Interior, 30, 129, 157, 182, 258; fear of Ghost Dance, 181–82; on Fetterman disaster, 171; policy of, 30, 68, 79, 100, 130, 210; relations with War Department, 61, 67, 70–73, 100, 130, 172–73, 182, 216–17; role in education of Indians, 62–64
U.S. Government, 6, 10; depiction of Native tribes, 15, 54, 129; and federal authority in West, 21, 23, 129; peace commission, 68–69; policies of, 11, 52, 55–79, 247; role of Congress in Indian policy, 55–56, 58, 247; role of Supreme Court in Indian policy, 57–58; vaccination programs, 253–54, 287n11
U.S. War Department, 60, 118, 179–80; and Bureau of Indian Affairs, 61, 67; casualties during Indian Wars, 252; relations with Interior Department, 61, 67, 70–73, 100, 130, 172–73, 182, 216–17; strategy of, 70, 118, 222
Ute Indians, 162, 171, 180, 203, 276n9
Utley, Robert, 123, 162, 184, 203, 206

Velyka Obukhivka, Ukraine, 194
Victorio, 216–19, 247
vigilantes, 16, 27, 117, 124, 161–62, 172, 185, 197, 209, 246
Volksgemeinschaft (People's Community), 11, 13
volunteers. See state militias

Walker, Francis, 210
Wannsee Conference, 95–96, 238, 257
Warbonnet Creek, 136
war literature (Germany), 43–45
Warsaw, 80, 82–83, 110, 143, 187
Warthegau, 81–82, 90
Washington, D.C., 14, 29–30, 141
Washita River, 123, 176
Wasichus (white people), 132, 202
Watson, Samuel, 119, 252, 263n27
Wehrbauern (soldier-farmers), 90, 96
Wehrmacht, 3, 15, 16, 39, 92; and anti-Semitism, 146, 154–58, 189, 192–94; and Baranivka Massacre, 191–95, 280n80; cooperation with SS and police, 45, 87–88, 143, 146, 151–53, 185, 190–92, 227–30, 240; and French Colonial troops, 186; General Quartermaster, 153; and Hitler, views of, 154, 276n97; invasion of Poland, 79–80, 142–48, 157–58; invasion of Soviet Union, 86–87, 148–58, 227–44; logistics problems, 149–50; and mass murder, 146–47, 151, 190–93, 228–30; military strategy of, 114–15, 142–55, 227–46; personnel shortage, 192; and Polish campaign, 143; and Polish POWs, 145; propaganda literature, 44; propaganda units, 42, 189; reprisals, 144–45, 186, 189, 193–97, 227–29, 236–37, 245–46; and settlements in the East, 90; Sinti and Roma, treatment of, 192, 245; Soviet POWs, treatment of, 150–51, 229–30
Weigley, Russell, 116
Weiss-Wendt, Anton, 262n13

Weltherrschaft (global domination), 38
Wentworth, John, 22
West, Elliot, 10, 17, 21, 119
western dime novels, 24, 31–35, 44, 129
Wheeler, Andrew C., 32
Whipple, Bishop Henry, 30
White, Richard, 59, 62
Whitside, Samuel, 182
Whoa (Nedni Apache chief), 220
Wild West, Rocky Mountain, and Prairie Exhibition, 35–36
Williams, Robert A., Jr., 266n2
Wilson, Henry, 76
Winter, Leopold, 230
Wolfkiller, 171
Women's National Indian Association, 28
Wooden Leg, 131
Worcester, Samuel, 57–58
Worcester v. Georgia, 57–58
World War I, 18, 40–42, 79, 144, 152; influence on views of mass killing, 178
Wounded Knee Massacre, 24, 160–61, 179–85, 198, 252, 259; historical interpretations of, 278–279n47
Wovoka, 180
Wright, J. George, 279n49
Wyoming, 129, 132

Yague Indians, 31
Yakima Indians, 164
Yavapai Indians, 213–14
Yellow Hand (aka Yellow Hair), 136, 274n53

Zulick, Conrad, 249
Zyklon-B (prussic acid), 94

www.ingramcontent.com/pod-product-compliance
Lightning Source LLC
Chambersburg PA
CBHW020829160426
43192CB00007B/580